Understanding the Globalization of Intelligence

Also by Adam D.M. Svendsen

Intelligence Cooperation and the War on Terror: Anglo-American Security Relations after 9/11

The Professionalization of Intelligence Cooperation: Fashioning Method out of Mayhem

Understanding the Globalization of Intelligence

Adam D.M. Svendsen
Intelligence and Defence Strategist, Educator and Researcher

palgrave
macmillan

First published 2012 by
PALGRAVE MACMILLAN

Palgrave Macmillan in the UK is an imprint of Macmillan Publishers Limited, registered in England, company number 785998, of Houndmills, Basingstoke, Hampshire RG21 6XS.

Palgrave Macmillan in the US is a division of St Martin's Press LLC, 175 Fifth Avenue, New York, NY 10010.

Palgrave Macmillan is the global academic imprint of the above companies and has companies and representatives throughout the world.

Palgrave® and Macmillan® are registered trademarks in the United States, the United Kingdom, Europe and other countries.

ISBN 978–0–230–36071–6

This book is printed on paper suitable for recycling and made from fully managed and sustained forest sources. Logging, pulping and manufacturing processes are expected to conform to the environmental regulations of the country of origin.

A catalogue record for this book is available from the British Library.

A catalog record for this book is available from the Library of Congress.

10 9 8 7 6 5 4 3 2 1
21 20 19 18 17 16 15 14 13 12

Printed and bound in Great Britain by
CPI Antony Rowe, Chippenham and Eastbourne

To my parents, Penny and David Svendsen

Contents

Illustration and Plates

Figure

Plates

Abbreviations and Acronyms

9/11	11 September 2001 – Terrorist attacks on the US
7/7	7 July 2005 – London bombings
21/7	21 July 2005 – Attempted London bombings
ASEAN	Association of South East Asian Nations
'C'	Chief of the Secret Intelligence Service (UK)
C_4I[SR]	Command, Control, Communications, Computers and Intelligence/Information [Surveillance and Reconnaissance]
CBRNE	Chemical, Biological, Radiological, Nuclear, and (high-yield) Explosive agents/weapons (WMD)
CI	Counter-Intelligence
CIA	Central Intelligence Agency (US)
COBRA	Cabinet Office Briefing Room 'A' (UK)
COIN	Counter-insurgency
COMSEC	Communications security
CP	Counter-proliferation
CSEC	Communications Security Establishment of Canada
CSIS	Canadian Security Intelligence Service
CT	Counter-terrorism
CTC	Counter-Terrorism Center (US CIA)
DCI	Director of Central Intelligence (US)
DHS	Department of Homeland Security (US)
DIA	Defense Intelligence Agency (US)
DIS	Defence Intelligence Staff (UK)
DNI	Director of National Intelligence (US)
DoD	Department of Defense/the Pentagon (US)
DoJ	Department of Justice (US)
ECHR	European Convention on Human Rights
ELINT	Electronic intelligence

EU	European Union
EUCOM	European Command, RAF Molesworth, Cambridgeshire, UK (US)
FBI	Federal Bureau of Investigation (US)
FCO	Foreign and Commonwealth Office (UK)
FEMA	Federal Emergency Management Agency (US)
G8	Group of Eight
GCHQ	Government Communications Headquarters (UK)
GEOINT	Geospatial intelligence
HEU	Highly Enriched Uranium
HUMINT	Human intelligence
IA	Information assurance
IAEA	International Atomic Energy Agency (UN)
IC	Intelligence community
ICT	Information and Computing/Communications Technology
IISS	The International Institute for Strategic Studies
IMINT	Imagery intelligence
INFOSEC	Information security
IP	Internet Protocol
IR	International Relations
ISC	Intelligence and Security Committee (UK)
IS[TA]R	Intelligence, Surveillance [Target Acquisition] and Reconnaissance
JAC	Joint Analysis Center, EUCOM (US)
JIC	Joint Intelligence Committee (UK)
JTAC	Joint Terrorism Analysis Centre (UK)
'Legat'	FBI Legal Attaché (US)
M_4IS	Multinational, Multiagency, Multidisciplinary, Multidomain Information Sharing
MASINT	Measurement and signature intelligence
MILINT/MI	Military Intelligence
MI5	The Security Service (UK)

MI6	The Secret Intelligence Service (UK)
MLAT (1)	UK-USUK–US Mutual Legal Assistance Treaty
MLAT (2)	Multilateral Legal Assistance Treaty
MoD	Ministry of Defence (UK)
MoU	Memorandum of Understanding
MP	Member of Parliament (UK)
NATO	North Atlantic Treaty Organisation
NCTC	National Counterterrorism Center (US)
NGO	Non-governmental organization
NIC	National Intelligence Council (US)
NIE	National Intelligence Estimate (US)
NPT	(Nuclear) Non-Proliferation Treaty
NSA (1)	National Security Agency (US)
NSA (2)	National Security Adviser (US)
NSC	National Security Council (US)
ODNI	Office of the Director of National Intelligence (US)
OPSEC	Operations security
ORCON	Originator Control
OSC	Open Source Center (US)
OSCE	Organization for Security and Co-operation in Europe
OSINF	Open source information
OSINT	Open source intelligence
PKI	Peacekeeping Intelligence
PM	Prime Minister
PR	Public relations
PSCI	Permanent Select Committee on Intelligence (US)
PSI	Proliferation Security Initiative (US)
RAF	Royal Air Force (UK)
RESINT	Research-originating intelligence
RMA	Revolution in Military Affairs
RUSI	Royal United Services Institute for Defence and Security Studies (UK)

SAS	Special Air Service (UK)
SBS	Special Boat Service (UK)
SF	Special Forces (see also SOF)
SIGINT	Signals intelligence
SIPRNet	Secret Internet Protocol Router Network (US)
SIS	Secret Intelligence Service or MI6 (UK)
SitCen	European Union Joint Situation Centre
SO15	Police Counter-Terrorism Command (UK)
SOCA	Serious Organised Crime Agency (UK)
SOCOM	Special Operations Command, Tampa, Florida (US)
SOF	Special Operations Forces
SOIA	Security Of Information Agreement (US)
SSCI	Senate Select Committee on Intelligence (US)
SSR	Security Sector Reform
TTIC	Terrorist Threat Integration Center, later NCTC (US)
UAV	Unmanned Aerial Vehicle ('Drone')
UK	United Kingdom of Great Britain and Northern Ireland
UKUSA	'Five-eyes' (UK, US, Australia, Canada and New Zealand) SIGINT arrangement
UN	United Nations
UNODC	United Nations Office on Drugs and Crime
UNSC	United Nations Security Council
UNSCR	United Nations Security Council Resolution
US	United States of America
WMD	Weapons of Mass Destruction
WoT	'War on Terror' or 'War on Terrorism' or 'Global War on Terror' (GWoT)

Source Abbreviations

ACA	*Arms Control Association*
AFP	*Agence France-Presse newswire*
AFPI	*American Foreign Policy Interests*
AP	*Associated Press newswire*
AR	Annual Report
BAS	*Bulletin of the Atomic Scientists*
BASIC	British American Security Information Council
BBC	*BBC News Online*
BJPIR	*British Journal of Politics and International Relations*
Brookings	Brookings Institution, Washington, D.C.
CFR	US Council on Foreign Relations, New York
CH	Chatham House, the Royal Institute of International Affairs, London
CL&SC	*Crime, Law & Social Change*
CNN	*CNN.com*
CNPP	Carnegie Non-Proliferation Programme
CREST	CIA Research Tool (US)
CRIA	*Cambridge Review of International Affairs*
CRS	*Congressional Research Service Report for Congress*
CS	*Comparative Strategy*
CSI	*CIA Studies in Intelligence*
CSP	*Contemporary Security Policy*
CUP	Cambridge University Press
DH	*Diplomatic History*
DT/ST	*Daily Telegraph/Sunday Telegraph* (UK)
FA	*Foreign Affairs*
FAS_SN	*Secrecy News*, published by the Federation of American Scientists (US)

FP	*Foreign Policy*
FT	*Financial Times*
GSN	*Global Security Newswire*
GU	*The Guardian*
HIR	*Harvard International Review*
HP	*The Huffington Post*
IA	*International Affairs*
IHT	*International Herald Tribune*
IISS	International Institute for Strategic Studies
IISS_AP	*IISS Adelphi Paper*
IISS_SC	*IISS Strategic Comments*
IISS_SS	*IISS Strategic Survey*
IJICI	*International Journal of Intelligence and CounterIntelligence*
INS	*Intelligence and National Security*
IS	*International Security*
ISC	Intelligence and Security Committee (UK)
ISN_SW	*ISN Security Watch*
ISP	*International Studies Perspectives*
JC&CM	*Journal of Contingencies and Crisis Management*
JCMS	*Journal of Common Market Studies*
JCS	*Journal of Conflict Studies*
JDI	*Jane's Defence Industry*
JDW	*Jane's Defence Weekly*
JFR	*Jane's Foreign Report*
JIAA	*Jane's Islamic Affairs Analyst*
JID	*Jane's Intelligence Digest*
JIDR	*Jane's International Defence Review*
JIR	*Jane's Intelligence Review*
JIW	*Jane's Intelligence Weekly*
JME	*Journal of Military Ethics*
JTS	*Journal of Transatlantic Studies*
JTSM	*Jane's Terrorism and Security Monitor*

LAT	*Los Angeles Times*
LRB	*London Review of Books*
Mail	*The Daily Mail* (UK)
MUP	Manchester University Press
NPR	National Public Radio (US)
NPS	*New Political Science*
NSAr	National Security Archive (US)
NYRB	*New York Review of Books*
NYT	*New York Times*
OD	*OpenDemocracy*
OUP	Oxford University Press
PSJ	*The Policy Studies Journal*
PSQ	*Political Science Quarterly*
PSR	*Political Studies Review*
RDS	*RUSI Defence Systems*
RHS&RM	*RUSI Homeland, Security and Resilience Monitor*
RIS	*Review of International Studies*
RJ	*RUSI Journal*
RUSI	Royal United Services Institute for Defence and Security Studies, London
SC&T	*Studies in Conflict & Terrorism*
SMH	*Sydney Morning Herald* (Australia)
SO	*Spiegel Online* (Germany)
SpyTalk	*SpyTalk – C.Q. Blog*
TA	*The Australian*
TAA	*The Age – Australia*
TL	*The Local* (Sweden)
TNPR	*The Nonproliferation Review*
TO	*The Observer* (UK)
TPQ	*The Political Quarterly*
TPV	*Terrorism and Political Violence*
TSO	The Stationery Office, Norwich, UK

TST	*The Sunday Times* (UK)
TWF	*The Washington File – US INFO*
TWQ	*The Washington Quarterly*
TWT	*The World Today* – Chatham House, London
UPI	*United Press International*
USIP	*US Institute of Peace*
USN&WR	*US News & World Report*
WB	*Wired.com (Danger Room) Blog*
WP	*Washington Post*
WSJ	*Wall Street Journal*
WT	*Washington Times*

Author Notes

Non-attributable sources

While researching for this study (and its companion volumes, Svendsen, 2010a and 2012e), over 60 (elite) interviews (i) were conducted in the United Kingdom and the United States of America. In a variety of ways, at least a further 60 prominent people were consulted (c), and kindly provided helpful insights and guidance in varying forms. Several meetings, conferences, workshops and training courses were also attended across the UK, and in the US, Italy, Ireland, Canada, Sweden, Norway and Denmark. Naturally, due to the sensitive nature of this subject, the majority of these interactions took place 'off the record' and/or under the Chatham House Rule. The label 'non-attributable source' is used in endnotes to identify contributions from these sources.

A further note on sourcing, referencing and terminology

Contemporary historians and analysts of intelligence find themselves increasingly dependent upon, and 'triangulating', sources such as published official strategy documents, think-tank and media output, as well as the semi-structured ('elite') interviews they have conducted, particularly as they become more up-to-date in their work.

The extensive references and endnotes provided in this study reflect engagement with those trends. For clarity, the references have been collected and presented together at the end of this study in a 'Select Bibliography' to constitute a form of reference library. Throughout the text, the key and strongest reference is generally cited first in any list of references, with subsequent references being ordered alphabetically, i.e. (Smith 2001 [strongest source]; see also Auld, 2009; Cotton, 2008; Dexter, 1999).

On the explicit use of *'vis-à-vis'* in this study: this term is particularly used to mean 'in relation to' in order to draw a distinction both with and between the term *'versus'*, which instead means 'against' or 'in opposition to'. The term *'vis-à-vis'* is used as a different 'operator', which particularly matters in domains such as politics and international relations, where sensitive nuances can impact significantly on prevailing developments.

Acknowledgements

In the UK, thanks go to: my family, Penny, David and Zoë Svendsen; Richard J. Aldrich at the University of Warwick; and to Philip H.J. Davies, at Brunel University, Uxbridge (especially for his organization of the 'Intelligence and Globalization' workshop, held during June 2009). Many thanks also go to: Stuart Croft (Warwick); Wyn Rees at the University of Nottingham. In the USA, many thanks go to: Daniel Byman at the Center for Peace and Security Studies (CPASS), Edmund A. Walsh School of Foreign Service, Georgetown University, Washington, DC (for sponsoring my visiting scholarship during June–September 2007). In Denmark, the Centre for Military Studies (CMS), in the Department of Political Science (IFS) at the University of Copenhagen (KU), provides an excellent research environment; and many thanks go to the other staff and to my fellow-students at all these universities for their support. Thanks also go to the interviewees, and to everyone else I have consulted when constructing this study, especially to Christina M. Brian and Julia Willan at Palgrave Macmillan.

Adam D.M. Svendsen

Preface: Intelligence *and* Globalization

The purpose of this book is manifold. Covering much subject terrain, two aspects particularly stand out: while seeking to (i) provide a concise general introduction to the complexities of contemporary Western Intelligence and its dynamics during an era of 'globalization writ large', this book more specifically offers (ii) arguments towards facilitating a general understanding of the distinct process of the 'globalization of intelligence'. Several timely insights are provided.

The central unifying thesis is clear. This book argues that the overall process of the 'globalization of intelligence' is accomplished through: *enhanced intelligence and information cooperation, which is conducted in a focused, directed and purposeful manner in various overlapping multi-functional operational contexts across the globe*. More technically, this type of interaction is officially known as 'liaison'. Accordingly, the phenomenon of *international* or *foreign* intelligence liaison, as it occurs in both theory and practice, forms the main focus of this study.

Summarizing the core findings presented in this book: the general trends strongly suggest that intelligence liaison is on 'a continuum with expansion' in the early twenty-first century. Significantly, these activities connect and add up through their various degrees of 'fusion', collectively contributing towards the readily observable overall increased globalization of intelligence.

Reflecting a 'complex coexistence plurality' of several different and overlapping concepts in action, this challenging process emerges as: (i) essential for complex issue management purposes during a globalized era characterized by transnational terror, crises (man-made and natural), and organized crime; while (ii) simultaneously raising several valid accountability and oversight concerns (Born *et al.*, 2011; see also 'Intelligence accountability' in Johnson, 2010b).[1] These factors make the exploration of the globalization of intelligence and its related phenomena, such as intelligence liaison, stand out as important.

Further evaluation is offered. Together with providing some detailed insights into the intelligence world and into how international interactions occur in – and, equally, how others overlap with – this frequently secretive domain of activity, several potentially useful lessons are proposed. These include: (i) some operational-to-strategy- and policy-orientated suggestions regarding the possible enhanced future governance and management of intelligence liaison extending to the 'globalization of intelligence'; and (ii) considering some closely related aspects, such as how intelligence collection, analysis and assessment/ estimate activities more generally can possibly be further optimized as the twenty-first century progresses.

In this study, aims are fulfilled through: (i) further developing the concept of '*reach*' in the intelligence and security context (defined as essentially the familiar idea of 'intelligence and security coverage', but with added *active influence potential* value attached); and then (ii) assessing the *dynamics* associated with that 'intelligence and security reach', termed '*reach dynamics*'.[2] Acknowledging the nature of the 'highly sensitive' subject of intelligence, and more specifically intelligence liaison, and that some realms might continue to be more 'fenced-off' due to secrecy considerations, this book also offers several directions ripe for future research (Svendsen, 2010a, p. 102).

A broad canvas is adopted to communicate several ideas. Continuing in an exploratory manner, attempts at the greater connection of the intelligence liaison phenomenon, extending to the 'globalization of intelligence', with a range of 'mainstream' bodies of 'theory', as well as the more direct 'theorization' of intelligence liaison itself, are then undertaken to try to further enhance our understanding. Ultimately, I intend to advance an overarching and literature-spanning analytical framework, with the initial population of that space. Many conclusions are offered for consideration.

With its emphasis on the dynamics of targeted communication and information flows, this book will also be of interest to those involved in similar interactions occurring in domains beyond merely the ('pure') intelligence sector and community (and the work it conducts, the material it handles, and the products it delivers). This includes being of interest to those people who are involved in any form of *critical information flow* processes, such as, most notably, crisis and civil protection managers and emergency planners, as well as being of interest to those working in the fields of communications, globalization and governance studies. Developments unfolding in multi-functional operational contexts ranging from war to peace have considerable relevance. In various ways, several key themes overlap and fuse (Miskel, 2008; see also Avant *et al.*, 2010; Gray, 2007b; Svendsen, 2011b).

Throughout this book, the following two key themes are prominent:

First: in an era of 'globalization writ large', the general phenomenon of international intelligence liaison is evolving in harmony with the trend of being on 'a continuum with expansion' (Svendsen, 2010a, pp. 42, 170, 172, 2012a). Through a management lens, this is so that multi-dimensional *intelligence and security reach* across and into multiple domains of operation and human activity at home and abroad can be enhanced, as well as extended into 'new' areas. Ideally, this 'reach' enhancement is accomplished in an appropriately proportional manner to that of the targeted threat, hazard, or risk. In the process, this opens up a whole range of *intelligence and security 'reach dynamics'* to being worthy of consideration, including 'outreach' movements (Treverton, 2009b). As Martin Libicki of RAND has observed: 'Those with the most attractive systems – in terms of information, knowledge, services, and reach – have an inherent advantage.' (Libicki, 2007, p. 3) When comprehensively explored, collectively these 'reach dynamics' provide a powerful explanatory prism through which contemporary intelligence, its activities, and its related phenomena, such as intelligence liaison and surveillance, can all be understood in a suitably interconnected manner.

Second: manifest as a proactive response to the familiar general long-term historical trend, recently more rapidly accelerated, of: (i) 'globalization writ large' (essentially what we generally understand by the term 'globalization' (see Chapter 1 (12.0), below)); and (ii) the impact of 'globalization *on* intelligence' – most notably the influence of all of globalization's well-known 'nasties', felt especially post-1989 and after the Cold War (see Chapter 6, below);[3] (iii) the 'globalization *of* intelligence', occurring especially in the early twenty-first century and post-9/11, can be discerned (Svendsen, 2010a, pp. xx–xxi; see also Svendsen, 2008a, b). Arguably the most direct manifestation of 'intelligence *and* globalization', including delving most deeply into what globalization means *for* intelligence, the *globalization of intelligence* is emerging through the mechanism of enhanced international intelligence liaison, together with being facilitated by the developments occurring both within and beyond those arrangements. This process includes factors such as 'intelligence and security reach dynamics' (as introduced above), and developments extending beyond merely the *regionalization of intelligence* processes, including overlapping with 'glocalization'[4] (Svendsen, 2011c; see Chapter 3 (2.1), below).

In their impact, all of these issues very much concern present intelligence activities, requiring careful close consideration by intelligence communities well into the future (Dorn, 2010; see also Aldrich, 2010).[5] Appropriately following soon after the centennial anniversary year of British Intelligence (2009–2010), these key, closely inter-related, themes will now be examined further.

Part I
Background

1
Unpacking Intelligence and Liaison
Understanding basics, drivers and underlying mechanisms

1.0 Introduction

Liaison is clearly central to intelligence. More widely, when occurring on broader bases, it is also clearly a major contributor to the overall process of the globalization of intelligence. As US intelligence scholar Loch K. Johnson has remarked:

> By combining their intelligence efforts with those of their allies, nations are able to trim intelligence costs and compensate for gaps in their own surveillance; yet fear that the other service has been penetrated by a common foe, and an awareness that the ally (however close) is likely to have some divergent objectives, keep the romance at arm's length.

Underlining the presence of nuances: 'The proposition warrants a corollary: the greater the perceived common danger, the more likely an effective liaison.' (Johnson, 2003, p. 17)

When evaluating the globalization of intelligence and its building blocks of 'liaison', delineating some study parameters is helpful. As the first Director General of Intelligence, UK Ministry of Defence (1964–1966), Major-General Sir Kenneth Strong, astutely observed in 1968: 'The initial point of any discussion of Intelligence is of course a definition of the word.' (Strong, 1968, p. 242) Accordingly, in order to better uncover 'drivers' and further explain 'underlying mechanisms' behind the globalization of intelligence, this chapter begins with some baseline definitions.

With acute relevance to the wider and higher occurring 'globalization of intelligence' process, if only by their close association, firstly, what is meant by 'intelligence' and 'liaison', and their subsequent fusion in the distinct phenomenon of 'intelligence liaison', is established. This chapter then continues by presenting some generalizations about intelligence liaison. Methodologically, adopting the starting position of 'basics', and then systematically building up the analysis in this study from those roots, emerges as a useful way forward.

To begin, better acknowledging its existence and its extended functioning in our contemporary globalized era, what does the word 'intelligence' actually mean? A suitably broad-ranging and multi-layered definition, appropriately tuned to the globalized context in which it strives to operate, is fashioned next. Helping to form the basis of later discussion, 'strengths' and 'weaknesses' are similarly delineated (see Chapters 4 (5.0) and 6 (9.0), below). The word 'intelligence' in the security context clearly continues to benefit from being further examined in our increasingly globalized circumstances.[1]

2.0 A definition of 'intelligence' – 'cloak, dagger... and skulduggery?'

What is precisely meant by the word 'intelligence' is still widely contested (Treverton *et al.*, 2006; see also Goodman, 2006; Taylor, 2007). This book focuses on the English-speaking Anglo-Saxon (UK–US) understandings.[2] However, even here differences are found. UK intelligence scholar Philip H.J. Davies argues that: 'The difference between British and US concepts of intelligence is that the US approaches information as a specific component of intelligence, while Britain approaches intelligence as a specific type of information.' (Davies, 2002, p. 64)

Much energy has been spent on defining 'intelligence' (McLachlan, 1968, p. xiii; Strong, 1968, pp. 241–242). Ultimately, the final, most acceptable, definition depends on your position, and on how far and in which direction the definition is taken. As Michael Warner argues: 'the term is defined anew by each author who addresses it, and these definitions rarely refer to one another or build off what has been written before.' (Warner, 2002) This is a useful place to start a discussion.

In 1987, UK academic Ken Robertson declared that: 'A satisfactory definition of intelligence ought to make reference to the following: threats, states, secrecy, collection, analysis and purpose.' (Robertson, 1987, pp. 46–48) It is also worth noting former UK intelligence officer Michael Herman's comment that: '"intelligence" in government usually has a more restricted meaning than just information and information services. It has particular associations with international relations, defence, national security and secrecy, and with specialised institutions labelled "intelligence".' (Herman, 1996, p. 1)

Warner's own definition of intelligence – 'Intelligence is secret, state activity to understand or influence foreign entities' (Warner, 2002) – will be added, here, with slight modification (Wilson, 2005, pp. 91–92), as it brings in more of the important dimension of 'intelligence' as a form of *power* – since 'knowledge is power' (Evans and Newnham, 1998, p. 255). Indeed, the interesting notion of intelligence as a form of power, akin to economic power, derives from the work of Michael Herman (1996). Neither is intelligence solely concerned with secrets, with the 'familiar secrets/mysteries dilemma' often featuring (Hennessy, 2003, p. 25; Treverton, 2009a, p. 3).

2.1 Intelligence characteristics

Intelligence comes in myriad forms (Lowenthal, 2006, pp. 68–108; Shulsky and Schmitt, 2002, pp. 11–40). These range from technical (TECHINT) – including signals intelligence (SIGINT), electronic intelligence (ELINT), communications intelligence (COMINT),[3] measurement and signature intelligence (MASINT),[4] imagery intelligence (IMINT),[5] and geospatial intelligence (GEOINT),[6] namely the 'scientific' dimension of intelligence – via human intelligence (HUMINT),[7] notably the 'artistic', even 'cultural', dimension of intelligence, to open-source intelligence (OSINT).[8] Broadly, these 'INTs' are the intelligence 'collection disciplines' (Svendsen, 2010a, pp. 12–13; see also Hall and Citrenbaum, 2012; HQUSAA, 2012).

Intelligence is also conceptualized as a *process*. Commonly known as the 'intelligence cycle', this process, in its narrowest and supposedly most perfect conception, consists of the steps of: determining the information intelligence consumers require (tasking); collecting the data needed to produce this intelligence (collection or harvesting); analysing the collected data (analysis or packaging); and disseminating the resulting intelligence, now in *product* form embodied in assessments (UK) or estimates (US), to consumers (dissemination, delivery, marketing or producing) (Berkowitz and Goodman, 1991, p. 30; Herman, 1996, p. 39). Added to this can be the step of 're-evaluation'; for example, if new intelligence has emerged during the process. This helps to answer the 'What is it?' question, and address 'What does it mean?' queries during analysis and assessment. Although in reality the intelligence cycle is often more complex, arguably the concept still performs a useful entry point for students of intelligence (Clark, 2009; Hannah *et al.*, 2005, pp. 1–3; Herman, 2001; Lowenthal, 2006, pp. 1–10; Shulsky and Schmitt, 2002, pp. 1–9; Wiebes, 2003, pp. 14–16).

Intelligence *product* again takes many different forms. The 'finished' assessments and estimates, essentially arising out of the analysis stage of the intelligence cycle, can range from being 'single-source' to being 'all-source' based. They also sit on a spectrum of being 'tactical' to 'strategic' (Lowenthal, 2006, pp. 41–73).[9] Intelligence product in tactical form ('Tactical Intelligence') is arguably 'rawer', and figures as the most actionable and operationally viable or 'serious' intelligence. Hence, it tends to be tightly controlled by its owners (originators) and is made available for dissemination on the most restricted bases. Strategic Intelligence, meanwhile, consists of slightly more 'sanitized' product. Therefore, it has some greater potential for wider dissemination. This is due to particular sensitive sources, methods, and their provenance, being less explicitly revealed in the information communicated, thus helping to contribute to the mitigation of counter-intelligence (CI) and other security concerns (Svendsen, 2008a, p. 134; see 2.2, below).

Interestingly, embedded in the spy fiction of British novelist Eric Ambler are some usefully painted insights. For instance, in *The Mask of Dimitrios* (1939), the different 'intelligences' that exist, for example, 'tactical' and 'strategic', are illustrated effectively when a crime scene is evaluated (Ambler, 1939, p. 50; Svendsen, 2009a). Closely overlapping are different configurations of, respectively, 'security intelligence' ('SI') and 'risk intelligence' ('RI'). In their different handling and calibrations, SI is largely reflective of pursuing 'see and strike' imperatives and RI is mostly representative of adopting 'wait and watch' approaches (see Chapter 5, Section 5.0, below).

'Business Intelligence' ('BI') similarly exists. In its own diverse mixtures, BI consists of varying combinations of both 'modes' of intelligence as outlined above (Petersen, 2012; Svendsen, 2012e). Ultimately, many different intelligence 'qualities' can be conveyed. Several different ranging ('near'/'central' and 'far'/'peripheral') 'targets' and 'leads' that interest and concern intelligence likewise emerge. All of these aspects are deserving of further examination.

2.2 Intelligence in action

Once produced, intelligence has to be transferred. How intelligence is securely conveyed from A to B, and is otherwise exchanged, shared or accessed, draws us into the domain of Communications Security (COMSEC) or Information Security (INFOSEC), today termed 'Information Assurance' (IA). Common standards in this area are often the bedrock of formal liaison.[10] Officially, according to the US Government, COMSEC consists of 'measures and controls taken to deny unauthorized persons information derived from telecommunications and [to] ensure the authenticity of such telecommunications', and includes the four categories of: (i) 'cryptosecurity' – resulting 'from the provision of technically sound cryptosystems and their proper use'; (ii) 'emission security'; (iii) 'physical security' – 'The component of [COMSEC] that results from physical measures necessary to safeguard classified equipment, material, and documents from access thereto or observation thereof by unauthorized persons'; and (iv) 'transmission security'.[11] Within this domain of activity, distinct intelligence 'systems' and 'architectures' acquire relevance, including closely associated operations (or operational) security (OPSEC) considerations. OPSEC is most pressing when handling operations (or operational) intelligence (OPINT), which, in the totality of OPINT's scope, includes (to various degrees) the fusion of the different qualities of intelligence or the 'intelligences' that exist (Warner, 2009a, pp. 11–37; see Svendsen, 2010a, p. 18; 2.1, above).

Intelligence is also *institutionalized*. In institutional terms, intelligence services can be both 'defensive' and 'offensive' in their deployment, encompassing 'covert action'. Arguably, covert action is the 'dagger' wielded by the 'hidden hand', with RAND analysts Hannah *et al.* able to observe that: 'while not an actual category of intelligence, covert action should also be considered as part of intelligence activities, as it is generally undertaken (in this context) for intelligence purposes (i.e. either driven by or attempting to generate intelligence).' (Hannah *et al.*, 2005, p. 2)[12] As UK intelligence scholar Len Scott has noted: 'For many writers ... on British intelligence, special operations are integral to the study of the subject. But for others they are not.' (Scott, 2004a, p. 323)

Denial, disruption, deception, disinformation, misinformation and propaganda activities – more popularly known as 'spin' – can also be added (Daniel, 2005, pp. 134–146; see also Allen, 2008, pp. 91–92; Harding, 2009; Wirtz, 2008, pp. 55–63).[13] In parallel there is the 'psychological dimension' of intelligence, which includes influence, persuasion, information and psychological operations (INFOPs/PSYOPs), at times also known as 'Military Information Support Operations' (MISOs), intended to win over 'hearts and minds' (Thornton, 2007, pp. 70–75; Cialdini, 2010; Deary, 2001; Duyvesteyn, 2011; Libicki, 2007).

Covert action can be further explained. Drawing on the definition frequently cited:

> 'Covert action' is defined by US law as activity meant 'to influence political, economic, or military conditions abroad, where it is intended that the role of the United States Government will not be

> apparent or acknowledged publicly.' Covert actions are thus distinct from clandestine missions: whereas the term 'clandestine' refers to the secrecy of the operation itself, 'covert' refers to the secrecy of its sponsor; the action itself may or may not be secret. (Kibbe, 2004; see also Lowenthal, 2006, pp. 157–173; Shulsky and Schmitt, 2002, p. 76; Treverton, 2009a, pp. 207–234)

The UK definition is more obscure. Over time it has moved 'from "special operations" to "special political action" to "disruptive action".' (Scott, 2004a, p. 325)

Often, covert action is carried out in the form of paramilitary activities, usually conducted by some type of 'special' military or civilian-quasi-military unit. There are the US Department of Defense (DoD)/Pentagon's 'Special [Operations] Forces' (SOF), including the US Army's 'Delta Force' and the US Navy's SEALs (Sea-Air-Land),[14] the CIA's 'Paramilitary Operations' or 'Special Activities Division/Staff';[15] and, in the case of the UK, the British Army's Special Air Service (SAS) and the Royal Navy's Special Boat Service (SBS), which are closely guided by intelligence from, and feed back intelligence to, the Secret Intelligence Service (SIS/MI6) and the UK Government Communications Headquarters (GCHQ) (Aldrich, 2005, pp. 341–342; Finlan, 2009; Svendsen, 2010a, pp. 78–91 and 158–164).

Frequently, UK Special Forces teams consist of a mixture of personnel from different units. These include participants from SIS and GCHQ, depending on what expertise and skill-sets are required for the particular operation, diplomatic or military, to be undertaken (see Chapter 5 (2.0), below). Currently, covert action is very much back in fashion, having been employed extensively in Afghanistan, Iraq and elsewhere, due to the recent so-called 'War on Terror' and 'Long War' (Kibbe, 2007, pp. 57–74);[16] as 'high-value targets' (HVTs), such as, most notably, Saddam Hussein (captured) and Osama bin Laden (killed), have found out personally (Svendsen, 2010a, p. 163; Schmidle, 2011).

However, these activities continue to remain highly sensitive politically, and remain fraught with other difficulties, such as of a legal and technical nature (Sepp, 2010).[17] Some widely publicized 'extraordinary renditions', and unmanned aerial vehicle (UAV) 'drone' attacks in countries such as Pakistan and Yemen, have involved CIA (paramilitary) Special Forces following up the leads fed from the CIA's Counterterrorism Center (CTC).[18]

A final category of intelligence is 'counter-intelligence' (CI). This is defined as: 'intelligence activities concerned with identifying and counteracting the threat to security posed by hostile intelligence organizations or by individuals engaged in espionage or sabotage or subversion or terrorism.' (http://wordnetweb.princeton.edu/; Ehrman, 2009; Redmond, 2010; Sims and Gerber, 2009) Or, in the rather grand UK definition, it is 'the defence of the realm' (Smith, 2004, p. 11). Here, too, liaison can perform an important role.[19] Since 1989, efforts to thwart 'economic/industrial espionage' by states have figured strongly in this area (Hagelin, 2009).[20]

2.3 Summarizing 'intelligence' and presenting a definition

Former US intelligence oversight practitioners, Abram N. Shulsky and Gary J. Schmitt, provide a helpful summary of 'intelligence' in their book, *Silent Warfare*. 'Intelligence' is characterized as: 'certain kinds of *information, activities*, and *organizations*.' (Shulsky and Schmitt, 2002, p. 1) Standing on the shoulders of Sherman Kent, the US doyen of philosophizing about intelligence, they elaborate: 'The word "intelligence" is used to refer to a certain kind of knowledge, to the activity of obtaining knowledge of this kind (and thwarting the similar activity of others), and to the organizations whose function is to obtain (or deny) it.' (Shulsky and Schmitt, 2002, p. 169)[21]

Meanwhile, former US Assistant Director of Central Intelligence for Analysis and Production, Mark Lowenthal, usefully defines 'intelligence' as: 'the process by which specific types of information important to national security are requested, collected, analysed, and provided to policy makers; the products of that process; the safeguarding of these processes and this information by counterintelligence activities; and the carrying out of operations as requested by lawful authorities.' (Lowenthal, 2006, p. 9)

After this brief survey of 'intelligence', the definition that will be drawn upon in this book is:

> the collection and processing (analysis) of information that is particularly of military and/or political value, and which especially (and purposefully) relates to international relations, defence and national (extending to global, via regional) security (threats). It is also usually secret (covert and/or clandestine), state activity conducted by specialized 'intelligence' institutions to understand or influence entities.

Most comprehensively, 'intelligence' can be best summarized as being: (i) a *process* ('the means by which certain types of information are required and requested, collected, analyzed, and disseminated, and as the way in which certain types of covert action are conceived and conducted'); (ii) a *product* ('the product of these processes, that is, as the analyses and intelligence operations themselves'); as well as being (iii) *institutionalized* or an *organization* ('the units that carry out its various functions') (Lowenthal, 2006; see also Johnson, 2012). After this 'globalization-friendly' definition of 'intelligence', what is precisely meant by 'liaison' is unpacked next.

3.0 A definition of 'liaison'

Definitions of 'liaison' are less contested. It is often characterized as a 'relation, link', stemming from the French language and the original 'Latin *ligationem* ... "a binding"' (Klein, 1967, p. 885), and as an 'illicit intimacy... (mil.) co-operation of forces.' (Onions *et al.*, 1966) The word 'liaison' perhaps also implies an element of prohibited courtship, something a bit mysterious, maybe even *risqué*, a private link. Here, the full intimacies, indeed the fact of the connection itself and who it may be with, is not intended to be revealed to a wider audience.[22] In the military context, as agreed by the US Department of Defense (DoD) and the North Atlantic Treaty Organization (NATO), 'liaison' is defined more precisely as: 'That contact or intercommunication maintained between elements of military forces to ensure *mutual understanding* and *unity of purpose and action*.'[23]

Distinct parameters emerge. During liaison, optimally shared perceptions, *fused* or *integrated* in a 'milder' incarnation and in a 'hub-and-spokes' manner, are acceptable. However, *over*-shared and *converged* perceptions are not. This is especially the occasions when (i) the sharing of perceptions extends too far, to what can be regarded as a 'group-think' extent, and when (ii) they have been too 'forced', resulting in a form of 'intelligence liaison blowback', reflecting a form of *overreach*. Meanwhile, questions concerning the *proportionality* and *sustainability* of those movements are also raised (Svendsen, 2010b). Elsewhere, 'liaison' has been denoted more officially in the *CIA Insider's Dictionary* as:

> (1) in governmental, military and intelligence usage, close and regular contact between counterpart units, organizations or agencies having complementary, supplementary or overlapping functions, responsibilities and areas of interest, usually on a lateral level, with a view toward facilitating and enhancing communications, coordination and effective cooperation in pursuit of common or similar goals; (2) in the intelligence and security sectors, international intelligence liaison between the intelligence and security agencies of the two

> nations or between two component agencies of the same national intelligence community. N.B. Liaison, especially for the purpose of exchanging sensitive information, is ideally, but not exclusively, maintained through cross-assignment of liaison officers (LOs), q.v. (Carl, 1996, p. 348)

Meanwhile, the LO role has been defined as: 'in governmental, military and intelligence usage, an officer of one agency, organization or unit who is assigned to a counterpart entity for the purpose of serving as the focal point of contact' (Carl, 1996). But, 'liaison' is not solely about communication. As noted in a US Army definition dating from October 1951: '13. Foreign liaison – Provides the official channel of liaison between the Army and foreign military representative on duty, visiting or training in the United States.'[24] Other functions become manifest.

3.1 Liaison 'functions'

Liaison has undergone some further analysis. The American intelligence scholar, H. Bradford Westerfield, provides a useful insight into 'liaison' in the intelligence context, by listing its *functions*. In his 'functional definition', he describes 'liaison' as comprising

> a wide range of forms and degrees of collaboration, across international boundary lines, between intelligence services governmental and/or nongovernmental. In the cross-national liaison, these services may share information and operations, provide support (training, advice, and supplies) and access to or for facilities, and participate in crypto-diplomacy – any of these functions. (Westerfield, 1995; 1996, p. 523)

Officially, in the UK, 'liaison' is referred to in several different, but overlapping, ways. For the UK SIS, it is referenced as: 'Foreign intelligence services with which SIS cooperates.'[25] In the UK *Butler Report* (July 2004), 'liaison' is defined as: 'the term used to indicate a collaborative relationship between the intelligence services of different countries, as in "liaison service" or "liaison source".' (Butler Committee, 2004, p. xi) In the US, 'foreign liaison' has been defined by the *Joint Inquiry into the Terrorist Attacks of September 11, 2001* (December 2002) as: 'Efforts to work with foreign government intelligence services, including law enforcement agencies that gather or carry out intelligence-related activities.' Its definition continued: 'Examples of foreign liaison include sharing information, joint collection efforts, and the arrest of suspected terrorists by foreign governments using US-supplied information.' And demonstrating its wide extent of use: 'Every major US intelligence agency has some form of liaison relationship with foreign governments.' (US PSCI and SSCI, 2002, p. 428)

The depth of liaison can vary. On some occasions, it can be characterized by a formal agreement. In this respect, intelligence services often behave like mini-states, negotiating their own treaties and sending out their own 'intelligence ambassadors and attachés'. Because of its tangibility, formal liaison is also the mode of liaison that can be most effectively investigated. At other times, as former CIA Inspector General (1990–1998), Frederick P. Hitz, has succinctly argued: 'Formal intelligence liaison relationships between cooperating services are seldom reduced to writing, even between long-term allies. The less said the better is the norm. The relationships go forward on the basis of mutual benefit and back-scratching.' (Hitz, 2008, p. 158)

The underlying *rationale* for the liaison can be easily recognized: 'when it is a case of each service making use of its comparative advantage in a given location to advance an agreed-upon goal, then such an arrangement clearly pays off' (Hitz, 2008). It can act as a 'force multiplier', complementing other intelligence efforts being undertaken elsewhere.[26] Case-specific variations exist.

3.2 Defining the 'double-edged sword' of 'intelligence liaison'

The term 'intelligence liaison' is expansive. It offers synonymy with the interchangeable terms 'intelligence cooperation', 'intelligence sharing', 'intelligence pooling', 'intelligence alliance', 'intelligence collaboration', 'intelligence integration', 'intelligence fusion', 'intelligence access' and 'intelligence exchange'. As a useful starting point, the nature of intelligence liaison is intrinsically diverse and can be characterized as being: 'simple and complex', 'symmetric and asymmetric', 'adversarial', and 'bilateral or multilateral' (Sims, 2006, pp. 196–202).

Discernible within intelligence liaison relationships, extending to the globalization of intelligence, are eight different, yet interrelated, levels of activity and experience. They each offer many different insights, and can hence be subsequently used for analysis purposes. Ranging from 'high' and 'macro' to 'low' and 'micro', these levels comprise: (i) the ideological level; (ii) the theoretical level; (iii) the strategy level; (iv) the policy level; (v) the operational level; (vi) the tactical level; (vii) the individual (as 'professional') level; and (viii) the personal level. These levels will constantly be encountered throughout this study during evaluation and should be kept in mind (Svendsen, 2010a, pp. 167–170, 2012e).[27]

In this book, 'intelligence liaison' is a direct composite of the words 'intelligence' and 'liaison' as defined above in 2.3 and 3.0–3.1. It means:

> relevant communication, cooperation and linkage between a range of actors, usually at (but not limited to) the official intelligence agency level, on intelligence matters – essentially exchanging or sharing information, particularly of military and/or political value, and which especially (and purposefully) relates to national (extending to global, via regional) security. It also includes: usually secret (covert and/or clandestine), state activity conducted by specialized 'intelligence' institutions to understand or influence entities.

The presence and preservation of secrecy surrounding the liaison, especially its details, is generally regarded as essential.[28] This is particularly if there is an associated illicit element and an intimacy involved that needs to remain hidden away, perhaps even from internal authorities.[29]

4.0 Liaison and outreach

Intelligence liaison can arguably be conceptualized as being a covert form of 'outreach'. Interpreted as 'soft liaison' – and hence less encumbered with the necessary operating restrictions and constraints of 'hard liaison' – most usefully 'outreach' is defined as: 'reach further than ... the extent or length of reaching out... an organization's involvement with the community.'[30] This conceptualization of intelligence liaison as a covert form of outreach is also present in at least one national intelligence community[31] (see also Johnson, 2006, esp. Figure 2.3, p. 89). Meanwhile, in the UK, and in other contexts – for example, in NATO – on occasions the term 'reach-back' is used to describe supporting intelligence interactions and information flows between headquarters level and the operations being conducted out-in-theatre and in forward battle-spaces.[32]

Adopting this route, the phenomenon of liaison is, therefore, subject to some of the traits associated with the phenomenon of outreach – such as, most notably, 'reach dynamics'. These include 'overreach' (more unfettered sharing or interactions) and 'under-reach' (more stunted sharing or interactions) (see Chapter 4 (5.0), below). But, arguably, at least in theory, by figuring in its harder form, the outreach behind the cloak of liaison can be more formal and tightly controlled. Frequently, this is accomplished by invoking the all-important so-called 'third-party rule' (also known interchangeably as the 'confidentiality rule' or 'control principle') in intelligence liaison interactions – a protocol designed to preserve the confidentiality of secret exchanges of information between different parties (see Chapter 2 (2.1 and 3.1), below). These qualifiers reflect the requirements stipulated by processes such as, notably, the 'professionalization' of liaison (Svendsen, 2012e).

How effectively these requirements are implemented in reality across all 'levels' of interaction remains debatable (see 3.2, above; Svendsen, 2010a, p. 167). As former US intelligence officer Robert David Steele has claimed, critically: 'Professionalism and "foreign liaison" constitute an inherent oxymoron.'[33] This is a tension not least apparent in a context where a plethora of informal arrangements exist in parallel, as Hitz has already suggested (Svendsen, 2010a, p. 4, 2012e). Often these arrangements or agreements exist outside and beyond the authorities that are technically supposed to 'govern' intelligence liaison relationships. Crucially, this allows for some more essential flexibility of operation.

The implications that flow from this adaptability range far. They can be good, bad, and/or ugly, or, equally, a complex dual or pluralistic combination of these qualities within and across all levels of intelligence liaison activity and experience (when taken together as a whole during moments of analysis). The balance of these qualities also varies over time in evaluations as intelligence liaison systems constantly change (Svendsen, 2010a, from p. 167; see also 3.2, above).

5.0 Characterizing intelligence liaison

Intelligence liaison has multiple characteristics. It can therefore offer much multi-functional utility to foreign policy, defence and security practitioners, including law enforcement and safety-focused personnel. This is particularly helpful when they are trying to navigate highly dynamic operational contexts (Svendsen, 2011b). There can be a single link ('simple liaison'), a network or matrix of links ('complex liaison'). The links can be of a formal and regulated, informal and ad hoc, continuing or temporary, enduring or brittle, institutional and/or personal nature.[34] The links can also be deeper, acquiring relationship attributes, extending to a 'special' relationship nature – depending on the presence and extent of conditional factors, such as trust and mutual interests and/or values (Zinn and Taylor-Gooby, 2006, pp. 61–63; Yang *et al.*, 2010, pp. 231–241). Through regulation, the link(s) may also be subject to some form of internal self-oversight or accountability mechanism. For example, this can be undertaken within and by the participating intelligence agencies, both jointly and on an individual national basis.

A broader definition can be tabled. Depending on the actors or parties involved, on an expanding continuum, this includes liaison occurring between law enforcement (police) forces, between embassies' and armies' legal, defence, and military attachés, and can include cross-sector, different level, and different organization contacts (Gerspacher, 2008, pp. 169–184; see also Alpert and Dames, 2011, pp. 104–106; Dearlove, 2010, p. 45; Deflem, 2010; Vagts, 1967). It can range from a shared and pooled database to people talking. Intelligence liaison can be extended into the domain of diplomacy, such as being a form of readily deniable 'clandestine diplomacy' or 'crypto-diplomacy' through using 'back-channels' (Westerfield, 1996, pp. 523–560; Scott, 2004a, p. 330; Wilson, 2005, p. 93).[35] It can be regarded as a form of covert action (Scott, 2004a, p. 324), or, adopting a yet wider focus, it can even include essentially any form of cross-boundary contact where 'intelligence' is exchanged – also featuring in the important intelligence community (producer) and user (customer or consumer) relationship (Herman, 1996, p. 44; Lowenthal, 2010, p. 437; Shukman, 2000, p. xix). Communication dynamics are essential.

Liaison has much relevance in relation to all stages of the 'intelligence cycle'. This includes the collection and analysis of material. However, intelligence liaison is simultaneously not neatly or easily categorizable in generic terms without a degree of distortion. As it takes place in multiple locations, it cannot be sited in a specific stage of the intelligence cycle. As former US intelligence practitioner Arthur Hulnick has observed: 'the cyclical pattern does not describe what really happens ... The Intelligence Cycle also fails to consider either counter-intelligence or covert action.' Equally, liaison can be added to his list. He continued: 'Taken as a whole, the cycle concept is a flawed model.' (Hulnick, 2006, p. 959; see also Evans, 2009; Clark, 2009)

The range of subjects covered by the liaison can also vary. So can the extent they are interacted over. Here, intelligence liaison often works on a *quid pro quo* basis. As Hitz has remarked: 'Except between the oldest and most interdependent allies, the working principle will most often boil down to a *quid pro quo* exchange in the context of "what have you done for me lately?"' (Hitz, 2005, p. 157; Clough, 2004; Reveron, 2006, p. 467) Intelligence liaison can operate at the national and international (bilateral through to pluri- and multilateral) levels (Rudner, 2004b). Perhaps most controversially, it can take place with foes. As *Jane's Islamic Affairs Analyst* noted in July 2007, the US–Syria intelligence relationship 'is an example of "adversarial liaison".'[36]

Intelligence liaison is also a useful mechanism for keeping tabs on friends. This is especially as the 'friends' may simultaneously be regarded as a competitor, for instance in the economic arena (Schweizer, 1993; see also Alexander, 1998).[37] Intelligence liaison helps to grant an insight into their activities, their future intentions, whether they are adhering to treaty obligations, and so forth.[38] Differing views persist.

6.0 Intelligence liaison dynamics

Intelligence liaison boasts multiple dynamics. Intelligence liaison or its cessation, or the threat thereof, can be used as a 'bargaining chip'. This is in order to help try and persuade a rethink or change of policy, for instance, at the highest government level of a current, former or potential intelligence partner. In May 2005, Syria announced that it was ending military and intelligence cooperation with the USA to underline its objections to US policy (Reveron, 2006, p. 466).[39] Other examples include the 'withholding' of some intelligence on Bosnia by the USA over UK–US differences on the issue during the 1990s (Wiebes, 2003, pp. 59–60), as well as the brief official US withdrawal of the supply of US SIGINT to UKUSA partner New Zealand after their differences over nuclear matters in 1985.[40]

Intelligence liaison can raise some awkward ethical and moral questions. These require compromises on one or both sides in order for the liaison to work most effectively (Wirtz, 1993; see also Lowenthal, 2006, pp. 255–273).[41] In 2009, the former UK Ambassador to Uzbekistan (2002–2004), Craig Murray – who had earlier in 2005 raised concerns about the UK and US use of Uzbekistani intelligence (allegedly) obtained by torture (Svendsen, 2010a, p. 71) – claimed that 'it was "schizophrenic" to condemn torture but use its "fruits".'[42] Hitz has also raised the concern that: 'There are ... many issues that need to be resolved respecting the CIA's use of "dirty assets".' (Hitz, 2008, p. 165)[43]

When navigating these circumstances, the 2010 UK *National Security Strategy* observed: 'Protecting our security requires us to work with countries who do not share our values and standards of criminal justice.' It stressed that: 'In working with them to protect our country from terrorist attacks and other threats we do not compromise our values. We speak out against abuses and use our own conduct as an example.' However, these interactions are not all smooth. The Strategy, likewise, went on to emphasize the dilemmas involved in these interactions: 'But we have to strike a balance between public condemnation of any deviation from our values and the need to protect our security through international cooperation.' It continued, acknowledging: 'Striking these balances is not always straightforward, and reasonable people can differ on how to do it. In recent years it has not proved easy to find this balance in some cases.' Indeed, on these issues, engagement was officially sought, so that a suitable arrangement could be found 'to scrutinise modern day national security actions effectively without compromising our security in the process.' (UK HMG, 2010, p. 23)[44]

Several 'paradoxes' are evident. The 'double-edged' nature of intelligence cooperation, which can 'cut' (work or not) both ways, negatively and positively, is again demonstrated.[45] Clearly in some circumstances – especially when striving to reach the goal of 'for the greatest good' in terms of collective security and public safety during certain cases (see Chapter 2 (2.0), below) – through compulsion the British may reluctantly have to put aside individual human rights concerns regarding intelligence material liaised over, that may have been obtained through the use of unsavoury and controversial methods.[46] Arguably, these dubious methods can extend to (i) being counterproductive in other areas of activity, (ii) work against (clash with) policy stipulations, and (iii) indeed be 'unlawful'. This is notably during the occasions that involve 'torture', and include 'extraordinary renditions' and distinctly unpleasant 'intensive interrogation' techniques, such as 'waterboarding'.[47]

Much stress is involved. Intelligence operators frequently encounter 'no-win' situations where in their work they are 'damned if they do' (allegedly becoming associated with torture and other unsavoury methods); and 'damned if they don't' (possibly sacrificing potentially useful investigative 'leads', which might have (at least a modicum of) valid warning and informing qualities) (Turner, 2011).[48] These situations are somewhat drily described by practitioners as being where the expression of 'dare to share' prevails.[49] In their *Renditions* report of June 2007, when conducting its intelligence oversight and accountability work, the UK Intelligence and Security Committee (ISC) regretfully noted that: 'What the U.S. rendition programme has shown is that these ethical dilemmas are not confined to countries with poor track records on human rights – the UK now has some ethical dilemmas with our closest ally.'[50] Intelligence liaison work is clearly challenging.

Imperfections frequently reign. The liaison may equally be with an unpalatable person or organization. More explicitly, this introduces the concept of so-called 'dangerous liaisons' (Aldrich, 2002; Treverton, 2005, p. 25).[51] Moreover, in order to liaise effectively, the intelligence officers involved have to be 'declared' or 'authorized'. Thus, by being 'outed', they reveal their identity to another party, increasing the chances of being exposed as a spy or being otherwise compromised (Scott, 2004a, p. 331; see also Lefebvre, 2003; Warrick, 2011).[52]

Both structural and cultural obstacles can feature. As the ISC *Renditions* report remarked by way of contextualization: 'Despite the value that intelligence sharing can bring, working with a foreign intelligence service is not always straightforward for the UK Agencies.' It went on to elaborate: 'Other countries have different legal systems and different standards of behaviour to the UK, and their intelligence and security services have varying levels of capability, capacity and professional standards. These factors must be taken into account when working with foreign liaison services.'[53] Closely overlapping with wider 'professionalization'-associated movements, agreed 'international standards' and 'best practices' being applied within liaison interactions by all the parties involved, clearly come in useful (see 11.0–12.0, below; Svendsen, 2012e).

Observations extend further. So-called 'realist' perspectives tend to compare the intelligence liaison process with a professional business relationship. Intelligence, as a commodity or product, is carefully negotiated, marketed, and traded over (Herman, 1996, pp. 217–218). We can even discuss the 'economics' of intelligence, including IPE (international political economy) resonating dimensions (see Chapter 4 (4.1), below). As US Intelligence scholar Jennifer Sims has argued: 'Although sometimes equated with intelligence sharing, intelligence liaison is actually better understood as a form of subcontracted intelligence collection based on barter.' (Sims, 2006, p. 196) The control and ownership of the intelligence liaised over, and of the source originating that intelligence, can be contentious and complicated. This is to varying degrees, depending on a complex mixture of circumstances and the terms of the liaison 'deal' struck. So-called 'Originator Control' considerations ('ORCON'), as well as their rigorous application in interactions, can also get introduced. For instance, as the UK *Butler Report* found in 2004:

> In oral evidence to our Review in May, the Chief of SIS [Sir Richard Dearlove] said that [the] source's reports had been received through a liaison service and that he had not therefore been under the control of SIS. SIS had been able to verify that he had worked in an area which would have meant that he would have had access to the sort of information he claimed to have. But they had not been able to question him directly until after the war. (Butler Committee, 2004, p. 101)

Similarly to any business deal, the final agreement under some circumstances is occasionally evaded, with details being interpreted slightly differently by each party involved.[54] Insights into some of the micro-intelligence management controls in UK–US intelligence liaison relations can be glimpsed in ISC reports. For example, during one episode, the ISC observed: 'The telegram was correctly covered by a caveat prohibiting the U.S. authorities from taking action on the basis of the information it contained.'[55]

Ultimately, each of the interactions outlined above generates its own politics. These warrant further in-depth exploration, particularly when currently, both domestically and in international affairs, there is quantitatively more intelligence liaison underway than witnessed previously (Hitz, 2005, p. 156; Tebbit, 2006, p. v, no.15; Walsh, 2009).

7.0 Exploring the depths of intelligence liaison

This book argues that intelligence liaison is a form of 'overt-covert action'. Or, to borrow Michael Herman's phrase, used in relation to how diplomats view intelligence generally, it is 'a slightly fenced-off mystery' (Herman, 1996, p. 215).[56] The iceberg analogy resonates. The aspects describable as 'hidden dynamics' are rarely revealed, or at least tend not to be probed until after a significant passage of time. Even then, accounts can be constrained, in part because of the methodological problems encountered, as characterized above.

Although having been better addressed by 2012, intelligence liaison, including its wider closely related trends, such as extending to the globalization of intelligence, continues to be a very unevenly researched area. The writing on intelligence liaison in all mediums, from media articles to the academic and (former-) practitioner literature, can be described as diverse and is mainly longer-term, historically orientated. It offers an almost exclusively *empirical* evaluation of liaison, reflecting an overall dearth of *theory* in this area of contemporary intelligence studies.[57]

As UK intelligence scholar Len Scott noted in 2004 about 'clandestine diplomacy', an aspect of intelligence liaison, it 'is a neglected area of enquiry.' (Scott, 2004a, p. 330) In the following pages, with particular focus on *international* or *foreign* intelligence liaison, this book aims to continue to contribute towards addressing that shortcoming (Sims, 2006).[58] As Scott concluded: 'The problems of learning about covert action (and clandestine diplomacy) will nevertheless persist, as the need to evaluate and judge them will undoubtedly grow.' (Scott, 2004a, p. 338; see also Finlan, 2009, pp. x–xi) Intelligence liaison, extending more widely to the globalization of intelligence, can also be legitimately added to his list. As these broader related trends are further unpacked, a useful place to begin an extended analysis is by attempting some generalizations about intelligence liaison. Further insights into the globalization of intelligence soon follow.

8.0 Intelligence liaison generalizations

Generalizing about intelligence liaison presents multiple challenges. Yet, despite confronting these generalizability issues, some efforts to this end are still worth trying (see Chapter 3, below). Intelligence liaison is important to various processes – not least, as already seen, and most relevantly for the analysis undertaken in this book, the globalization of intelligence. In its fullest form, intelligence liaison can convey multiple meanings.

Indeed, as a multi-purpose or multi-functional tool to help achieve desired ends in the form of a *modus vivendi*, including in wide-ranging areas such as politics and international relations, intelligence liaison is arguably one of the most effective *modi operandi*. Intelligence liaison also boasts substantial impact in more specific domains. For instance in the US military context, as the US Joint Chiefs of Staff noted while emphasizing the utility of liaison: 'Robust liaison facilitates understanding, coordination, and mission accomplishment.'[59] Similarly, it performs an important role in the emergency planning/management, civil protection (emergency preparedness), and disaster and crisis management domains of activity (e.g., Alexander, 2002, p. 90).[60] Intelligence liaison also featured prominently in General Michael Hayden's US Congressional confirmation hearing for the post of the head of the CIA in May 2006 (Ward and Hackett, 2006; see also Jones, 2007, pp. 384–401).[61] In the UK, at least at the highest levels, a substantial amount of the heads of the intelligence agencies' time is expended on managing liaison. These relationships are all deemed to be extremely valuable (Jones, 2010a; McKeeby, 2006; Tenet, 2007, p. 34; UK HMG, 2010, p. 25, para.3.4).[62,63]

Intelligence liaison takes place in multiple locations. Indeed, it is remarkably widespread, depending upon how broadly it is conceptualized. At its least, it offers decision-makers an extensive range of options of deployable *types and forms* and *functions* (see Chapter 4 (2.0), below). We next examine its strengths.

9.0 Intelligence liaison strengths

Intelligence liaison boasts many strengths. For instance, as an issue navigation aid, it can be the ultimate enabler. Often it is cloaked in intense secrecy, staying hidden in the background, away from scrutiny and subsequent accountability. This feature adds to its appeal as a tool, according it more flexibility and dynamism of operation. Showing attitudes of the time, as Sir John Bruce Lockhart, former deputy Chief of the UK SIS (MI6) in the 1960s, declared: 'The essential skill of a secret service is to get things done secretly and deniably.'[64]

Intelligence liaison is an essential component. It can be one of the key means of acquiring and communicating knowledge, as well as conveying the *power* associated with knowledge. Intelligence liaison can also be a means for using that resulting 'intelligence power'. Therefore, in the post-9/11 and increasingly globalized security environment, it is unsurprising that, to a greater degree than previously, countries are increasingly reliant upon intelligence liaison that extends across the globe.[65]

Intelligence hegemony is vital. Thereby, at least a degree of 'intelligence supremacy' can be best realized. For the US, the intelligence hegemony is essential for: (i) acquiring and maintaining primacy; (ii) persuading other parties into a collective and cooperative orbit; and (iii) helping to provide leadership and effective global management in international affairs. It increases the potential for a 'rapier', rather than a 'bludgeon', to be applied in governance contexts (Omand, 2005; see also Brennan, 2010). This significantly assists in the 'smart power' calculation regarding the potentially most advantageous deployment of 'hard' and 'soft' power (Nye, 2004; O'Hanlon and Campbell, 2006 Mooney and Evans, 2007, p. 120).[66] Currently, a global hegemony of intelligence power and resources is central to helping sustain the multi-challenged status quo of *Pax Americana* and its derivatives.[67] But, several 'weaknesses' also exist.

10.0 Intelligence liaison weaknesses

Despite the positive attributes of intelligence liaison, several potential pitfalls are involved. These have been shown by the recent intelligence controversies concerning the 9/11 attacks and surrounding the issue of supposed Iraqi weapons of mass destruction (WMD). Intelligence liaison can be a powerful tool, but it is only as effective as those who use it.[68] Equally, the *effects and outcomes* of intelligence liaison can be complicated and ambiguous (Johnson, 2003, p. 17; Lefebvre, 2003). This prompts the recommended essential qualification: 'proceed with caution'.

Indeed, US defence expert Derek Reveron has observed: 'Nowhere is "trust, but verify" as important as in intelligence-sharing relationships.'

(Reveron, 2006, p. 468) Moreover, as US intelligence practitioner Warren Mulholland noted in the 1970s: 'on balance we benefit from liaison with other services, and that although we use great caution in what we teach and give to them, we must face the fact that even the simplest and most basic of clandestine techniques can be used against us just as readily as against a common adversary.' (Mulholland, 1973, p. 23)

Despite its importance, intelligence liaison should not induce over-dependence. International intelligence liaison arguably works best when deployed in a *supporting* role, complementing other *unilateral* intelligence efforts (Hitz, 2008, pp. 157–158).[69] Intelligence liaison also contributes towards the generation of shared perceptions. Ironically, if international intelligence liaison is too close, or if a particular intelligence liaison relationship becomes too much of an 'end' in itself, then intelligence 'reach' excesses and deficits become more pronounced. Intelligence *convergence* occurs. Episodes of 'intelligence liaison blowback', namely 'groupthink' (Davis and Persbo, 2004; Hill, 2003, pp. 115–116), can result, as well as other problems that at least contribute to other well-known intelligence analysis-related 'flaws', such as 'mirror-imaging', 'perseveration', 'transferred judgement', and other cognitive shortcomings (Davis, 2002; Lowenthal, 2006, p. 8). Several dangers lurk.

In a 'traditional liaison' context, there can also be concerns about participants going too 'native', suggesting the complicating issue of 'split loyalties'.[70] These wide-ranging issues can increase the likelihood of some form of 'intelligence failure' emerging (Taylor, 2007, p. 256; Hatlebrekke and Smith, 2010, pp. 147–182; Lowenthal, 2006, pp. 109–144; Shulsky and Schmitt, 2002, pp. 41–73). However, the absence of intelligence liaison, together with the lack of the communication of knowledge, resulting in ignorance, is worse. The purpose of providing adequate contextualization contributing to overall situational awareness and mission accomplishment is lost.

Not infrequently, risk management considerations emerge. This is typically where foreign services are given permission to carry out an operation on sovereign national territory (Gerber, 2007, pp. 227–238; see also Fuchs-Drapier, 2011, pp. 184–197; Chapter 4 (3.0, point 6), below). Intelligence liaison involves risk, but its absence would involve greater risk. Trade-offs figure. Ultimately, successful intelligence *fusion* is the objective.

11.0 Distilling the important operational parameters

International intelligence liaison can be demanding. For it to function, at least an element of 'homogenization' and 'international standardization' needs to be present. Usually conceptualized as some form of agreement established between all parties involved in the liaison,[71] including somewhere the presence of at least mutual interests and/or values, this arrangement helps to foster a foundation level of *trust* (Gupta and Becerra, 2003, p. 25; Kydd, 2005; Lubell, 2007, pp. 237–250). This is the essential enabling condition for *substantial liaison* to take place, and for providing the most stable underlying bond of the relationship. Trust, too, allows the prospect of increased liaison and related phenomena, such as 'jointery' (used to describe the joining up of the three military services – the army, air force, and navy – in response to the trend that 'military power has been increasingly recognised as a unity' (Herman, 2003a, p. 51)), into the future (Gardner, 2006, p. 30).

In the case of the UK–US intelligence liaison relationship, a mosaic of agreements formally achieves this process, including those associated with the UKUSA arrangement (see Chapters 2 (2.2 and 3.2) and 3 (9.0), below). More widely, as Michael Herman stresses: 'This importance of standards spreads well beyond the English-speaking communities and applies to intelligence's internationalization.' (Herman, 2004, p. 187)[72] While in the rapidly growing peacekeeping intelligence (PKI) context, PKI 'seeks to establish standards in open-source collection, analysis, security, and counter-intelligence and training, and produces unclassified intelligence useful to the public.' (Carment and Rudner, 2006; Steele, 2007, p. 167)[73] On similar bases, standards perform an important role, as bedrocks, in the overall globalization of intelligence (Aldrich, 2009a, p. 34; Svendsen, 2008a, b).

12.0 Essential terminology definitions

Clarifying the key terms encountered in this study is now helpful. The term 'homogenization', introduced above, means making 'of the same kind... consisting of parts all of the same kind; uniform' (Swannell, 1992, p. 508; see also Mooney and Evans, 2007, pp. 123–124) or, at least, *approaching* that condition. The other term referenced, 'international standardization', has a similar meaning, although it is not quite the same as 'homogenization'. This is because at its most *formal* and in its most *pure* form, it can correspond to the work undertaken by the International Organization for Standardization (ISO),[74] with 'the ISO' of intelligence having already been suggested (Steele, 2004; see also Murphy and Yates, 2009).

Meanwhile, as already outlined above in the Preface, the term 'globalization' has several potential meanings when employed in relation to intelligence (Ripsman and Paul, 2010, pp. 5–10). To recap, three closely overlapping forms particularly stand out and are referred to throughout this study: (i) the general consideration of 'globalization writ large', including claims that we seem to be 'competing with everyone from everywhere for everything' (Sirkin *et al.*, 2008; see also de Blij, 2009);[75] and, more specifically, (ii) the more direct impact of globalization *on* intelligence; and, finally, (iii) the globalization *of* intelligence.

Developed in response to (i) and (ii), the focus of this book, (iii) the *globalization of intelligence*, can mean much. Essentially, when distilled, it refers to the greater interconnectedness and interdependence of intelligence and its institutions across the world. This is as well as referring to intelligence cooperation occurring more widely and in greater depth, whether between individuals, organizationally, technologically, and so forth.

Elsewhere, 'globalization' has been defined relevantly to the world of intelligence as: 'A historical process involving a fundamental shift or transformation in the spatial scale of human organization that links distant communities and expands the reach of power relations across regions and continents...' (McGrew, 2005, p. 24), and as the 'de-territorialization – or... the growth of supraterritorial relations between people.' (Scholte, 2000, p. 46; see also Fairclough, 2006; Gallaher *et al.*, 2009; Liu *et al.*, 2012; Ritzer, 2009; Steger, 2009). Special Forces analyst Alastair Finlan notes: 'Globalisation, arguably one of the most contested concepts in international relations, has through specific technologies related to transport and communications effectively shrunk time and space on a global scale.' (Finlan, 2009, p. 112) Several changes to the overall contemporary landscape of intelligence are apparent.

Ultimately, in the intelligence realm, a complex web of various intelligence liaison and outreach arrangements emerges overall. Collectively this networked web provides a form of global intelligence coverage. Each reflecting different degrees of 'specialness', the arrangements work by overlapping in key metropolitan centres, such as London and Washington, and by being governed by a mosaic of agreements ranging in nature from formal to informal. Particularly when examining intelligence and information flows through these channels, the globalization of intelligence becomes increasingly evident, including the attempts towards its improved management. Many timely observations arise.

Part II
The Globalization of Intelligence in Action

2
The Burgeoning Globalization of Intelligence
Intelligence cooperation in practice

1.0 Introduction

During November 1944, General William J. Donovan, head of the US Office of Strategic Services (OSS), wrote in a memorandum to US President Franklin D. Roosevelt: 'Your correspondent suggests that OSS has been penetrated by the English Intelligence Service.' He continued: 'If by penetration is meant that we have worked closely together with that Service in the spirit of cooperation that you have urged upon us, then the statement is true; but if more than that is meant, the statement is not true and on the contrary we have greatly profited by our working with the British and at the same time we have maintained the integrity of our organization.' Concluding, he remarked: 'In point of fact you would be interested to know that both our Allies and our enemies know less about our inner workings than we do about theirs.'[1]

Building on that witnessed earlier in the twentieth century, this chapter evaluates some of the international intelligence cooperation that has been under way in the early twenty-first century (Aldrich, 2011a; Clift, 2010). Especially examined is the intelligence liaison, extending to the globalization of intelligence, that has been witnessed during the so-called 'War on Terror' era (*c.* 2001–2009) and beyond. Anglo-American and other Western countries' intelligence liaison interactions, together with their closely associated multilateral intelligence liaison activities with other countries across the globe, form the main subjects of focus in this chapter.

Particularly discussed are the two key and closely interrelated thematic and functional issue-areas of counter-terrorism (CT) and WMD counter-proliferation (CP), over which intelligence liaison most frequently occurs (Svendsen, 2010a, p. 33). In the contemporary globalized security environment, maintaining focus on CT and CP continues to be of much relevance. As the IISS *Strategic Survey 2007* noted: 'In 2008, managing nuclear proliferation and terrorism will remain the priorities.' (IISS, 2007, p. 402) In 2012, and into the foreseeable future, those concerns persist.[2] Some consideration of intelligence liaison on organized crime issues is also included.

By exploring the interactions outlined in this chapter, collectively the burgeoning 'globalization of intelligence' can be readily and empirically observed as being in action. Complementing the 'theoretical' dimensions of discussion undertaken later, several insights are provided.

2.0 Counter-terrorism as the lead issue

To fully appreciate the driving momentum behind the increase in intelligence cooperation, contextualization is helpful. In recent years, 'general issues' emerged foremost in UK–US and other countries' intelligence liaison on counter-terrorism (CT) (Pollard, 2009, pp. 117–146; Svendsen, 2010a, pp. 39–100). Alongside the overarching 'responsibility to protect' ('R2P') governance principle, pursued both at home and abroad, the goal of public safety continued firmly in its ascendancy after 9/11 (Dias, 2011; Hunt and Bellamy, 2011).[3] This included civil protection and emergency preparedness activities, also involved against civil contingency-impacting concerns, such as floods, farm livestock 'foot-and-mouth' disease and fuel-shortages (Alexander, 2002; Burgess, 2008).[4]

As the former UK Cabinet Office Intelligence and Security Coordinator, Sir David Omand, and others have commented, in our contemporary era of complex and rapid globalization we have moved (some legacies aside) from the 'secret state' model of the Cold War to the 'protective state' (Hennessy, 2007, 2010; Aldrich, 2005; Cook, 2009; Hayman with Gilmore, 2009; Selverstone, 2010). The motto 'protect and serve', as adopted by agencies such as the Los Angeles Police Department (LAPD), increasingly dominates in the Public Safety era (Inkster, 2010a, pp. 203–209; Jenkins and Godges, 2011; Omand, 2010).[5]

States have launched several initiatives in an attempt to realize the better management of threats, hazards and risks, as well as the responses to them. Together with their other partners, in both the UK and US, successfully fulfilling 'public safety' aspirations has remained a strong 'top-down' political impetus. It also remains a forceful governmental-to-intelligence and security operational driver (Foley, 2009b; Newbery *et al.*, 2009). Indeed, the general pursuit of 'public safety' was especially energized after the 9/11 attacks, as the homeland security paradigm burgeoned (Ransley and Mazerolle, 2009; Shapiro and Darken, 2010, p. 288; Svendsen, 2010c).[6]

At times, it also became more of a 'politicized' objective, including all the inherent negative connotations (Pillar, 2010; Treverton, 2010).[7] The goal of public safety was sought more widely, and its implementation was attempted in a timelier manner, on improved *a priori* and 'forward' bases (Brattberg, 2012; Daalder, 2007; Dershowitz, 2006; Hegghammer, 2010; Rasmussen, 2006, p. 94).[8]

Enactment of the above rationale could even challenge the law, sometimes substantially.[9] This has been most apparent in the case of the United States. CIA 'intensive interrogations', 'extraordinary renditions' and 'secret prisons' have been the most emblematic of those trends (Blakeley, 2011b; Hitz, 2008, pp. 159 and 164).[10] These were actions deemed essentially legitimized, at least to some participants and observers, as several – believed to be exonerating – 'crisis' circumstances were encountered and needed successful navigation (Hitz, 2008, pp. 166–167).[11]

The UK confronted similar challenges. Particularly as witnessed domestically, as well as attempted internationally, the UK strove to appropriately maintain its proportionality considerations while simultaneously more widely seeking to realize the goal of public safety (Svendsen, 2010a, p. 70).[12] This attempt to maintain a 'sense of proportion' was especially acute in the situations judged to be requiring a *crisis management* or an *emergency response* approach (Perry, 2009; Smith and Elliot, 2006; Svendsen, 2010b; Whetham, 2011). These were the situations believed to necessitate approaches beyond mere regular *risk management*. For instance, in the UK, this required the 'activation' of the civil contingencies (emergency management)-associated Cabinet Office Briefing Room 'A' (COBRA) mechanism, such as used on 7/7 and 21/7 (2005) during the terrorist attacks on London; while, in the US, the Federal Emergency Management Agency (FEMA) was used (Hennessy, 2010, pp. 360–389; Miskel, 2008).[13]

But, quickly generating scope for further inquiry, difficult trade-offs were involved.[14] Not least, this was on individual bases, especially in terms of individual human rights versus the wider overall objective of public safety (Foot, 2006; Gade, 2010; Gearty, 2005).[15] This was apparent when, in the domain of human security, the more collective-leaning, utilitarianism-influenced 'greatest good and happiness for the greatest number' (Blackburn, 2003, pp. 75–80)[16] was one of the prominent prevailing underlying philosophies emergent in the overall mix of expressed governing ideas.[17] As the 2010 UK *National Security Strategy* observed: 'To protect the security and freedom of many, the state sometimes has to encroach on the liberties of a few: those who threaten us. We must strike the right balance in doing this, acting proportionately, with due process and with appropriate democratic oversight.' (UK HMG, 2010, p. 23; see also Miller, 2011) Aspirations rode high as both 'containment' and 'rollback' activities featured.

2.1 The legal dimension gathers momentum

Impacting on several interactions, legal tensions were rapidly encountered both between and within the UK, the USA, and other partner countries. These continued to increase over the years from 2002. Indeed, they became paramount (Blank and Noone, 2008; Kennedy, 2004; Roberts, 2002; Sands, 2006; Scott, 2004b).[18] Countries, such as Canada (Hitz, 2008, pp. 159–162; Svendsen, 2010a, p. 74),[19] Australia,[20] and those in Europe and elsewhere were not exempt.[21] By 2004, and indeed continuing to the present time, the law itself – including accountability and oversight activities (Born and Leigh, 2005; Born *et al.*, 2005)[22] – was now having to 'catch-up', and rapidly (e.g. Foley, 2009a; Hemming, 2010; Wittes, 2009).[23] This process was most pressing with regard to the sheer volume of enhanced public-safety-led political and operational requirements that had been adopted vigorously and quickly on both sides of the Atlantic, especially post-9/11 (Armstrong *et al.*, 2012; Wacks, 2008, pp. 121–153).[24] They had also been adopted more broadly globally.[25] This development was particularly apparent when intelligence and security operations were being conducted abroad by the full-spectrum of intelligence, law enforcement and military agencies (Morris, 2010, p. 104).[26] Liaison adjustments became necessary.

It is particularly interesting to examine developments in the 'hotbed' of the UK (Svendsen, 2010a, pp. 50–52; Vidino, 2011).[27] As reported in October 2009: 'During the *in camera* evidence session', held in February 2009, 'to a sub-committee of the Commons home affairs select committee,' head of the Office of Security and Counter-terrorism (OSCT) in the UK Home Office, Charles Farr, 'confirmed there were CIA agents operating in Britain, and that Britain had a "very close" relationship with the US intelligence community.' The report continued: 'Asked if CIA agents and other "outside organisations" were working in Britain, Farr replied: "Most certainly, yes. Are they declared? Yes. They are in regular dialogue with our agencies here. The cornerstone of this is the American relationship."' Offering some further contextualization for these interactions, Farr went on to explain: '"Why? For two reasons, I think, above all: because of the huge American capability that can be brought to bear on counter-terrorism, and has been since 9/11. Secondly,"' he continued, '"because people who pose a threat to this country are six hours away from the eastern seaboard, something which the Americans are acutely aware of, as are we, and therefore take a very close interest in."'[28] The obligations of being a close ally were apparent.

Many changes were required. Simply rapidly increasing the numbers of 'legal advisors' embedded within agencies and departments reflected insufficient movements by governments. Arguably, the law needed some essential adjustments of its own, not least so that the fullest range of interactions, extending to conducting multiple intelligence liaison relationships, could be maintained smoothly (Roberts, 2009). Again, these attempts were undertaken in both the UK and USA, as well as elsewhere, such as in Australia (Denemark, 2012; Head, 2002; Michaelsen, 2010).[29] In part, this was done in order to better accommodate, as well as to attempt to control in an appropriate manner, the latest developments.[30] However, quickly eluding the grip of traditional and conventional governance-control mechanisms, these developments rapidly increased in their multitudes. Frequently, this was in high-tempo and condensed-space operating environments, as witnessed in various states' major cities, as well as in important theatres abroad, notably Afghanistan (from 2001) and Iraq (from 2002).[31]

Several dilemmas were involved in many domains of activity. This included the striking of complicated and controversial trade-off balances, and not all the 'right' balances were struck.[32] Both before and continuing after 9/11, the authorities encountered exponentially steepening 'learning curves'.[33] During the so-called 'War on Terror' (*c.* 2001–2009), it proved very challenging to reconcile unsettling operational realities experienced on the ground and in the field, with – at least at first – comfortable geographically and politically distant home-country-based policy and legal and ethical stipulations.[34]

In terms of homeland security, particularly after 9/11, problems first found on the doorstep were soon encountered elsewhere. The issues were brought substantially and individually closer to several countries' publics, as was highlighted in Spain with the 11 March 2004 Madrid attacks and in the UK with the 7/7 (7 July 2005) London bombings (Dolnik, 2010; Reinares, 2010).[35] By 2005, regional security in Europe was also looking increasingly shaky. No perfect answers were forthcoming (Cilluffo *et al.*, 2010).[36]

Different approaches were attempted. Some of the dilemmas being confronted within both the UK and US intelligence communities, as well as between them, concerned the *publicizing of intelligence*. Liaison would again perform a central function in these 'risk communication' interactions (Nicoll, 2010b).[37] Publicizing intelligence product, or information derived from that source, including in published national and international intelligence-based (terrorism) threat warnings, frequently sets several quandaries for governments. Most obviously, 'sensitive' sources and methods, including explicit and specific areas of 'intelligence interest' beyond merely general bases, could be exposed and become compromised (Ellis and Kiefer, 2004, p. 109).[38]

The extent to which intelligence (and other sensitive information or data) should be shared is always a topic of considerable and persisting debate.[39] Among the concerns are: whether the sharing is between intelligence agency departments internally, with other government agencies, with another liaison service, more widely with the public, or multilaterally – rather than just bilaterally – with other countries (Svendsen, 2010a, pp. 64–67).[40] Both domestically and internationally, liaison between agencies, and intelligence 'fusion' efforts, continue to be key. They are also still open to further extension, and tactical-to-strategic optimization.[41]

Persisting legal concerns made some further inroads. In the UK, during 2009 and extending into 2011, so-called 'control orders' against alleged terrorist suspects continued to be legally challenged.[42] This included when the disclosure of sensitive 'secret evidence' against suspects was regarded as highly undesirable; even during trial in court, for various 'security reasons', because security authorities asserted such disclosures could potentially compromise operations. For example, there might be ongoing covert surveillance operations about which the authorities did not want targets to be 'tipped-off'.[43] During early 2011, after a UK governmental review, 'control orders' subsequently become subject to some adjustment and re-branding as 'Terrorism Prevention and Investigation Measures (TPIMs)'.[44]

The use of 'intercept evidence' in courts in the UK has confronted similar concerns. Several lines have become blurred.[45] To many, intelligence has 'exceptional' qualities and it is *not* the same as 'evidence'.[46] Instead, intelligence merely provides 'leads' and 'tips', ready for future investigative follow-up and other subsequent associated future tasks, such as robust evidence acquisition, which can then be used to support legal cases and/or for launching other operations.[47]

Perhaps most critically, the important 'third party rule' in intelligence liaison interactions has also become increasingly besieged. Indeed, the 'third party rule', 'confidentiality rule' or 'control principle', intended to protect the confidentiality of secret exchanges, figures as an internationally-shared and applied principle, which, in itself, sometimes has greater value in being preserved than the actual value of some of the intelligence shared and protected by it (Svendsen, 2012b; see also Chapter 1 (4.0), above).[48] This rule has come under considerable pressure from legal quarters to be 'rolled back', at least at times. Arguably, this has been seen most starkly in the recent 'Binyam Mohamed affair' (2008–2010) in the UK, which involved damaging allegations of the UK's 'complicity' in torture. Canada has encountered similar problems in not-too-dissimilar circumstances (Gaskarth, 2011; Svendsen, 2012b).[49]

Ultimately, the matter under consideration often results in a series of finely balanced trade-offs. Ideally this is so that the excesses and deficits of intelligence and security reach (including outreach), respectively overreach and under-reach, can be best managed in as many directions and areas as possible.[50] As the US Office of the Director of National Intelligence (ODNI) argued in a statement concerning the early February 2010 UK legal judgement finding in the Binyam Mohamed case, and after the UK Government's appeal on national security grounds had been lost: 'The protection of confidential information is essential to strong, effective security and intelligence cooperation among allies. The decision by a United Kingdom court to release classified information provided by the United States is not helpful, and we deeply regret it.' The statement continued: 'The United States and the United Kingdom have a long history of close cooperation that relies on mutual respect for the handling of classified information. This court decision creates additional challenges, but our two countries will remain united in our efforts to fight against violent extremist groups.'[51] Blows to relations were softened.

The British Government agreed. In its response to the UK Intelligence and Security Committee's own expression of worry concerning this episode, repeating its legal defence, the UK Government observed that it 'shares the Committee's concern.' This was especially as, in its view, 'The principle that intelligence belonging to another country should not be released without the agreement of that country underpins the intelligence-sharing relationships that are vital to our national security.' In part to reassure its partners during this time of flux, it went on to stress that: 'The Government is committed to protecting the intelligence it receives from its partners and the maintenance of the "control principle".'[52] The weathering of this issue would be robustly managed.

There were further complexities. Arguably, as a form of 'blowback protection' for its UK partner, acting on its awareness of the UK's legal obligations as stipulated strongly under the European Convention of Human Rights (ECHR), the USA was allegedly somewhat 'evasive' on the topic of supplying to the UK the fullest details of the controversial issue of its treatment of detainees (Svendsen, 2010a, pp. 70–76 and 89).[53] However, as the UK Government observed: 'The Government acknowledges the importance of verifying assurances in circumstances where new information comes to light. As the [Intelligence and Security] Committee noted, we did this with the US following the new information that came to light in February 2008 about the [US] use of [the UK's] Diego Garcia' (as a transit point for at least two CIA rendition flights (Svendsen, 2010a, p. 74)). It continued, trying to offer some greater contextualization: 'Nevertheless, the Government believes that we must avoid proceeding with our bilateral partners on the basis of mistrust or a presumption of deceit, and must instead make considered judgements on the basis of careful analysis and foreign policy expertise.'[54]

Complicated 'trade-offs' again featured centrally in relations, as a pragmatic risk-management-based approach was maintained for the way forward. Although interactions were largely sustained, and substantive information flows continued to a sufficient extent, evidently the 'problems' encountered and requiring their finer navigation had multiplied (Svendsen, 2012b).[55] We turn there next.

2.2 Enhanced liaison risks and management solutions

Qualitatively, the risks associated with liaison have become extended in recent years. Unsurprisingly, this has gone hand-in-glove with the observed quantitative increase in liaison and with the burgeoning of the globalization of intelligence (see Chapter 3, below). Indeed, the contemporary history of intelligence presents some emblematic examples concerning liaison. Some of the most serious shortcomings in the Western handling of counter-terrorism (CT) intelligence were exposed after the October 2002 Bali terrorist attacks. These problems occurred both in the UK and in other countries, such as in one of the UK's key global CT partners, Australia (Svendsen, 2010a, pp. 53–54; Vandepeer, 2009).

The above developments also pointed towards the growing influence of globalization-related factors, such as, most notably, the impact of 'glocalization'. Boundaries between several different domains were becoming increasingly blurred, and 'traditional/conventional' lenses and frameworks for issue analysis and management were increasingly merging (see Chapters 3 (2.1), 5 (2.0–3.0) and 6 (2.0; 6.0), below). Following a special inquiry conducted by the Intelligence and Security Committee

(ISC) that reported in December 2002, the UK CT threat-assessment system was judged to be flawed (Broderick, 2007; Svendsen, 2010a, p. 64).[56] To improve both the national and international coordination of UK CT intelligence, an intelligence fusion centre was set up. This became the Joint Terrorism Analysis Centre (JTAC), established in MI5 headquarters at Thames House during June 2003.[57]

The intention of JTAC was to facilitate the cross-agency communication of CT intelligence. This was to be accomplished through better integrating the government agencies specifically focused on the CT task. To achieve this objective, JTAC included members from the three UK intelligence agencies – MI5, SIS (MI6) and GCHQ – as well as drawing on members from other relevant UK Government departments and agencies, such as the Department for Transport's Transport Security and Contingencies Directorate (TRANSEC), and the police. By 2004, reflecting on the developments undergone, the ISC noted that: 'because [JTAC] allows all counter-terrorism intelligence to be processed centrally, [it] has significantly improved the UK intelligence community's ability to warn of terrorist attacks, and this concept is now being copied by several countries.'[58] Jointery in intelligence was established as the way forward.[59]

The USA invested in a similar model. Operating beyond the CIA's own internal Counterterrorism Center (CTC), during May 2003 a multi-agency Terrorist Threat Integration Center (TTIC), spanning the US Intelligence Community (IC), was set up (Treverton, 2009a, pp. 90–95). The USA had been studying, and had learnt some useful lessons from, the then proposed UK JTAC model when thinking about establishing its own TTIC.[60] Later, by December 2004, the US TTIC became re-branded as the National Counterterrorism Center (NCTC) (Richelson, 2008, pp. 464–466).[61]

From the end of 2005, the strategy being generally promoted on the domestic front for the US Intelligence Community was greater 'integration' and 'standardization'. The further 'nationalization' of intelligence was sought, and intelligence 'fusion centers' would be central.[62] These fusion centres were established in many different configurations, with important overlaps in various areas, such as structurally and organizationally. Moreover, in the manner of their work, they deal with differently calibrated and ranging intelligence product, offering the potential for extended insights.[63] The act of intelligence fusion was having more of an impact (Svendsen, 2010a, pp. 56–57).

Prior to JTAC being operational, the UK's threat-assessment process remained firmly under the spotlight in 2002 as further terrorist attacks occurred. Following the Kenya attacks of 28 November 2002, an increasing political dispute arose in the UK about the type of warning issued to UK nationals (citizens) abroad concerning Mombasa and terrorism. The UK Foreign Secretary, Jack Straw, was prompted to declare in Parliament that 'no information was available to the UK, the USA or Australia which could have prevented the attacks which took place.'[64]

Some insights into international intelligence liaison were provided. This was a cast of countries that again underscored the important partnership between the 'English-speaking countries' in CT intelligence gathering and pooling (Rudner, 2002, 2004a; Svendsen, 2008b, pp. 661–678, 2010c; Wark, 2004–2005).[65] As the Canadian Security Intelligence Service (CSIS), later observed around 2006, concerning its intelligence liaison relationships: 'Internationally, the Service cooperates with Canada's allies, sharing intelligence to counter global threats such as terrorism and the proliferation of weapons of mass destruction.' It continued, showing the breadth of its intelligence interactions and how these are managed: 'CSIS also provides information to a number of other countries and foreign agencies. Such international intelligence sharing is governed by strict standards and guidelines. It must receive ministerial approval and is closely monitored by the Security Intelligence Review Committee and [(until reportedly 'abolished' in April 2012)] the Office of the Inspector General.'[66] Intelligence oversight and accountability considerations were more or less involved as part of the overall intelligence management process (Lefebvre, 2010; Svendsen, 2012e).

More widely, challenging questions arose in several countries, with the security and sharing dilemma being intensely debated. This took place at the same time as figuring out how best to achieve an optimum balance in these liaison interactions both domestically and internationally.[67] While subsequent adjustments have clearly been made in the UK since 'deficiencies' were exposed in the autumn of 2002, concerns about such difficult 'glocalization-related' questions continue to persist to date (Svendsen, 2010c, pp. 309–316).

Moreover, as there are no quick and easy answers to these challenges, at least some of the issues raised will generate some considerable and sustained discussion into the foreseeable future (Moore and Turner, 2010).[68] Not least this is because many substantial developments are ongoing and rapidly unfolding in dynamic, real-time contexts, while management 'solutions' continue to be worked out.[69] Significantly, participation in multilateral efforts coexisted as part of several other general multilateral CT initiatives (Svendsen, 2008a, b).[70] Focus now moves on to that aspect.

3.0 Multilateral UK–US intelligence liaison on counter-terrorism

Multilateral efforts were similarly essential to CT efforts. In May 2005, US Acting Assistant Secretary for Diplomatic Security, Joe Morton, declared that: 'We must cooperate to interdict terrorists.'[71] Faisal Devji, historian and author of *Landscapes of the Jihad*, also added fuel to arguments concerning why international intelligence liaison on a global scale was needed in the CT efforts. He highlighted that a truly global 'solution' was required to tackle al-Qaeda and its sympathizers: 'The issues of concern to them are strictly global. They cannot be dealt with by solutions at national level, or even by internationalist solutions – those take too long.'[72]

In its 2005 CT strategy document, the UK Government similarly acknowledged: 'We must accept that the threat will persist for some time ... we cannot act alone.' More widely, 'We must work with our international partners to make it: harder for terrorists to travel undetected; harder to communicate without being overheard; harder to finance their operations by moving money across borders.'[73] Those policy aspirations now had to be operationalized.

Several of the multilateral arrangements were organized to work on a 'bottom-up' or 'democratic' basis. Collective cooperative and human-shared security dimensions were emphasized. These would conform more towards 'ideals' in their delivery. Pragmatic operational 'realities' were not too far behind, however (Schell, 2003; Svendsen, 2010a, pp. 41–42).

Both the UK and USA subscribed to several multilateral CT efforts. An increase in international intelligence sharing throughout the world was quickly identified as being a 'practical help' to the USA in its response to the 9/11 attacks. This was particularly as a long-term so-called 'war against terror' was planned (US PSCI and SSCI, 2002, p. 271).[74] Significantly, in November 2005, with reference to the CIA's 'Alliance Base' in Paris, US journalist Dana Priest of the *Washington Post* revealed that 'the CIA [had] set up a network of secret joint operations centres [Counterterrorism Intelligence Centers (CTICs)] with two dozen foreign intelligence agencies to hunt down suspected terrorists in the years after September 11 2001.'[75] The importance of international cooperation on CT to the CIA after 9/11 was publicly exposed.

3.1 Collective efforts: 'Less exclusive' multilateral intelligence liaison

Familiar distinct trends quickly presented themselves as more multilateralism was adopted. At least initially, most of the multilateral moves appeared to be made on the wider, 'less exclusive' multilateral CT front. In contrast to the bilateral and more exclusive multilateral intelligence liaison – such as that under way within the UKUSA signals intelligence (SIGINT) arrangement, which operates on more of a 'need-to-share and pool' basis between the carefully included participants (see below in 3.2) – 'less exclusive' multilateral intelligence liaison is conducted on much more of a tightly controlled 'need to know' basis.

With originator control (ORCON) consideration factors figuring, this calibration is often determined 'top-down' by those in possession or control of the intelligence. On the international stage, by default, this is usually the USA, due to the sheer magnitude of its intelligence 'industry' and resources (Svendsen, 2010a, p. 31). At least a degree of 'hegemony' over 'intelligence power' is enabled, and – when compared with other, for instance, 'flatter' and 'more-exclusive' arrangements – 'hierarchies' within these structures, including their associated dynamics, are rendered more important (Walsh, 2009; see also 3.2, below).

Notably, many of the initiatives at the multilateral level on CT were either US, UK or jointly UK–US led. As former UK intelligence officer Michael Herman noted in 2002, after 9/11: 'The coalition of 50 nations was formed in the first instance through US-UK intelligence briefings, and intelligence has subsequently been the glue holding it together.' He continued: 'Terrorism has brought about a greatly changed level of cooperation between unlikely collaborators ... The [9/11] effect has therefore been to confirm [the] position [of intelligence] as a worldwide growth industry.' (Herman, 2002, pp. 227–228) Management of these more multilateral initiatives also significantly increased the volume of UK–US bilateral intelligence liaison (Svendsen, 2010a, pp. 40–42 and p. 78).

The less exclusive multilateral intelligence liaison takes place in many locations. Featuring more as *information-sharing* – due to the nature of the sanitized intelligence products involved – it is forum-/arrangement-specific. It is under way in a wide range of different structural and cultural forms. Significantly, its configuration is determined directly by the nature of the arrangement within which it is taking place. This is influenced by the COMSEC/INFOSEC/IA, counter-intelligence, and other data and security considerations encountered (Henderson, 2003, pp. 353–356; Svendsen, 2010a, pp. 41–42). The globalization of intelligence remains a not unfettered process.

The UK and/or the USA are parties in most of these frequently overlapping arrangements. There are efforts through: the G8 (Bensahel, 2003; Penttilä, 2003);[76] with the European Union (EU) (Nicoll, 2010a, pp. 64–81, esp. pp. 75–77; Svendsen, 2011c) (including EUROPOL

(Fägersten, 2010));[77] other European geographic region or sub-region-focused arrangements – including: the Club of Bern (*Club de Berne*), the Counter Terrorist Group (CTG), the Middle European Conference (MEC) (Svendsen, 2011c), and ASEAN;[78] and within international organizations, such as the UN, including the International Atomic Energy Agency (IAEA) (Chesterman, 2006),[79] the Organization for Security and Co-operation in Europe (OSCE),[80] and, with a strong military operation-orientated focus, the North Atlantic Treaty Organization (also including the involvement of the NATO-supporting 'Intelligence Fusion Centre' based at RAF Molesworth, UK) (Kriendler, 2006; Reveron, 2006, p. 461).[81] INTERPOL focuses on international police and law enforcement intelligence and information sharing (Clutterbuck, 2006; Walsh, 2011).[82] Bilateral UK–US intelligence liaison through their conventional channels again supports all of these arrangements (Bensahel, 2003; UK HMG, 2010, pp. 59–63).[83]

The overall effectiveness of the less exclusive multilateral moves in relation to intelligence liaison has been more limited. This is especially when outcomes are taken and analysed on merely individual bases, over a short time-frame; rather than when the initiatives are examined more collectively (due to their important overlap), and over a longer-term timespan (due to their gradual evolution).

On the whole, as already witnessed, the movements on the wider, less exclusive multilateral front have not been as extensive as the moves made on the more exclusive bilateral bases (Siry and Reveron, 2001; Wiebes, 2003).[84] The multilateral sharing of intelligence still remains (strictly) limited, despite being more extensive since 9/11 (Lansford, 2007).[85] This also re-emphasizes the overall haphazard and uneven characteristic of the regionalization extending to the globalization of intelligence processes, as they have gradually unfolded, and indeed as they continue to develop.[86]

In Europe, intelligence liaison concerns remained evident during late 2001. Despite several immediate initiatives post-9/11, worries prevailed that intelligence-sharing within Europe, and across the Atlantic between European countries and the USA, was not as extensive as had been hoped. They were starting from somewhat of a low base. Transatlantically, in relation to Washington, European intelligence and security officials lamented that there was 'a "one-way flow" of intelligence information.'[87] Concerns persisted into 2003, and were subject to being addressed into the future (Aldrich, 2009b; Rosenau, 2006; Svendsen, 2011c).[88]

After the Madrid bombings of 11 March 2004, there were more demands for greater intelligence sharing within Europe itself. This was especially as various intelligence services within several European countries had held potentially useful different pieces of the jigsaw relating to the attacks, which had not been aligned.[89] Now, events had compellingly shown that increased intelligence liaison, extending to enhanced intelligence 'fusion', was critically needed. This was in order to facilitate adequate information connectivity and 'joining-up' to effectively underpin both European homeland and regional security.[90]

By 2005, several problems still remained with limitations in CT intelligence sharing at the European level.[91] These would continue to be gradually addressed into the future, with, as discussed below, further intelligence-orientated capacity and capability-enhancing initiatives being launched (Argomaniz, 2011; Pany, 2012).[92] Going beyond merely the regional level, even by March 2006 overall global multilateral efforts focused on countering terrorism continued to be hampered by the fact that, as the UN Office on Drugs and Crime (UNODC) noted: 'There are 12 major multilateral conventions and protocols related to states' responsibilities for combating terrorism. But many states are not yet party to these legal instruments, or are not yet implementing them.'[93]

Extended UN efforts were required. During April 2006, according to the UNODC, the UN Secretary-General 'issued recommendations for a global counter-terrorism strategy, which led to the unanimous adoption by the General Assembly, on 8 September 2006, of the *United Nations Global Counter-Terrorism Strategy*.' Significantly, as the UNODC continued: 'The strategy marks the first time that countries around the world agree on a common strategic approach to fight terrorism.' With a 'plan of action' being fashioned and intended 'to address the conditions conducive to the spread of terrorism; to prevent and combat terrorism; to take measures to build state capacity to fight terrorism; to strengthen the role of the United Nations in combating terrorism; and to ensure the respect of human rights while countering terrorism',[94] this global strategy continues to be implemented over time. Underpinning the implementation of the UN global strategy, various configurations of liaison and outreach would again perform an important role.[95]

Not everything changed after 9/11. Some commentators simultaneously expressed scepticism regarding the extent of wider international cooperation. Former US National Security Advisor, Zbigniew Brzezinski, argued in November 2001 that:

> [G]rand illusions obscure a realistic appreciation of the global consequences of Sept. 11. ... [including] that the emergence of a broad coalition against terrorism marks a shift away from US

> preponderance in world affairs toward genuinely cooperative interdependence ... individual European states are doing what they can ... notably that of Great Britain, that even entails direct participation in some of America's actions against terrorism (as well as not-so-subtle efforts to influence US decisions).[96]

Inevitably, some national self-interest did prevail in the post-9/11 international arena. However, these sentiments were not alone: indeed, the complex trade-offs having to be made between national intelligence compartmentalization and the more 'collective security'-imbued approach towards the greater sharing of intelligence, were highlighted in reports. The tensions between security and sharing, or individual security *versus* collective and human security, together with various configurations of human rights at different levels of activity and experience, persisted. Again, this was where aspects of utilitarian philosophy ('the greatest happiness for the greatest number' (Heywood, 2004, pp. 243–244)) often came forcefully into play when trying to govern.[97] Few 'quick-fix' solutions were going to be forthcoming, with developments instead evolving on more gradual bases. This was so that trust, or at least mutual interests and/or values, could be better established as the bonds to facilitate and strengthen interactions.

By the end of November 2001 some changes had occurred in Washington. Overall, international collaboration was reportedly judged to have 'improved dramatically since September 11.' Indeed, one CIA official went on to claim that: 'The extent of co-operation with other intelligence agencies around the world is unprecedented, as is the willingness on the part of many governments – including some unexpected ones – to co-operate.'[98]

While some impediments remained, other ways of facilitating greater intelligence sharing, in a manner less compromising to operations, were attempted. For example, some greater scope existed for the sharing of more 'finished' or 'processed' and longer-ranging 'strategic' intelligence assessments and estimates. This is where 'rawer' individual sources and their provenance are harder to identify in the suitably fused and sanitized all-source end product eventually disseminated (Sims, 2007).[99]

For similar reasons, both the establishment and the development of open source intelligence (OSINT) arrangements also figured largely, and could likewise boast sufficient scope for being extended into the future. These arrangements most notably include the 'International Open Source Working Group' (IOSWG), which involves the participation of several countries across the globe, and the regional Europe-associated

'Budapest Club' OSINT partnership established in 2007 (Svendsen, 2010a, pp. 19–20; see also Chapters 1 (2.1) and 3 (2.0)). Trends pertaining to the 'regionalization' and to the 'globalization of intelligence' increased (Svendsen, 2011c).

Yet, despite these positive developments, central dilemmas continued to be highlighted. Into the future, sustaining momentum behind the initiatives being introduced after 9/11 was a factor that needed to be taken into account by managers. As British journalist Jimmy Burns of the *Financial Times* warned: 'maintaining such heightened co-operation will be difficult.'[100] The familiar issues of 'turf battles' were cited (Aid, 2012; Svendsen, 2010a, pp. 32, 90, 136).[101]

Arguably, these hampering factors reassert themselves to varying degrees over time. This occurs as the most immediate (and mutual) 'emergency' or crisis stimulus of terrorist attacks ebbs away more into the distant past, fading increasingly from minds as shocks dull.[102] Added to this, before the US Federal Bureau of Investigation (FBI), for instance, underwent all of its changes witnessed since 9/11 (Svendsen, 2012c; see also Graff, 2012),[103] reportedly: 'some in Washington argue that the powerful domestic culture of the FBI ... makes it hard to collaborate internationally.'[104] Further adjustments were required.

During 2002–2003, greater recognition emerged that change had to occur. Unless the currently existing more exclusive and hierarchical multilateral intelligence pooling and sharing arrangements, such as UKUSA, became more inclusive, the potentially most successful multilateral sharing of intelligence could not be more fully realized. Current hierarchies within these intelligence liaison arrangements needed 'flattening', even becoming increasingly 'equalized' (Lander, 2004; Schraagen *et al.*, 2010). This was especially while operating in a context where alternative structures were not yet forthcoming, as reportedly towards the end of 2001: 'there is no agreement on a multilateral institution with internationally agreed powers to pool, disseminate, and act on intelligence.'[105]

Beyond more general 'information' handling, these features essentially do not (generally) exist in arrangements such as NATO, the UN, or the G8 (see, e.g., Carment and Rudner, 2006; Chesterman, 2009; de Jong *et al.*, 2003; Dorn, 2010).[106] This is perhaps apart from some more recently developed operations-focused information-sharing arrangements being expeditiously established, mainly due to pressing multi-functional military and law enforcement requirements. However, these are: (i) generally embedded in operational contexts abroad – such as in Afghanistan; are (ii) more limited in their scope (for example, in terms of their activities); and (iii) on the whole conduct their business on more confined bases and more cloistered away from wider-interacting and increasingly strategic-leaning headquarters (see references to 'Alliance Base' and CIA 'Counterterrorism Intelligence Centers' (CTICs), cited above at the end of 3.0; see also references to the Joint Narcotics Analysis Centre (JNAC), based in Afghanistan, in Svendsen, 2010a, p. 24, 2011f).[107]

More specifically, showing the contemporary thinking, the observation surfaced in late 2001 that: 'within the US and British intelligence communities there is a reluctance to pursue multilateralism for its own sake.' The report continued: 'officials on both sides of the Atlantic insist that the key to good intelligence sharing is that it is done on a "need-to-know" basis.'[108] A high-degree of *purpose* had to be present before intelligence 'controls' were more 'relaxed' or adjusted. In mindsets, 'functionalism' was central (see Chapter 3 (8.0), below; Netten and van Someren, 2011).

In September 2002, a year after the 9/11 attacks, scepticism lingered concerning liaison. In the view of one analyst, Andy Oppenheimer, genuine '[i]nternational co-operation is yet to get off the ground, with intelligence sharing between agencies, and between countries, still in its infancy.'[109] Later, in 2003, an article in *Jane's Foreign Report* declared that: 'the bottom line is that, in the war against terrorism, US and British intelligence services remain in a unique position. All others contribute if and when Washington considers it necessary. The situation is unlikely to change in the near future.'[110] Previous barriers and hierarchies were proving hard to erode and flatten.

There were further concerns. During March 2004, soon after the Madrid attacks, the so-called 'third-country rule', the convention that controls wider intelligence sharing beyond the preferred bilateral basis intended for best source and method protection, was claimed to be acting as an obstacle 'hurting [the] war on terrorism'.[111] By early July 2005, some of the same scepticism concerning international intelligence cooperation surfaced. UK journalist and former military intelligence officer Michael Smith reported that: 'Intelligence-sharing failures hamper war on terrorism.' He maintained: 'The 11 September 2001 attacks in the USA may have focused the world's attention on the need to share intelligence, but despite measures being put in place and bodies established, countries are mainly paying lip service to the exchange of information.' (Smith, 2005)

While intelligence cooperation *structures* were by now increasingly in place, more *cultural* obstacles remained. Smith continued: 'Washington, in particular, is guilty of this ... multilateral sharing of intelligence on terrorist groups remains sporadic at best ... real co-operation only exists on the basis of bilateral relationships between organisations that have traditions of working with each other, or personal relationships between officers themselves.' (Smith, 2005) Significantly, while gradually improving over time on evolutionary bases, some prevailing scepticism surrounding broader multilateral intelligence sharing continues to date (Svendsen, 2011c).

Narrower relationships fared better. The importance, as well as the exceptional nature, of the bilateral UK–US intelligence liaison axis in the progression of the so-called 'War on Terror' continued to be asserted (Svendsen, 2010a). In 2003, calls also continued over time for increased and more effective broader intelligence and information sharing.[112]

The prevailing 'calls' were soon heard and some actions were taken. The shortcomings of 'bottom-up' and the more 'democratic' and 'less exclusive' multilateral intelligence liaison arrangements were quickly anticipated. Consequently, a way to make these arrangements more effective, and to exert a degree of further control over them, was to take a more constructive lead in their shaping. Perhaps paradoxically, heading in the direction towards greater 'exclusivity' was to be the way forward. This was accomplished through applying a more rigorous 'top-down' directing and management approach. Some strategic thinking was advanced. The USA and UK-led top-down intelligence liaison efforts on the issue of CT were initially focused on (what can be termed) the increasing 'homogenization' and 'international standardization' movements. Essentially, these formed what could be regarded as 'Part One' of a wider process – namely, the 'regionalization', extending to the 'globalization', of intelligence (Svendsen, 2008a; see Coletta, 2008; Chapter 3 (7.0), below).

As part of this wider process, after 'Part One' came 'Part Two'. In essence, Part Two focused on intelligence liaison arrangement 'optimization' movements, and included the eventual 'flattening' of hierarchies. This occurred when implementing Part Two was no longer deemed too risky a strategy to pursue, because the 'best practices', established earlier in Part One, were by now in position and were already being followed (Svendsen, 2008b; see Chapter 3 (8.0), below). A cautious, stepped, path during adjustments was adopted due to the nature (which and who) and/or the number of liaison parties involved. Further steps towards the carefully managed increasing 'globalization' of intelligence were gradually undertaken on incremental bases (see Chapter 5 (2.0), below).

The 'homogenization' and 'international standardization' processes extended widely. Moreover, these processes were not symptomatic of mere political rhetoric. Operational relevance was also present.

As demonstrated throughout this chapter and highlighted below in Chapter 3 (7.0), individual UK and US, as well as joint UK–US (and, in various combinations, other countries') programmes heading in this and similar directions have evidently been under way (see Chapter 3 (9.0), below). Continuing to date, these have been implemented to varying degrees of effectiveness. Adopting various configurations, they are achieved through international intelligence liaison alongside other (perhaps more 'overt') diplomatic tools and means, such as outreach, confidence building, and capacity/capability training activities.[113]

Further developments are apparent. Establishing 'best practice' methods, for example through training and in the handling of intelligence – OPSEC/COMSEC/INFOSEC/IA – then better allows favourable conditions for further intelligence liaison to take place. The greater sharing of intelligence is enabled and helps to contribute towards facilitating working together more effectively, allowing for enhanced 'jointery' and interoperability.[114] As the ISC annual report of 2006 noted in some detail:

> The additional funding for SIS allocated from the SIA [Secret Intelligence Account] will be spent on enhancing front-line counter-terrorism operations overseas and developing the capacity of liaison services in CONTEST [UK CT strategy] Priority 1 countries. These developments will provide SIS, working in co-operation with its liaison partners, with a greater degree of operational access into countries of interest. We have been told that this access and influence will be a key part of SIS's worldwide counter-terrorism strategy and will strengthen long-term relations with liaison services and the security of SIS staff overseas.[115]

These 'reach-enhancement' processes are occurring in multiple locations. The enterprises involved are not all 'new' initiatives, however (Gal-Or, 1985).[116] The top-down, US-led 'international standardization' and 'homogenization' processes can be seen to have been a relatively long-term and integral part of the US CT strategy. As Morton noted: 'Under the [1983] Antiterrorism Assistance Program that we run at Diplomatic Security, the United States trains foreign law enforcement and security officers in the latest antiterrorism techniques.' Indicating the capacity-building elements of the programme, he continued: 'Most countries that receive Antiterrorism Assistance training are developing nations that don't have the resources necessary to maintain an effective antiterrorism program.' Long-term impact was likewise apparent: 'In 20 years, we've trained more than 48,000 officials from 141 countries in airport security, bomb detection and disposal, hostage rescue, and crisis management. That training has paid enormous dividends ... we are all safer because of it. International cooperation on many fronts is essential in the global war on terrorism.'[117]

Demonstrating the long-term cooperative trends, in a previously classified article, which appeared during 1976 in the CIA's Center for the Study of Intelligence (CSI) publication, *Studies in Intelligence*, US intelligence practitioner, W.R. Johnson, remarked: 'the history of our Service, from its first feeble squirming in the arms of its old British aunt, has been dominated in many ways by liaison.' He continued: 'Indeed, we have created whole national services, internal and external, from one end of the world to the other, trained them, vetted them, funded them, in order to be able to conduct liaison in their countries, and to get them to do work that we, though expending vast sums in training and subsidy of operations, thought we were too small or too poor to handle ourselves.'[118]

Out of the four principles of US CT policy, 'principle four' has the most implications with regard to foreign liaison and the wider 'globalization of intelligence'. Notably, as the fourth principle remarks: 'the counterterrorism capabilities of countries allied with the United States, and those that require assistance in fighting terrorism, must be bolstered.'[119]

Interoperability between countries was becoming increasingly important. As the US Joint Chiefs of Staff remarked in March 2007: 'Interoperability is an essential requirement for multinational operations. Nations whose forces are interoperable can operate together effectively in numerous ways.' Furthermore, the interoperability extended widely: 'Although frequently identified with technology, important areas of interoperability may include doctrine, procedures, communications, and training.' Within this domain of activity, standards again performed an important role: 'The establishment of standards for assessing the logistic capability of expected participants in a multinational operation should be the first step in achieving logistic interoperability among participants.'[120]

These processes were then considerably expanded and extended after 9/11.[121] More explicit intelligence activities similarly were not exempt. In 2003, an FBI briefing demonstrated some greater US-led 'homogenization' and 'international standardization', with: 'the FBI is working with its partners across the world to standardize expertise in financial investigations.' Demonstrating the extent of internationalization undergone, the FBI revealed that: 'Investigators from the FBI and agencies in the

UK ... [and other European countries] and Europol are now working on each other's forces to better coordinate joint investigations.' Moreover, 'FBI specialists are teaching a terrorist financing/money laundering crimes curriculum to investigators in 38 different countries – with subjects like handling evidence in document intensive investigations, major case management techniques, forensic examination tools, and methods of terrorist financing.'[122]

In a speech to the UK House of Commons, soon after the October 2002 Bali bombings, UK Prime Minister Tony Blair made reference to similar movements being put into effect by the UK. Working in the Asia-Pacific region, Australia and the USA were also closely involved. Many efforts were evidently under way. At length, Blair drew attention to joint 'Western'-led, 'top-down' moves relating to the continuing 'homogenization' and 'international standardization' of intelligence in other countries through the mechanism of multi-level intelligence liaison and security sector reform (SSR).[123]

Significantly, Blair emphasized the cooperative security trends. The important contributions of both regional and global initiatives were again signalled. At the same time, other globalization-associated shortcomings were highlighted, such as 'money laundering, illegal border crossing and [the] illegal trade in arms'[124] – essentially reminding us that terrorism, although it often forms the lead issue, is not the only security-driving concern faced. This is despite, perhaps even to a worrying extent, CT work arguably attracting the lion's share of intelligence and security services' staff time and absorbing the majority of resources (Taylor, 2007, p. 263).[125]

More could be done. Further related developments prevailed. Later during 2003, the persisting trend towards the greater 'homogenization' and 'international standardization' of intelligence systems and other security and law enforcement initiatives was further apparent. Notably, these processes appear to take place most markedly when they are intended to carry out the same or similar functions (Svendsen, 2010a, p. 4). Some general 'homogenization' and 'international standardization' efforts were highlighted in the US *National Strategy for Combating Terrorism* of early 2003. Again, these objectives were intended to be far-reaching: '[R]idding the world of terrorism is essential to a broader purpose. We strive to build an international order where more countries and peoples are integrated into a world consistent with the interests and values we share with our partners – values such as human dignity, rule of law, respect for individual liberties, open and free economies, and religious tolerance.' The strategy continued: 'We understand that a world in which these values are embraced as standards, not exceptions, will be the best antidote to the spread of terrorism. This is the world we must build today.'[126]

As already witnessed, a similar form of 'international standardization' and 'homogenization' was clearly also on the UK agenda.[127] This was demonstrated in the UK's own CT strategy document of 2005, with the declaration that: 'This strategy must be pursued internationally.' Most significantly, the document observed that: 'Our people and interests around the world are at risk, as are the people and interests of other nations. Effective protection depends on international co-operation and international standards. The UK therefore works closely and effectively with its partners both bilaterally and multilaterally.'[128]

Dealing with the issue of organized crime, in 2009 the UK's Serious Organised Crime Agency (SOCA) adopted a similar route. Significantly, this has included fostering so-called 'vetted units', consisting of approved local law enforcement personnel located across the globe in several strategically important countries.[129] Close cooperation on organized crime issues between the FBI and specialized UK London Metropolitan Police units, as well as with other agencies, likewise continues.[130] During 2011, Charles McMurdie, head of the London Metropolitan Police's e-crime unit, observed: 'It is, I think, getting easier to commit cyber crime ... The internet does not sit nicely within UK borders so we work a lot with international partners and law enforcers. We also have joint investigation treaties ... and all the UK agencies who deal with cyber crime and cyber security will pull together to provide a more joined up and co-ordinated response.'[131]

As already seen, overall these types of joint movements took many forms. These included working with the 'international community' through the UN, the EU, the G8, and the close police and law enforcement and intelligence liaison with counterparts overseas (Deflem, 2010). The 2005 UK strategy document continued by highlighting the top-down directed approach adopted, by noting the support given to countries less experienced with countering terrorism. In harmony with UN Security Council Resolution (UNSCR) 1373, unanimously passed soon after 9/11 (Svendsen, 2010a, pp. 40–41), this was in order 'to strengthen their counter-terrorist capabilities through programmes of training, of support with protective security and of help with preparedness and crisis management.'[132] As the IISS *Strategic Survey 2009* recalled:

> [I]n 2001 al-Qaeda did represent a security challenge to the status quo different from anything previously experienced. It was a global

> insurgency which linked and inspired many different terrorist groups and required a coordinated, global, security-focused response. In that regard the United States played the central role, with the [CIA] taking the lead in knitting together a global coalition of intelligence and security services. With their assistance Washington was able to start mapping out the dimensions of the post-Afghanistan al-Qaeda threat and to begin to create the circumstances in which it could be contained.

As the Survey continued:

> No other nation could have achieved this. Although over time the United Nations did much to create an institutional framework that provided a context for and legitimisation of international counter-terrorism efforts, the UN could never have coordinated the requisite operational response. (IISS, 2009, p. 38)

Nationally, through to regionally and globally, over time these developments collectively have had an important impact.

Some meaningful inferences can be presented. In a compelling manner, the UK and USA (together with, in various combinations, other countries, organizations and institutions) are arguably making increasing moves towards the greater globalization of intelligence. This is by introducing the top-down, directed homogenization and international standardization processes through UK and US international intelligence liaison (together with, in various configurations, other countries', organizations' and institutions' liaison activities) – as a 'means' mechanism (see Chapter 3 (4.0), below). Since more final 'closure' to the problems encountered remains elusive, through these processes the path is being laid, and favourable conditions are being established, for further international intelligence liaison in the future – more in the form of an enduring issue management 'end' and 'solution' (see Chapter 3 (3.0), below; Svendsen, 2008a and 2008b). Toiling alongside were some narrower and *more* 'exclusive' multilateral efforts attempting to combat terrorism on a global basis. These are examined next.

3.2 Hubs and Spokes: 'Exclusive' multilateral intelligence liaison

Further progress was made during the summer of 2005. There were notably some positive developments regarding more exclusive intelligence liaison focused on the issue of CT. Again, in their 'newer' form, these interactions extended beyond occurring merely on bilateral bases.

In June 2005, a tripartite UK–US-France meeting was held, focusing on achieving closer cooperation on CT. France also had long-term experience with terrorism, and had learned several useful, communicable lessons. Perhaps more relevantly than the UK's Northern Ireland and IRA terrorism experience, because of its former colonial Algerian connections, France had especially experienced *jihadist*-related terrorism, particularly during bombing campaigns in Paris in the 1990s (Adamson, 2006, p. 166; Kepel, 1997).[133] According to Reuel Marc Gerecht, a former CIA officer: 'There's only one country in Europe that worked terribly hard on this issue before September 11 and that was France.'[134]

The year 2005 was bleak for the so-called 'War on Terror'. After the meeting, reportedly: 'a French participant ... said France had been encouraged by the new US approach, particularly the idea of dropping the phrase "war on terror".' Some optimism existed as hopes abounded that 'the recent ... meeting ... is thought to mark a shift in US strategy towards encouraging moderate Muslim groups to discredit violent Islamic extremists, while moving away from a purely military-focused campaign.' A seeming 'strategic shift' by the USA more towards the European strategic position of engaging more with moderate Muslims, while opposing the extremists, was speculated upon.[135] But, as seen in 2009–2010, that shift took a while to become more fully manifested.

In 2005, the pursuit of successful and extensive multilateral intelligence liaison quickly demonstrated that it was a central and invaluable tool. This was especially so for the post-7/7 (7 July 2005) London bombings investigations. Even with all the associated risks accounted for, this liaison work was helpful for acquiring leads and was soon shown to be worth the participatory effort. Gathering intelligence from a wide range of partners was a useful asset for both collection and analysis purposes. Shortly after the attacks, a weekend meeting was reportedly held with 'Police, intelligence agents and forensics experts from 27 countries' who were 'asked to assist with every aspect of the inquiry.' These experts included 'American investigators [who] flew to London within hours of the bombings.'[136] Moreover, as former CIA operative and Inspector-General, Frederick P. Hitz, has noted: 'the forensic support [the intelligence cooperation] supplied ... enabled the London police to identify the perpetrators of the ... attacks in several days.' (Hitz, 2008, p. 163; Weston, 2009, pp. 19–20)[137]

Relationships were extended. The US State Department's coordinator for counter-terrorism, Henry Crumpton, declared shortly afterwards in September 2005 that for the US: 'Cooperation ... with America's international counterterrorism partners is "the key element to victory ... It's not just information-sharing, not just cooperation, but interdependence".'[138] Further intelligence liaison and cooperative arrangement-driving 'evangelical' sentiments in relations were articulated. A philosophy receptive towards conducting enhanced liaison, extending to the greater globalization of intelligence, was clearly present.

Yet, concerns simultaneously prevailed amongst observers. Contemporary worries that this high degree of UK–US intelligence interdependence was ebbing, due to the impact of other external factors, were quick to be articulated by some American commentators. This was felt to be due mainly to the prevailing UK discomfort over the highly visible sacrificing and eroding of the moral high ground by the USA during the progression of the so-called 'War on Terror' (Hitz, 2008, p. 167; McMaster, 2010). This scenario was interpreted along the lines that the attractiveness of the 'European dimension' to the UK might instead increase in the pursuit of its foreign policy. Worries prevailed that such a shift would adversely affect the more specific UK–US intelligence relationship. Would these 'friends and allies' remain as close?[139]

However, the commentators considerably underestimated the importance to the UK of continuing to successfully pursue its 'bridging-role' between Europe and America. This approach has remained a central pillar in the foreign policy of the UK as the twenty-first century has progressed (Svendsen, 2010a, p. 5; Svendsen, 2011d). Likewise, despite the increased legal and ethical difficulties being encountered in UK–US intelligence and security relations (discussed above in 2.0–2.2), UK involvement in at least aspects of US-led rendition operations persisted into 2010–2011.[140] Indeed, the process of rendition remains a valuable tool, especially when qualitatively it really is 'extraordinary', quantitatively it is not overused, and particularly when it appropriately overlaps with bodies of law, such as that established by extradition treaties.[141]

Ultimately, as Reuters correspondent William Maclean has observed: 'International intelligence cooperation is too important in tackling a transnational, networked foe like al Qaeda to allow tactical differences to grow into major disputes, analysts say.'[142] Often the whole (processes such as the 'globalization of intelligence' and its associated 'dynamics') is greater than the sum of its parts (the various international intelligence liaison relationships involved). This is mainly due to the 'overlap' of those relationships and to them acting in a 'complementary' manner in their interactivity (see Mark Lowenthal's observation in Chapter 3 (2.0), below).

Elsewhere, familiar patterns were apparent. Already well-established exclusive intelligence liaison arrangements continued to retain and demonstrate their significance. For instance, the UKUSA arrangement was an especially important component in UK–US intelligence liaison on CT. The SIGINT resources and efforts of fellow UKUSA members, including Australia and Canada, were quickly and firmly brought into the collective so-called 'War on Terror' soon after 9/11. As later observed in the Australian Government's 'Flood Report' (*Report of the Inquiry into Australian Intelligence Agencies*) of 2004: '[I]n an age of increasing globalisation, intelligence gathered in distant places can have direct and crucial relevance to Australia's interests and to the security of Australians at home and abroad.'[143] After a visit to the UK–US/UKUSA SIGINT station RAF Menwith Hill in North Yorkshire, former Chairman of the US Senate Intelligence Committee (2001–2003), Senator Bob Graham, also later perceptively observed: 'Such information may well be more important than armaments in this new century.' (Graham, with Nussbaum, 2008, p. 86)[144]

Exchanging SIGINT was important and valuable to all UKUSA partners' CT activities (Aid, 2009; Aldrich, 2010; Rudner, 2007).[145] Intercepted telephone calls, e-mails and fax records could be relayed amongst the partners. As an example, the value of SIGINT, at least to the UK and US, was demonstrated around the 2003 Christmas and New Year holiday period regarding the targeting of British Airways flight 223 from London to Washington, when a series of sufficiently specific terrorist warnings were picked up by UK–US intelligence agencies from SIGINT 'chatter'. Remedial actions were then taken on the basis of the contribution from this source of intelligence.[146]

More recently, in 2010, the high value target (HVT) Osama bin Laden, for over a decade the USA's 'No. 1/Most Wanted' terrorist suspect (Svendsen, 2010a, p. 47), was reportedly successfully traced by the USA to a compound in Pakistan through this method, namely the use of a telephone. Eventually, he was killed during a US Navy SEALs operation in early May 2011, after months of monitoring by several US intelligence agencies (Inkster, 2011a, pp. 5–10; Schmidle, 2011).[147]

Earlier in 2001, however, the SIGINT system appeared flawed. There were some 'exclusive' multilateralism shortcomings. Immediately after 9/11, the full CT value of the UKUSA systems was questioned. Perhaps they were not looking quite as 'effective' as had previously been claimed? (Baer, 2002, p. xvii; Bamford, 2002, p. 410)[148] As part of the widespread 'intelligence failure' accusations circulating after 9/11, the US National Security Agency (NSA) came under some criticism for not helping to prevent the attacks (Ball, 2002, p. 60; Dahl, 2005; Hersh, 2004, p. 73).[149]

In their subsequent investigations, both the UK Government Communications Headquarters (GCHQ) and NSA – together with input from the Communications Security Establishment of Canada (CSEC) and the other UKUSA partner SIGINT agencies – translated thousands of previously intercepted communications for any potential leads. The lack of evidence prior to the attacks was attributed by commentators to searches not being targeted specifically enough and to unfocused 'information overload'. This was rather than (alleged) 'missed clues' being due to problems with the physical UKUSA systems themselves *per se* (Marrin, 2011a; Svendsen, 2010a, p. 13).[150] In December 2002, the US Joint Inquiry report noted that 'many' US intelligence community members 'felt that the prioritization process was so broad as to be meaningless.' (US PSCI and SSCI, 2002, p. 220; see also Aid, 2003) On *qualitative* bases, the sheer *quantity* of intercepted intelligence had overwhelmed systems (Svendsen, 2010a, p. 14).[151]

Other early criticisms were soon forthcoming. In 2002, former GCHQ officer Michael Herman observed that: 'The arrangements in the anti-terrorist campaign still appear to be mainly bilateral and *ad hoc*.' He acknowledged: 'Intelligence is exchanged, but there is as yet no machinery for collective agreement on what it means.' More tellingly, 'Britain has been an intelligence partner, but its position remains exceptional. In intelligence, as in other things, the main pattern is of the US as the hub and others as the spokes.' (Herman, 2002, pp. 234–235, 2003a)[152]

In early 2003, Matthew Aid, a US expert on SIGINT, agreed that there were shortcomings. Indeed, he noted that SIGINT CT efforts were currently somewhat beleaguered. A CIA official he quoted argued: 'We've got to be serious about this: our intelligence world can't be this nice private club of English-speakers any more.' Aid continued, there was an 'evident lack of international cooperation among national Sigint agencies... [with] multinational Sigint joint ventures ... [being] practically non-existent.' (Aid, 2003, pp. 109–111; Vucetic, 2010) However, despite these characteristics, Aid acknowledged that SIGINT, 'whatever difficulties it faces, will remain an important tool for intelligence agencies in the ongoing war on terrorism.' (Aid, 2003, pp. 109–111) As already witnessed, it was indeed remaining an important tool.[153] With a few adjustments, it could be made potentially more powerful in the future, thereby enhancing its contribution to overall CT efforts (Aid, 2009; Aldrich, 2010; Richelson, 2010).[154]

Much could be done. In his article, Aid continued by highlighting that: 'The rationale for greater international Sigint cooperation against terrorism is a fairly simple one.' Not least, costs are reduced and the reach of intelligence is extended. While appropriately addressing the COMSEC/INFOSEC/IA concerns, greater SIGINT sharing on a wider multilateral basis could also bring 'regional expertise, technical skills and geographic access.' (Aid, 2003, pp. 109–111)

Many countries have acquired significant SIGINT capabilities in recent years. In some cases, this has been with commercially available equipment, combined with the significant advantage of local language expertise and abundant manpower: India, for instance, can be highlighted (Todd and Bloch, 2003, pp. 184–185).[155] Towards the end of 2004, the former Director General of the British Security Service (MI5) (1996–2002) and Chairman of SOCA (2004–2009), Sir Stephen Lander, proposed that there should be 'a new UKUSA Treaty involving not just sigint, nor just the Five Eyes [US, UK, Australia, New Zealand and Canada] allies, but also the key European players.' (Lander, 2004, p. 493; Svendsen, 2010a, pp. 172–173)[156]

These arguments were more or less heeded. During the summer of 2004, more 'joining-up' was attempted (Doig, 2005). International CT-related intelligence experienced further moves in the direction of trying to improve joint performance. In order to collectively consolidate CT threat assessment evaluation across the globe, reportedly the UK JTAC (established June 2003), the US TTIC (established May 2003) and the Australian National Threat Assessment Centre (established October 2003) were to be increasingly connected.[157] The Canadian Integrated Threat Assessment Centre (ITAC), operational since 15 October 2004, and the New Zealand Combined Threat Assessment Group (CTAG) have also since been connected to these.[158] Again, this process emphasized the importance of close UK–US intelligence liaison and wider cooperation with trusted international and UKUSA intelligence partners at the exclusive multilateral level to combat terrorism. Indeed, from its outset, UK officials disclosed that JTAC 'made it a priority to liaise closely with the [US] Terrorist Threat Integration Center.'[159]

Gradual moves in a more positive direction were apparent. Although to some critics, these needed to be extended much further. These efforts again needed to go beyond just the 'traditional' UKUSA and 'Five-Eyes' partners or 'English-speaking club'. As former US intelligence officer Robert David Steele has forcefully argued: 'Bottom-up collective public intelligence is here to stay, and the new standard, defined by the Swedish Ministry of Defence, is Multinational, Multiagency, Multidisciplinary, Multidomain Information Sharing (M4IS).' He went on to highlight that: '"Sharing, not secrecy, is the operative principle."' (Steele, 2007, p. 167) With the increased international integration, at least most immediately, of the key UKUSA partners' nationally based terrorist threat analysis centres (intelligence fusion centres), attempts at some more collective forms of terrorism analysis were being advanced by the leading Western intelligence powers.

Together with these efforts, again arguably a form of the tentative 'flattening' of hierarchies was being attempted. This was especially apparent within the exclusive UKUSA arrangement between the UK, the USA and Australia, as well as with other international partners beyond being increasingly included, as time progressed. These other partners included countries such as Germany and Denmark, for instance, with the greater international integration of their national terrorist and threat analysis centres into the overall 'network'.[160]

Some further 'flattening' was witnessed elsewhere. Notably, there was a flattening of previous hierarchies within the UKUSA arrangement itself, as well as in the bilateral Australia-US intelligence relationship. The erosion of merely UK–US exclusivity at the highest level of UKUSA was witnessed with the continuing 'rise' of Australia in the 'English-speaking intelligence club' and beyond (Svendsen, 2008b, pp. 663–667). Indeed, Australia's 'rise' had been especially notable since the 9/11 attacks and throughout the so-called 'War on Terror', and particularly since the shared experience of the October 2002 Bali attacks and the presence of other mutual threats located in the Asia-Pacific region. Moreover, this upwards trajectory would continue to be followed into the foreseeable future (see above in 2.0).[161]

Other identified intelligence liaison-related infrastructure shortcomings were being addressed towards the end of 2005. As *Jane's* analyst Andrew Koch noted: 'Faced with continuing criticism that its system of sharing relevant intelligence and other battlefield information with allies is flawed, the US is looking to augment and eventually replace the current network.' The so-called 'Multinational Information Sharing (MNIS) programme' was essentially being upgraded 'to ease the flow of data and intelligence between allies.'[162] These moves came as the USA acknowledged the value of intelligence and information sharing with its coalition allies in its military-dominated CT and counter-insurgency (COIN) operations. This was both across the globe, and particularly in high-tempo and condensed-space operational theatres such as in Iraq and Afghanistan (Mackinlay, 2002, 2009; Reveron, 2008).[163] Operationalizing such movements, at least in some areas, has continued to be replete with difficulties.[164] Into 2009–2012, these have continued to be worked out, along with balancing other 'deals', 'capturing' and 'killing' as ongoing issue management 'solutions' (Svendsen, 2011e, pp. 34–35).

3.3 The challenges of greater 'connectivity'

Amid all of the 'connecting-up' activities, another vexing question soon materialized: Would the increasing 'homogenization' and/or 'collectivization' of intelligence analysis and assessment be an entirely beneficial move? Instances of 'groupthink', symptomatic of dangerous overreach and convergence in the liaison, could arise, as, more forcefully, differences are increasingly tidied and omitted to reach some form of workable 'consensus' in such forums, arguably reflecting a 'lowest common denominator' result. Distinct pitfalls are apparent.[165]

Or, instead, would different interpretations be shared more widely? Thereby, this last, freer and more 'open-minded', process would actually help to foster diversity, and to inform and formulate a more inclusive, cohesive and coherent CT strategy based on better-fed 'shared perceptions'. Efforts towards the careful *'fusion'* of aspects, rather than the greater forced *'conversion'* or *'convergence'* of the whole, ideally had to be pursued amongst international intelligence liaison partners.[166] Trends again tended towards being on 'a continuum with expansion'.

Extending into 2010 and beyond, the rationale for continuing intelligence cooperation on a 'global' basis remained clear. After the shocking attacks in Norway, with the bombing in Oslo and the shooting on the island of Utøya on 22 July 2011, Norwegian Intelligence found intelligence liaison a valuable tool while conducting its *post facto* investigations.[167] Ultimately, as the IISS *Strategic Survey 2009* observed: 'While arguments about the scale and strategic nature of the threat from terrorism will continue, a primary task for intelligence agencies and security forces remains countering the dangers that present themselves around the world.' After all, 'many conflicts have historically featured the use of terrorist tactics, and continue to do so.' (IISS, 2009, p. 35)[168]

Simultaneously, intelligence liaison developments were increasingly flourishing in the domain of WMD counter-proliferation. Attention is now turned to that dimension.

4.0 WMD counter-proliferation as the lead issue

There are several UK and US WMD counter-proliferation efforts in existence. These extend to also include multiple wider multilateral international arrangements with other countries. Interactions concerning these arrangements occur regularly, frequently on a daily basis. While having already been partially explored elsewhere, two recent particularly high-profile cases, on which there was considerable UK–US intelligence liaison – together with some other important overlapping international intelligence liaison interactions – can be especially highlighted for further evaluation: first is the case of the A.Q. Khan 'nuclear network' (the decades-long clandestine nuclear proliferation activities of the business-like network associated with the prominent Pakistani nuclear scientist and 'father' of Pakistan's nuclear bomb, Dr Abdul Qadeer Khan, which included the secret transfer of classified nuclear technology and 'know-how' to countries such as Iran, Libya, and North Korea, and which was eventually 'shut-down' by a UK and US-led operation during 2003–2004); and secondly, the issue of supposed Iraqi WMD and related programmes (the central claimed *casus belli* for launching the 2003 war in Iraq) (Albright, 2010; Kroenig, 2010; Svendsen, 2010a, from p. 101).[169]

These cases have been selected for several reasons. While their consequences are still being experienced, respectively, they overall represent contrasting examples of: (i) a generally successful WMD counter-proliferation case (on the whole 'how-to-do-it', namely the '*gradual* counter-proliferation and rollback' of WMD); and (ii) a less successful case (broadly 'how-*not*-to-do-it', namely the '*shock and awe* counter-proliferation and rollback' of WMD (Steinberg, 2007)) (Arnold, 2008; Chandler, 2002; Katz, 2008).

Because of their comparable qualities, these cases should be evaluated together. This observation resonates only insofar as the controversial issue of Iraq and its supposed WMD can be regarded as a 'genuine' WMD counter-proliferation case;[170] rather than a case of policy- and decision-makers becoming more sidetracked by 'regime-change', or even grander plans for reshaping the Middle East region. (As UK journalist Robert Fisk has argued, in 2002–2003 with respect to the issue of Iraq: 'it was also clear that the Bush plans for the Middle East were on a far greater scale than the mere overthrow of the Iraqi leader.' (Fisk, 2005, p. 1097; see also Curtis, 2003; Freedman, 2008; Haass, 2009))[171] The example of the A.Q. Khan network emerges as more of a genuine WMD counter-proliferation case, where the counter-proliferation of WMD was generally the leading and agenda-setting issue.[172]

The case of the A.Q. Khan network has other commendable features. Interestingly, it largely unfolded in parallel to (at the same time as) the example of supposed Iraqi WMD; and, generally, it was left more to the professionals and experts – such as diplomats, security and intelligence officers and their agencies – to follow through and solve privately at more of their own pace. This was with less top-down and direct intervention from their 'political masters' in London and Washington. A condition of 'due process' predominated (Svendsen, 2012e).

Indeed, the A.Q. Khan case remained cloaked in the shadows, even from many of the policymakers, until its public exposure in early 2004.

Disclosure occurred after acceptable tangible and verifiable ends had essentially been achieved (Svendsen, 2010a, pp. 104–105). The A.Q. Khan case was managed quite differently from the issue of supposed Iraqi WMD, which notably became notoriously: (i) over-politicized (bringing with it all the negative aspects of that condition); (ii) more of a highly-publicized political *cause célèbre*, especially for politicians in London and Washington – being played out live in real-time in the full glare of the media spotlight, rather than being reported subsequently; and (iii) during which the most relevant experts were frequently bypassed, if acknowledged at all. These events all occurred to an unfortunately detrimental extent (see 4.3, below; Jervis, 2010a).

Extending beyond those already communicated elsewhere, wider instructive lessons from these cases can be readily conveyed. These lessons are still directly relevant to intelligence liaison interactions today.[173] They also flag up areas that should be carefully kept in mind when engaging with wider and higher complex processes like the 'globalization of intelligence'. A useful place to begin is with a general survey.

4.1 Surveying the strategic terrain

UK and US strategies regarding counter-proliferation efforts are generally manifold and complex (Graham *et al.*, 2008).[174] A significant part of the UK and US counter-proliferation strategies involves signing up to several, sometimes overlapping, multilateral arrangements and non-proliferation 'regimes'.[175] Some of these non-proliferation 'regimes' have existed for decades and are international organization-led. Others are comparatively recent and are at times more US-led initiatives (Ogilvie-White and Santoro, 2011; Spear, 2011).[176]

Many of the recent initiatives have been introduced in order to try and address perceived problems and gaps found in the earlier non-proliferation regimes (Bourne, 2011; Hibbs, 2011; Kupatadze, 2010).[177] This is especially concerning those regimes that pre-dated the latest rapid globalization and technological developments, such as the Nuclear Non-Proliferation Treaty (NPT) of 1968, whose shortcomings were particularly exposed in recent years by the WMD-related cases highlighted in this chapter (see 4.2 and 4.3, below; Gill, 2011; Krause, 2011).

Both national and international security concerns were generated.[178] As UK non-proliferation scholar Wyn Bowen observed in 2006: 'The apparent shortcomings of the current non-proliferation regime with regard to deterring and thwarting illicit nuclear activities have also been placed into sharp relief.' Continuing, he observed that: 'In large part, concerns about the non-proliferation regime's effectiveness derive from its traditional focus on controlling the nuclear-related activities of state actors and government-to-government transfers.' (Bowen, 2006, p. 83; Perkovich, 2006)[179]

Contemporary multilateral counter-proliferation efforts worthy of emphasis, and to which both the UK and USA adhere with other countries, include: (i) the US-led Proliferation Security Initiative (PSI) of May 2003 (Valencia, 2006; Yost, 2007; TNPR Editorial, 2006);[180] (ii) the G8 Global Partnership Against the Spread of Weapons and Materials of Mass Destruction of 2002 (Bergenäs, 2010a, pp. 150–152; Cornish, 2007a);[181] (iii) efforts through the UN – such as the UN Charter Chapter VII-mandated UN Security Council Resolution (UNSCR) 1540 of 28 April 2004 (Bosch, 2004, pp. 6–8; Bosch and van Ham, 2007; Stinnett *et al.*, 2011);[182] (iv) efforts with and by the EU;[183] (v) the Nuclear Non-Proliferation Treaty (NPT) and the International Atomic Energy Agency (IAEA), including the IAEA Safeguards;[184] as well as (vi) the Biological and Toxins Weapons Convention (BTWC);[185] (vii) the Chemical Weapons Convention (CWC);[186] and, more focused on delivery systems, (viii) the Hague (or International) Code of Conduct against the proliferation of ballistic missiles;[187] and (ix) the Missile Technology Control Regime (Nicoll, 2012).[188] The UK has also ratified (x) the Comprehensive (Nuclear) Test Ban Treaty (CTBT). Although having signed the CTBT, the USA has not – yet[189] – ratified it.[190] To 'improve integration' and coordination amongst all the different above agreements, the US-Russian-led Global Initiative to Combat Nuclear Terrorism was launched in July 2006 (Frost, 2005).[191]

A complex series of intelligence liaison arrangements takes place in the background behind these counter-proliferation regimes. Among many tasks, these activities perform a supportive role, including helping to verify that the agreements are being upheld (Bentley, 2011; Berridge, 2010, p. 87). Due to all the risks inherent in intelligence liaison, unsurprisingly the intelligence liaison and associated interactions on proliferation issues often operate in a similar manner as witnessed over other issues, such as counter-terrorism (CT) intelligence-sharing (see, for example, references to the US 'National Counterproliferation Center' in Richelson, 2008, p. 466). As Jason Ellis and Geoffrey Kiefer have observed, highlighting the risk management considerations involved:

> [I]ntelligence sharing is a potentially risky, if sometimes necessary, enterprise. When undertaken, intelligence-sharing or data exchanges must be conducted with a full appreciation of the potential risks

> involved. Yet despite the obvious downside potential, intelligence sharing need not be dismissed as a pointless exercise or one that is so fraught with danger that it should never be attempted. As in other policy areas, decision makers will be required to prioritize objectives and resources, making difficult trade-offs when necessary. (Ellis and Kiefer, p. 143)

The highest volume of intelligence liaison on the issue of WMD counter-proliferation is witnessed bilaterally, for instance, between the UK and the US. The exclusive multilateral UKUSA SIGINT arrangement also performs a demonstrably important role. Frequently involving more *information* sharing – due to the 'sanitized' forms of intelligence involved in the interactions – some other intelligence liaison occurs elsewhere on the issue of WMD. This occurs both bilaterally and multilaterally with other countries, and plurilaterally with international organizations, such as the International Atomic Energy Agency (IAEA) and NATO.[192] Overlapping 'globalized intelligence' flows continue to reflect their complexity.

4.2 Evaluating UK–US intelligence liaison on the A.Q. Khan network

All policies and strategies tackling WMD counter-proliferation involve 'a series of difficult policy trade-offs' (Ellis and Kiefer, 2004, p. 4). This is apparent not least when central tools such as intelligence liaison are involved. The main UK–US intelligence cooperation against the A.Q. Khan network appears to have taken place on the basis of existing bilateral UK–US intelligence liaison mechanisms, as well as through the exclusive multilateral UKUSA SIGINT arrangement. Into the future, as with the CT investigations, these intelligence liaison arrangements will remain key. They will also take on, in a complementary fashion, the tasks generated by newer cooperative arrangements established by more recent policies coming on-stream, such as the US-led PSI.[193]

The stalking and dismantling of the A.Q. Khan network appears to have been overall a *partial* success for UK–US intelligence liaison and their collaborative efforts (Corera, 2006; Svendsen, 2010a, pp. 103–116). The actual outcome remains somewhat ambiguous and is sometimes contested.[194] Indeed, the answer is arguably not even as clear-cut as 'partial success', as UK and US intelligence were grappling with such complex issues.[195] Insofar as it is actually possible to judge WMD counter-proliferation operations in such absolutist terms as 'success' and 'failure', as the UK *Butler Report* found in July 2004, the results of

WMD counter-proliferation activities, prior to the supposed Iraqi WMD case, had been largely 'successful' (Butler Committee, 2004, pp. 19–20; Svendsen, 2010a, p. 105, p. 115).

Notably, in previous WMD counter-proliferation activities, the important micro and lower operational and tactical levels had tended to succeed more alongside the macro and higher strategy and policy levels. Simultaneously, the micro and lower levels had greater opportunities to inform more successfully the macro and higher levels over time, and had continued to do so. This scenario was rather than the macro and higher levels being increasingly *disconnected* from the micro and lower level considerations, as was the case witnessed in the example of supposed Iraqi WMD (on the different 'levels', see Chapter 1 (3.2), above).[196]

Consisting of dualities, extending to pluralities, *mixed results* endure in the final outcomes, involving at least some persisting ambiguity. Generally, therefore, familiar patterns continue in counter-proliferation operations. A condition of 'complex coexistence plurality' continues to be reflected overall.

On occasions, some UK and US debates and differences were witnessed on how to best proceed with the investigations into the A.Q. Khan network. These were both domestic and international in their nature, such as between diplomats and different security and intelligence communities. However, these debates are arguably natural. This is especially when trying to grapple with such a complex phenomenon, which has no exact, easily agreeable end or solution, and instead requires constant management as it has ongoing ramifications. Significantly, the disagreements that surfaced appear not to have been so severe as to detrimentally prevent any later joint activities, or to counter-productively hamper the intelligence investigations into the A.Q. Khan network (Svendsen, 2010a, pp. 109–110).[197]

Indeed, the unravelling of the A.Q. Khan network through UK–US intelligence liaison is most appropriately evaluated as *approaching a partial success*. This status is accorded to that episode because of the presence of the ambiguities, including the 'too-slow-to-act' argument raised by critics, who stressed that the 'shut-down' of the network took decades too long (Albright and Hinderstein, 2005).[198] At a minimum, several useful lessons were extracted from the A.Q. Khan example. These should be carefully heeded for their potential application in future counter-proliferation operations and international intelligence liaison interactions.[199]

Further conclusions emerge. That there were any instances of especially significant UK–US intelligence reach deficits and excesses within their intelligence liaison on this issue is not apparent. Neither, on the whole, did the intelligence have to 'conform' to one absolutely fixed, unyielding or unqualified policy agenda stance. The intelligence thus had at least some opportunities to continue to *inform* decision- and policy-makers. This was both *before*, and in an updating manner *after*, the tipping-points, 'decision shut-off points' or episodes of 'cognitive closure'. Some essential flexibility and dynamism was preserved in the implemented response. This allowed for more inclusiveness and the better consideration of the actual complexities being confronted. There appears not to have been any overwhelming discernible detrimental shortcomings, or intelligence liaison 'blowback', in the *effects and outcomes* of the UK–US intelligence liaison on the issue of the A.Q. Khan network.[200]

This scenario, however, appears not to have been the case in relation to the issue of supposed Iraqi WMD and related programmes. Instead, here, intelligence and security reach excesses and deficits within the UK–US intelligence liaison were considerably more evident. This included those traits extending into relevant domains beyond, in both their other individual and joint intelligence liaison interactions, in terms of both their intelligence-gathering and analysis efforts. Moreover, in the Iraq example, there was no sufficiently compelling opportunity, or intelligence 'moment', that could have feasibly shifted the overly rigid decision and fixed response made at the tipping-point, 'decision shut-off point', or occasions of 'cognitive closure', by the key policy- and decision-makers (Dorey, 2005; Svendsen, 2012e).

Indeed, transcending merely the widespread individual 'policy failure' and/or 'intelligence failure' arguments, overall the case of supposed Iraqi WMD can be better conceptualized. This case stands out as being one of multi-level and multi-dimensional-emphasized *policy* – and, to a lesser extent, intelligence – reach deficits and excesses (Byman, 2008). This example will now be evaluated in more detail.

4.3 Evaluating UK–US intelligence liaison on supposed Iraqi WMD

In early July 2004, shortly before the Butler Report was released, an authoritative article in the *Financial Times* noted that: 'As [UK and US] records are examined, the fortunes of the intelligence agencies of the two countries will to some extent rise and fall together.' More specifically, 'While their assessments of the threat posed by Iraq in 2002 did not agree on everything, they shared an enormous amount of raw information and co-operated closely on the analysis. Inevitably, intelligence co-operation across the Atlantic will come under intense review.'[201] An oversight and accountability gap persists, especially concerning liaison questions. These will now be discussed.

Intelligence is well known to often be an imperfect 'science' and 'art'. Verification is difficult. Intelligence frequently results in several differences of interpretation (Chesterman, 2008).[202] Often, this is a healthy sign and should not be dismissed. Although, likewise, there will always be people who will try to shape intelligence – as well as its analyses – to better 'fit' their own preconceived agendas.

Concerning the supposed Iraqi WMD case, the doubts and the caveats were there (Wilkie, 2004, pp. 75–102).[203] They were especially present and enduring amongst the wider and experienced cohorts of the UK and US intelligence communities, and they were 'located' at especially the lower and micro operational, tactical, individual (as professional) and personal levels of intelligence activity (see Chapter 1 (3.2), above). This was evident with the concerns particularly expressed by former senior UK Defence Intelligence Staff (DIS) official, Dr Brian Jones, and those of the late WMD expert Dr David Kelly *et al.*: 'Jones ... told the *Independent* newspaper the DIS's "unified view" was for there to be careful caveats about assessments of Iraq's chemical and biological weapons. But they had been overruled by the heads of the intelligence agencies. Mr Blair said Dr Jones' concerns had been considered by the head of defence intelligence, who decided the dossier's wording was correct.'[204] (see also Jones, 2010a; Svendsen, 2012e)

Inevitably some differences between the UK and US intelligence assessments were apparent. But, it appears that – along with the other original caveats and doubts – several of these divergences were suppressed and removed at more 'senior', macro issue-focused and higher-level managerial meetings (Immerman, 2011, pp. 166–167). Perversely, these essentially appeared to occur beyond the reach of the intelligence world. As the BBC reported: 'Mr Blair said the disputed claim over Iraqi weapons strikes within 45 minutes was entirely the work of the JIC' (the UK Joint Intelligence Committee).[205] Arguably this was done so that the politically cognizant intelligence services could best fulfil their obligations to their users and customers in both Washington and London. They were tasked to 'produce' or 'deliver' in harmony with their users' political agenda. Dilemmas and disconnects were quickly encountered (Corera, 2011; Svendsen, 2010a, pp. 120–122).[206]

Interestingly, again according to the BBC: 'Analysts in the [DIS] in the Ministry of Defence did question the 45-minute claim because of the vagueness ... They also raised concerns about claims about Iraqi production of chemical agents.' Yet these concerns were dismissed by more senior managers: 'But their bosses, who sat on the [JIC] but were not intelligence specialists, agreed the DIS experts should not see intelligence which came in during the latter stages of the dossier's drafting and which MI6 said overrode their concerns.' Unfortunately, as the report continued, 'The late intelligence is now thought to have been unreliable.'[207] Different 'level'-orientated fissures became increasingly apparent.[208]

Overt 'pressure' exerted by the politicians in both the UK and USA was perhaps not necessary *per se*.[209] The 'intelligence machines' in both the UK and USA generally worked successfully as they were intended. Namely, this was delivering, as tasked, to customers' requirements. However, information beyond the narrowly drawn requirements was frequently omitted. This was while some mis-flows of information variously polluted, with further diversions occurring for public political case-building ('propaganda' or 'spin') purposes. Furthermore, arguably sufficient pressure to 'conform' came from, at least 'politically-aware' or 'politically-sensitive', senior intelligence managers. This was in order to fulfil successfully the role that was expected of them by their most important customers, their political masters. Undoubtedly, this was a pragmatic move, especially when there was still a career to be made (see, e.g., 'Bureaucratic Pressure Theory' in Taylor, 2007, p. 264; see also Jervis, 2010b; Rovner, 2011b).[210]

Indeed, as the Butler Report later recommended: 'We see a strong case for the post of Chairman of the JIC being held by someone with experience of dealing with Ministers in a very senior role, and who is demonstrably beyond influence, and thus probably in his last post.' (Butler Committee, 2004, p. 144; Svendsen, 2010a, p. 236)[211] Actual 'pressure' was essentially not so necessary when perceptions of political-to-policy and ideological desires were adequate, and when expectations, in the form of the requirements that were provided, were enough to encourage sufficient conformity. As the BBC's security correspondent Gordon Corera found: 'The process was ... subjected to the "operational imperative to produce results". In the case of Iraq, Sir Richard Dearlove, the chief ['C'] of SIS until ... summer [2004], also made clear there was a "pressure on the [Secret Intelligence] Service [(SIS/MI6)] to produce" as it tried to ramp up its coverage of Iraq from mid-2002.'[212]

In this broken context, constrained by narrow-remits, short time-frames, and forced disconnects, intelligence liaison could not function properly. Consequently, it failed to enact one of its core 'functions' and act as an adequate 'force multiplier' (see Chapter 1 (3.1), above).

illustrating one of the many paradoxes associated with intelligence liaison: elements of its 'professionalized' qualities were both present *and* lacking (Svendsen, 2012e). With all the enforced distortions, the power intelligence liaison could potentially bring became diverted. In these circumstances, it instead acted more as a false verifier. A veritable smörgåsbord of any range of sources was provided, which could then be more easily selected or 'cherry-picked' from in order to conveniently produce – at least seemingly – adequate support for the desired case attempting to be fashioned.[213] Perverted information flows dominated.

Other features became evident. This scenario also made it easier to bury non-supporting sources, as well as to obscure the counter-arguments and contradictory facts presented in their reporting. Due to poor, including overly refined, and/or distorted intelligence management and coordination – stemming from trying to help advance the prescribed political case, as delineated from up high, without too many obstacles posed by properly verified details and thoroughly developed and vetted sources – governments were able to effectively double-cross themselves with their own intelligence.[214]

Worse scenarios were apparent. Governments were able to be effectively double-crossed by inadequately vetted external sources ('CURVEBALL' – the codename for the unreliable and mismanaged Iraqi defector and dissident source on biological weapons, Rafid Alwan (Svendsen, 2010a, p. 233, col.2)), perhaps even triple-crossed (claims that Iraq had sought Niger uranium/'yellowcake' (Svendsen, 2010a, p. 235, col.1)), through variously overlapping and dangerously converged international intelligence liaison channels in London and Washington.[215]

The intelligence management process clearly instead needs to remain neutral, de-politicized, objective, and as wide-ranging or 'open-minded', as far as is humanly and technologically possible. Indeed, as the retired first Director General of Intelligence at the UK Ministry of Defence (1964–1966), Major-General Sir Kenneth Strong, remarked in 1968: 'A true Intelligence appreciation ... is a balanced fusing of all the ingredients which contribute to an understanding of international relations. It is also objective ... Intelligence is – or should be – free of pressure or prejudice, whether engendered within government or by groups outside the government.' (Strong, 1968, pp. 242–243) In the case of supposed Iraqi WMD, those benchmarks, even professional 'standards', were clearly lacking (see Thomas Fingar's comments in Chapter 5 (1.0), below; Svendsen, 2012e).

The interactions over the source CURVEBALL also nicely exposed some of the dynamics that can be encountered when engaging in wider international intelligence liaison exchanges. Not least, this is especially when operating in contexts where intelligence becomes increasingly 'globalized'. This is together with revealing episodes when different international intelligence liaison arrangements significantly overlap, both individually and jointly, in London and/or Washington, and in capitals beyond.[216] The episodes concerning CURVEBALL therefore have much illustrative value when discussing liaison (Svendsen, 2010a, p. 233).

These liaison interactions, as well as their close associates, can then go in either a positive or negative direction depending on the other surrounding circumstances involved. This includes the political climate and its forcefulness, in terms of influence, within, and the tempo at which these interactions are being undertaken. Evidently, in such contexts, higher-level intelligence management and coordination considerations – or indeed even equally their lack thereof – also have an important role to perform. This is especially in helping to shape the 'final' *effects and outcomes* that eventually emerge from the liaison.

Other areas under stress can be highlighted. The most important levels in the world of intelligence generally, and indeed more specifically intelligence liaison – namely the micro and narrow personal and individual (as professional) and operational and tactical levels – were essentially bypassed. Or else, they were 'cherry-picked', if unquestionably favourable for the purpose of building the desired political case trying to be fashioned publicly. Albeit in different configurations, this happened in both the UK and USA – implemented, in other words, in order to help reach agreement at the macro and broader, higher policy and strategy and theoretical and ideological levels of activity (Pillar, 2006; Svendsen, 2012e).

The enhanced internationalization, extending to the 'globalization', of the intelligence liaison appeared to help. This process seemingly lent the case being advanced greater credibility. Not least, this was as more foreign liaison partners were able to 'sign on' to the overall case being advocated. This process was undertaken in order to try and capitalize upon the general flow of intelligence, potentially for gains for themselves (Svendsen, 2010a, p. 142). As former chief UN weapons inspector and US Marine Scott Ritter observed, what UK and US intelligence did effectively deliver together was more of a kinetic 'shock and awe rollback' disarmament case. This was in the form of regime change (Svendsen, 2010a, p. 135). Eventually, Saddam Hussein – the target who threatened to provide an ongoing proliferation problem well into the future – was successfully removed. A 'counter-proliferation paradigm' was translated into action. The problem was, however, that its activation was clearly dubious in terms of garnering sustainable and widespread support into the future. Not least, this was because it was activated on distinctly weak legal bases, a poor foundation which was publicly exposed to all observers (Svendsen, 2010a, pp. 132–134 and 155).[217]

Specifically on Iraqi WMD, as chief UN weapons inspector Dr Hans Blix himself recorded during early summer 2003, there was an 'open verdict'.[218] Concerning wider global non-proliferation efforts, the US-led invasion of Iraq, with all the associated strong whiff of international illegality, has had distinct shortcomings.[219] Without at least a second clearly legitimizing United Nations Security Council Resolution, as an 'insurance policy' or another form of commensurable support, an unhelpful 'message' has essentially been presented.[220] We are now in a 'newer' proliferation era, where – as seen especially with the A.Q. Khan nuclear network – more 'selfish' entrepreneurialism is the dominant driver. This is together with a commensurate overlooking, even dismissal, of legal, moral and ethical dimensions. These are the established value-system qualities that should ideally act as a most effective check on proliferation activities (Langewiesche, 2007; Thornton, 2007, pp. 16–19).[221]

Strategically, a recalibrated, but not entirely reformed, response is required. Arguably, intelligence, through efforts towards its greater 'professionalization', similarly needs to be better harnessed. This includes the 'professionalization' occurring within intelligence liaison relationships, domestically and internationally, and extending to the globalization of intelligence (Patrick, 2010; Svendsen, 2012e).[222] Likewise, intelligence, in all senses of its meaning, needs to be better deployed, in order to more effectively realize that more sophisticated response in a sufficiently adequate and timely manner (Cooper, 2011).[223]

As encountered in the overarching realm of CT, arguably the highly crucial so-called 'ideas war' has again been more 'lost' than 'won' (if those terms are sufficiently applicable). This rather dubious state of affairs was accomplished through implementing a policy that suffered from distinct acontextualization traits, and displayed inadequate sensitivity to the full plethora of details and subtle nuances of the actual chaos of 'reality' (Kutz, 2008, pp. 6–8).[224] Clearly, rather than blaming 'everybody', only top leadership and their close bespoke-selected advisers could be held most accountable.[225] Ultimately, despite any claims to the contrary, this was because that was where the most responsibility was sited in a strongly concentrated form. Moreover, this was especially apparent in the context that emerged, where any 'lower level' concerns were patently overruled and were not allowed enough of an informing voice (Svendsen, 2010a, pp. 133–135 and 154–155).[226]

This troubling trend needs to continue to be comprehensively addressed, through undertaking greater or enhanced contextualization efforts, for instance, facilitated through undertaking increased research-originating intelligence ('RESINT') activities (see Chapters 3 (1.1) and 5 (5.0), below). What happened with Iraq arguably serves to suggest to 'regimes of concern' that they should actually speed-up WMD programmes, and should increase stockpiles of lethal weapons, including conventional weapons (Bergenäs, 2010b; Dalby, 2011).[227] Actual, unambiguously known possession of WMD arguably brings with it the greater national and international security deterrence threat of more effective retaliation in the form of approaching mutually assured destruction (MAD), as witnessed during the Cold War (Gaddis, 2005, p. 326; Haddick, 2009; Long, 2008).[228]

Again, as seen in the past, it is highly likely that MAD will help contribute towards, at least potentially, deterring the USA (and the UK, and other countries) from: (i) adopting and adapting actions that were taken against Iraq (namely, invasion and regime change); and from (ii) applying the same actions towards other 'states of concern', such as, notably, Iran and North Korea (Bowen and Brewer, 2011; Knopf, 2008; Ogilvie-White, 2010).[229] The passage of more time will have to take place to ascertain whether, despite appearances, the invasion of Iraq can be evaluated as having been more of a 'success'. Whatever 'metrics' are used, this is especially in the long-term concerning the issue of WMD, and indeed additionally of conventional weapon, counter-proliferation, and in overall security and safety terms (Chivers, 2011; Cooper and Mutimer, 2011).[230]

The vivid failings of policy-makers aside, the Iraq war case also exposes numerous limits of intelligence. Overlapping with the frequently raised technology versus 'human factors' arguments, technical intelligence (TECHINT), consisting of signals intelligence (SIGINT) and imagery intelligence (IMINT), could only be used so far (Svendsen, 2010a, pp. 27–30).[231] The crucial centrality of intelligence liaison and human intelligence (HUMINT), in helping to fill in the remaining blanks of the WMD puzzles, was highlighted (Hitz, 2008, pp. 1–2).[232] This was together with exposing all of the associated limitations of liaison, when intelligence sources were trying to be stretched and re-configured to fit most desired pre-existing and politicized frames. With such high stakes in play, the onus upon all involved is heightened, and patience and acute sensitivity to detail are rendered even more crucial in such circumstances (Berkowitz, 2003). Better balancing is required.

The more micro operational, tactical, individual (as professional), and personal levels are essential. The reliability of the HUMINT reporting in such circumstances has to be *even more* robust. It needs to be subjected to tougher validation criteria and processes, and cannot be rushed or moulded, with caveats jettisoned. This is not least the case when a policy of pre-emption is trying to be pursued. Otherwise, as seen with the example of the 2003 Iraq war, the 'case' made on the basis of available intelligence, (mis-)used as 'evidence', can rapidly disintegrate and collapse in the wider, acontextualized, operating environment (Svendsen, 2012e).[233]

In the process, even the best intentions could be destroyed. This is no matter how passionately, and indeed messianically, including with alleged 'blind faith', they are believed and pursued.[234] As John le Carré succinctly observed in an interview in October 2005: 'Actually ... I believe the sin was greater than simply taking us [Britain] to war [in Iraq]. It destroyed our relationship with the Middle East and with south-east Asia and took us on a flight of fantasy about our relationship with the US.'[235] Strong insights were provided.

4.4 Cooperative WMD counter-proliferation efforts beyond Iraq

Further relevant contemporary developments concerning global-extending cooperative WMD counter-proliferation efforts are now examined. A case suggesting the presence of greater US-led top-down 'homogenization' and 'international standardization' processes within this domain of intelligence activity can also be argued convincingly.

A mode of enhanced cooperative activity concerning WMD counter-proliferation efforts is particularly seen in relation to agreements such as the US Proliferation Security Initiative (PSI). This is especially whereby the PSI has been officially denoted as: 'a set of activities... best understood as a set of partnerships that establishes the basis for cooperation on specific activities when the need arises.' The US State Department briefing continued: 'It does not create formal "obligations" for participating states, but does represent a political commitment to establish "best practices" to stop proliferation-related shipments.' The initiative likewise included: 'PSI interdiction training exercises and other operational efforts [that] will help states work together in a more cooperative, coordinated, and effective manner to stop, search and seize shipments.'[236] More crucially, the PSI's officially reported challenging task has been to 'bring together nations with a similar purpose: to implement practical steps to interdict dangerous weapons and technologies in transit.' In detail, 'PSI activities consist mostly of training exercises and tabletop simulations, which evolve from discussions of an operational group of experts (OEG) [*sic.*] who have been meeting quarterly since July 2003.'[237]

The cooperation coalescing around the structure of the PSI framework was valuable in intelligence liaison terms. As a 2008 RAND report found: 'Through intelligence sharing and cooperation in interdiction, a PSI participant is more likely to learn that one of its flagged ships is carrying illicit WMD items; it is also more likely to be able to obtain immediate help in inspecting cargo beyond its reach.' The report continued, demonstrating where potential 'added value' in interactions could be reaped: 'Additionally, PSI exercises help improve participants' interdiction procedures and capabilities. PSI affiliation also offers the qualitative benefit of contributing to more-cooperative strategic relations with other PSI participants.' (Wolf *et al.*, 2008, p. 27) Again, a whole range of beneficial cooperative activities is suggested (Hamel-Green, 2009). Reform of Central and Eastern European intelligence agencies and their Special Operations Forces (SOF) in the post-Cold War era by the Western intelligence agencies and SOF, most notably under the guise of police, intelligence and security sector reform (SSR) initiatives, can also be referenced. This is along with other similar developments occurring in other countries across the globe (Roberts, 2006, pp. 129–131; Watts, 2004; see also the US-led 'Container Security Initiative' (CSI) in Svendsen, 2010a, pp. 21 and 58).

Finally, as the *Butler Report* remarked: 'A number of common threads have become clear from our examination of each [non-proliferation] case ... [including] the powerful multiplier effect of effective international (in many cases, multinational) collaboration.' (Butler Committee, 2004, p. 26, para.108) Long may this quality last in a manner *complementing* unilateral intelligence efforts. However, intelligence liaison, extending to the globalization of intelligence, can be a double-edged sword that cuts (or works) both ways (see Chapter 1 (6.0), above). All the risks and downsides, for instance in the form of intelligence and security reach deficits and excesses in such interactions, also need to be more fully accounted for and be appreciated by all parties. This is especially when navigating intelligence investigations focused on highly complex issues such as WMD counter-proliferation. Moreover, this is not least when the navigation is undertaken in a dynamic domain where the stakes now and for the future are high – especially while operating in high-tempo environments where operating spaces are simultaneously condensed (Mutimer, 2011).[238]

For policy-makers and intelligence operators alike, a more enduring non-proliferation regime can be constructed. This is by adopting, for instance, a greater – and more coherent and coordinated, indeed *strategic* – emphasis on mainstream economic market mechanisms, used for sanctions ('stick') and incentive ('carrot') purposes (Ifft, 2007;

Luongo and Williams, 2007).[239] However, in the 'smartness' of their targeting (judiciously balancing 'hard' and 'soft' components), the economic sanctions have to be comprehensive in their scope as well as being suitably connected strategically (Taylor, 2010; Whang, 2011).[240]

Intelligence, when sensibly and legitimately used to *inform* and *direct* policy- and decision-making in a timely and updating manner, can considerably aid in these efforts. This is important as, worryingly, today more individual-focused 'entrepreneurialism', with the simultaneous increased overlooking and dismissal of the legal, moral and ethical dimensions, such as demonstrated effectively by the example of the A.Q. Khan 'nuclear network', has emerged as the dominant driver in contemporary WMD proliferation activities (see above in 4.3).[241]

Overall conclusions are now drawn.

5.0 Conclusions

To help avoid distinctly liaison-damaging and distorting implications, several cautionary notes are now offered.

Most concerningly, a bleak scenario may be confronted in the future. This is increasingly apparent if the type of trajectory travelled on during the so-called War on Terror (*c.* 2001–2009) ever returns and again dominates (N. Davies, 2009; Rosenberg and Feldman, 2008).[242] Arguably, this was where there appeared to be – at least occasionally – an increasing *disconnect* between, on one hand, the macro and high, and, on the other hand, micro and low levels of experience, activity, and analysis. In such unbalanced circumstances, detrimentally, the goal of 'operational policy' – located firmly within the 'mid-' or 'meso-level' domain (where the macro and micro 'quartets of levels' should most harmoniously connect or fuse) – becomes increasingly difficult to achieve; and with that last scenario emerging, with the simultaneous presence of distinct paucities within that zone, the realization of overall 'success' becomes increasingly elusive (see Chapter 3 (6.0), below).

Meanwhile, counter-productive consequences are experienced within the more specific domains of intelligence liaison and the globalization of intelligence. As ramifications, the disadvantageous conditions of 'overreach' and 'under-reach' are increasingly reflected on the occasions when the increasingly toxic and imbalanced, even over-politicized, environment (as described above) prevails, notably as demonstrated during the run-up to the 2003 war in Iraq (Pillar, 2011a). Liaison interactions cannot be artificially removed or even isolated from the overarching context in which they are embedded and are occurring.

Unless carefully managed and addressed, the downturns become wide-ranging, occurring both operationally and strategically, as well as in policy terms. Amid the consequent disconnects and imbalances, what can be regarded as a condition (indeed the most optimal condition) of intelligence and security equilibrium disintegrates (Nye, 2011b).[243]

Certainly, by the end of 2008, instead of being more like coerced firefighters and emergency first-responders, intelligence, security and law enforcement services (including the military), in at least both the UK and USA (extending at times to their close partner countries), needed to return to being more akin to *architects* and *engineers* in their risk and threat management and responses. Extended re-balancing efforts were necessary (Treverton, 2009a, pp. 100–133).

Consequently, an urgent re-think and re-adjustment of policy and strategy was increasingly required by 2009. This was together with the enhanced generation of those constructs, for providing some better future leadership and guidance (Gray, 2007a; Smith, 2006; Strachan, 2010; Svendsen, 2010b).[244] The USA particularly needed such moves, and, especially relating to its close association in the UK–US alliance, so did the UK. It looks highly likely that we are now beginning to witness at least some of this much-needed change. This has come with the advent of the Obama administration in early 2009, and with the consigning of the so-called 'War on Terror', or at least its 'blunter' components, to history.

Positively, its associated 'terminology' has been dropped. Albeit somewhat 'slow' and 'fitful', there are also increased gradual movements towards addressing its 'symbols', including Guantánamo Bay prison (Aughey, 2011; Grayling, 2009; Treverton, 2009a, pp. 235–261; Wittes, 2010).[245] Emphasizing more 'emergency preparedness' and greater '*defensive*-defence', rather than so much a mode of '*offensive*-defence', would, more-or-less, be the re-fashioned way forward (McCauley and Moskalenko, 2010; McCrisken, 2011; Woodward, 2011).[246]

In its Conclusion, the IISS *Strategic Survey* of 2009 remarked that: 'The intellectual habit in the West has recently become to align national or alliance strategic interests with the delivery of a global public good.' (IISS, 2009, p. 387) Liaison interactions extending up to the globalization of intelligence likewise increasingly strive towards attaining that goal (Svendsen, 2010a, p. 173).[247]

Other conclusions are already clear. Increasingly, absolutist thinking akin to that reflected in former US Secretary of Defense Robert McNamara's claim (from soon after the October 1962 Cuban Missile Crisis) that: 'Today, there is no longer such a thing as strategy, there is only crisis management', is bankrupt.[248] Whenever operating, a mode of strategy and policy is needed (or indeed needs to be better fashioned) that is considerably more intimately tied to the 'lower' considerations. This is as those considerations are both directly and indirectly encountered at the micro and lower levels of activity and experience, such as at the operational and tactical and individual (as professional) and personal levels. Both systematically and systemically, being overall *better connected* has clear benefits.

Intimately including the careful deployment of liaison and outreach components for all their purposes, an enhanced *intelligence methodology* is also therefore required. This is together with a greater listening to the results that a more advanced intelligence methodology can yield, as well as fostering a wider understanding of what intelligence can appreciably offer (Immerman, 2011, p. 179; see also, e.g., Chapters 5 (5.0) and 6 (4.0 and 7.1), below; Svendsen, 2012e).

Notably, adopting this more sophisticated approach towards intelligence would (i) boost its strategic impact, and, going beyond merely operational bases, would (ii) allow intelligence to perform an improved *informing, warning* and *directing* role. Being merely 'surveillance-led' is insufficient, resulting in distinct problems (Chesterman, 2010; Laidler, 2008).[249] By mid-2007, involving their re-connection, a degree of 'high'/'macro' and 'low'/'micro' level adjustment appeared to be at least beginning to emerge somewhat more effectively. This re-configuration included the UK and the USA in their general relations (Hastings Dunn, 2008; Svendsen, 2011d).[250]

Doubtless such enhanced intelligence efforts could be extended further, both structurally and culturally (Gray, 2007a, 2010a; Russell, 2007a; Strachan, 2010).[251] This was still highly evident in 2009–2011, even if developments such as the launch in March 2008 of the UK's first *National Security Strategy* and the UK's *National Risks Register* (published in November 2008), and subsequent updates into 2010–2011, were taken into account (Cronin, 2010; Porter, 2010). The establishment of a UK National Security Council in May 2010 looks to be a step in a positive direction towards addressing at least some of these concerns. However, time is still needed to see how this new 'structure' will fully work, including in cultural terms (Davies, 2011; Dearlove, 2010, p. 88; see also Chapter 5 (3.0), below).[252] Helping to shape opportunities needs extension (Dupont and Reckmeyer, 2012).

The globalization of intelligence as an overall concept and construct now benefits from being further examined. This forms the main focus of the next chapter.

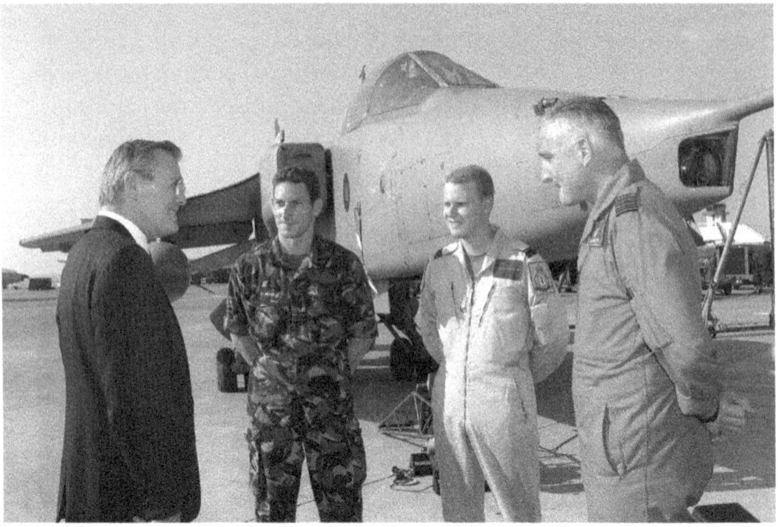

Plate 1 US Secretary of Defense Donald Rumsfeld talks to members of the British Royal Air Force, enforcers of the no-fly zone in northern Iraq, in June 2001. Photo: US DoD

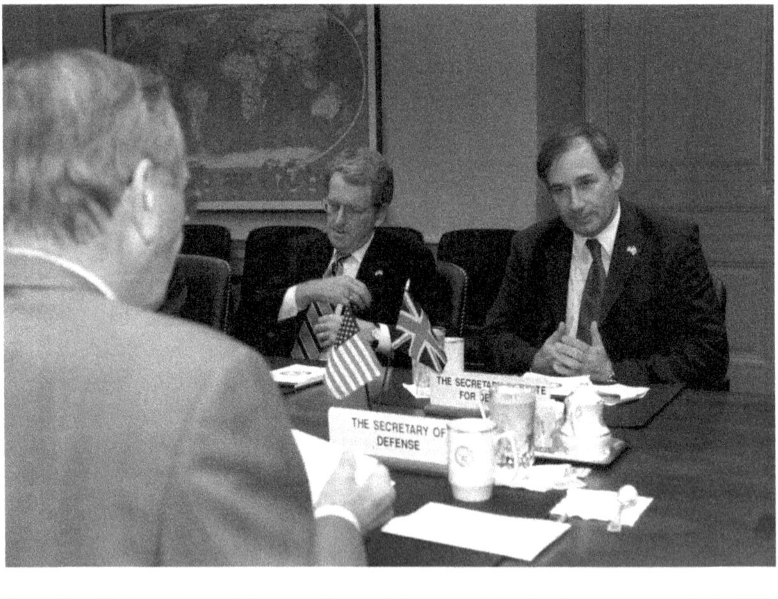

Plate 2 US Secretary of Defense Donald Rumsfeld holds discussions with British Secretary of Defence Geoff Hoon (right) and British Ambassador to Washington Sir Christopher Meyer (centre) in October 2001. Photo: US DoD

Plate 3 British Chief of the Defence Staff (CDS) Admiral Lord Michael Boyce (right) inspects US troops with US General Richard B. Myers, Chairman of the Joint Chiefs of Staff, and Lt. Col. Tracy Bryant, Commander of Troops, in November 2002. Photo: US DoD

Plate 4 US Secretary of Defense Rumsfeld selects a question while British Secretary of Defence Hoon looks on. Photo: US DoD

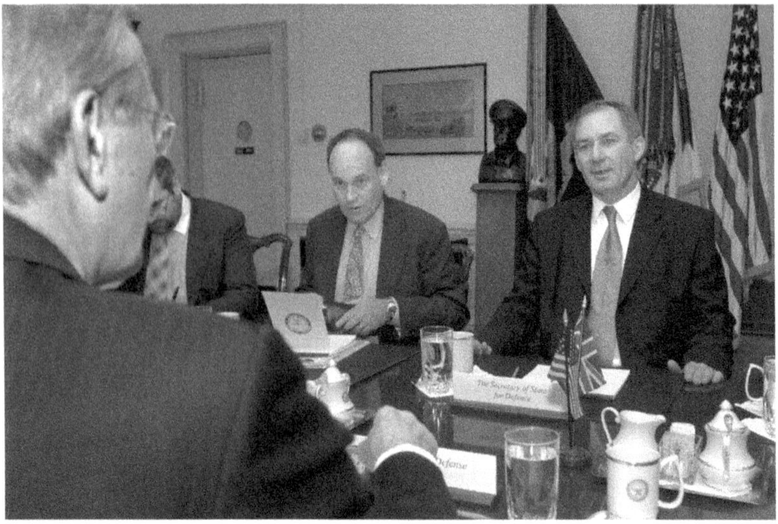

Plate 5 US Secretary of Defense Rumsfeld and British Secretary of Defence Hoon hold talks in January 2004. Photo: US DoD

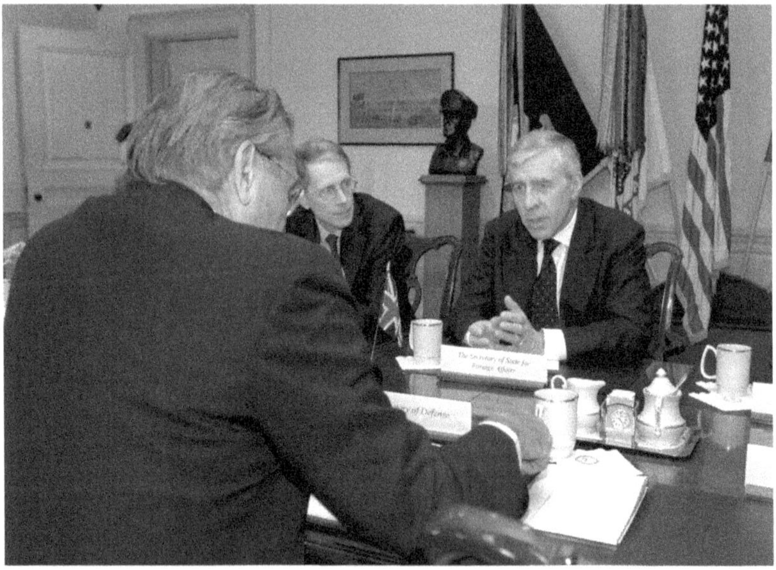

Plate 6 US Secretary of Defense Rumsfeld and British Foreign Secretary Jack Straw hold discussions in May 2005. British Ambassador to Washington Sir David Manning looks on. Photo: US DoD

Plate 7 British Prime Minister Tony Blair and US Secretary of State Condoleezza Rice pose for the press during Rice's visit to the UK and Europe in March 2005. Photo: US State Department

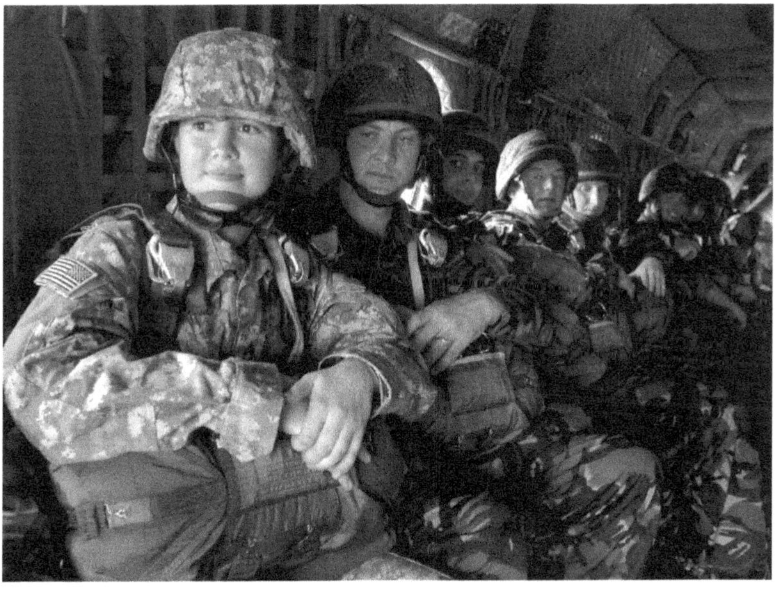

Plate 8 US and British troops deploy together in July 2007. Photo: US DoD

3 Overview

From intelligence to *globalized* intelligence during an era of terror, crises, and organized crime

1.0 Why intelligence matters

Today, intelligence is especially important. So is its study, in order to enhance our understanding of the phenomenon in our contemporary, globalized era (Treverton and Agrell, 2009, pp. 1–8; see also Aldrich and Davies, 2009, pp. 887–888). We can observe this because, as former UK intelligence officer Michael Herman has remarked: 'The main change has been the dramatic increase in intelligence's own importance after September 11, 2001.' (Herman, 2004, p. 184; see also Dearlove, 2010, pp. 85–86)[1] Moreover, intelligence is central to the doctrine of pre-emption, a trend dominant in the security and foreign policies of several countries, most notably the US and the UK (Hill, 2003, pp. 66–69).[2]

Part of what Canadian Intelligence has dubbed a 'New Intelligence Order' (Roberts, 2006, p. 135), this trend has been markedly in the ascendant since the 9/11 attacks in the US, during the subsequent so-called 'War on Terror' and 'Long War' (*c.* 2001–2009), and beyond (Kahn, 2006; Lebovich, 2011; O'Brien, 2009). Intelligence often dominates the media headlines in a context where tackling 'new' terrorism and other pressing associated global security challenges, such as organized crime and the proliferation of Weapons of Mass Destruction (WMD), sit at the top of national and international agendas (Giegerich, 2010; Gills, 2010).[3]

In the early twenty-first century, there have also been several high-profile inquiries into intelligence 'failure' (Phythian, 2005, pp. 361–363; see also Jervis, 2010a; Svendsen, 2010a, p. 139). These have publicly emphasized the central importance of intelligence, as well as the other activities of secret services, to wider political processes. Arguably, intelligence has changed. It has morphed from being mainly a peripheral *supporting* activity to being more of a *centrally involved* activity. Rather than delivering merely an *informing* and *warning* contribution, intelligence is performing more of a *leading* and *directing* role – a change encapsulated by the frequently used phrase 'intelligence-led' (Ratcliffe, 2008; see also Crawford, 2011; Nicoll, 2010c).[4]

Inevitably, this development has implications. This is especially apparent when operations are more technologically 'surveillance-led' in an *a priori* and pre-emptive manner. As US intelligence scholar Stan A. Taylor has noted: 'The modern security environment (terrorism, nuclear proliferation, cross-national drugs and crimes – all occurring during unprecedented globalization) has brought about calls for stronger intelligence activities while at the same time it has created concerns about the unintended consequences of intelligence activities.' (Taylor, 2007, p. 267)[5]

As a result, intelligence has moved increasingly out of the shadows and into the public spotlight. Moreover, reflecting its enhanced status, within academe, intelligence should instead be considered more broadly and form a greater part of any consideration of mainstream government, foreign policy and wider international affairs, including globalization. Transformative shifts have occurred.[6]

1.1 Extending the academy

There is also a need for a more purposeful, active and *applied* form of contemporary intelligence studies. We need to further develop a well-funded branch of '*functional* intelligence studies', which is more operational-to-strategy/policy-orientated and impacting in its nature.

In other words, the intelligence studies field needs to become better operationalized. At the least, aspects of intelligence studies need to get more ahead of the prevailing curve of events and developments. This is instead of the field of intelligence studies being merely mostly reactive and being more 'behind', albeit at times closely, what is occurring in the real-world (see also as discussed below in 2.0).

Improved shaping can occur and be advanced. Thereby, in contemporary intelligence activities, greater and more timely 'all-source-ready' material, such as research-originating input ('RESINT'), could be offered to policy- and decision-makers. Demand for this support is continuing to grow as we are all grappling with the same issues (Svendsen, 2010d; see also Martin and Wilson, 2008; Wirtz and Rosenwasser, 2010). The utility, relevance, and, hence value, of the intelligence studies field and of the work it produces will then be substantially enhanced beyond, in the main, merely its own circles. Greater delivery potential is offered.

Both strategically and operationally, further adopting this 'action-research'-related approach would be useful for contextualization and multiple issue-management purposes during an era characterized by complex globality (Marrin, 2011b).[7] Not least, this movement is important as the developments associated with the complex globalization process take place well beyond the scope of control of individuals and single agencies, while practitioners are striving to navigate intense multi-functional operational contexts from war to peace. Much of tangible value to practitioners can be, and needs to be, conveyed in an ever-timelier manner during an era of 'globalized strategic risk' (see Chapters 2 and 5; Atkinson, 2010; Russell, 2007b; Sims, 2007; Sloan, 2012; Watters, 2011).[8]

We also need to keep pushing forward with constantly challenging the 'intellectual bases' of the intelligence studies field. This is so that complacency does not ensue, while, today, previously identified 'missing dimensions' and other areas of paucity concerning intelligence are being better addressed (Andrew and Dilks, 1984; see also Aldrich, 2010, p. 362, 2011b, p. 143; Svendsen, 2012e). This further work also needs to be more concerned about the *dynamics* of intelligence (henceforth termed 'intelligence dynamics') and their near-to-far-ranging influence – such as, in this study, focusing on the globalization of intelligence and better understanding its impact (Svendsen, 2011e).

In summary, we can highlight and advance the utility of the intelligence studies field towards, at a minimum, helping both scholars and practitioners reach an improved understanding of contemporary issues and developments (Svendsen, 2009b; see also Hood *et al.*, 2004, pp. 145–186). More widely, in part with reference to burgeoning 'Collective Intelligence' or 'COLINT' developments (Svendsen, 2012d), the public can similarly be kept better informed through mechanisms such as their greater educative engagement (see Chapter 5 (4.0–5.0), below). Greater communication efforts remain essential.

2.0 Enhancing connections and reach: Why intelligence cooperation matters

The rise of cooperative activities in the 'intelligence world' is clearly perceptible. In the current context, arguably the 'hidden hand' of intelligence liaison has emerged as the most significant dimension of intelligence (see Chapter 1 (3.2), above; Crawford, 2010). As *Jane's Intelligence Digest* noted in 2006: 'Since the terrorist attacks of [9/11] made Al-Qaeda's global reach evident, much attention has focused on improving intelligence-sharing and law-enforcement co-operation.'[9] US intelligence scholar Jennifer Sims has similarly observed that: 'Since [9/11], the role of foreign intelligence liaison has taken center stage in the global war on terror' (Sims, 2006, p. 195), while the *Economist* reported in 2005 that: 'Most of the new powers granted to the spooks have to do with surveillance and information-sharing.'[10]

Over time, many different practitioners, civilian and military alike, have frequently stressed the usefulness of intelligence liaison (Gardner, 2006, p. 30; McKeeby, 2006).[11] Symbolically, although more recently subjected to changes during the so-called Arab Spring/Reawakening of 2011 (Johnstone and Mazo, 2011; see also Freeman, 2011; Haass, 2011), 'Intelligence cooperation between Muslim Arab governments and the United States has become critical for countering Islamic terrorist threats to both parties.'[12] The centrality of liaison to recent and current intelligence activities is enhanced.[13]

Rationales are clear. These actions have primarily been effected to enhance the responsive *reach* of intelligence and security agencies. Generally, the intention is for their extended intelligence and security reach to be implemented across all the areas where intelligence operates and in which it has an interest.[14] With both thematic/functional (including time/tempo and space/spatial) and geographic/regional (including global) constructs mattering, this 'reach' can be readily observed; particularly where it overlaps with more familiar and established concepts such as intelligence coverage.[15] During 2010–2011, the UK Secret Intelligence Service (SIS/MI6) told the UK Intelligence and Security Committee (ISC), that 'the [international terrorism] threat is evolving, but that they were able to keep abreast of the scale of the challenge. With their *global coverage and network of foreign liaison partnerships*, they regard the threat as "broadly contained".'[16]

Distinct 'reach' markers emerge. As senior RAND analyst Gregory Treverton has emphasized:

> Terrorists who are willing to die for their cause as suicide bombers, for example, cannot be deterred from acting in any way similar to the way that states could. Thus, there is even more pressure on intelligence, which now has to be not merely good enough to structure deterrent threats. Rather, *it also needs to reach deeply into small groups* – their proclivities and capabilities – to provide an understanding that can lead to preventive action. (Treverton, 2009a, p. 2, emphasis added)

The 'reach-enhancement' process takes place in both the domains of domestic and international affairs, including within intelligence and security organizations themselves. Firstly, it manifests itself specifically in terms of the direction, scale, and persistence of intelligence and security activities and investigations, simultaneously ushering in related challenging questions of 'proportionality' (Svendsen, 2010b).[17] Secondly, the reach-enhancement process is ideally implemented in a directly competitive, as well as ultimately 'winning', manner versus targets and risks.

Overall, an active 'extended-boundaries' approach is reflected, characteristic of trying to be 'ahead of the curve' of events and developments, rather than being more passive and 'behind' that curve (Cronin, 2002/03). Its advocates generally promote the adoption of a more dynamic 'forward' stance, often in tandem with partners. Both strategic and operational impact is apparent (see Chapter 2 (2.0), above).

More widely, the importance of liaison can be readily highlighted. In April 2008, the Director of the FBI, Robert S. Mueller, acknowledged that: 'The essential components to confronting [terrorist] threats are intelligence and partnerships.' He continued: 'Today ... the vast majority of the FBI's terrorism cases originate from information developed by our partners overseas – even those cases in which the suspected terrorists and the potential targets are all on American soil.'[18] Extending further, as was emphasized by the Office of the US Director of National Intelligence (ODNI) in 2007: 'The IC [US intelligence community] cannot win against our adversaries on its own ... its necessary work with foreign intelligence and security services must proceed on a planned and prudent basis.'[19]

Clearly, that work had already been central. In 2005, in testimony to a closed US Congress committee session, the CIA deputy director of operations reportedly revealed that 'virtually every capture or killing of a suspected terrorist outside Iraq since the Sept. 11, 2001, attacks – more than 3,000 in all – was a result of foreign intelligence services' work alongside the agency.'[20] In evidence for the UK ISC's Renditions report of June 2007, Sir David Pepper, the Director of the UK Government Communications Headquarters (GCHQ) (2003–2008), succinctly remarked: 'When we talk about use of intelligence, that would include passing it to liaison services.'[21] As a former US Assistant Director of Central Intelligence for Analysis and Production, Dr Mark Lowenthal, has also observed: 'When assessing different intelligence services, keep in mind that most have liaison relationships with other services, thus increasing their capabilities. The degree to which these relationships complement or overlap one another is important.' (Lowenthal, 2006, p. 303) Disconnects also feature.

The centrality of liaison to contemporary intelligence is thus firmly demonstrable. Indeed, networks – whether they are composed of intelligence officers and/or (their) agents – as well as the process of networking, have always been key to intelligence, as well as representing how intelligence is organized (Stephenson, 1976, p. xi and p. xiii; see also Montgomery Hyde, 1962). One commentator has even remarked: 'Ours is the age of the network. Whether framed in socio-economic, technological or ideological terms, our present times are increasingly seen as characterized by the rise and spread of fluid, decentralized forms of social organization in which information and telecommunication devices play key roles.' (Bousquet, 2008, p. 915; see also Bolt, 2009; Bousquet, 2009; McChrystal, 2011; Maoz, 2011)

The impact of the Internet, globalized media, citizen journalism, digital and social media, and all of their information flows, can similarly be evoked. Hand-in-glove with their burgeoning significance, these 'networked' trends, and the clustered interactions surrounding them, have quickly increased on exponential bases, both mirroring and forming part of the proliferation of general globalization trends. As relevant rapid technological developments have shrunk space constructs (condensing them geographically, territorially, and spatially), the impact of time constructs have also increased, particularly in terms of the rate and tempo at which events occur, intentionally and otherwise (West, 2011).[22]

Inevitably, intelligence has been affected by these overarching trends and developments. This has necessitated some further intelligence change and transformation in both core collection/gathering and analysis/assessment activities for the plethora of different information and intelligence 'communities' that exist in their variously interconnected ways. As former CIA analyst Richard L. Russell has argued, with a close referential eye on the CIA, 'modern institution[s]' are needed that are 'capable of efficiently operating in the globalized information-technology era.' (Russell, 2007a, p. 151)[23]

On both structural and cultural bases, networks and the qualities they possess – such as their organization and the diverse flows of information between them (however exactly configured and calibrated) – have become increasingly important, and they continue to remain so as they keep constantly morphing into the future (see Chapter 6 (8.0), below; Clift, 2003).[24]

In the contemporary globalized era, and undoubtedly continuing into the future, these networks continue to need to be better connected and exploited through their enhanced facilitation. This is best accomplished both at the human and technical levels, and vertically and horizontally, again including in geographic/regional and functional/thematic terms, forming closely interconnected matrices.[25]

As an integral part of these 'networked' processes, the significance of liaison is thus further elevated. Liaison is *what* those networks do, including *how* they can pursue their activities. Subject to some similar trends, a 'softer' form of liaison, featuring as *outreach*, has also flourished in parallel, particularly in the important open source (OS) and overt intelligence realms (see Chapter 1 (4.0), above).

Indeed, more generally, the OSINF/OSINT realm and its associated arrangements represent the areas where the trends of the regionalization and the globalization of intelligence extend to their furthest in the covert intelligence world (Svendsen, 2010a, pp. 19–20, 2011c; see also Chapters 1 (2.1) and 2 (3.1), above). Frameworks and their associated dynamics for structuring and facilitating responses have relevance.

2.1 The changing landscape

Rarely probed in detail and frequently remaining highly secret, intelligence liaison has increased exponentially, albeit unevenly. Traditional, bilateral international intelligence liaison has increased particularly rapidly. For Western states and their intelligence and security services, this has brought with it a diverse range of new and sometimes non-traditional, even 'unlikely', partners. Underlining the sheer fluidity of the processes being examined, this has even included (at least for a time) partnerships with (various different entities in) Libya and Sri Lanka, and, especially since 2009, Yemen (Ward and Hackett, 2006; see also Dutch Review Committee, 2009, p. 44, para.14.8).[26]

While these trends and relationships vary over time, particularly in their details, they have been useful (Svendsen, 2010a, p. 6 and 8). As former US Deputy Secretary of State Richard Armitage observed in 2002: 'Probably the most dramatic improvement in our intelligence collection and sharing has come in bilateral cooperation with other nations – those we considered friendly before 9/11, and some we considered less friendly.' He continued: 'This is a marked change, and one that I believe results not just from collective revulsion at the nature of the attacks, but also the common recognition that such groups present a risk to any nation with an investment in the rule of law.'[27] Highlighting the persistence of these trends, later in April 2004, US Secretary of State Colin Powell made a similar observation.[28] Treverton, too, in 2009, acknowledged 'the corresponding expansion in the consumers of intelligence.' (Treverton, 2009a, p. 3)[29]

Some greater multilateral intelligence liaison has also been witnessed. Frequently referring to multi-parties involved in variously interconnected intelligence arrangements, rather than so precisely to the nature of their interactions *per se*,[30] this multilateralism has been seen both geographically and organizationally within regional frameworks such as the European Union (EU) and the Association of South East Asian Nations (ASEAN). The *regionalization* of intelligence is represented effectively (Svendsen, 2011c; see also Bergenäs, 2010c).[31]

There has also been cooperation between and beyond these regionally focused arrangements, allowing the discussion of the globalization of intelligence.[32] For instance: 'At the 9th ministerial meeting of the ASEAN Regional Forum (ARF) in Bandar Seri Begawan on 30 July 2002 ... the ARF participating states and organization (the EU) agreed on concrete steps that included: freezing terrorist assets, *implementation of international standards, cooperation on exchange of information and outreach, and technical assistance*.'[33]

Although multilateral intelligence liaison has been increasing, inevitably it has increased more incrementally, more gradually, than other more confined configurations of liaison (bilateral or trilateral). This is because of a range of familiar, persisting security and counter-intelligence anxieties concerning the protection of sources and methods that arise in such multilateral contexts (Zartman and Touval, 2010; see also Svendsen, 2010a, pp. 16 and 41–42; Chapter 2 (3.1), above).[34]

Further extended intelligence cooperation trends include developments occurring at the plurilateral level between different parties, again particularly focused on counter-terrorism, such as between the USA and the EU, and the USA and ASEAN (Rees, 2006, 2011; Chapter 1 (5.0), above).[35] Frequently, the concept of 'uneven and combined development' is reflected (see 10.0, below).[36]

Perhaps more remarkably, post-9/11 direct linkages between the local (domestic and internal) and international (foreign and external) have emerged (Graham, with Nussbaum, 2008, p. 85).[37] This simultaneously points towards identified phenomena such as 'glocalization', which suggests a greater 'contraction of "global" and "local",' and 'refers to the increasing entanglement of these two spheres' (Mooney and Evans, 2007, pp. 117–118; Nussbaum, 2007; Swyngedouw, 2004)[38] – essentially describing situations whereby events and developments occurring locally have more of a direct and wider impact globally than previously.[39] The 'glocalization of intelligence' might be discussed as another related dimension (see Chapter 6 (2.0), below).

3.0 International intelligence liaison as increasingly an 'end'

Some recalibration has occurred, involving the increased 'strategizing' of liaison. Whereas international intelligence liaison previously played more of a supporting role in intelligence activities, today it is evidently playing an increasingly directing role. No longer is it: (i) merely performing the more peripheral role of a 'means' or 'method', sited at the micro operational and tactical levels of intelligence efforts; instead it is also (ii) more effectively performing an ever-more-central role as an 'end' or 'solution' and ongoing issue-management tool, located at the macro strategy and policy levels of intelligence activities (George, 2010; see also Pouliot, 2011; Svendsen, 2011b; Chapter 1 (3.2), above).

Overall, liaison acts as an operating mechanism that delivers strategically. Indeed, again highlighting the importance of intelligence liaison and the enhanced use of associated 'back-channel' mechanisms, the claim has surfaced that: 'Intelligence liaisons can become the primary channel of communications between two governments, a function that is supposedly reserved for embassies, ambassadors, and heads of state.'[40]

It is a potent tool for issue navigation and continues to constantly evolve. Insightfully, early in 2007 the ODNI revealed that: 'We are still building the foreign intelligence relationships to help us meet global security challenges'. Offering some further details of the developments undergone, the ODNI report maintained: 'Progress has been made. In fact, the IC partnered with the Department of Defense to provide Commonwealth partners [for example, the UK and Australia] access to information on a classified US system [for example, SIPRNet – the US Secret Internet Protocol Router Network (Svendsen, 2010a, pp. 29–30)] to improve our combined ability to fight the wars in Iraq and Afghanistan.'[41]

Operational concerns were not the only considerations. At the higher strategic level, the ODNI also 'completed the first-ever inventory of all US intelligence liaison relationships, and is using the knowledge gained to maximize our reach and minimize the real and potential costs of working with foreign partners', with helpful input coming from its 'Foreign Relations Coordination Council (which includes members from around the IC)'. Furthermore, as its report continued, the ODNI revealed that: 'Two issues are of particular concern: how to set policies to expand and govern sharing of information and secure network access with foreign partners, and how to find the resources and access to assess the strengths and weaknesses of current and potential partners.'[42] By

2010, some further management solutions had since been forthcoming (see Chapter 5 (2.0), below).[43]

Important liaison relationship considerations also formed a concern for SIS/MI6. This was apparent during the calculations underlying its increased withdrawal from involvement in managing certain operations against organized crime. As the Chief ('C') of SIS (2004–2009), Sir John Scarlett, remarked in testimony to the UK ISC in early 2007:

> We [SIS] have become deeply involved in the setting up and management of quite complex... operations. Now these have been established, there clearly is an argument for saying "well, the management and running of these is not something which naturally falls to SIS. It is certainly something which could in theory be done by SOCA [the UK Serious Organised Crime Agency]." At the same time, they are so important, they achieve such results, they have such a strategic impact, and therefore they have such a political profile that they are not just police operations. They have real political and strategic significance. For us to just pull out of them would risk ... undermining the bilateral relationship quite seriously.[44]

In an increasingly globalized context, intelligence is becoming a greater actor in its own right. Self-evidently, this enhances its importance. Thus, at least to a degree, it requires ever-greater macro extending to micro management. As US intelligence scholar Stan Taylor has observed, in the US, 'The most significant intelligence reform since the creation of the CIA in 1947 came about in 2005 with the creation of a National Intelligence Director (NID) along with a large support office.' He continued: 'The bulk of these institutional and/or procedural reforms are meant to increase intelligence coordination within each nation *and* greater intelligence cooperation between nations.' (Taylor, 2007, pp. 263–264, emphasis added; Svendsen, 2011e, pp. 36–43; Wilson, 2007)[45] Prominent wide-ranging, even multi-ranging, developments exist.

In the UK, the ISC *Annual Report 2006–2007* again emphasized the importance of liaison. This was particularly where the ISC noted the direction of (still classified) expenditure flows. The funds were 'used to enhance front-line counter-terrorism operations overseas ... and to develop the capacity of liaison services in priority countries ... with further capacity-building work planned in key areas of the *** region and the ***.' Moreover, the funding was useful as it also 'enabled SIS to put more personnel on the ground in areas where British forces are operating', thereby contributing towards the enhancement of its reach.[46]

Intelligence coverage- and influence-related concerns have come to the forefront. Again, clearly driving these developments is the security and intelligence agencies' need for enhanced reach, across the full spectrum of their diverse activities. In addition, there is a persisting need for 'new' insights into traditionally more closed-off and sensitive realms (Herman, 2002; see also Chesterman, 2010; on 'reach dynamics', see Chapter 4 (5.0), below).[47] Not least, as already seen, this includes extended intelligence and security reach into various communities, foreign countries' domestic spheres, and indeed even into individuals' own homes and lives. As databases have proliferated, as they have become increasingly interconnected, and as the widely varying information they store and provide access to – namely data intelligence ('DATINT') (Svendsen, 2010a, p. 14) – has substantially burgeoned, closely overlapping privacy concerns likewise loom large. Privacy limits and parameters are continuously challenged.[48]

In an era of generally rapidly increasing globalization ('globalization writ large'), the pressures encountered occur to a considerably greater degree. This results from an erosion of traditional distinguishing categories (internal and external or domestic and foreign) and from increasingly porous conventional barriers, such as states' borders (Gavrilis, 2010).[49] Substantial concerns remain as 'solutions' are gradually worked out.

4.0 International intelligence liaison increasing as a 'means'

Liaison is on an upward trajectory. Undeniably some rhetoric is present in public pronouncements and surrounding discourse regarding its growth. However, operationally there genuinely is a substantial increase which can be mapped over time. In 2005, the *Washington Post* authoritatively reported that: 'The CIA has established joint operation centers [Counterterrorist Intelligence Centers (CTICs)] in more than two dozen countries where U.S. and foreign intelligence officers work side by side to track and capture suspected terrorists and to destroy or penetrate their networks.'[50] Moreover, highlighting the increase in intelligence sharing, these CTICs reportedly include 'secure communications gear, computers linked to the CIA's central databases, and access to highly classified intercepts once shared only with the nation's closest Western allies.'[51]

The liaison has also become more regularized. Merely *ad hoc* movements have been added to, with there being: 'daily decisions on when and how to apprehend suspects, whether to whisk them off to other countries for interrogation and detention [rendition], and how to disrupt al Qaeda's logistical and financial support.'[52] Other countries, even small ones such as Denmark, have similarly witnessed a growth in their international intelligence liaison relationships in recent years, and continue to remain focused on optimizing that task (Tebbit, 2006, p. v, no.15; see also Chapter 2 (3.2), above).[53] According to Dutch intelligence scholar Cees Wiebes in 2004: 'Since the end of the 1990s ... co-operation between the monitoring services of France, Germany and the Netherlands has grown and the countries exchange "Sigint" [signals intelligence] daily. Together with Denmark and Belgium, a "Group of Five" is slowly taking shape.'[54] In the covert intelligence realm, intelligence liaison is the central mechanism contributing to the increasing regionalization and eventual extended globalization of intelligence.

Several developments commend themselves for examination. Alongside the outreach developments occurring in parallel in the *overt* intelligence realm, these evolutionary processes are clearly under way in the *covert* intelligence world. Again, this is for a range of reasons: in summary, they reflect a growing recognition of essential collective and cooperative security means as an adaptive response to the notoriously difficult transnational and noisy globalized security threats confronted in the early twenty-first century (Crelinsten, 2006, pp. 3–6).[55]

As Treverton has highlighted, there is 'the increased number of needs for – and, therefore, types of – intelligence across a variety of time horizons from immediate warning to longer-term understanding.' (Treverton, 2009a, p. 3) These trends are emergent so that, in harmony with a doctrine of pre-emption, more comprehensive pictures of the challenges confronted can be constructed. This is in an ever-more-timely manner for delivery, a highly useful asset in our globalized, so-called 'just-in-time', society (see Chapter 2, above).

Yet, despite these observed developments, considerable shortcomings remain in our understanding. Both in wider public international affairs and within the academic fields of inquiry of international relations and intelligence studies, the intelligence liaison phenomenon, extending to the globalization of intelligence process, remains substantially under-studied and under-theorized. Indeed, as Swedish intelligence scholar Wilhelm Agrell argued in 2006: 'there is no generally established theory of intelligence and hence no given theoretical framework for the analysis of intelligence liaison.' (Agrell, 2006, p. 635) Still, by 2012, efforts contributing towards the tackling of these observed paucities require extension (Hughes-Wilson, 2010, pp. 83–84; Peake, 2011, pp. 32–33;

Webb, 2010, pp. 1–3). This consideration forms another associated aim of this study.

Intelligence liaison, extending to the globalization of intelligence, needs to be both better and more widely understood. This is because intelligence liaison occurring in an era of increasingly globalized intelligence now concerns not just intelligence specialists, but everyone – including, not always comfortably, the wider public. With the increasing emphasis on cyber and critical national infrastructure (CNI) protection, individuals in private companies – such as the utilities and airlines – can be both consumers and providers of intelligence (Graham, with Nussbaum, 2008, pp. 85 and 175).[56] In short, the 'Collective Intelligence' ('COLINT') paradigm is growing – particularly its more 'grounded' aspects (Svendsen, 2012d; Tovey, 2008).

Today, the onus on intelligence generally, and on intelligence liaison specifically, has been significantly increased. This is particularly in our era of a precautionary doctrine of preventative pre-emption in states' foreign and security policies (see Chapter 2 (2.0), above).[57] Furthermore, as Canadian intelligence scholar Martin Rudner has remarked: 'The imperative for intelligence co-operation can sometimes make strange international bedfellows, and can have *profound implications for foreign policy, civil society and human rights*.' (Rudner, 2002, emphasis added)[58] Highly dynamic processes, such as the 'globalization of intelligence', warrant closer examination.

Arguably, the acceleration of liaison, extending to the burgeoning of the globalization of intelligence, is leading to somewhat of an imbalance. Intelligence liaison is now being used more extensively across the globe, and it is playing an ever-greater role in international relations as a whole, as well as featuring more centrally in states' and the private sector's foreign and security policies (Aldrich, 2009b; Aydinli, 2010). Alongside, however, we have seen the emergence of a correspondingly large deficit in intelligence liaison accountability and oversight. Increasingly, liaison occurs beyond the scope and ability of single entities, even including individuals and states, to police merely their own activities (Aldrich, 2009a).[59]

Prominent events in the early twenty-first century have served to further emphasize the need to better understand the phenomenon of intelligence liaison, extending to the globalization of intelligence. Recent significant episodes closely involving intelligence have also underlined the need to communicate that understanding more widely in the mainstream of academic and public inquiry. Notably, the wars in Afghanistan (launched in 2001) and in Iraq (2003), the 9/11 and WMD intelligence inquiries and surrounding controversies – ethical and otherwise – including concerning 'torture' allegations and CIA 'secret prisons', the 'normalization' of 'extraordinary renditions', and 'intensive interrogations', all have significant implications to impart (Jones and Sheets, 2009; Weaver and Pallitto, 2010; see also Chapter 2, above).[60]

Intelligence liaison requires to be better understood beyond solely the niche field of intelligence studies. This applies whether it is conceptualized broadly (as in this study, including extension into areas of *information* cooperation) or whether it is analysed more narrowly. Moreover, intelligence liaison, extending to the globalization of intelligence, needs to better find its place in the broader schema of international relations, globalization, governance, communications, and information studies (Aldrich, 2011b, p. 145). Several areas resonate.

5.0 The 'secrecy-sharing dilemma' features ever more acutely

For the intelligence liaison relationships to function most effectively some essential secrecy must remain (Miller, 2010).[61] As officially observed by the UK *National Security Strategy* of October 2010: 'Our security and intelligence agencies play a vital role in protecting our country from threats to our way of life. It is inherent in their work that most of it has to be done in secret to protect those who risk their lives for our security, and to maintain the confidence and cooperation of partners overseas.' The Strategy continued: 'For the same reasons the exercise of oversight, whether by Parliament or through the courts, also has to involve a measure of secrecy. Here too we must strike a balance, between the transparency that accountability normally entails, and the secrecy that security demands.' (UK HMG, 2010, p. 23)[62]

Inevitably, the balances struck are not always perfect. On occasions, some of the secrecy involved does need to be carefully reviewed and adjusted. This is so that it does not extend too far, even to what can be regarded as a counter-productive extent (Bowman, 2006–2007; Heisbourg, 2011).[63] Outreach activities in the overt intelligence realm can help to compensate and facilitate here (Omand, 2009; Shapiro and Siegel, 2010).[64] By allowing the ushering in of some greater transparency overall, they complement the developments occurring in the covert intelligence realm. Valuably, in an educative manner, they have the added benefit of helping to engage and inform an ever-wider audience of the diverse requirements of intelligence, and its overall 'job' or 'mission(s)' and, to a certain extent, its capabilities. Thereby, 'intelligent customers' can also be better fostered. This enables intelligence to perform an educational, informing and directing role, essential for mission accomplishment and adequate contextualization (Svendsen, 2011b).[65]

An important caveat has to be remembered, however. This is as long as quantitatively there is not too much outreach, and qualitatively it does not extend too far, resulting in overreach (or more unfettered sharing and interactions). Otherwise, the contribution of intelligence liaison in its 'harder' outreach, and hence more 'controlled', covert form is eroded (see Chapter 2 (4.3), above).[66] Some form of 'structure' also needs to be present for the outreach efforts to be constructive and sustainable, including in cultural (even philosophical) terms.[67]

Other dangers can be highlighted. There will be negative consequences if, firstly, there is failure to further engage and address the balance of the extent of openness; and if, secondly, efforts are lacking to further and better understand intelligence liaison, extending to its related processes of outreach and the globalization of intelligence.

Collectively, these observed paucities will result in increased risks being taken more blindly, or less consciously, in the future. Furthermore, this scenario will increase the likelihood of highly detrimental episodes of 'intelligence liaison blowback'. This suggests a situation where intelligence and security reach 'deficits' and 'excesses' feature prominently (Posner, 2004). Overall, particularly in an era of 'mass' WikiLeaks (and equivalents, such as 'OpenLeaks' (Clemente, 2011, p. 19)), and with the presence of the international hacking group 'Anonymous', the globalization of intelligence has to be carefully managed.[68]

6.0 Neglecting this topic 'is *not* an option'!

A passive reaction to the concerns raised above is insufficient. There will be negative consequences if gaps and imbalances are allowed to flourish. Efforts to prevent the counter-productive disconnect between, on the one hand, the closely interrelated higher or macro and, on the other hand, lower or micro 'levels' of experience, and hence analysis, will also be hindered without the presence of some greater, yet carefully refined, openness (for the different 'levels', see Chapter 1 (3.2), above). This consideration still applies even if that greater openness is merely internal (private, intelligence agency or community or government-limited) in nature, rather than external (public).[69]

Successful connection between the 'macro' and 'micro' levels is crucial in the secret world of intelligence liaison. This is because in the intelligence world as a whole, and especially in intelligence liaison relationships and their associated interactions – extending to the globalization of intelligence – the specifics and details of micro levels (the operational, the tactical, the individual (as 'professional'), and the personal levels) matter significantly (Sims, 2006).[70] In these micro level domains of activity, much is at issue: precise sources and pieces of intelligence are carefully negotiated over in minute detail; and operations are under way. Including the several balances and trade-offs centrally involved, these developments are often at stake in high-tempo, condensed-space operating environments where time-frames are short, staff are limited and resources finite.[71] Much vulnerability is evident (Svendsen, 2012e).

The risks encountered at the micro levels are therefore increased. This is most apparent in finely targeted counter-terrorism (CT), counter-proliferation (CP) and counter-insurgency (COIN) enterprises (see Chapter 2, above). At the least, the micro levels need *viable opportunities* to be able to inform and direct the macro levels of activity (the ideological, the theoretical, the strategy and the policy levels). This is as well as the micro levels being suitably enabled to perform those tasks in a potentially ongoing and updating manner (see also references to the important 'customer, consumer or user–producer relationship' in Chapters 1 (5.0) and 4 (3.0, point 3), above and below).

Adequate 'intelligence percolation' is needed. The most desirable condition to strive for is successful fusion in the region of the mid-/meso-levels. The aim should be to realize a form of operational policy that results in widely recognized operational-to-strategic success (see Chapter 2 (5.0), above).

A larger 'intelligence methodology' is required. Otherwise, the overall mission of intelligence, extending to the globalization of intelligence, will be increasingly jeopardized. However conceptualized, whether in terms of 'law enforcement', 'public safety', and/or 'national security', without suitable adjustments, the achievement of those intelligence objectives will be missed.[72] We cannot afford that scenario.

7.0 Establishing liaison frameworks and defining operational parameters

Several developments within the domain of intelligence liaison are unfolding. These impact more widely on the 'globalization of intelligence', underlining their reference here. Moreover, they are contributing to what can be ascertained as 'homogenization' and 'international standardization' processes occurring within those arrangements and enterprises (see Chapter 1 (11.0–12.0), above). In summary, these developments include:

(i) Trends apparent in intelligence, law enforcement and security sector reform (SSR) (Hannah *et al.*, 2005, p. iii; Wilson, 2005 and 2007) involving the provision of training and other assistance to foreign intelligence and security services by Western, and in particular by UK and US, intelligence services on key issues, such as on counter-terrorism and WMD counter-proliferation (Bayley, 2006).[73]

(ii) The UK–US and other countries' encouraging of greater accountability systems and legal frameworks – such as for former Communist Eastern European countries' intelligence and security services (Watts, 2004; Martin, 2007; Roberts, 2003, 2006).[74]

(iii) The encouraging of 'good' or 'best practice' in intelligence communications and information security and 'information assurance' (COMSEC/INFOSEC/IA) – such as at the North Atlantic Treaty Organization (NATO) level, and NATO members becoming NATO Security and Evaluation Agency (SECAN) compliant (Morffew, 2006, pp. 48–51).[75]

These multiple and wide-ranging 'homogenization' and 'international standardization' processes (or at least attempts towards those objectives) offer more than merely symbolic value. In short, they represent 'Part One' of a move towards the increased international interconnectedness and, with it, interdependence, of intelligence through international intelligence liaison (Svendsen, 2008a).[76] See Figure 4.1 below.

The globalization of intelligence is not far away. The processes of homogenization and international standardization help to establish the frameworks for intelligence liaison arrangements and to define their operational parameters. In a useful 'multiplier-effect' manner, they create a patchwork of overlapping facilitators. In parallel, greater outreach efforts are discernible in the overt intelligence world. For instance, many intelligence agencies and communities now explicitly conduct forms of 'academic outreach' with universities, even interacting with schools (see also 11.0, below).[77] Thereby they also contribute, at least in part, to the overall globalization of intelligence trends. Essentially, while different rates of progress are reflected, particularly in specific areas of broad-ranging intelligence activity, these trends are in harmony with being on 'a continuum with expansion' (Svendsen, 2010a, p. 20, 2012a).[78] Several notable developments come to our attention.

8.0 The optimization of intelligence liaison arrangements

Further relevant developments are apparent. Building on 'Part One', the establishing of frameworks and the definition of operational parameters (as discussed above), 'Part Two', contributing towards the overall globalization of intelligence, can be facilitated (Svendsen, 2008b; see also Gruber, 2000, pp. 5–10). Part Two consists of the optimization of intelligence liaison arrangements. Frequently, this involves the flattening of hierarchies (Friedman, 2005; see also Arquilla and Ronfeldt, 2001; Schwab, 2006). This occurs within the now 'exclusive' arrangements, including those which extend globally, following – perhaps paradoxically – greater inclusion through exclusivity on the basis of the by now operationalized 'best practices'. In turn, these best practices address security and counter-intelligence concerns, by becoming increasingly consolidated or 'normalized' in operations (see Chapter 2 (3.1–3.2), above; see also Figure 4.1, below).

Necessarily, a degree of the compartmentalization of intelligence for security purposes is continued. These restrictions are intended for maintaining at least some counter-intelligence (CI) protection and associated intelligence control through regulation (Bowman, 2006–2007). However, arguably, this compartmentalization of intelligence is less pressing than witnessed in history during the Cold War (Aldrich, 2001; see also Aldrich, 2010; Hennessy, 2010). This is because the contemporary context is different. Most notably, the threat from mirror-imaging, high-grade, hostile, state-actor intelligence services is somewhat lower – though, of course, not completely removed. Some 'penetration' and other agency 'infiltration' risks and threats do remain.[79] However, the compartments that exist instead now have multiplied and tend towards being larger and broader in their scope.[80]

In essence, Part Two is gradually implemented over time. The central condition for intelligence liaison, extending to the globalization of intelligence, is trust (or, at least, mutual interests and/or values),[81] and this is incrementally built up through these 'confidence-building', then maintaining, stages (Wilson, 2005, p. 101). Once these relationships are being conducted, and over time are increasingly 'optimized' in their operation, intelligence can then be shared in a more regularized manner. This follows more of a routine 'need to share and pool' rationale, which is based more on institutionalized values. Along with the presence of a constructive 'need to use' rationale towards intelligence and information sharing, this last scenario extends interactions. This enables them to occur further than more constrained exchanges, which instead take place on merely more of an *ad hoc* and more restricted, particular episodic or investigation-confined, 'need to know', or 'narrower' *quid pro quo*, basis (Atkinson, 2010, p. iv). Many insights are apparent.

9.0 The globalization of intelligence and its 'location'

The 'globalization of intelligence' and where it is 'sited' is readily characterizable. As demonstrated in 2.1, when the above trends are confined to solely geographic regional bases the mere increasing *regionalization of intelligence* is observed. When these trends extend beyond the confines of regional bases, and are operating more 'out-of-area' – geographically and/or organizationally, including technologically – the increasing *globalization of intelligence* is witnessed (Williams, 2008; see also Brzezinski, 2009; Kitchen, 2010).[82]

To varying degrees, regionalized intelligence arrangements contribute to the globalization of intelligence. This is especially apparent when different regionalized and/or other forms of intelligence liaison arrangements overlap across the globe through commonly linked participants. A useful example to highlight here is the United Kingdom. Significantly, pointing to its 'hub' role, the UK is a party in various European-region (Club of Bern, etc.) and EU (SitCen, etc.) intelligence arrangements, NATO, as well as UKUSA, while also enjoying extensive agreements with Commonwealth countries and bilateral arrangements with countries in Africa, Asia and Latin America (Barkawi, 2006; Richelson, 2008, pp. 342–346).[83]

When exploring the globalization of intelligence and 'where' it is manifest, initially the main focus is most appropriately placed on the key UKUSA countries. These include the 'Five-Eyes' of the UK, US, Australia, Canada and New Zealand (Hager, 1996; Ball, 2011).[84] Particular concentration should be on the interactions of the UK and US, which sit at the pinnacle (see 11.0, below). Indeed, looking through the prism of the more specific and important bilateral UK–US intelligence liaison relationship is a useful place to begin to undertake an exploration of the wider intelligence liaison trends and efforts, up to the 'globalization of intelligence' (Svendsen, 2010a, p. xix; see also Dearlove, 2010, p. 4, fn.1; Svendsen, 2012e). As Stan A. Taylor notes: 'In the contemporary world, only the US, UK, and Russian services can claim to have truly global intelligence coverage and activities.' (Taylor, 2007, p. 253; see also Lowenthal, 2006, p. 14)[85] Especially in recent years, the intelligence services of China can be added to his list, not least due to the abundant manpower they can call upon (Lowenthal, 2006, pp. 294–296).[86]

Significantly, the UKUSA countries are instrumental in leading the discernible regionalization and globalization of intelligence developments. This is the case both within and beyond the confines of the exclusive multilateral UKUSA arrangement, as well as through other regional groupings, such as the EU and NATO, and through close cooperation with other established regional groups – for example, as already witnessed, with ASEAN (see 2.0, above; Haacke, 2009).

The UK and the USA are clearly not the only countries participating in the regionalization, extending to the globalization, of intelligence. Valuable contributions figure from other Western countries, such as the Netherlands, France, Germany and Sweden (with the Swedish Ministry of Defence's 'Multinational, Multiagency, Multidisciplinary, Multidomain Information Sharing [M_4IS]' approach (Steele, 2007, p. 167; Chapter 2 (2.1), above))[87] as cited throughout this study (see also for Romania, Watts, 2011).

Instructive observations emerge. In short, the most effective international intelligence sharing takes place within trusted and exclusive bilateral and, occasionally (though more often than previously), in multilateral intelligence liaison arrangements. To date, within the *covert* realm of intelligence, the exclusive intelligence liaison arrangements represent the sites where the greatest regionalization – extending to the overall globalization of intelligence – has occurred, and is continuing to develop. We can now try to further capture the 'globalization of intelligence' trends in some greater depth.

10.0 'Uneven and combined development'

Different interpretations of the trends persist. How evenly the globalization of intelligence extends remains more debatable, and will remain contested into the future. These factors vary extensively from specific case to case, and the debate is surrounded by much conjecture. At a minimum, the 'final' evaluation depends on: (i) the international intelligence liaison relationship under scrutiny; (ii) at which point in time, and (iii) in which context. The globalization of intelligence is a constantly morphing and fluid entity, making it challenging to capture, harness, and manage. As it is subject to many changes over time, complexity prevails.

Indeed, the current degree of the globalization of intelligence appears to be very haphazard, both in terms of the rate at which it is happening and how far it extends: it certainly is not uniform. However, while trends can be mixed – particularly in terms of their deepening, and in more intangible cultural, spiritual or philosophical ways – they are not ambiguous. This is especially apparent in terms of arrangements widening and developing in tangible structural or physical manners. The globalization of intelligence appears to be taking place most markedly at the macro levels of relations, and in the overt intelligence realm. Today, the micro levels and the covert intelligence realm are also increasingly included, as hierarchies involved become increasingly 'flattened' (see Chapter 2 (3.1–3.2), above).

The globalization of intelligence is multi-causal. Significantly, the pressing contemporary threats and issues being regularly confronted are asymmetric, transnational and global in nature and scope. They are, therefore, increasingly difficult to target, requiring ever-more-sophisticated responses (Svendsen, 2011b; see also Heuser, 2010; Lonsdale, 2008, p. 36).

In detail, the threats and issues include: so-called 'new' terrorism, the proliferation of Weapons of Mass Destruction (WMD) and conventional weapons, illegal immigration and people trafficking, drugs (narcotics) and other organized crime (including gangs), the demands of peacemaking and peacekeeping (stabilization) and other humanitarian operations – especially post-conflict reconstruction – as well as cyber issues and anti-globalization movements (Adamson, 2006; Farrell, 2010, p. 308; Feiling, 2009; Felbab-Brown, 2009; Galeotti, 2005; Madsen, 2009; Shelley, 2010; Thornton, 2007).[88]

Many of the driving pressures come from below, or they manifest themselves from the bottom up. This is both from the public and operators who are directly and individually experiencing the driving factors on the front line or fault-lines (Weber *et al.*, 2007; see also Mazarr, 2008; Mittelman, 2010; Riedel, 2011b; Scholte, 2005, pp. 279–315).[89]

A whole range of 'top-down', up to strategic, reactions are also prompted. These range from national through to regional, extending to global, responses spearheaded by states. This is particularly the case when an end goal of 'public safety' is the main driver (see Chapter 2 (2.0), above). Some of these top-down responses observed in the intelligence and security sector realm, both offensive and defensive in nature, form the main focus of inquiry in this study. As the Canadian Security Intelligence Service (CSIS) noted in 2002: 'In the era of globalization, isolation is not an option for the intelligence service of a democratic country, but rather a recipe for failure.'[90]

Observations such as this one have not gone unacknowledged, but have fed directly into intelligence, security and law enforcement activities in the early twenty-first century. Indeed, as UK Foreign and

Commonwealth Office minister Ivan Lewis remarked on the BBC Radio *Today* programme in August 2009, as some of the sharper and more stressful international interactions came into focus: 'We always make it clear that torture is unacceptable and abhorrent ... however, in a modern world you cannot counter terrorism by acting in isolation; we have to work on a global basis with many other countries.'[91]

Niceties become challenged under pressure. In some circumstances, the risks of at least a modicum of unhelpful (alleged) association with dubious methods of activity cannot be entirely avoided.[92] As noted in a Dutch independent intelligence oversight committee report from 2009: 'In actual practice, however, precluding all and any cooperation with [unsavoury] services in advance could lead to undesirable and even disastrous situations.' The report continued: 'At the same time GISS [Dutch General Intelligence and Security Service (AIVD)] should not lose sight of the fact that it is bound by the parameters and restraints imposed by law.' (Dutch Review Committee, 2009, p. i) Put simply, these circumstances form one of the necessary risks of 'doing' intelligence that have to be carefully navigated.[93]

11.0 Overlapping factors: The centrality of the United States

The US role is pivotal in the above processes. Arguably, US global hegemony in the realm of intelligence has been substantially maintained in this relatively novel arrangement of increasingly globalized intelligence (Norrlof, 2010). This has been accomplished by attempting to steer these processes through international intelligence liaison, extending to including participation in outreach efforts. As a result, what Michael Herman has perceptively termed 'intelligence power' is less completely devolved and freely pooled amongst other countries (Herman, 1996; see Chapter 1 (9.0), above; Wark, 2003, pp. 4–5). Overall, the purpose is to ensure that as many of the positive attributes of intelligence protectionism as possible can be maintained. Sustaining this control status occurs in conjunction with balancing the gradual introduction of positive attributes of increased intelligence cooperation.[94]

US 'intelligence hegemony' claims can nevertheless be contested. The prevailing trends simultaneously reveal that the USA has developed enhanced dependence upon international intelligence liaison with intelligence partners spread widely across the globe. Indeed, demonstrating their importance, 'Foreign Partners' form one of the four pillars of the October 2007 US *National Strategy for Information Sharing*.[95] Some new and non-traditional partners can be included, who are regarded as essential contributors to US and global security, particularly after 9/11. According again to the findings of *Washington Post* journalist Dana Priest, 'Today's CIA is desperately seeking ways to join forces with other governments it once reproached or ignored, to undo a common enemy.'[96]

Naturally, these changes, together with some added diversification to help maintain agility, have entailed some nuanced adjustments (Todd and Bloch, 2003, pp. 71–99).[97] Not least, greater connectivity has emerged between the various internal and domestic security agencies, such as the British Security Service (MI5), and important metropolitan police services, such as the New York Police Department. The strengthened links are apparent both at home and abroad. Frequently, today, each of these agencies enjoys international liaison networks as comprehensive as their counterparts, who are instead focused on exploiting foreign intelligence, such as MI6.[98]

As the IISS *Strategic Survey 2009* summarized: 'The means available to and used by security agencies to address terrorist threats have evolved considerably. For example, there is much greater cooperation between the agencies of different countries, and recognition of the need to obtain and share actionable intelligence', while it also rightly cautioned: 'though this is never going to be as complete or automatic as some might wish.' (IISS, 2009, pp. 35–36)

Multiple implications from these developments abound. In his response to the question, 'Do you think the CIA is too reliant on foreign liaison services?', former CIA Director General Michael Hayden (2006–2009) observed: 'No. I know that's an accusation that's out there. But there's a reason all those [foreign intelligence] people come visit us at CIA Headquarters.' He continued: 'We're big, powerful, technologically savvy, global, and we have a broad global context into which we can put events.' Meanwhile, on the other hand, he noted: 'Our liaison partners are local, focused, and culturally nimble. That's good partnership. Those things complement one another.' (Mansfield, 2010, p. 5, col.1) Again, several balances have to be adroitly struck.

Collectively, what transpires is complex. There is an overarching web of interconnected intelligence liaison arrangements. These arrangements, extending to including other forms of outreach and not just 'formal liaison', provide a form of global intelligence coverage. This is especially true for the US, which remains more or less at the top and centre, continuing to perform (with persistently varying effectiveness) its pivotal 'hub' role (Roberts, 2006, p. 139). A range of *ad hoc* and informal through to regularized, institutional, and formal agreements – including those associated with UKUSA – governs and establishes the tone for these arrangements (Svendsen, 2010a, p. 4 and 25).[99]

Adopting network terminology, frequently these arrangements substantially overlap in national capitals, forming hubs – notably in London and, especially, Washington. They, and the product that flows through them, also seek fusion within structures such as national intelligence, security and law enforcement agencies, and, more recently, in those agencies' 'fusion centres', which, within the above hubs, are intended to act as nodes, both for domestic and international purposes (see Chapter 2 (2.2 and 3.2), above; Taylor, 2004).

This fusion can be useful. As analysts Perry and Moffat from RAND have noted with regard to information flows and the fostering of knowledge: 'Information sharing among nodes ideally tends to lower information entropy (and hence increase knowledge) partly because of the buildup of correlations among the critical information elements. That is, information can be gained about one critical information element (e.g., missile type) from another (e.g., missile speed).' (Perry and Moffat, 2004, p. xv)

Further related developments occur in the overt intelligence realm. Transnational 'knowledge network' clusters – consisting of complex, potent mixes of public and private, commercial and non-profit sector, academic, government and non-government organization (NGO) stakeholders – then form around these points of contact, participating variously (Stone, 2008).[100] Notable phenomena, which can be identified and summarized as intelligence dynamics (see 1.1, above), become stronger and have more of an impact.

Through the close UK–US alliance, the UK is closely associated with all of these developments. Beneficially, it is also able to tap significantly into, as well as contribute towards, the US resource of global hegemony of intelligence power across all these strata. Over time, other close UK–US intelligence partners, notably Australia and Canada, can be observed as being increasingly included. Respectively, beyond each mutually sharing various 'regional security' concerns in areas such as the transatlantic and/or Asia-Pacific regions, this upwards trend is due to the close involvement of Australia, as with the UK, in both Afghanistan and, until recently, Iraq operations, and due to Canadian involvement in Afghanistan and its shared North American 'continental security' with the US (DeKeseredy, 2009; see also Chapter 2, above).[101]

Indeed, here, the globalization of intelligence can largely be argued as being synonymous with the 'Americanization' or 'Westernization' of intelligence, rather than it representing a 'purer' form of globalization *per se* (Chapters 3 and 4 of Ritzer, 2009; Vucetic, 2010).[102] As already introduced, even the theme of US 'intelligence hegemony' can be validly raised for discussion, becoming further unpacked later in Chapter 6 (5.1). Yet, when comprehensively examining the theme of the globalization of intelligence, these more constrained constructs quickly show themselves to be insufficient. As with general globalization considerations, so much more is readily observable. Occurring beyond merely 'Anglosphere' confines, many additional meaningful and relevant intelligence activities and their associated developments, including those made by several other countries, also clearly prevail (see, for example, their earlier references in 9.0, above). Therefore, when taken as a wider construct with broader participation, the globalization of intelligence continues to emerge in a compelling manner beyond merely figuring so much in the abstract. Authenticity exists.

4
Anatomy and Introducing Theory

Why 'reach' matters

1.0 Introduction

To valuably extend our understanding of the globalization of intelligence, the 'intelligence liaison' phenomenon is now disaggregated. In this chapter we will break down intelligence liaison into eight attributes or variables, followed by an explanation of how it at least appears to work and its rationale. This systematic analysis of intelligence liaison is offered to explain what constitutes the 'building blocks' that collectively contribute to the process of the globalization of intelligence. Common threads and seams exist, and so have enduring relevance in helping us reach an understanding of the globalization of intelligence.

An examination of closely associated *'intelligence and security reach dynamics'* is also included. The following challenging question is asked: *Can reach dynamics be considered as contributing towards a viable 'intelligence paradigm' that also explains liaison and its related activities, extending to the globalization of intelligence?* We begin with an overview.

2.0 Introducing a reference guide: The components of intelligence liaison

The anatomy of intelligence liaison can be conceptualized as having *eight* closely interrelated, systemic attributes or variables. These are: (1) *internal influences/factors*; (2) *rationale*; (3) *types and forms*; (4) *conditions and terms*; (5) *trends*; (6) *functions*; (7) *external influences/factors*; and (8) *effects and outcomes*. More fundamentally, these eight attributes or variables provide useful criteria that can be employed for benchmarking and theory-testing in this book.

Naturally, these 'benchmarks' are not too dissimilar to those found in mainstream foreign policy analysis (FPA) studies (Hill, 2003). They are used as analytic filters to accept and, through exposing limitations and parameters, reject at least aspects of the other bodies of theory and approaches consulted. This process of theory-testing is an effective way of trying to better explain the phenomenon of intelligence liaison, and to better answer the general question of *why* it occurs (see 4.1, below).[1] Indeed, adopting this advanced analytical approach also helps explain how and why the globalization of intelligence materializes. This helps to reinforce the observation of close linkages and shared characteristics with intelligence liaison. Much is proposed.

A brief summary follows in the next section, demonstrating what each of the eight attributes or variables introduced above consists of, through their detailed unpacking. This summary brings together many key dimensions covered throughout this study, some of which have already been discussed. It will also be useful for future reference purposes.

3.0 Unpacking the eight attributes of intelligence liaison: A quick reference

1. The *internal influences/factors* are extensive. Primarily, they comprise the specific countries or actors and agents involved in the intelligence liaison together with all the associated factors they bring. These include: (i) the nature and culture of the intelligence communities and agencies involved (Davies, 2004a; see also McFate, 2010; Rees and Aldrich, 2005; Svendsen, 2009b, pp. 723–725; Thornton, 2007, pp. 168–173);[2] (ii) their *modi operandi* and their intended ends; (iii) the people involved – their personalities, their interpretations, philosophies, ideologies, and roles (including as liaison officers and defence or military or legal attachés); (iv) organizational, managerial, structural, and bureaucratic factors – such as inertia, time-lags, and 'red-tape'. As an example of organizational factors having an impact with regard to intelligence liaison, overlapping lines of command can be unhelpful. This generates tensions as people can clash, making proper liaison impossible, as seen at times in history, for example at Bletchley Park during the Second World War (Grey, 2012).[3] For the purposes of this book and its companion volumes, the UK and USA form a main focus as key actors (Svendsen, 2010a, 2012e). Also within this internal influences/factors category, the agency–structure debate found vexing mainstream international relations (IR) theory arguably has its most

relevance in relation to intelligence liaison (Evans and Newnham, 1998, p. 9; Bieler and Morton, 2001; Hill, 2003, pp. 25–30).

2. The *rationale* behind intelligence liaison usually operates at several levels. These range from the generic to participant-specific. For example, in both a 'means' and 'end' or 'solution' form, intelligence liaison figures as the mechanism for: (i) responding to the current national(-ized) (homeland), regional(-ized) to global(-ized) security concerns; (ii) fulfilling and managing coerced, mutual or similar aims and interests and/or values; (iii) supplementing intelligence collection or analysis weaknesses or limitations, filling knowledge gaps; (iv) widening and deepening access (that is, extending intelligence and security reach, both within relationships and between, across, and into entities/organizations); and (v) implementing the *functions* and achieving 'means' and desired 'ends' – perhaps on a financially cheaper basis than if it had to be done alone (unilaterally) (see Chapter 3 (3.0–4.0), above). Throughout, the driving desire for enhanced intelligence and security outreach is central. This in turn contributes towards trying to attain greater optimized balances both in terms of overarching intelligence and security (general) reach and (more specific) outreach. This is notably in a directly 'winning', and ideally proportionate, manner against threats in the form of targets, hazards and risks (Svendsen, 2010b).[4]
3. The *types and forms* of intelligence liaison are again numerous. They can be broken down into: (i) *domestic* – intelligence liaison between: (a) the intelligence agencies within one country's intelligence community – essentially more intelligence liaison between these leads to greater integration and fusion within the national intelligence community; and (b) between intelligence agencies (producers) and users, for example, politicians and businesses, resulting in the greater '*nationalization* of intelligence' (see Chapter 5 (2.0), below)[5] – and (ii) *international*. International intelligence liaison is further divisible into: (a) *bilateral* – two parties involved; (b) *trilateral* – three parties involved; (c) *multilateral* – when four or more parties are involved (even if interacting on a 'hub-and-spokes' basis (see Chapter 3 (2.1), above)); and (d) *plurilateral* – which can be bilateral to multilateral, but between different *forms* of parties, such as the European Union (EU) and the USA (a supranational entity and a state, respectively; see Chapter 3, above). As well as being a form of integration and interdependence, facilitating greater collective and common security, intelligence liaison also involves a businesslike relationship (see towards end Chapter 1 (6.0), above). Intelligence liaison can be selective or

a partnership. It can espouse other characteristics as outlined throughout this chapter, often determined by the *conditions and terms*.

4. The *conditions and terms* determine when (time factors) and where (spatial/location factors) intelligence liaison takes place. This is done through establishing the frameworks for the arrangements and defining the operating parameters for the intelligence liaison (see Chapter 3 (7.0), above). They are set up when the *rationale* for the intelligence liaison is present. The central condition forming the basis for intelligence liaison is 'trust', or, at the least, the existence of mutual interests and/or values (see Chapters 1 (5.0) and 3 (8.0), above). These constructs form the underpinning bond of the interaction undertaken. As seen earlier, trust is established when (some form of) an agreement, which is acceptable to all the parties involved, has been adopted, thus allowing for confidence building and then maintaining over time. This 'contract' establishes the standards, rules and guidelines for the process and/or for the use of the product of intelligence liaison (see Chapters 1 (2.2, 6.0 and 11.0–12.0) and 3 (7.0), above).[6] In the case of substantial liaison, the agreement is usually formal and some examples exist of this type of liaison being underpinned by written agreements (see 3. *types and forms*). The UKUSA agreements and other related memoranda of understanding (MoU) can be cited as examples (Svendsen, 2010a, p. xix; see Chapter 3 (9.0 and 11.0), above).[7] The 'contract' is arrived at through the processes of bargaining and negotiation. The contract determines and regulates the *functions* of the intelligence liaison, and their nature, and establishes the various *quid pro quo*s (including at which 'levels' of activity they are sculpted and whether 'areas of responsibility' are developed (Svendsen, 2010a, p. 167)), as well as forming the framework for homogenization and (international) standardization processes. As observed generally by a Dutch independent intelligence oversight committee report in 2009:

> Before starting to cooperate with a foreign intelligence and/or security service GISS [Dutch General Intelligence and Security Service (AIVD)] must first assess carefully whether the service qualifies for cooperation. Criteria to be considered are respect for human rights, democratic anchorage, the tasks, professionalism and reliability of the service, the advisability of cooperation in the context of international obligations, enhancement of the performance of statutory tasks and the degree of reciprocity (*quid pro quo*). (Dutch Review Committee, 2009, p. i; see also Svendsen, 2012e)

Meanwhile, when interacting with the USA in the defence realm, as Alasdair Roberts notes, the 'conditions that govern the handling of shared information are laid out in bilateral Security of Information Agreements, or SOIAs.' As he continues: 'The practice of negotiating SOIAs was formalized in the United States in 1971 by National Security Decision Memorandum 119, which prohibits the sharing of military information with a foreign government that has not signed a legally binding SOI agreement.' (Roberts, 2006, p. 132)[8] Additionally, alongside these formal and regulated arrangements governed by *rules*, more informal arrangements can coexist. These include those agreements more loosely governed by *guidelines*, which can potentially allow some greater room for careful individual interpretation, flexibility and agility, depending upon factors such as the precise circumstances encountered by practitioners.[9]

5. The *trends* range from revealing and understanding the history of intelligence liaison through to thinking about possible future directions and scenarios. They include lessons learnt from a range of sources (for the importance of history in the intelligence context, see Wark, 2003; also Andrew, 2004; Popplewell, 1995a). They also allow for conceptualization, hypothesis formulation and the posing of questions, such as: 'Is the British Empire and Commonwealth intelligence system witnessed in the past a useful model for effective globalized and multilateral intelligence liaison in the future?' (Popplewell, 1995b; Svendsen, 2012e). These trends can vary substantially in terms of how abstract or 'long-ranging' they can be. Hindsight and foresight activities figure centrally within this domain (see Chapter 5, below; Hennessy, 2011).
6. The *functions* detail some of the operating dynamics of intelligence liaison (see Chapter 1 (3.1), above). Functions include: influence or control of overall policy; the sharing of information, operations and facilities; support through training, advice and supplies; clandestine or crypto-diplomacy (for 'covert diplomacy', see Shpiro, 2004; for 'back-channels', see Chapter 3 (3.0), above); evading national and/or international restrictions; and monitoring. Including the controversial 'friends spying on friends' dimension of intelligence activities (Hitz, 2008, p. 163; see Chapter 1 (5.0), above),[10] monitoring: (i) ensures that neither side has broken any agreements – for instance, through foreign intelligence partners conducting 'black' or unilateral (especially active) intelligence operations *sans permission* on the host country's territory, and thus making them *persona non grata* through violating the sovereignty of that country (Baer, 2002, pp. xv–xvi; Dutch Review Committee, 2009, p. 43, para.14.1; Lowenthal, 2006,

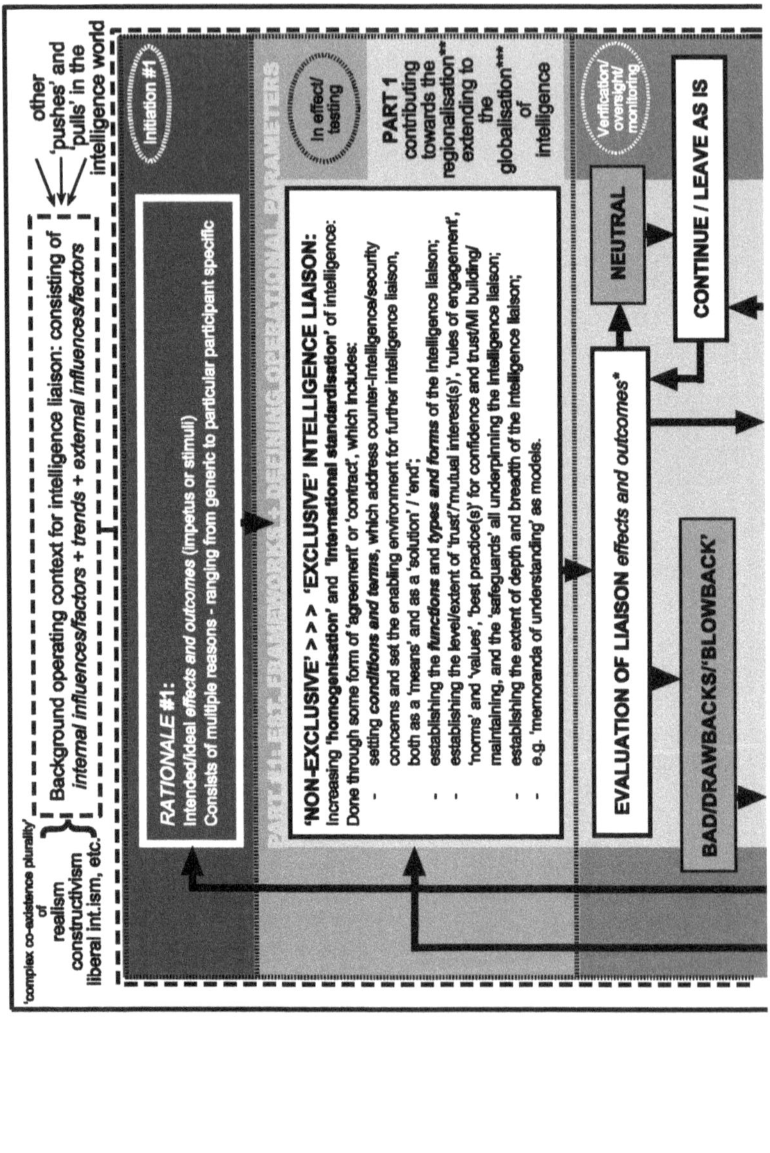
'complex co-existence plurality' of realism constructivism liberal int.ism, etc.
Background operating context for intelligence liaison: consisting of internal influences/factors + trends + external influences/factors
other 'pushes' and 'pulls' in the intelligence world
Initiation #1
RATIONALE #1:
Intended/ideal effects and outcomes (impetus or stimuli)
Consists of multiple reasons - ranging from generic to particular participant specific
PART 1) ESTABLISHMENT FRAMEWORKS + DEFINING OPERATIONAL PARAMETERS
In effect/ testing
'NON-EXCLUSIVE' > > > 'EXCLUSIVE' INTELLIGENCE LIAISON:
Increasing 'homogenisation' and 'international standardisation' of intelligence:
Done through some form of 'agreement' or 'contract', which includes:
- setting conditions and terms, which address counter-intelligence/security concerns and set the enabling environment for further intelligence liaison, both as a 'means' and as a 'solution' / 'end';
- establishing the functions and types and forms of the intelligence liaison;
- establishing the level/extent of 'trust'/mutual interest(s)', 'rules of engagement', 'norms' and 'values', 'best practice(s)' for confidence and trust/MI building/ maintaining, and the 'safeguards' all underpinning the intelligence liaison;
- establishing the extent of depth and breadth of the intelligence liaison;
- e.g. 'memoranda of understanding' as models.
PART 1 contributing towards the regionalisation** extending to the globalisation*** of intelligence
Verification/ oversight/ monitoring
EVALUATION OF LIAISON effects and outcomes*
NEUTRAL
CONTINUE / LEAVE AS IS
BAD/DRAWBACKS/'BLOWBACK'

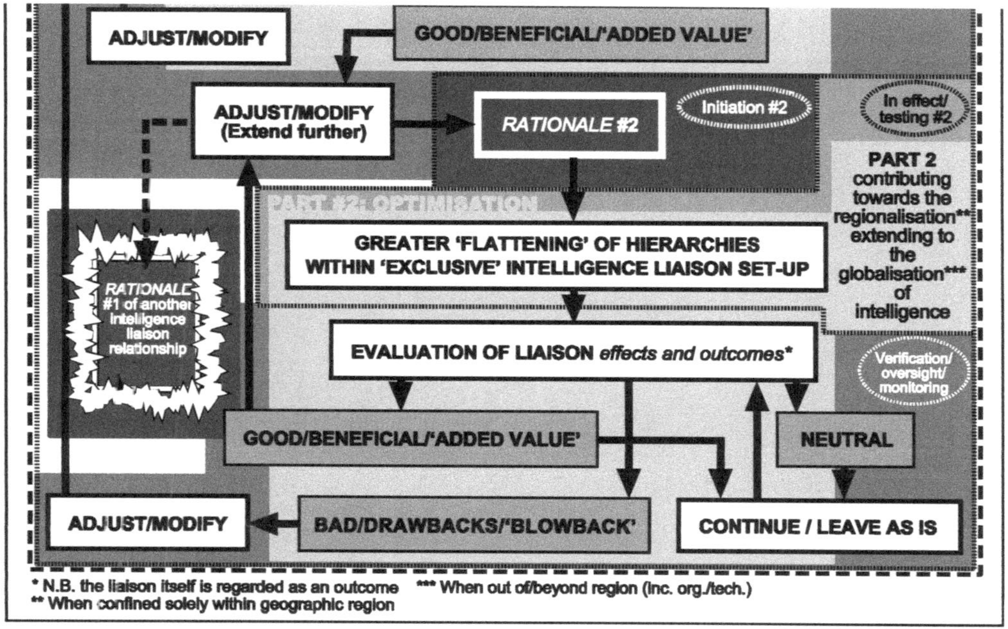

Figure 4.1 An international intelligence liaison relationship in operation in theory, contributing towards the 'regionalization' and 'globalization' of intelligence.

p. 5);[11] (ii) offers reassurance against penetration (Rimington, 2001, pp. 206–208);[12] (iii) grants insights into future intentions of 'allies' and 'foes';[13] and (iv) allows for the managing of an internal oversight, self-policing, self-regulation and accountability system – that is, for instance, using intelligence liaison to oversee other areas of the intelligence liaison (see Chapter 5 (2.0–3.0), below).

7. *External influences/factors* contribute towards establishing the operating context for intelligence liaison. This includes anything 'external' to the intelligence liaison, and includes other relationships, such as political, economic, and defence relationships. In this book, with its substantial focus on the Anglo-American intelligence relationship for illustrative purposes, the overall UK–US alliance and its associated dynamics figure centrally (Freedman, 1995; Svendsen, 2010a). *External influences/factors* also include: circumstances, the wider international affairs context and its influence – such as globalization (writ large), the so-called 'War on Terror' and 'Long War', and the earlier Cold War; the impact of 'domestic' politics and their influence on the intelligence agencies and communities conducting the liaison (Wirtz, 1993);[14] foreign policy influences, for example the UK trying to play its Atlantic-'bridging' role and treading a fine balance between maintaining closeness to both Europe and the USA (Svendsen, 2011d); the media, domestic and international public opinion, and any form of *external* oversight, regulation and general accountability system of intelligence (that is, essentially operating outside of the intelligence agencies and communities participating in the intelligence liaison) (Dover and Goodman, 2009); as well as relationships with other countries and, closely related to this, other countries' influence(s) (see, for example, the USA and the UK *vis-à-vis* Pakistan in Svendsen, 2010a, pp. 107–108).
8. What results from the intelligence liaison is identifiable as the *effects and outcomes* of the intelligence liaison. In analyses of the observed and recorded *effects and outcomes* of intelligence liaison, a form of risk assessment is undertaken. The *effects and outcomes* can also have an impact on the other attributes and variables – for example, if an outcome affects the linked *external influences/factors* or the *internal influences/factors* in any manner.

Taking an overall 'organizational/systems theory' perspective, normally the influence of each of the eight attributes or variables on one another is seen as being essentially about the same, or 'in balance'. Highlighting the complexities involved, a particular attribute or variable, or part of an attribute or variable, only gains 'special' or more influence or is particularly expressed on the overall intelligence liaison 'system' or 'regime' (*modus vivendi*) at a particular moment in time and/or in particular circumstances (see also Dupont and Reckmeyer, 2012).

Equally, the issue of 'ethics' can enter the overall equation at several points. Ethics can be attached to several different parts of the attributes or variables, such as relating to the *modi operandi* deployed during the intelligence liaison (Herman, 1999; see also Andregg, 2010; 'Intelligence and Ethics' in Andrew *et al.*, 2009; Hennessy, 2007; Herman, 2004; Omand, 2006; Whetham, 2011). This includes concerning the use of 'extraordinary renditions', evidence obtained by 'torture', and so forth. When under way on broader bases, these factors and their associated considerations likewise impact on the wider and overlapping, higher-occurring, globalization of intelligence (see Chapter 2, above).

For further and visual explanation, see Figure 4.1.[15]

4.0 Explanatory analytical frameworks

Analysis of intelligence liaison, extending to the globalization of intelligence, can be extended. Intelligence liaison in all its myriad forms, up to and including the globalization of intelligence, reflects the chaotic real and constructed worlds in which we live. Concepts such as 'complex interdependence' are also effectively represented (Keohane and Nye, 1998). Furthermore, the spread of intelligence liaison to the globalization of intelligence can, in part, be explained by the influence of a pragmatic problem-solving (Lindblom, 1959 and 1979) and risk management mentality (Ale, 2009; see also Bell, 2007; Coker, 2009; Gibson, 2005; Rasmussen, 2006).[16] As the UK Government's response to the ISC's 2007 *Renditions* report highlighted: 'the [UK Intelligence] Agencies have adapted their procedures to work round problems and maintain the exchange of intelligence that is so critical to UK security.'[17]

However, the presence of these factors alone still does not yet offer the fullest explanation for both *why* and *how* intelligence liaison, extending to the globalization of intelligence, occurs. Both phenomena are more complex. To help think at a higher level and 'out of the box', more theoretical dimensions of discussion are now engaged.

4.1 Intelligence liaison, theory and approaches – and why its own theory is required

Theory can have some utility in explaining, firstly, intelligence liaison, and, then, the overall globalization of intelligence. Building on the findings from earlier work, several different bodies of pre-existing theory, as well as different approaches that can be adapted to the study of intelligence-related phenomena, appear to contain significant analytical potential for explaining intelligence cooperation (Svendsen, 2009b).

Indeed, variously abstract or 'ranging' mainstream theories of alliance and balance of power, of diplomacy, of international political economy (IPE), of bureaucratic politics, and of securitization, together with theories concerning business, risk and negotiation – even cybernetics – can all be appropriately drawn upon in relation to the phenomenon of intelligence liaison. With a few adjustments, these can likewise be extended and extrapolated up to help explain the globalization of intelligence (on problem-solving and risk, see as cited above in 4.0; on the pact of restraint, see Elie, 2004, p. 174; Schroeder, 1976; on alliance theory, see Snyder, 1990, p. 103; Plümper and Neumayer, 2009; Weitsman, 2004; for bureaucratic theory and politics, see Chapter 6 in Peters, 2001; Dupont, 2003, p. 34; on security and securitization, see Hough, 2008; also Buzan *et al.*, 1998; Buzan and Hansen, 2009; for intelligence and cybernetics connection, see Taylor, 2007, p. 250; for IPE theories, see O'Brien and Williams, 2007; on diplomacy, see Ross, 2007; Berridge, 2010).[18]

However, what is also clear is that, when taken *individually*, each of these theories and approaches is insufficient – be they long-range, mid-range or short-range in their nature. This is revealed during processes such as their 'testing' in and against the intelligence liaison phenomenon (as conceptualized in this book), and when using the benchmarking criteria outlined above in 2.0 (for their in-depth testing, see Svendsen, 2009b).

Remarking upon this status is certainly not to devalue or dismiss the different theories and approaches – they can actually be quite useful at times – but merely to reveal, firstly, their 'limitations'; and, secondly, where those limitations and their parameters can be sited against the specific phenomenon of intelligence liaison. While aspects may variously fit, when taken alone, these theories, together with the adoption of solely individual approaches, fail to explain the full range of complexities that can be observed within and surrounding intelligence liaison, extending to the globalization of intelligence, at every moment in time (Munton, 2009; also Matei, 2009; Valtonen, 2010). This shortfall is even apparent when each of those theories is employed in their most extensive forms (Svendsen, 2009b, pp. 713–714).

Moreover, the shortcomings are particularly evident when analysis is taken yet further. This is particularly the case when the intelligence liaison phenomenon is broken down into its eight different systemic attributes or variables (as above in 2.0), and when it is also analysed at and across all of its different identified eight 'levels' of activity, experience and analysis (see Chapter 1 (3.2), above). Therefore, to start explaining the amalgamated phenomenon of intelligence liaison more comprehensively with these other theories and approaches, they need to be employed *more collectively*. Significantly, this is most satisfactorily accomplished by those theories and approaches being deployed in a condition of 'complex coexistence plurality'. When extrapolated up, the same conclusion can be drawn and be applied, even *a fortiori*, to the wider and higher overall globalization of intelligence process (Svendsen, 2009b).

We can then try to go beyond this characterization. Once the parameters and limitations of these other bodies of theory and approaches have been ascertained through their testing, we can attempt to refine our understanding of the intelligence liaison phenomenon, extending to the globalization of intelligence, yet further. 'Short(er)-range' theorization can next be tried. This paves the way for some more detailed attempts at directly theorizing the phenomenon of intelligence liaison itself. This goes together with assessing how intelligence liaison as a phenomenon in practice, as well as a subject for study, for instructive and educative purposes, is better approached.

Wider and higher related processes, such as the globalization of intelligence, can likewise be appropriately studied by adopting a similar and more sophisticated approach (Svendsen, 2009b; also Hedström, 2005; Hedström and Bearman, 2009). Ideas heading in that direction are tabled next.

5.0 'Reach dynamics': An 'intelligence paradigm' that also explains liaison?

When further explaining intelligence liaison, extending to the globalization of intelligence, intelligence and security 'reach dynamics' also have relevance (see Chapter 1 (4.0), above). Owing to perceived extended threats and risks, enhanced *intelligence and security reach, into, within*, and *across* all activities that concern intelligence and security, is frequently demanded as a management solution.[19] Indeed, arguably the craft of 'doing' intelligence as a whole, including in a globalized context, can be best explained by a generic theory of *optimized (intelligence and security) reach*. Or, at their least, attempts by practitioners at striving towards trying to effectively realize that objective.[20]

The power of this 'theory' reveals itself in several respects. Not least, by thinking of intelligence in terms of its functional *reach*, all the stymying definitional problems and disagreements associated with trying to precisely define 'intelligence' can be escaped (see Chapter 1 (2.0), above). When examining intelligence and security reach factors and calculations, and information flows between the centre and the periphery of activities, by association *'intelligence and security reach dynamics'* can be highlighted. This is a reference to the configurations of the conditions of 'reach' experienced or encountered (i) qualitatively within, and (ii) quantitatively across, intelligence- and security-related interactions, and between different entities. Namely, this is whether intelligence and security overreach and/or under-reach are reflected (see below). As US intelligence scholar Jennifer Sims has argued:

> Protecting the intelligence infrastructure for tomorrow's decision makers also means, however, that *intelligence professionals must try to prevent the kind of blowback that occurs when the intelligence business goes awry – as a result of either substandard performance* [(for example, conceptualized in this study as a form of 'under-reach')] *or overreach.* This point is particularly important for democracies such as the United States during periods of high threat and aggressive intelligence reform. (Sims, 2005a, p. 17, emphasis added; see also Svendsen, 2012e)

Indeed, thinking of intelligence in terms of *intelligence and security reach and its associated dynamics* offers further qualities. It allows the provision of a suitable domain where intelligence and related concepts, such as surveillance, can closely connect through their overlap (Warner, 2009a, p. 19; also Ball and Webster, 2003; Chesterman, 2010; Lyon, 2007).[21] Furthermore, when conceptualized in terms of intelligence and security reach, the overall 'holy grail' goal of intelligence – or the 'intelligence paradigm' – emerges as being one of: ***trying to acquire optimum (intelligence and security) reach***. This is frequently characterized (albeit perhaps misguidedly) as attempting to attain 'the truth', which can ideally then be 'spoken unto power.' (Lowenthal, 2006, p. 7; see also Lynch, 2011; Smith, 2009)

5.1 The parameters of 'reach'

However, some limits are already distinct. Due to the imperfect nature of the world, most realistically only an *optimized reach* balance in the overall condition of 'intelligence and security reach' can ever hope to be attained. This condition arises as intelligence and security 'reach requirements' constantly fluctuate over time, and particularly markedly so in extreme times of 'war', 'emergency', or 'crisis'. Nevertheless, the persistent quest for the higher ideal goal of *optimum reach* should be maintained. This is for driving and steering all of the intelligence collection, gathering, and analysis and assessment processes.

In fact, the continuous quest for the 'holy grail' of *optimum intelligence and security reach* should feature prominently in *all* intelligence interactions and activities, across and within all the domains in which those activities occur, both physically and virtually. This is so that ultimately, in practice, intelligence agencies can expeditiously fulfil their core requirements in a comprehensive, well-balanced and proportionate manner.

Maintaining this balance is crucial with regard to sensitive surrounding issues, such as civil liberties and human rights. This enables agencies to retain the *moral high ground*. Indeed, the sacrifice of the 'moral high ground' is inimical to any wider and longer-term enduring intelligence and policy efforts, especially to their future operation, and to any opportunity generation and exploitation (see Dearlove's comments in Svendsen, 2010a, pp. 92–93; Gray, 2010b; Mumford, 2012; Pinto, 1955/1961, pp. 20–23).[22] Again, overall balance is key and should be stressed (Svendsen, 2010b).[23]

5.2 The rationale for 'reach' engagement

Striving for 'optimum intelligence and security reach' has added merit. In intelligence and security operations, and in closely associated domains of activity beyond, this core driving rationale of intelligence increases many leverage and negotiation possibilities, particularly during the occasions when any form of externalized *outreach* figures. This is especially important with regard to relations and interactions between intelligence 'friends and allies', and with other countries which need to be consulted for assistance purposes, relating to both the outflow and inflow of information, expertise and/or training (Treverton, 2009b).[24]

Moreover, as an article published in *Jane's Islamic Affairs Analyst* commented in 2007: '[a]lthough intelligence links are often conducted independently of broader foreign relations, they cannot ignore the realities of state interests.'[25] Such an overarching rationale again helps to explain: (i) the duality of the cooperative ('altruistic') and competitive ('egoistic') dimensions found within intelligence activities – and more specifically in intelligence liaison interactions; as well as (ii) those aspects associated with the (albeit often haphazard, *ad hoc* through to regularized) 'widening' and 'deepening' trends, all occurring during an era of increasingly globalized intelligence (Thomas, 1988, pp. 233–235; see also Chapter 6 (8.0), below).[26]

At least in theory, the 'optimized intelligence and security reach' balance contributes to intelligence success. Meanwhile, *reach flaws* come to the forefront, for example, through the neglect and/or the bypassing of the goal of an 'optimum reach balance' – albeit even if that scenario occurs accidently or unconsciously. This trait is notable in 'cherry-picking' situations, for instance (Svendsen, 2010a, pp. 116–158). The 'reach flaws' in turn contribute to intelligence 'failure'. This failure is encountered either in particular domains, at specific analytical levels of activity and experience, or even overall, systematically and more systemically (Hatlebrekke and Smith, 2010).

Providing further insights, the most prominently recognized intelligence 'failure' includes the familiar concept of 'strategic surprise' (Betts, 1982; Levite, 1987; Kam, 1988; Betts and Mahnken, 2003; Bracken *et al.*, 2008; Wirtz, 2009; Betts, 2009). For example, often this is due to under-reach in intelligence collection and poor coordination.[27] Indeed, discernible within episodes of 'intelligence failure' are two notable *intelligence and security reach flaws*: (i) too much reach, namely *overreach*, reflective of *reach excess(es)* or more unfettered activities; and (ii) too little reach, namely *under-reach*, representative of *reach deficit(s)* or more stunted activities (see Chapters 1 (4.0), 2 (2.1 and 3.3) and 3 (5.0), above).

Extended evaluation is helpful. Both intelligence and security reach excesses and deficits demonstrably feature centrally in: (i) intelligence analysis and assessment shortcomings – for example, mirror-imaging and groupthink, and so forth; as well as figuring in (ii) intelligence collection limitations – for instance, blind spots, a form of under-reach; and in (iii) data and information-overload situations[28] – for example, resulting in '*blanch* spots' or 'white-outs', a form of overreach. Phenomena, such as intelligence and security *overstretch*, can also be directly mapped *vis-à-vis* the intelligence and security reach flaws, and thus can be seen to be closely associated (Black, 2006).[29] Further connections are apparent.

5.3 Measuring 'reach'

An important question now emerges: how can we best benchmark the intelligence and security 'reach' condition, or determine whether reach is excessive and/or deficient? The most compelling answer appears to be that: *there are **no** rigid or generic criteria that can be universally applied*. Therefore, measuring intelligence and security 'reach', and agreeing on its extent (both in terms of its width and depth), can remain ambiguous, and even hotly contested.[30]

In short, determining the 'reach condition' depends heavily upon 'weak' constructs, such as (to adopt a colloquial phrase) 'where the line is drawn' in terms of judgements and decisions. At best, only a 'rolling' (subject to being constantly refined) risk management-associated analysis/assessment framework approach and methodology can be adopted in these circumstances (UK HMG, 2010, p. 37).[31] This simultaneously resonates with the persisting ambiguities that can be empirically discerned in intelligence liaison interactions, within the wider globalization of intelligence process, and, indeed, even with regard to these processes' analyses (see also 'Defining and Identifying "Disproportionality"' in Svendsen, 2010b, pp. 370–71).[32]

Contextual considerations remain key. Any criteria for measuring *intelligence and security reach* are most appropriately applied specifically, on a case-by-case basis. The criteria must be determined according to the particular entity being evaluated and its operating parameters. Again, the importance of contextual details and specifics is highlighted. This is together with the requirement that these need to be effectively represented or reflected in some form – such as caveats or footnotes – in the final and overall products (assessments or estimates) that are synthesized. If these details and specifics, and the knowledge they can communicate, are lost, evaluations unravel; if they are subsumed or buried, they cease to warn and inform.[33] Intelligence then loses the value it can potentially bring to overall developments.

A fix is available. Presenting a portfolio that includes the fullest range of insights that prevail allows for capturing the ambiguity or uncertainty involved. For instance, this can be accomplished through using a greater 'scenarios methodology' (see Chapters 5 and 6, below; Fingar, 2011). This narrative approach enables agencies to educate and inform decision-makers of the complexities involved during the 'sense-making' process. However, it can be argued that a form of intelligence and security under-reach figures in circumstances where ambiguity and uncertainty is persistently too deep and/or too wide for comprehensive 'sense-making'.

In summary, in these situations, there is not enough (or compelling enough) data present to sufficiently underpin: (i) a 'final' judgement, (ii) an agreed consensus, and (iii) the decision-cut-off and/or tipping point (or an episode of 'cognitive closure'). This is especially important when taking place at the 'policy level'. Consequently, adjustments have to be made to try and address that 'reach imbalance' (Immerman, 2011, pp. 166–7).

5.4 The implications of 'reach'

Greater impact is recognizable. Thinking in terms of 'reach' and its dynamics in the intelligence and security context is instructive. Some diversification into its descendent phenomena of internalized *'inner-reach'* and externalized *'outreach'* is allowed (especially see 'Reaching deep into markets' in Sirkin *et al.*, 2008, from p. 110). Again, these closely concern both the collection and analysis domains of intelligence. These can be evaluated as follows: (i) 'inner-reach' – that is, 'know thy self', which is internal (Treverton, 2009a, p. 5) – for example, manifested in the intelligence world as any form of *internal* intelligence management, including concerning how issues of data and information overload are handled within intelligence and security organizations and communities (Sims, 2005b; also Gill, 2007); while (ii) 'outreach' denotes 'know others – thy friends, allies, opponents, enemies'.

Outreach is concerned with the *external*. For example, most formally this figures in the intelligence world as 'intelligence liaison' (at least in the *covert* or *clandestine* intelligence world), and explicitly as the well-worn phrase 'outreach' (as mainly seen and used in the *overt* or *open source* – *OS* – intelligence world) (Sims, 2005a, from p. 14).[34] A form of outreach is also involved in any 'external' intelligence management, such as in human-to-human (human intelligence – HUMINT) interactions, for example during interviews and interrogations (Mackey, with Miller, 2004; see also Frantzen, 2010).[35] Both in virtual and physical terms, intelligence liaison constructs extend across the globe.[36]

Significantly, both intelligence and security reach 'excesses' and 'deficits' feature in 'inner-reach' as well as within 'outreach' interactions. As senior RAND analyst, Gregory Treverton, has observed: 'As military planners would state, it is impossible to understand red – that is, potential foes – without knowing a lot about blue – ourselves – that is, our own proclivities and vulnerabilities.' (Treverton, 2009a, p. 5)

Simultaneously, employing an 'optimized (intelligence and security) reach theory lens' helps to resolve 'puzzles' that can be empirically observed concerning the intelligence world. For instance, it helps to answer the question of why, frequently, in the wake of an 'intelligence failure', instead of cutbacks *more* resources (often in the form of increased staff and boosted monetary budgets) are devoted to the intelligence and security sector. This can be explained by those measures being justified in order to better address the perceived mis-configurations and mis-calibrations of reach present at various levels and junctures of intelligence activity, both spatially and in terms of time (Dahl, 2010).

In turn, some form of inquiry or review frequently ascertains the mis-configurations and mis-calibrations of reach. This is accomplished through pinpointing their location and finding their 'centre of gravity' (Hitz, 2008, p. 3).[37] Furthermore, adjustments are made in order to attempt to strike a better balance in terms of the discernible intelligence and security reach 'deficits' and 'excesses'. For instance, this includes those evident in intelligence and security investigations and activities, and where they extend in terms of their width, depth, and direction, when pursuing intelligence 'tips', 'leads' and 'targets'.[38]

Notably, the intelligence budget 'cuts' of the early 1990s can also be explained in these 'intelligence and security reach-scale' terms. This is not least as the cuts came in the wake of a so-called 'intelligence success', namely the West's claimed 'victory' in, and the end of, the Cold War (see Chapter 6 (1.0), below; Glenny, 2008, p. 4). Many observations emerge emphatically.

6.0 A survey of the landscape so far

Some preliminary conclusions readily surface. Working on the premises discussed above, the drivers behind international and foreign intelligence liaison (and indeed the overall globalization of intelligence as a whole) can, therefore, be explained comprehensively by a descendent or related theory of *optimized intelligence and security outreach*. More arguably, in the contemporary early twenty-first century context, that *optimized outreach* features as occurring on an *exponential* basis (see Chapter 6, esp. (9.0–11.0), below).

Especially in the post-9/11 and globalized security environment, enhanced intelligence and security outreach is demanded in several different areas. This is in order to try and strike a better-optimized balance in terms of the general intelligence and security reach present across, and into, the multiple domains of operation, and areas of technical and human activity, in which intelligence has an interest (see Chapter 3 (2.0), above).[39]

Particularly prior to 9/11, some of these domains were hitherto deemed more 'sensitive' and 'closed-off'. Hence, they were treated carefully with a greater 'hands-off' approach. No longer is this type of approach so acceptable. At least politically, this is especially the case in an era of (at least perceived) heightened risks, threats, and uncertainty, and not least where the precautionary principle of preventative pre-emption is a dominant mode of operating across the globe (Svendsen, 2010a, p. 51).[40]

The trends outlined here can simultaneously trigger concerns. In a disproportionate manner, the intelligence and security reach – including outreach – could extend too far. In the process, this exacerbates all the associated risks of such a scenario. Some of these 'problems' have already been discussed in this study.[41] Furthermore, methodologically, while the extent of its *predictive utility* might be contested, the resulting 'theory' that can be constructed surrounding the concept of 'intelligence and security reach' – and, by association, through the phenomenon of related 'intelligence and security outreach', intelligence liaison extending to the overall globalization of intelligence – can still be valuably instructive; albeit with the presence of some informing hindsight being required in some form or other, such as adopting and adapting 'lessons learnt from history' (see 3.0, point 5, above).

In this book, the theory-development process samples from a diverse range of what can be termed most fittingly as 'empirical and interpretive extrapolations'. This allows both the 'scientific' and 'artistic' capture of intelligence-related phenomena. In the process, this also appropriately reflects the nature of intelligence itself, as well as helping to dilute any overly-positivist rendering. A range of foresight activities, as well as the process of undertaking them, similarly can have demonstrable utility within the intelligence domain of activity, as is discussed in the next chapter. This is together with acknowledging that areas of intelligence, such as intelligence analysis, are open to becoming increasingly 'scientized' in terms of their method and approach (on the 'scientization of intelligence', Chapter 5 (5.0), below; on 'professionalization', Svendsen, 2012e). Some operational-to-strategy- and policy-orientated suggestions regarding the pressing question of 'where next?' are now offered.

Part III
Conclusions

5
Where Next?
Suggestions for the future

1.0 Introduction

In 2000, Rocco Rosano, a commentator on US Intelligence, observed succinctly: 'This topic is a very interesting one. While it can be demonstrated that "Intelligence Liaison" is imperative, it can be shown equally well that it is [no] substitute for other, more traditional defensive and offensive source programs and operations.'[1]

Today, the study of intelligence liaison has matured, sufficiently for many potentially viable operational and strategy-to-policy-orientated suggestions for intelligence liaison, extending to outreach and the globalization of intelligence, to be offered. Thanks to the concentrated efforts of other analysts of the phenomenon (for example, J.E. Sims, G.F. Treverton, R.J. Aldrich, and J.I. Walsh, and see also Wippl, 2012), some suggestions already abound in the public domain.

Moreover, as the Deputy Director for National Intelligence for Analysis and Chairman of the US National Intelligence Council (NIC), Dr Thomas Fingar, stressed in March 2008: 'we need to teach people. What we do is too important to [merely] rely on on-the-job training... it's more efficient, more effective to teach people than it is to critique them after they have done it wrong.' (Fingar 2008, p. 13; see also Bar-Joseph and McDermott, 2008; Fingar, 2011; Kerbel, 2008; on the ODNI *c.* 2005–2011, Svendsen, 2011e, p. 37)[2] Fingar continued: 'there's no substitute for sound tradecraft, good analytic methodologies, rigorous adherence to the laws of evidence and inference... One [part] is the articulation and enforcement of standards. We didn't have them before. The law required me to establish them. We have.' (Fingar, 2008, p. 12; see also Bernkopf Tucker, 2008, p. 51; Clauser and Goldman, 2008; Immerman, 2011; Lowenthal, 2008; Svendsen, 2012e)[3]

Further operational-to-strategy and policy-orientated suggestions can be readily identified. Advocating the effective harnessing of the 'positive' and 'beneficial' aspects of globalization within the intelligence domain, many of these proposed suggestions have potential 'added value' (Gibson, 2009; Miskel, 2008).[4] Beginning by presenting some *domestic* (national) intelligence liaison suggestions, this chapter continues by tabling some suggestions for *international* intelligence liaison, extending its analysis into the realm of the globalization of intelligence.

Some greater 'centralization' (or central, even strategic, management) of liaison is raised, also highlighting that the important input from more 'peripheral' or 'local' and operational considerations is simultaneously considered adequately, both in terms of the overall calculations and the 'operational policy' balances being struck.[5] The chapter finishes with a discussion of the promotion of an improved 'scenarios methodology' and the enhancing of 'risk resilience'. Room for optimization remains.

2.0 Domestic (national) intelligence liaison suggestions

Domestically, enhanced intelligence 'nationalization' is key. A continuing focus on further integration and cooperation within home intelligence communities (IC), as well as between national intelligence agencies deployed out in operational contexts abroad, is recommended (Editorial, 2010).[6] Adopting this approach includes continuing to address deeply entrenched cultures, increasing the emphasis on 'community values' and allowing them to extend further in terms of their influence. In the process, previous barriers – such as 'turf battles'[7] and intelligence compartmentalization-related 'stove-pipes' or 'silos' – are addressed, paving the way for the improved sharing of intelligence (Sepp, 2010, pp. 135–136).[8] This approach is currently being advanced within the US Intelligence Community, for example as articulated early on in the US *National Intelligence Strategy* of October 2005, and with the creation of US intelligence 'fusion centers' and other US 'Information Sharing Environment' (ISE) components.[9]

These areas form a domain where the philosophy of 'responsibility to share' ('R2S') is strongly promoted, and where there are attempts to better navigate potentially restrictive originator control ('ORCON') considerations (Treverton, 2009a, pp. 185–206).[10] As a major RAND report on counter-insurgency (COIN) observed in 2008: 'Although the creation of the Office of the Director of National Intelligence has improved sharing among intelligence agencies, channels in the field between the operating military and civilian and intelligence agencies remain clogged.'[11]

It is, therefore, helpful for similar integrative strategies to be pursued and extended, both at home and out in operational contexts abroad.[12] Issues of compartmentalization can still be tackled both structurally and culturally.

During 2008, some progress was made by the US. This occurred as the ODNI claimed to have: 'Developed innovative IT solutions to enable information sharing across the IC.' This included 'iVideo, which allows imagery to be shared, Intellipedia, the Community's secure wiki, and Inteldocs, a Web-based document-sharing system.'[13] During August 2009, the updated US *National Intelligence Strategy* disclosed that 'EO ['Enterprise Objective'] 2: Strengthen Partnerships' and 'EO 4: Improve Information Integration & Sharing' would continue to be pursued by the US Intelligence Community.[14] As the ODNI argued in 2010: 'More generally, the underlying technology for private information retrieval holds the potential for broad application and can expand the policy options available for dealing with information sharing, coalition operations, and international cooperation throughout the IC.'[15] To help facilitate the meeting of the wider intelligence liaison 'end' objectives, several technological 'solutions' were being advanced.[16]

There were similar initiatives in the UK, including the extended presence of mechanisms such as 'Executive Liaison Groups' (ELGs). As described by the UK ISC, ELGs 'are unique to major covert terrorism investigations.' Notably, 'An ELG provides a secure forum in which MI5 and the police work closely together. They enable MI5 to share safely secret, sensitive and, often, raw intelligence with the police, on the basis of which decisions can be made about how best to gather evidence and prosecute suspects in the courts.'[17]

Furthermore, as the UK ISC found in 2010: 'GCHQ staff are now integrated in Security Service and SIS Counter-Terrorism Teams, are seconded to the Joint Terrorism Analysis Centre, perform a liaison function with the [London] Metropolitan Police Service's counter-terrorism [SO15] work and are deployed overseas with the military: this represents genuine progress in collaborative working across the counter-terrorism community.'[18] In the case of the policing of cyber issues, 'While intelligence sharing currently follows a fairly informal format,' Charles McMurdie, head of the London Metropolitan Police's e-crime unit, explained, 'the process of exchanging resources between agencies such as the [Ministry of Defence], [GCHQ], the Metropolitan Police force and the Serious Organised Crime Agency is constantly evolving.'[19]

In terms of technological interconnectivity, the UK Government declared that: 'Work on CLiC (Collaboration in the Intelligence

Community) continues to progress well.' Providing some insights into the overall methodology pursued, the UK Government continued: 'The incremental approach that has been adopted is delivering results at a relatively low cost and with manageable risk levels. The Government intends to continue with this incremental approach to enhancing intelligence-sharing capabilities.'[20]

Meanwhile, during June 2011, reports noted that the UK's Chief of Defence Intelligence (CDI), Air Marshal Chris Nickols, called for a 'single intelligence environment (SIE), which enables collaborative working across organisations and security levels, producing easy-to-use products from multiple sources with analysts working from a single terminal', emphasizing 'that there is a far greater chance of getting better intelligence assessments if all sources are combined.'[21]

However, these movements must not be made in isolation and/or be too rushed. They must be closely tied to expanded and reinforced intelligence liaison (extending to outreach) verification, monitoring, oversight and accountability mechanisms (Müller-Wille, 2006; see also Born *et al.*, 2005; Born and Leigh, 2007; Zegart, 2011).[22] These also need to be more effective at probing the lower and micro levels, where the deepest intelligence liaison interactions occur. Thereby, detrimental and problematic outreach related phenomena, such as overreach or underreach, may be detected, and identified sooner (Svendsen, 2012e).[23]

Moreover, the oversight and accountability focus also has to be 'well-placed' (Lotrionte, 2008). In more of a 'risk pre-emption' manner, the 'problems' could be mitigated before they generate wider counterproductive outcomes and impacts, thereby facilitating greater risk resilience (Cornish, 2007b; see also Ale, 2009; Fischhoff and Kadvany, 2011; Gray-King, 2009; Jackson, 2008; Lupton, 1999; Warner, 2009b). Arguably, a newer operating mantra concerning information-to-intelligence exchanges should be along the lines of: *'if you can defend sharing it, share it!'* Simultaneously, risks relating to intelligence liaison are more distributed, if such an approach is adopted on a sufficiently widespread scale, and the justifiable reasons for the sharing are suitably recorded.

Oversight monitors for intelligence liaison could be employed in order to conduct this oversight on an ongoing basis. Acting akin to 'auditors' found in other sectors of human enterprise, they should ideally: (i) possess appropriate skill-sets for their task (such as being a recently retired senior official from another government department or intelligence agency), in order to bring in some greater independence of operation (beyond influence), but with some liaison-related experience, and hence suitably cognisant and amenable to the requirements and risks entailed in such interactions; (ii) be employed for a fixed term of service; as well as (iii) be subject to a form of cross-party parliamentary or congressional approval; and (iv) report to the intelligence oversight committees of those bodies – albeit *in camera* with their testimony remaining classified, due to the sensitive nature of these types of interactions. Similar practices could be implemented internationally. Focus now turns to that dimension.

3.0 International intelligence liaison suggestions

The process of the globalization of intelligence can readily be extended. Promoting greater creativity and leadership, in the form of refined directing, is required. Effective 'business cases' can be made for the pursuit of grander and more connected international intelligence liaison strategies (Boulden, 2002; Gray, 2007a),[24] paving the way for the greater sharing of intelligence, both more widely and extensively on multilateral bases.

Prevailing information 'monopolies' can be better configured. Suitably facilitated, firstly, structurally (introducing operational frameworks), and then culturally (including philosophically, through following 'optimization' processes), this increasingly 'globalized' mode of sharing includes intelligence featuring in some increasingly 'actionable' and 'rawer' forms at the lower and micro levels of multilateral international intelligence liaison, such as at the operational and tactical levels (Cardillo, 2010; Frankel, 2011). These more 'serious' international intelligence liaison movements could be built incrementally by following and developing the trends already observed as being under way. They can be accomplished by following the different stages tabled below; advanced, perhaps, more explicitly and in a more connected manner. Adopting a more *strategic approach* again has relevance.

More can be done. Accountability and oversight considerations again figure prominently (Aldrich, 2009a; Born *et al.*, 2011; Raab, 2011; 'The Global Perspective' in Lefebvre, 2012, pp. 211–212). In the newer arrangements of increasingly globalized intelligence, arising from increased international intelligence liaison, implementation of these stages would be carried out under a sharper, more consistent critical eye (or, better yet, *eyes*), rather than relying on the mechanisms previously adopted. Some form of refereeing of the judgements reached by operators at the different levels, by means of enhanced coordination, could also be implemented. Arguably, this would help to prevent counterproductive instances of non-optimized and under-optimized intelligence and security reach balances, including at the higher levels of activity.[25]

The critical eyes should examine the depths of intelligence liaison with greater degrees of effectiveness. This activity should not be constraining; in fact, it can be further empowering. For example, monitoring needs to be sensitive to the nuances and complexities that can be encountered in intelligence liaison interactions, particularly at the important low and micro levels of intelligence liaison, as well as with regard to more 'peripheral' or 'local' activities and issues.

Again, in more of a 'risk pre-emption' manner in this domain of activity, problems of intelligence liaison (extending to outreach) – including potential 'intelligence liaison blowback' – can then be detected and tackled earlier, and *as* they surface (on *a priori* bases), rather than being engaged later, *post facto*, when they have already surfaced, and when it is harder or too late to effectively address them, and their wider ramifications. Again, these activities should be undertaken in more of a forward manner that is 'ahead of the curve' of events and developments (Cronin, 2002–2003).[26]

Specially appointed intelligence liaison monitors could also be recruited for use internationally, operating by overseeing (at least) their own country's side of, and participation in, the international liaison. Acting in concert with counterparts appointed in partner countries would be beneficial, facilitating the increased internationalization of the oversight.

Concerning oversight generally, as *Atlantic Monthly* correspondent James Fallows has commented: '"Hindsight is not a strategy," President Bush said in his State of the Union address in 2006. But accountability, and any hope of learning from errors, requires an honest look back at what has occurred.' (Fallows, 2006, p. 229)[27] As vividly seen in the issue of supposed Iraqi WMD, the intelligence 'failure' angle has already been considerably scrutinized by the various inquiries that have reported to date. However, until the *policy 'failure'* angle has been better probed, large, disquieting gaps in the historical record will remain.[28]

Indeed, while some efforts are under way, further activity in this area is required before both the UK and the USA can properly advance from the controversies surrounding the prelude to the 2003 war in Iraq (Hannay, 2009).[29] The policy dimension, being founded on the basis of a so-called 'coalition of the willing', takes the crown of being the most flawed dimension of the run-up to the 2003 Iraq war (see Chapter 3 (4.0–4.3), above; also Finlan, 2009, p. 139; Svendsen, 2010a, p. 116). As Mark Lowenthal, a former US Assistant Director of Central Intelligence for Analysis and Production, has stressed when describing the state-based machinery of intelligence: 'Intelligence and the entire process by which it is identified, obtained, and analyzed respond to the needs of policy makers.' (Lowenthal, 2006, p. 2; Treverton, 2011) For all these reasons, therefore, even conceding all its undeniable shortcomings, the intelligence dimension of the case of Iraq and its supposed WMD cannot be held to be as responsible as the policy dimension. Iraq demonstrated that there was something that could go disquietingly awry at the core of UK and US foreign policy-making machines (Hennessy, 2005).[30] Supposition trumped consideration and consultation.[31]

Today, this paucity still needs to be addressed. This is particularly necessary in an era of complex globality in international affairs, where the margin for such 'errors', in the form of poor or acontextualized policies and strategies, is considerably reduced (Fallows, 2006; Svendsen, 2010c). This is especially when acting in high-tempo and condensed-operating-space environments with finite resources available, when confronting high-tech empowered opponents, including suicide bombers, and where, in war situations 'amongst the people' (Smith, 2006), destructive 'collateral damage'[32] can easily occur (Hafez, 2006 and 2007; Kutz, 2008; Mckenzie, 2012).[33] High stakes figure (Dover and Phythian, 2011).[34]

The example of supposed Iraqi WMD offers further instructive lessons. It effectively represented an episode of '*knowledge* failure', particularly on behalf of decision- and policy-makers. This was where the full operating context was not appreciated, and – indeed worse – efforts towards understanding it were even to a substantial extent dismissed and overlooked,[35] perhaps as part of trying an 'experiment'.[36] So-called '*intelligent customers*' (see Chapter 1 (5.0), above) were scarce – arguably apart from specific individuals in the UK, such as former Foreign Secretary Robin Cook, and, in the USA, former NATO Commander General Wesley Clark (Svendsen, 2010a, p. 146; also Pillar, 2012). Into the future, there was now a clear need for more concerted efforts towards the fostering of 'intelligent customers' by intelligence services (Svendsen, 2010a, p. 98; Wilder, 2011).[37] The 'mission' of intelligence has again become considerably enlarged. Not only has inevitable mission 'creep' been encountered by intelligence (and its closely associated activities, such as Special Operations), in contemporary globalized circumstances it is also experiencing a substantial degree of mission 'gallop'.[38]

The question of how and when intelligence is used, especially in both the UK and US, lies at the centre of this wider concern. Indeed, frequently, the very relevance of intelligence itself is subject to much dispute. This is along with, for instance on the issue of Iraq, the persisting questions surrounding the extent of the relevance of the UK's supposed influence, and even the then UK Prime Minister Tony Blair's personal input in relation to the Bush administration and the US's burgeoning action against Iraq (Ralph, 2011).[39]

The need for a *greater strategic role* for intelligence in contemporary international affairs and the management of those affairs is palpable, together with a better and higher understanding of what intelligence can tangibly offer.[40] As seen, for example, in the wake of the July 2004 *Butler Report* in the UK, governments have taken some note. However, to be more constructive, their efforts need to extend further and be more encompassing in their nature. Those comprehensive 'solutions' should also promote greater connectivity, together with better coordination, structure and direction. They need to better promote ongoing problem- or issue-'management tools' over time, also allowing for the facilitation of further cultural changes (Bracken *et al.*, 2008, p. 302). This is rather than rushing towards adopting 'quick fixes', where essential 'due process' might be lacking.[41] 'Knee-jerk' actions need to be avoided.

Positively, intelligence communities have recognized and grasped the need for further change. For instance, during 2009, the UK Cabinet Office disclosed that: 'In 2009, the Prime Minister, on the advice of the Cabinet Secretary, with the support of the three Agency heads and having consulted widely within Government, agreed to the recommendations of an internal review on strengthening the central intelligence machinery.' It continued: 'The review built on the changes to the central intelligence machinery announced by the Prime Minister in July 2007. One outcome of the review was a revision to the terms of reference of the Joint Intelligence Committee, building on the improvements in this regard since Lord Butler's 2004 report.'[42] Into 2012, further time is still required to see where recent developments go, and whether they extend far enough.[43]

'Only connect', emphasized the British novelist, E.M. Forster.[44] This is a simple phrase worth recalling in all intelligence activities and their study. Indeed, concerning the issue of organized crime, as journalist Misha Glenny claimed in 2008: 'most knowledge of the new wave of global crime was anecdotal at best. Nobody had joined up the dots.' (Glenny, 2008, p. 6) Highlighting further complexities, as former US intelligence officer Frederick Harrison has cautioned, in intelligence enterprises: 'Sometimes, truth is discovered not by connecting dots, but by determining that there are none.' (Harrison, 2006, p. 26)[45]

Therefore, *connections* are clearly important, however they might be manifested.[46] Moreover, these 'connection-associated' tasks should not be undertaken without some adequate *contextualization* helping verification. Sufficiently wide-ranging questions need to be asked in a timely manner better interrogating the familiar dimensions of 'problems', such as: 'who?', 'why?', 'what?', 'when?', 'where?', and 'how?' (Hobbs, 2009, pp. 24–25).[47] Contextual considerations remain key (see Chapter 4 (5.3); Dahl, 2011).

4.0 Using a greater 'scenarios methodology' and increasing risk resilience

Adopting a stronger 'scenarios methodology' offers much. Indeed, a range or portfolio of alternative scenarios can valuably be presented and considered where, at least at this early stage in the overall decision-making process, consensus is not required. This concerted and conscious (that is: cognisant/self-aware) delaying of 'cognitive closure' enables 'open-mindedness' to be maintained, and for different views to emerge in any analysis and assessment. Moreover, the greater sampling of divergent views is enabled, including allowing those at the lower and micro levels to inform and direct more, also in a greater 'due process' manner. In turn, the further cross-fertilization of diverse ideas is fostered, better highlighting what the future may hold if certain actions are undertaken (see Strong's comments in Chapter 2 (4.3), above; Svendsen, 2012e).

Further efforts are beneficial. Harnessing this proactive approach and rigorously pursuing the scenarios methodology, together with other 'horizon-scanning', 'strategic notice', and 'futures' methodologies, helps to strike better balances in intelligence and security outreach.[48] More democratic and greater 'grassroot' stakeholder ownership and 'buy-in' engagement into the overall process is also encouraged (Kull, 2011; see also Briggs, 2010; Egnell, 2010; Jarvis and Lister, 2010; Jones and Smith, 2010; Nagl and Burton, 2010).[49] Adopting this more 'collective' methodology aids the overcoming of intelligence and security overreach phenomena, such as 'blanch spots' or 'white-outs', and intelligence and security under-reach phenomena, such as 'blind spots'. Both of these can act detrimentally as blocks on, and in, the analysis process, and even feed back into and contaminate the overall 'intelligence cycle' (Shell, 2003, p. 16; see also Chapter 1 (2.1 and 5.0), above; Kent, 2010; Svendsen, 2012d, e).[50]

Moreover, robustly practising the scenarios methodology is essential in an era when international affairs are characterized by greater uncertainty, due to the contemporary globalized context; and when, in any analysis and assessment ('sense-making') processes, prevailing assumptions are, and also should be, increasingly challenged (Nolte, 2010; also Jackson, 2010; Mittelman, 2010).[51] As the scenario development team at Shell have argued: 'Scenarios can help in such situations. They can bring greater clarity to difficult areas of decision-making because they acknowledge and focus on what we don't know, encouraging us to explore the nature of uncertainties and helping us to understand where the need for judgement lies.' (Shell, 2003, p. 18; also Canton, 2008; Davis, 2010; Fukuyama, 2007, pp. 1–6; Svendsen, 2012e)

The input from intelligence liaison extending to outreach can be very powerful, both as part of the application of the scenarios methodology and in assisting with the scenario-development process. It provides an essential conduit for other, alternative views, such as from liaison partners, to enter the calculation; yet, at the same time, it provides suitable safeguards against those contributions having a disproportionate influence (both qualitatively and quantitatively), even possibly to a counter-productive extent, on the overall 'system'. Some cushioning is provided (see Chapter 4 (6.0), above; also Flynn, 2007, 2008; Riedel, 2011; Svendsen, 2012e).[52]

Scenarios assist considerably. By feeding into and providing a larger pool of assessments from which to sample during overall 'prediction' efforts, the enhanced scenarios methodology will help complement the 'forecasting methodology' pursued, for instance, by the UK Joint Intelligence Committee (JIC) arrangement (Gustafson, 2010; see also Habegger, 2009; Hennessy, 2011; Lindgren and Bandhold, 2009; Ringland, 2006). As Paul Bracken, Ian Bremmer and David Gordon have observed: 'prediction is one way to deal with uncertainty. But it is *only* one way of many.' (Bracken *et al.*, 2008, p. 304, emphasis in original) Adopting a greater scenarios approach would potentially contribute towards helping to further offset instances of 'groupthink' or over-reach from arising, and equally 'mirror-imaging' or under-reach from occurring (see Chapter 4 (5.2), above). In the process, this would help to neutralize, or at least dilute, the impact on the system of the 'shock' episodes of intelligence and security reach deficits and excesses present at each juncture of developments (Svendsen, 2012e).[53]

Furthermore, as the scenarios methodology necessarily involves a wider range of stakeholders contributing – with the associated counter-intelligence and security anxieties simultaneously suitably addressed – there is greater collective 'ownership' of the final analysis and assessment. This enhanced engagement is an important factor when awkward issues, such as State-undermining 'subversion' at home and 'insurgency' abroad, are being strategically confronted through use of the terrorism tactic (Kilcullen, 2007 a, b). There is also the potential for some greater accountability and oversight to be ushered in, at least internally (see, e.g., 2.0–3.0, above).

Adopting more of a 'scenarios methodology' similarly impacts on the important and multiple producer–consumer relationships. This is done through better connecting people at the lower and micro levels with those at the higher and macro levels (Ralston and Wilson, 2006, p. 37 and from 45; see also Chapter 3 (6.0), above). The development of a stronger scenarios methodology would also eventually help in refining targeting and prioritization, especially in terms of intelligence tasking and gathering, helping to further illuminate any potentially overlooked or under-considered intelligence gaps (Svendsen, 2012d, e).

More refined outreach calibration and configuration efforts can therefore be undertaken. In an increasingly globalized context awash with rapidly proliferating uncertainties and 'unknown unknowns', adopting this approach is an important consideration. The intelligence analysis and assessment capability and capacity of intelligence communities would simultaneously be expanded in a positive direction (see Chapter 4 (5.0), above).

5.0 Possibilities *and* probabilities

While the possibilities are covered, the probabilities also need to be considered. In the 'artistic' domain of intelligence, once the enhanced scenarios methodology is in operation – providing increased insights into the range of *possibilities* that *could* be expected, both in terms of their depth and breadth[54] – the 'scientific' dimension of intelligence, notably the empirical, quantitative and statistical data informing of the *probability* or likelihood of particular possibilities arising, can then be introduced into the overall creative developmental process. This latter area can be rationalized as the 'scientization of intelligence'; at least, *components* of intelligence, such as intelligence analysis, can become increasingly 'scientized' methodologically and in the manner of their approach (Rosenberg, 2008; also Clark, 2009; Marrin, 2011b; Prunckun, 2010). Further successful 'fusion' of these different overarching dimensions of intelligence, 'artistic' and 'scientific', is sought (Agrell and Treverton, 2009, from p. 265; Svendsen, 2012e).

Again, balance is key. The possibilities and probabilities should ideally be considered equally. The 'scientific', quantitative (or 'technocratic' or 'technology factor', even TECHINT) dimensions should not out-weigh 'artistic', qualitative and cultural (or 'humanistic' or 'human factor', even HUMINT) aspects (Roberts, 2010).[55] As Bracken *et al.* argue: '*Risk management is about insight, not numbers.* It isn't the predictions that matter most but the understanding and discovery of the dynamics of the problems.' (Bracken *et al.*, 2008, p. 6, emphasis in original)[56]

The 'problems' or 'issues' and their dynamics can be highly taxing. As sociological risk theorist Jens O. Zinn has remarked: 'Regularly, risks are contested.' (Zinn, 2008, p. 1) Risks, therefore, need to be unpacked as far as possible before a response is triggered. We must not: (i) abandon the tools of conducting refined and intelligent risk management that involve conventional intelligence methods (Arad, 2008; Warner (*et al.*), 2012); and (ii) jettison adequate contextualization (that is, comprehensively understanding the 'complex coexistence plurality' contexts confronted) by following an overly risk-averse approach. As Waldron states about the alternative 'One Per Cent Doctrine':

> [I]t's a striking methodology and a liberating one, and many people think it's the only way to respond to the threat of low-probability, high-impact events. With it, the endless evidence-gathering and analysis that characterises traditional intelligence policy gives way to clarity. Nothing any longer needs to be conditional. We no longer say, "If X has happened, then we need to do Y," with all our effort being devoted to finding out whether X has in fact happened or (in an uncertain world) what its probability is. Instead we say, "If there is the smallest significant chance that X has happened, then we have no choice but to do Y." If X may lead to a catastrophe that must be avoided at all costs (like a nuclear attack on an American city), then we need to swing into action immediately and do Y. No further questions.[57]

Ultimately, pursuing the more absolutist risk-averse route – including along the lines of 'one per cent doctrine' thinking (as described above) – can in fact lead to worse and uncontrolled or uncontrollable scenarios instead emerging (Suskind, 2006; also Furedi, 2006; Rasmussen, 2006). This is because the prevailing *status quo* (albeit even if disadvantageous and with potentially catastrophic portent from the outset) has effectively been further tangibly-to-intangibly upset during more instantly reactive, rather than more deeply considered, responses. Caution and 'due process(es)' should prevail, not a mode more akin to panic, or indeed arrogance, loaded by emotions (Coker, 2009).[58] Resilience is key (Inkster and Nicoll, 2010; also Aradau and Van Munster, 2011; Cole, 2010; Svendsen, 2012e).[59]

Moreover, *crisis management* techniques should not be adopted too hastily, at the expense of the continuation of approaches more akin to *opportunity* or *possibility management* in the overall regular *risk-management* approach. A greater perspective, both in terms of its breadth and depth of range, is required before event-switching or escalating (or so-called 'lesser evil' (Ignatieff, 2005)) judgements and decisions can be adequately made in governance contexts. As Bracken *et al.* have observed: 'Risk management is distinguished from other approaches to making decisions, such as using abstract ideals ("stability," "democracy") as policy drivers. And it differs from relying on rules ("do not reward bad behavior") to guide actions.' (Bracken *et al.*, 2008, p. 302)

They continued: 'Ideals are fine, but absent consideration of the likelihood of their success, or their costs and consequences, they can lead to catastrophic results. Rules also have their place. But ... when the strategic environment is changing fundamentally, rules cannot handle the increasing uncertainty.' Worse situations can develop, as they cautioned: 'Indeed, rules of thumb can become dangerous if they are employed mechanically, without considering how an evolving environment may respond.' (Bracken *et al.*, 2008, p. 302) Here, the powerful contribution made by research-originating material or 'RESINT' is abandoned at great peril. Its lessons, when properly applied, can help provide some useful operating guidelines, with sufficient scope remaining available for individual context interpretation and navigation (see Chapter 3 (1.1), above; Svendsen, 2012e).[60]

Overwhelmingly, with all of its kinetic,[61] the 'security/military methodology' of 'see and strike' has been the dominant mode of operating against a range of risks and threats in recent years. The 'intelligence methodology' of 'wait and watch' instead now needs to predominate. This is required both *before* any application of the security/military methodology as a 'means', as well as being maintained *during* its implementation, while trying to achieve security and law enforcement missions or 'ends' (Mathewson, 2010; see also Inkster, 2010b). Enhanced guidance and an overall *law enforcement* approach, including the facilitation of essential aspects such as 'proportionality considerations', can then be best reflected in overall actions (Svendsen, 2010b).[62] Otherwise, the ability to realize any viable and sustainable public safety and security into the future will commensurably haemorrhage. Any situation 'command-and-control' (C2) opportunities will similarly be lost rather than engendered, raising questions concerning governance ability (Eriksen, 2010; Svendsen, 2012e; Whetham, 2011).[63] Bolstering strategic and risk intelligence qualities and input is noteworthy.

When the proactive risk management route is followed, a 'highlighting' mechanism emerges. It assists in the refining of the overall targeting and forecasting efforts, helping in the identification and formulation of better judgements concerning what *should* be expected, and hence prepared and planned for in a timely manner by responders. Improved risk pre-emption and intelligent risk resilience emerges. Ideally, the artistic and scientific dimensions of intelligence should be given equal weighting. This is so that synergy, arising from the fusion of both dimensions, can be maximized. Moreover, this is undertaken so that those issues not so highlighted are not neglected or overlooked. In summary, the overall process should work by prioritizing like a medical 'triage' system (Alexander, 2002, pp. 200–211; see also Clemente and Marrin, 2005, 2006–2007; Dupont and Reckmeyer, 2012; Marrin, 2009).[64]

Again, uncertainty and even 'unknown unknowns' would similarly be better addressed through adopting such a well- or *better*-considered approach. In a more sustainable (and indeed democratic) manner, we would simultaneously be better prepared for confronting other prominent issues anticipated in the future, including the consequences linked to climate change, natural disasters and pandemic diseases (Notholt, 2009; also Clifford-Jones, 2009; McInnes and Rushton, 2010; Paskal, 2011).[65] Greater 'intelligence emancipation' can be realized (Booth, 2007, pp. 110–116; Svendsen, 2012e; Taylor, 2007, p. 267).

6.0 Conclusions

Current trends concerning contemporary intelligence and its dynamics continue to need to be further unpacked. This is as well as better understanding the potentially powerful role contemporary intelligence and its dynamics can perform, particularly if they are adequately and properly harnessed, both structurally and culturally.

Once better appreciation of the limitations of intelligence aspects has been attained, their strengths need to be better exploited, for instance, by enabling those 'intelligence strengths' to figure more centrally, performing a greater informing and directing role in the subsequent engineering processes (see Chapter 6 (4.0), below; Svendsen, 2012e). This is in addition to them continuing to perform their more traditional supporting and warning role. Further optimization opportunities need to be better capitalized upon. The globalization of intelligence is now opened up for some extended exploration in the next and final chapter.

6 Clarifying the Globalization Nexus

Explaining the 'globalization of intelligence' in the broader context and theory conclusions

1.0 The intelligence world and the wider globalized context

The post-Cold-War era ushered in a time of much soul-searching for intelligence. With the demise of the 'Soviet Issue', there was increased uncertainty about what the future might hold (Gray, 2008; see also Agrell, 2009; Betts, 2010; Davis, 2008; Lawson *et al.*, 2010).[1] This was especially apparent in the context of the post-Cold-War 'peace dividend' intelligence budget cuts witnessed in the early 1990s (Kennedy, 1993; Lowenthal, 2006, pp. 220–231).[2]

As the post-Cold-War era progressed, the trend of greater international cooperation gradually emerged. Both generally, and more specifically in the intelligence world, this trend became manifest as a response to the continuing general rapid globalization (writ large), and owing to the exponentially increasing 'complex interdependence' trends proliferating in international affairs (Waters, 1995; also Abbott *et al.*, 2007; Jones *et al.*, 2010).[3]

At least in some quarters, this trend was recognized early on in the transition from the Cold War to the post-Cold-War era. Capturing the increasing impact of 'globalization *on* intelligence', an article published in *Jane's Foreign Report* during 1989 remarked: 'Instead of regional issues, world leaders will be talking to each other about global ones, such as the environment, drug-trafficking, terrorism and the spread of nuclear weapons and ballistic missiles.'[4] Many 'nasty' factors were apparent (Cusimano, 2000; Sutherland, 2011, pp. 269–271).

Governments quickly became increasingly concerned. The focus of intelligence agencies, such as the US Central Intelligence Agency (CIA), was also later further sharpened on these issues as the 1990s progressed

(Tenet, 2000; also Lowenthal, 2006, pp. 232–254).[5] This was especially once (i) the earlier immediately dominating political 'economic espionage' concerns of the early to mid-1990s became a lesser priority (Adams, 1994; Schweizer, 1993); and as (ii) international intelligence *cooperation*, rather than *competition*, quickly emerged as the most useful mode of operating between states (Hulnick, 1991–1992; see also Alexander, 1998; Coker, 2002; Gannon, 2001; Gruber, 2000, p. xiii). The greater 'globalization *of* intelligence' was not far behind.

Other factors fuelling contemporary developments were soon forthcoming (Herman, 1996, p. 379; Murakami, 2002; Svendsen, 2010a, pp. 42 and 54). The trend of greater international cooperation has increased particularly rapidly since the events of 9/11. It has also been further spurred on in the wake of the other subsequent terrorist attacks, including during the 'emergency' conditions fostered by the so-called 'War on Terror' and 'Long War' (*c.* 2001–2009), and through the years since (Weber *et al.*, 2007; also Aydinli and Rosenau, 2005; Glenny, 2008, 2011; Gray, 2002; Harding, 2010; Held and McGrew, 2007, pp. 43–72; Leblond, 2005; Naím, 2005; Saul, 2009; Scholte, 2005, pp. 279–315).[6]

As US intelligence consultant Larry L. Watts observed: 'The 9/11 attacks accelerated [some already existing post-Cold War] efforts to transform the orientation of intelligence services from rivalry, both domestic and international, to cooperating against the new threats.' He underlined: 'This was an unprecedented situation for intelligence services where considerations of secrecy, trust, and national security made them the strongest bastion of the nation-state and its sovereignty against all other states and their institutions.' (Watts, 2004; see also Treverton, 2003a, b)[7]

In this context, complex trade-offs are increasingly prevalent. This includes the claim made by Jusuf Wanandi that: 'We are locked in a struggle for ideas and beliefs.' (Wanandi, 2002, p. 187; Blair, 2007)[8] Neither can the trade-offs be so easily avoided or postponed, as countries such as the UK, have increasingly found in their foreign policies in recent years (Hill, 2010; McCourt, 2010; Porter, 2010).[9] As the UK commentator Will Hutton has astutely observed: 'The lesson for the twenty-first century is that the fight for security, prosperity and justice can no longer be won on any one nation's ground. It is international.' Importantly, he continued: 'It requires a political narrative. It requires courage and leadership.' (Hutton, 2003, p. 464)[10]

Capturing overall landscape changes, as former CIA Inspector General (1990–1998), Frederick P. Hitz has remarked appropriately: 'This is a brave new world for Western intelligence agencies. It will demand in most instances close cooperation with the host spy service where the incident occurred or the perpetrator can be found. Liaison relationships thus become crucial, doubtless sometimes leading to overinvolvement with local brigands...' However, as he continued: 'Nonetheless, there is a long history of Western law enforcement dealing successfully with the criminal challenges of mob violence, terrorism, and drug trafficking domestically, so there is ample room for collaboration and a sharing of spy expertise with the gumshoes. It will just be a different world.' (Hitz, 2005, p. 183; see also Aydinli, 2010; May, 2005)[11] Intelligence practitioners have confronted several challenges. Closely reflecting the nature of the full-spectrum of 'problems' grappled, their navigation of those issues has often been mixed and uneven (Russell, 2007a; see also Aldrich, 2011b; Maddrell, 2009; Rovner, 2011a). Accordingly, significant adjustments have been required (Svendsen, 2011e).[12]

It is still necessary to find sustainable enterprises for viably tackling contemporary global security issues (Patomäki, 2008; Treverton *et al.*, 2012).[13] Moreover, they require further continual development (Various, 2010).[14] As UK academics Jon Moran and Mark Phythian have observed: 'As a result of the War on Terror [2001–2009] individual states have witnessed significant changes in security and intelligence policies, criminal law, the operations of security and police agencies (including the development of extended surveillance architectures), and immigration law.' They continued: 'Indeed, domestic and international security have come to represent different dimensions of the same core issues, and have generated controversy at both domestic and international level over the appropriate balance between liberty and security in a post-9/11 liberal-democratic context.' (Moran and Phythian, 2005, p. 327)[15] Sustainable security initiatives also need to better build upon and adapt earlier 'older' lessons from history, which still have at least some relevance (Etzioni, 2007; Andrew, 2004; Dover and Goodman, 2011; Popplewell, 1995a; Wark, 2003).[16]

Key debates persist. Certainly, lessons are being *identified*, but are they being sufficiently *learnt* and *applied*? Greater codification efforts, in the form of 'doctrine'-generation, are required (see Part I of Rid and Keaney, 2010).[17] Being mainly 'surveillance-led' and instantly reactive, with other intelligence-associated activities and degrees of reflection trailing further behind, is insufficient (Strachan, 2005).[18]

In summary, the importance of *Strategy* has been enhanced. Indeed, as the Danish political scientist Mikkel Vedby Rasmussen has concluded: 'We have stopped believing in lasting peace, what is left is only strategy – we had better be good at it.' (Rasmussen, 2006, p. 206; see also Freedman, 2006; Lehmkuhl, 2008; Strachan, 2008a, 2011; Till, 2008)[19]

In these circumstances, greater refined-quality *strategic intelligence*, for effectively underpinning those strategies, is increasingly demanded in an always-timely manner (Johnson, 2009; McDowell, 2009; Oleson, 2009; Treverton and Ghez, 2012). Advanced processes, such as the globalization of intelligence, offer much to decision-makers (see also Russell, 2007a, esp. from p. 149).

2.0 Under siege, encouraging change, but not overwhelmed

While still resilient, 'the state', as a primary actor in international affairs, is considerably besieged, due to the globalization-associated breaking down of traditional barriers, and their related categories of analysis and management allocation (Hislope and Mughan, 2012; Khanna, 2009; Ripsman and Paul, 2010; Zakaria, 2009).[20] Despite the presence of some privatization and outsourcing trends, together with 'public–private' partnerships becoming more widespread and important, intelligence (at its 'purest') still continues to be substantially linked to the state (Keefe, 2010; also Haddick, 2011; Petersen, 2012).[21] Intelligence, therefore, is also not disconnected from these wider developments or unaffected by them. Neither can intelligence overlook them. Indeed, the general flow of globalization trends ('globalization writ large') actually enhances the importance of intelligence, including in a capacity- and capability-extending manner. This is equally the case whether those trends are deemed positive or negative in their nature, or whether cooperation or competition is under way (Sirkin *et al.*, 2008; also Bergen *et al.*, 2011; Inkster, 2011b; Mendelsohn, 2011; Pillar, 2011b).[22] Qualitative and quantitative constructs have merged.

Aware of the increased centrality of its role, in 2007, the CIA evaluated the 'Strategic Environment' in the following bleak terms: 'We operate in an unstable and dangerous world where international terrorism, the rise of new powers, and the accelerating pace of economic and technological change will place enormous strains on the ability of states to govern and will sharply increase the potential for strategic surprises.' The CIA document then itemized:

- Our adversaries in the long war on terrorism are dispersed across the globe; they are resilient, ruthless, patient and committed to the mass murder of our citizens.
- The possession and proliferation of weapons of mass destruction threatens international stability and safety of our homeland.

- The rise of China and India and the emergence of new economic "centers" will transform the geopolitical and economic landscape.
- Weak governments, lagging economies, competition for resources, and youth bulges will create crises in many regions.[23]

Undeniably, in an operating context where threats and risk issues – and with them interests – go from national to regional then global, with there also often being a feedback loop to the individual and local (a manifestation of 'glocalization' (see Chapter 3 (2.1), above; Rogers, 2009)),[24] some sort of response is needed (van Creveld, 2006; Svendsen, 2011a).[25]

Responses have been witnessed. Frequently, 'the state' tries to maintain its primacy against the global concerns (Paul and Ripsman, 2004; Ripsman and Paul, 2005; Mabee, 2009).[26] These responses have attempted to be, at least reputedly, 'intelligence-led/driven', including launching the so-called 'War on Terror' and 'Long War' (Howard, 2006–2007):[27] a move in order to tackle the so-called 'new' global terrorism, as well as deal with 'rogue' regimes – such as Taliban-dominated Afghanistan (from 2001) and Saddam Hussein's Iraq (from 2003) – and other 'states of concern', notably Iran and North Korea (Indyk, 2009; see also Bowen and Brewer, 2011; Pollack, 2011).[28]

Neither can Pakistan be overlooked in Western-led counter-terrorism and counter-proliferation efforts. This is particularly because – in all of its globalization-empowered 'entrepreneurialism' – repeatedly several contemporary intelligence and security investigative roads, from all over the world, lead in its direction (see Chapters 3 and 4 of Svendsen, 2010a; also Bennett Jones, 2009; Kilcullen, 2009b; Riedel, 2008, pp. 12–13, 2011a).[29] During 2009–2012, Yemen and Somalia have also figured more centrally (Clark, 2010; Haywood and Spivak, 2012; Phillips, 2011).[30]

In short, the global concerns require 'global solutions'.[31] As UK Foreign Secretary Margaret Beckett declared in a speech during July 2006: 'the globalisation of economics and the globalisation of threats requires a globalised response – in other words multilateralism.'[32] If only by its close association with the state, intelligence also has quickly recognized, and then increasingly adopted, this last quality (see below in 4.0). During the multinational operations especially in Iraq and Afghanistan, in the domain of intelligence we have also witnessed, as US defence analyst Derek Reveron has remarked, that 'widely disseminated U.S. intelligence has become institutionalized... [including] a variety of new partners.' (Reveron, 2006, p. 465)[33] Changes to sovereignty have emerged.

However, limits remain. Sometimes, the state's reassertion is not always so well judged. At times, its responses can be characterized as 'disproportionate' (Svendsen, 2010b; Whetham, 2011). Disappointingly, this is often at the expense of (individual) human and constitutional rights, privacy and civil liberties, both at home and abroad (Moran and Phythian, 2005, p. 328; Moran, 2005).[34] As Wanandi cautioned: 'The danger is that as the role of the state increases, adherence to the rule of law, respect for civil liberties, and support for human rights may weaken. It could even delegitimize the fight against terrorism itself.' (Wanandi, 2002, p. 187; Cole and Dempsey, 2006; Todd and Bloch, 2003) These concerns include the risk of state-undermining 'subversion' increasing.

Worse, publics at home and abroad become commensurably disillusioned. This is manifested in: (i) their worries about intelligence and surveillance imbalances becoming prevalent, such as being 'over-spied' on, in a 'disproportionate' manner; (ii) their concerns that state security responses are overly militarized – including the use of 'extraordinary rendition' and 'intensive interrogation' techniques, as witnessed during the Bush administration era (2001–2009); as well as (iii) their worries that responses are insufficiently coherent (Svendsen, 2010a, pp. 91–100; see also Baker and Phillipson, 2011; Guelke, 2009; Lowenthal, 2006, p. 1; Nathan, 2010; O'Brien, 2010; Wark, 2003).[35] Forms of the condition of 'overreach' are nearby (Downes, 2010; see also Blakeley, 2011a; Ramsay, 2011; Sanders, 2011).[36]

3.0 Evolving 'norms'

The changes to previously existing 'norms' are readily perceptible. Clearly, intelligence also has not been immune from these general trends. On some occasions, it has perhaps even led the way. Former UK intelligence practitioner Michael Herman claimed in 2003 that from the globalization-associated developments 'comes the possibility of a new paradigm for intelligence.' He continued: 'In the international system of (normal) states, it is moving to becoming not a zero-sum contest, but a cooperative activity between them, directed against common threats and common concerns.' Furthermore, 'Even major policy disagreements ... are based on shared (or partially shared) evidence; Intelligence has become the material of world wide inter-governmental and public discourse.' Ultimately, 'The paradigm of cooperative intelligence activity and interpretation was implicit in the developments of the 1990s, but with 9/11 and subsequent events it can now be articulated.' ('How international?' in Herman, 2003b; 'Globalised intelligence?' in Herman, 2002, p. 234)

Great complexity remains in the realm of contemporary intelligence activity. Rather than a complete transformation (in a 'flattened' manner), some previous continuity with 'older' or traditional and more familiar trends ('spikiness' and 'hierarchies') persists in parallel. Arguably, today the prevailing picture can be conceptualized as being essentially a *more* (but not entirely) flattened and equalized 'complex coexistence plurality' (Naím, 2009; see also de Blij, 2009; Ghemawat, 2007; Legro, 2005, p. 186; Mithas and Whitaker, 2007; Walsh, 2009).

The nature of the overall 'complex coexistence plurality' balance depends on circumstances. Moreover, demonstrating its context-specificity, its calibration varies from intelligence liaison relationship to intelligence liaison relationship. For example, the balance struck in the UK–US intelligence liaison relationship is clearly different from that struck in the US–Pakistan intelligence liaison relationship, and so on (see also Eznack, 2011; Odgaard, 2012).[37]

At a minimum, the overall 'complex coexistence plurality' balance depends on factors, which include: (i) the nature and details of the eight attributes or variables of intelligence liaison (see Chapter 4 (2.0), above); and (ii) the different 'complex coexistence plurality' balances that emerge at and across all the different 'levels' of intelligence liaison: (a) at different points in time, and (b) in different contexts (including which 'sectors' the intelligence liaison is under way in – for example, law enforcement, intelligence agencies, conventional military, and Special Forces, etc.) (see Chapter 3 (6.0), above; Svendsen, 2010a, p. 167).

Demonstrating the persisting elements of continuity, the predominant 'intelligence paradigm' is still the functional one of *optimized intelligence and security reach*. More specifically, the 'intelligence liaison paradigm' arguably is a close relative and descendant, namely: *optimized intelligence and security <u>out</u>reach* (see Chapter 4 (3.0, point 2; 5.0–6.0), above). Although, today, due to observed phenomena – such as both the globalization and glocalization trends discussed earlier – the intelligence and security reach extends further, both wider and deeper. Also, in the dimensions of its different configuration, the intelligence liaison paradigm is occurring on greater and continuing exponential bases. Here is where change is most evident in the contemporary context (see Chapter 3, above; Feakin, 2009).[38]

4.0 Identifying and exploring roots, killing weeds

More combined global interests have emerged for several reasons. Reflecting the plurality involved in interactions, this is because: (i) US national security interests, and those of other countries, have converged; or (ii) they are sufficiently harmonizable, due to the same or similar threats being jointly and directly experienced by many states across the world – for example, in the form of the series of *jihadist*-related terrorist attacks witnessed during 2000–2005 and beyond; or (iii) it is out of convenience – for instance, for countries' own domestic purposes; or (iv) it is because interests have been compelled to become harmonized and converge by top-down coercion from the besieged, hegemonic US 'hyperpower' – as enunciated by the 2001 'Bush Doctrine': 'either you are with us or against us.' (LaFeber, 2002, p. 543; see also Byman and Waxman, 2002; Hirsh, 2002) The presence of (at least some) coercion also helps to account for the increase in international intelligence liaison on issues such as counter-terrorism with non-traditional intelligence liaison, or less-friendly, partners, such as – at least publicly for a time for the USA – Syria (see 'Mutual Coercion Mutually Agreed Upon' in Hardin, 1968; Chapter 1 (5.0 and 6.0), above; Jakobsen, 2011).[39] Again, there are many 'pushes' and 'pulls' that need to be factored in during adequate contextualization. Moreover, it is detrimentally reductionist to select just one reason for emphasis during analysis (Etienne, 2011; Jakobsen, 2012).[40]

Indeed, the presence of global interests opens up the possibility and increases the necessity for greater intelligence liaison on deeper and wider bases. As terrorists, traffickers, proliferators and other (organized) criminals have extended the reach of their influence, so have security, intelligence and law enforcement agencies had to similarly adapt. This route has been followed in order to, at the least, compensate (Manningham-Buller, 2007, pp. 43–45).[41] Today, arguably, they are trying to extend their intelligence and security reach yet further. This is to stay ahead, and thus better pre-empt, the globalization-empowered adversaries in a 'forward' manner (see Chapter 2 (2.0), above).[42]

A more globalized intelligence capability is needed, namely one that is able to comprehensively provide a more holistic and timely picture of the threats and challenges faced now and into the future. This is particularly the case today with many states opting to pursue potentially risky proactive and pre-emptive preventative security and foreign policies, which can be further provocative. As Harvard Law Professor Alan Dershowitz has observed, pre-emption is a 'knife that cuts both ways.' (Dershowitz, 2006; see 'cautions' in Harcourt, 2007; Whetham, 2011) Therefore, by applying a greater *intelligence methodology*, the scenario that eventually emerges can be increasingly *engineered* (Svendsen, 2012e).

Indeed, we can argue that by doing the enhanced engineering, better calibration efforts can be realized (Wallace, 2010).[43] This helps to ensure that the emergent scenario 'cuts' (works) more in the way desired in its effects and outcomes. Notably, this will facilitate the condition of 'operational policy' so it can have the best opportunity to succeed (see Chapter 2 (5.0), above). Any paucities are deeply damaging, as is often highlighted (Kilcullen, 2009a; Svendsen, 2012c).

5.0 Intelligence *and* globalization

The intelligence world is not isolated from other general trends. Closely associated are those observable as burgeoning in the corporate/business world (e.g. see Sirkin *et al.*, 2008). As Bruce McKern has argued: 'Managers are much more concerned today with communications laterally, across functions and across national boundaries, than with the vertical flows associated with the traditional hierarchy.' Continuing, he remarked: 'Managers have to deal with far greater complexity in the management of business than in the past, arising from the more rapid pace of change, the density of communication linkages and greater diversity in business lines, geography, personnel, and business partners' (McKern, 2003, p. 3; see also Collins, 2002; Stohl, 1995; on 'hierarchies and intelligence cooperation', see Walsh, 2007, 2009).[44]

Organizationally, as UK intelligence scholar Philip H.J. Davies notes: 'The presence of collegial and organic structures in a secret service is, in many respects, a counter-intuitive phenomenon... [especially] [i]n a field of activity where security and "compartmentalization"... must be paramount.' (Davies, 2004b; Berardo, 2009; Hastedt and Skelley, 2009; Hood *et al.*, 2004, pp. 3–19) Significantly, the intelligence world has not been divorced from further relevant developments, including the general 'boom' in the PR (public relations) industry.[45] Closely associated with intelligence and security outreach activities, both UK and US Intelligence have been participating in their own PR activities (Dover and Goodman, 2009; Svendsen, 2010a, pp. 65, 66–67, 157).

So, are we witnessing the 'globalization *of* intelligence'? Yes. As the US intelligence scholar Loch Johnson has observed: 'Indeed as globalization (interdependence) seems to bring in its wake a greater incidence of worldwide terrorist, drug, and criminal activity, victimized nations have proven more willing to provide some of their intelligence findings to one another and – a dramatic change in norms – to international organizations, in what Herman refers to as the "globalization of intelligence"' (Johnson, 2003, p. 17; Cooper *et al.*, 2008).

Even if we adopt a cautious perspective, distinct trends emerge. Gradually and unevenly, phenomena that can be characterized as moves that add up to the 'globalization of intelligence' can be seen to be under way. These uneven and often combined developments are frequently led and determined by the US, and the UK – through the prevailing hegemony of the close UK–US (extending to UKUSA) intelligence liaison relationship (see 5.1, below).

Or, if we adopt more of a sceptic's stance and define 'globalization' narrowly, at the very least, movements towards the globalization of intelligence can be seen to be *starting* to be made. Notably, this is in the direction of greater intelligence sharing and increased cooperation with other countries. These movements offer potential for being extended (Svendsen, 2008a, b).

How calculated or consolidated these 'globalization of intelligence' movements are is more of a moot point. This is particularly in terms of what can be conceptualized as an overall coherent and coordinated international intelligence liaison strategy. There are some pointers that indicate such an approach has been adopted to an extent (see Chapters 1 (11.0–12.0) and 3 (7.0), above).[46] Although, several key questions concerning this issue remain unanswered – for example, perhaps more debatable is: (i) how connected these moves are; (ii) how far they extend; (iii) how far are they being implemented beyond existing perhaps more in rhetorical and theoretical terms; and (iv) are they being implemented in more fragmented ways (in disjointed short-term tactical, or *ad hoc*, rather than connected longer-term strategic, or regularized, manners) (Aldrich, 2009c; Cronin, 2010)?

There are other uncertainties about these movements towards the globalization of intelligence. For instance, hard to unpack is: (i) whether and to what extent such an approach is entirely by design; or (ii) has it come about more naturally or organically; or (iii) essentially by 'accident', driven by circumstances – rather than being explicitly conscious? Most likely, reflecting the complexities involved, over time the current scenario appears to have arisen through a complex mixture of all these drivers, methodologies and approaches, including their different balances. Unevenness is therefore again reflected[47] (Cohen, 2008; see also Chapter 3, esp. (10.0), above; Svendsen, 2012e).

While also mixed, the globalization of intelligence movements, together with those of their facilitator, intelligence liaison, are not ambiguous. Admittedly, in the covert intelligence realm, they tend not to extend as widely or deeply, particularly when ORCON ('originator control') factors dominate; and when there is enduring reluctance to surrender the perceived sovereignty of 'intelligence property rights' or the 'ownership' of intelligence (see Chapters 1 (6.0) and 2

(3.1), above). These are developments that are especially evident at the pluri- and multilateral levels, and especially with regard to those actors deemed not so trustworthy, or where 'mutual interests' and/or 'values' are weaker.[48] Elements of *intelligence protectionism* continue, with a careful eye to counter-intelligence trends and security anxieties. This is in order to maintain some control over intelligence and to protect sources, as is particularly apparent in the domain of HUMINT (Svendsen, 2010a, p. 16).

Currently, 'collective intelligence' ('COLINT') and its associated trends, emergent since approximately 2007, also continue to be subject to substantial vetting and verification by intelligence and security communities. This is before COLINT features are more formally accepted on widespread bases by becoming increasingly established and further integrated into mainstream intelligence activities through their greater harnessing and exploitation (Svendsen, 2012d).[49]

In short, the best aspects of intelligence cooperation are gradually being traded-off carefully against the most favourable aspects of intelligence protectionism (Heath, 2006; Sullivan *et al.*, 2007). Unsurprisingly, in the *overt* intelligence realm, the globalization trends have tended to flourish considerably more freely. However, to be most useful, these efforts should not be structureless or entirely uncontrolled (see Chapter 3 (5.0), above). Many intelligence 'ownership' questions are raised and are discussed next.

5.1 Ownership questions: Whose 'globalized intelligence'?

Significantly, many of the moves towards the globalization of intelligence appear to be being made on rigorous UK–US-originating terms and conditions. Or, western, developed, and 'northern' (rather than 'southern') ('WDN') countries determine them. This is most perceptible in the domain of counter-terrorism, and during intelligence and security sector reform (SSR) initiatives. These contribute towards helping to define the operational parameters and establishing intelligence liaison arrangement frameworks. Moreover, these developments are shaped, at least in part, by the technological and information-originating factors involved (Graham and Hansen, 2007; Svendsen, 2010a, pp. 13–15, 27–30).[50]

Operation under such constraints helps to explain these developments' uneven advance. This is so that substantial US – and, by close association through the UK–US alliance, UK – command, control and hegemony over intelligence power, can be sustained into the increasingly globalized intelligence future (Brown with Ainley, 2005;

also Bisley, 2008; Guyatt, 2003; Norrlof, 2010). Those players wish to preserve some unipolarity and unilateralism (Calleo, 2008; Kerton-Johnson, 2008; Nye, 2011a).[51]

Some control, however, has been carefully traded-off. This is evident within internationally connected terrorist threat integration and analysis centres, such as JTAC in the UK, as well as within more operationally-focused arrangements, such as the CIA's 'Alliance Base' in Paris and in its Counterterrorism Intelligence Centers (CTICs) (see Chapters 2 (2.2–3.1) and 3 (4.0), above). This trade-off has been carried out in order to try to meet the pressing higher political requirements of tackling the globalized strategic risk concerns, including threats. As Watts has observed: 'After the Cold War, especially after the 11 September 2001 terrorist attacks on US soil, a new wave of reform focused more on effectiveness and functional coordination than on control *per se*.' (Watts, 2004; also Gruber, 2000, pp. xiv–xv; Lowenthal, 2006; pp. 274–288)

Simultaneously, McKern has noted a feature of the business world which resonates to some extent in the intelligence world: 'For most industries and for most firms, it is no longer possible to depend on a competitive position arising from monopoly, location, protection or privileged access to resources or markets.' (McKern, 2003, p. 3)[52]

Again, just how much intelligence control has been relinquished remains debatable. It does vary from case to case. We do see at least elements of the security sector trying to maintain at least a degree of protectionism. This is while other alternative, and frequently traditional, barriers (both virtual – ICT firewalls – and physical – border walls, such as Israel's security wall and the US-Mexican border fence) are being constructed – in order to reassert some greater state-centred, and individualistic security control amid the general erosions (Gavrilis, 2010).[53]

6.0 Persisting US intelligence hegemony?

As RAND senior analyst, Gregory Treverton, and colleagues have observed: 'The campaign against terrorism is inherently multi-lateral; no one state can protect itself on its own. And as nations build coalitions, one of the critical things they can offer would-be partners is information – or intelligence.' (Treverton *et al.*, 2006, p. 32) Greater international intelligence liaison, extending to including outreach, enables the US global hegemony of intelligence power and intelligence omniscience to be increasingly realized and maintained (Norrlof, 2010).

Yet, matters are not as clear-cut as this scenario might suggest. This is because the US hegemony of intelligence power is being increasingly challenged (Haass, 2008; see also Clinton, 2010; Dumbrell, 2010; Dunne and Mulaj, 2010; Young, 2010). As US Coordinator for Counterterrorism, Henry A. Crumpton observed in January 2006:

> Globalization and the related spread of free market economies, liberal values and institutions, and a developing global cultural network has provided unprecedented advancements in so many areas. This global interdependence, in the long run, will make us all more secure. ... Yet, this growing interdependence, inexorably linked to technology, poses risks because our infrastructure is increasingly more fragile. Our global interdependence makes us stronger, but also in some aspects, more vulnerable.[54]

To a greater extent than previously, the US is dependent upon its international intelligence liaison relationships, including outreach, for what then US Secretary of Defense Donald Rumsfeld called soon after 9/11 the 'scraps of information that people from all across the globe' can provide.[55] Paradoxically, this dependency is even helpful in sustaining America's traditional general insularity and 'isolationist' qualities.

Some frameworks have collapsed; however, all is not lost. Alternative frameworks have been constructed and continue to evolve. Essentially, the USA can continue its role of being the hub at the centre and top of the collective web of overlapping international intelligence liaison arrangements. How they connect is key (Lowenthal, 2006, p. 303). Adopting network terminology, the USA can also continue to boast some important 'nodes' within that 'hub' – most obviously the 17 US intelligence agencies that compose the formal US Intelligence Community (including the ODNI), as well as the US hosting other substantial and burgeoning intelligence-entities, such as the New York Police Department (NYPD) (see Chapter 3 (11.0), above).

Together, these networked mechanisms provide global coverage and reach, reflecting the outcome of the increasing globalization of intelligence. The 'intelligence power' acquired thereby is in turn additionally essential for the attempted pursuit of pre-emptive security and foreign policies. Moreover, through the diversification of intelligence liaison risks, there is at least some enhanced resilience. This is while simultaneously making oversight and accountability activities increasingly challenging, at least beyond single agencies. More complex trade-offs are encountered (Aldrich, 2009a; Svendsen, 2012e).[56]

7.0 The USA is not alone

While the USA essentially remains the hegemon in the realm of intelligence, its 'friends and allies' can also gain. In return for their liaison interactions sustaining the USA's greater intelligence power, 'special' or 'essential' partners – such as the UK and, to greater extents than previously, Australia and Canada – can increasingly tap into some of the US global hegemony of intelligence power and intelligence resources. This is facilitated through their close friendship and alliance with the USA. For instance, in May 2011, during US President Obama's state visit to Britain, close UK–US intelligence and security ties were re-emphasized.[57] Simultaneously, therefore, the collective and cooperative and human security dividends of the US intelligence power can then be deployed more widely, top-down, and paternalistically for the benefit of partners (Nye, 2002; also Altinay, 2011). In these circumstances, the US can act as a benevolent hegemon.

Ultimately and primarily, however, the intelligence power can be deployed for the US itself.[58] As the US *National Intelligence Strategy* of August 2009 concluded: 'Only as we [the US Intelligence Community] become a unified enterprise can we meet the unprecedented number of challenges we face and seize opportunities to enhance the security of the United States along with that of its allies, friends, and like-minded nations.'[59] These activities take place in a context that involves a convenient so-called 'coincidence of interests', again including the presence of 'mutual interests' and/or 'values' (Nicander, 2011).

At a minimum, a duality consisting of 'altruism' and 'egoism' continues firmly in place – extending to a plurality when involving their derivatives (Thomas, 1988, pp. 233–235).[60] As former CIA Inspector General, Frederick P. Hitz has observed: 'Even nations whose leaders propose different philosophical approaches to the problem find that their intelligence services cooperate fully and rapidly with one another on practical questions of information sharing on identities and evidence.' (Hitz, 2008, p. 162; see also Aldrich, 2009b) An important 'culture' of intelligence is once more apparent (Davies, 2004a; Chapter 4 (3.0, point 1), above).[61]

Once intelligence is increasingly globalized according to the model discussed above, a system that operates on more of a globally omniscient basis emerges. Of course it is not perfect, and – as with any other human endeavour – neither should we ever expect it to be.[62] However, this all- or most-seeing and *reaching* intelligence arrangement arguably helps to *better* deliver the ideal type of a more improved intelligence capability, reflecting a condition of increasingly optimized 'intelligence and security reach'. Again, this is a useful quality to possess when trying to most successfully pursue the precautionary and pre-emptive preventative security and foreign policies in the contemporary international environment during an era of 'globalized strategic risk'. This is also when trying to fulfil those policies and modes of operating in the least potentially provocative manner possible.[63] The aim is to avoid all forms of 'blowback'.

States and their governments can then focus on pragmatically trying to tackle the early twenty-first century global challenges into the future.[64] This includes acting in a more *a priori* and intelligence-informed *risk management* manner, promoting improved *risk pre-emption*.[65] Capitalizing upon enhanced *foresight* activities (including scenarios), offers the ability to be 'ahead of the curve' of events and developments to a greater extent; while more firmly undertaking *opportunity management*, allows for the improved seizing of the *architectural* and *engineering* possibilities (see Chapter 5 (4.0), above; Svendsen, 2012e).

These strategic approaches should figure prominently and be on the ascendancy, rather than intelligence and security services having to act more in a way akin to emergency first-responders, namely 'behind the curve' of events, and, as a consequence, having to adopt more extreme (and hence potentially more contestable) *crisis management* approaches *post facto* (Cronin, 2002–2003; Smith and Elliot, 2006). Unfortunately, particularly during the episodes where controversial 'disproportionality' is observed, the attempted strategy/policy efforts can flounder (Svendsen, 2010b; see also Gross, 2008).

Indeed, these episodes of 'failure' can also be measured in terms of the (mis-)configurations or (mis-)calibrations of *intelligence and security reach* involved. Factors, such as the 'speed' or rate of implementation, can be similarly included (Biddle, 2007). Richard Popplewell has even appropriately characterized these types of episodes as 'lacking intelligence'. Certainly, they arguably lack its reflective informing and directing qualities to an adequate enough extent (Popplewell, 1995a; Walsh, 2008).[66] The 'rule of law' also needs to succeed in a suitably accommodating manner (see Chapter 2 (2.1), above).[67]

7.1 Advancing an extended 'intelligence methodology'

A considerably enhanced intelligence methodology instead needs to prevail. As Hew Strachan, Chichele Professor of the History of War at the University of Oxford, reminds us: 'security is relative, not absolute.'

(Strachan, 2008b, p. 48)[68] A proposed model could be along the lines of a consecutively (or linearly) implemented three-step opportunity-generating risk-management programme, involving appropriately interlinked: (i) problem analysis; (ii) containment; and then (iii) roll-back (summarized as P-C-R). Equally resonating is the interconnected process of: (i) 'securitization'; (ii) 'politicization'; and then (iii) 'action' (summarized as S-P-A), against targeted issues. These models should be underpinned strongly throughout by an appropriately empowered intelligence methodology that, in turn, is fully heeded, deep, and wide-ranging, as well as being as 'objective' as possible. (Note, too, here, that not all 'politicization' is deemed as being automatically negative or 'bad' (on 'negative'/'extreme'/'capital-P' *Politicization* in the US context, see Treverton, 2009a, pp. 168–184; Riste, 2009). In some situations, it can also act as a valid stimulus on processes, driving them forward proactively.[69])

While prevailing in the domain of counter-proliferation, for instance, these models can then also be viably used in a range of other circumstances, including counter-insurgency (COIN) and counter-terrorism (CT) enterprises (see Svendsen, 2010b, 2012e, Rid and Keaney, 2010; Ringmose *et al.*, 2008).[70] Unless (and/or until) the 'problem analysis' dimension is considerably enhanced, through better and suitably informing contextualization efforts, the problem solving during the course of 'complex emergencies' and multi-functional operations cannot be commensurately improved. Simultaneously, potential 'solutions' remain increasingly elusive – for instance, in the form of well-considered management strategies (Mitchell, 2011; also Gregor, 2010; Sutherland, 2011, pp. 211–214).[71]

In our contemporary era, we have seen much-enhanced UK–US, and more widely extending, sometimes disconnected, securitization and politicization. Now, we arguably need to advance some further enhanced *'intelligence-ization'* (the process of providing more 'intelligence' input and a greater 'intelligence methodology') within and across all those entities and frameworks. Or, put another way, the tackling of highly complex issues in an era of exponential globalization needs to become more 'intelligence-ized'. This includes allowing intelligence to perform an improved *informing, warning* and *directing* role, as objectively as possible, across the whole portfolio of continuum-extending hazards-and-risks-to-threats currently faced (Posner, 2004; Svendsen, 2012e).[72]

Broader conclusions concerning the phenomenon of international intelligence liaison will now be considered. Further insights into the 'globalization of intelligence' are simultaneously provided.

8.0 Facilitator dynamics: Sketching international intelligence liaison

A two-dimensional diagram suggestive of *how* the multidimensional international intelligence liaison phenomenon works is portrayed in Figure 4.1, above. In the diagram, the theoretical basis of an international intelligence liaison relationship as it operates in practice is displayed. The key framework contributing towards the regionalization, extending to the overall globalization, of intelligence through the mechanism of international intelligence liaison is represented graphically. Albeit in all of its abstractness and 2D representational simplicity, this model also attempts to offer a coherent explanation for the way that intelligence liaison contributes to wider trends.

The theory articulated unashamedly paints intelligence liaison, and its contribution towards the globalization of intelligence, in an ideal form and way of operating. For example, this is logically as liaison and the globalization of intelligence appear to look, and arguably how they should look, in the calculations encountered at the highest and macro quartet of levels of intelligence liaison and its management (Priest, 2000).

However, distinct limitations remain. In terms of theorizing intelligence liaison, the analyst cannot get much beyond a general and functional theory of *how* intelligence liaison operates to attain one that more fully satisfactorily answers the core question of *why* intelligence liaison in its entirety occurs. This is because too many specifics and general considerations feature at all the different levels of intelligence liaison, and intimately vary from case to case (e.g., Fägersten, 2010; Matei, 2009; Munton, 2009; Svendsen, 2010a).

Contextual factors are key. International intelligence liaison is therefore on the whole beyond general theorization on that plane of analysis, as 'generalizability limits' are soon encountered. Other than to argue that international intelligence liaison occurs and is evolving because policy- and decision-makers increasingly need it as they operate in the rapidly globalizing context in international affairs, a general theory of international intelligence liaison starts to disintegrate. This happens as its depths start to be explored further, and therefore such long-ranging theorization is too vague and abstract to be of much greater utility than providing an obvious starting point for understanding the phenomenon in generic terms for guidance purposes.

Unsurprisingly, in practice, intelligence liaison in all its dimensions is considerably more complex and messy. In reality, it becomes significantly harder, in fact (virtually) impossible, to capture and unpack neatly in overarching terms as an analysis of the phenomenon becomes deeper – especially as particular contexts, and hence increasing quantities of raw details and specifics, are added in during the practice of intelligence liaison. This is particularly the case at the lower and micro levels of experience and analysis, where details and specifics appear to be more important, perhaps even gaining more of a momentum of their own – for example, as was demonstrated during the 'CURVEBALL affair' (Svendsen, 2010a, p. 233, col.2; see Chapter 2 (4.3), above).

Small wonder then that it is at these lower and micro levels that there appears to be greater potential for intelligence liaison to unravel, and for intelligence and security reach deficits and excesses, such as *under-reach* and *overreach*, as well as other 'mis-flows' of information, to emerge. These are developments that manifest themselves further away from even the most alert eyes (and/or grasp) of macro- and micro-managers, down in essentially less monitorable and harder-to-control depths of activity. Several limits become increasingly evident, requiring us to look elsewhere.

Most immediately, 'complexity theory' emerges as relevant. Particularly this is where, in his scholarship on the 'complexity of cooperation', Robert Axelrod lists the steps of: 'evolving new strategies'; 'coping with noise'; 'promoting norms'; 'choosing sides'; 'setting standards'; 'building new political actors'; and 'disseminating culture' (Axelrod, 1997, p. vii; Bousquet, 2008; Bousquet and Geyer, 2011; Svendsen, 2009b). More widely, re-focusing assists. We move there next.

9.0 Explaining intelligence liaison trends with the 'theory of optimized outreach'

Deploying a softer theory 'lens' during evaluation is most instructive. Set at a broader focus, this can be done in the form of employing a more abstract *theory of optimized outreach*. Indeed, this appropriately 'empirical and interpretive extrapolation'-based lens emerges as powerful in satisfactorily explaining the intelligence liaison phenomenon and some of its observed dynamics. It also more adequately explains the overall 'globalization of intelligence'.

The explanatory power of adopting this approach stems from the premise that a 'theory of optimized intelligence and security outreach' is not only valuable for explaining intelligence liaison phenomenon developments, but also – through its 'parent' of *intelligence and security reach* – those developments observed in the world of intelligence *as a whole* (see Chapter 4 (5.0), above). This is a conclusion that likewise extends to evaluating overall processes such as the globalization of intelligence.

Using the 'theory of optimized intelligence and security outreach' lens allows a necessary escape from being overly constrained by all the definitional problems and disagreements associated with trying to define the term 'intelligence', and by association, 'intelligence liaison' precisely (see Chapter 1 (2.0–5.0), above; Sims, 2005a, pp. 15–18). Increased consensus regarding what is meant by 'intelligence' and its purpose is possible.

Further conclusions are apparent. Adopting the *theory of optimized outreach* lens also allows for a more holistic understanding of intelligence liaison. Simultaneously, it informs us about other intelligence interactions, and, perhaps more significantly, offers an explanation for how intelligence liaison connects with the other interactions observed in the intelligence world (see, e.g., Chapter 4 (5.0), above), rather than isolating it and its dynamics artificially from wider developments during its analytical dissection. For instance, the central role international intelligence liaison performed as part of the wider run-up to the 2003 war in Iraq can be readily highlighted (see Chapter 2 (4.3), above; Chapter 4 of Svendsen, 2010a; Svendsen, 2012e).[73] Again, broader closely associated processes, most notably the globalization of intelligence, are not far behind.

9.1 Paving the way for better prediction?

More lessons prevail. Thinking in terms of *intelligence and security reach* (and, more specifically with regard to intelligence liaison, that of *intelligence and security outreach*) allows for the introduction of its associated phenomena or various conditions. These include: *overreach*, when there is too much present (see, e.g., 'groupthink' in Chapters 1 (3.0 and 10.0) and 4 (5.2), above); and *under-reach*, when there is too little (e.g., Svendsen, 2010a, p. 69).

A viable conceptual framework is now tabled for explaining *why* several developments occur. This framework also explains why several developments *have* occurred, and perhaps even offers tools – in the form of *suggestions* regarding what to look out for or to be sensitive towards – for how *intelligence and security (out)reach imbalances* could try to be better pre-empted, and hence avoided, *into the future*. An enhanced mode of *risk pre-emption* is promoted as part of the overall risk management of international intelligence liaison and the 'globalization of intelligence'.

Highlighting the last qualifier, this framework also, therefore, has some *predictive utility*. Again, the presence of some informing hindsight is helpful, such as in the form of remembering 'lessons learnt from history' (see 1.0, above; Koblentz, 2011). The setting of requirements can be aided most expeditiously by the provision of a lens through which the challenges and the responses to them can be examined; and whereby problematic areas or vulnerabilities can be identified, and then potentially addressed.

What is promoted is a risk-management strategy intended to *maximize risk resilience* and to advance the enhanced *minimization of vulnerabilities*. In intelligence liaison relationships, if there is too much or too little outreach present in interactions, some form of 'blowback' is likely to occur. The risks adopted in those domains are thus higher. Here, risk-management concerns connect closely with the outreach considerations (Gibson, 2005; see also Amoore and de Goede, 2008; Coker, 2009; Dupont and Reckmeyer, 2012; Zinn, 2008).

Further explanation is possible. If there is *overreach*, the outreach needs to be carefully rolled back. This needs to be done appropriately tuned to the specific operational circumstances. For example, this can be accomplished by undertaking reflective 'stepping-back' actions, and by having mechanisms in place so that the stepping-back can have a meaningful impact or at least a viable opportunity to inform. This can be done by introducing 'challenge-team' ('Red-Teaming' or 'A+B-Team') activities, or exchanging independently-'finished', rather than jointly undertaken 'in-progress', analysis and assessment (estimate) products. Adopting these approaches is generally a useful way to help contribute towards addressing intelligence analysis and assessment flaws (Svendsen, 2010a, pp. 57, 60 and 61; 2012e; Russell, 2010). They also help to ensure that wider processes, such as the 'globalization of intelligence', work in their most effective and productive manner.

Other scenarios exist. Alternatively, if there is *under-reach*, the outreach needs to be rolled forward carefully. In the domain of intelligence staff and personnel management, such a mechanism – for example, the appointment of counsellors by intelligence agencies – can be cited, so that, at least in theory, employees feel less compelled to vent their frustrations publicly through 'leaking' or 'whistle-blowing' activities in the media, for instance, where security considerations might be compromised.[74]

Again, whichever approach is adopted, it should be appropriately tuned to being *directly in harmony with the specific operating context*. In summary, all of these developments represent the quest for the 'holy grail' of intelligence liaison, and indeed the overall goal of the 'globalization of intelligence', namely: *optimum intelligence and security outreach* (*optimum outreach*). Here, in terms of 'intelligence balances', a form of 'intelligence liaison equilibrium' is sought (see also end of Chapter 5 (5.0), above).[75]

10.0 Summarizing key conclusions

As Swedish intelligence scholar Wilhelm Agrell argued instructively about intelligence liaison: 'in theory intelligence liaison should be guided by reason, logic and trade-offs. The actual conduct of intelligence liaison might be something quite different.' Continuing, he remarked: 'The pattern of liaison and the political setting of the intelligence relations are at best complicated and full of contradictions, at worst irrational, obscure and impossible to comprehend in terms of a coherent security strategy.' (Agrell, 2006, p. 636) A useful summary of the challenges confronted by the intelligence liaison analyst is offered.

As this book (together with its companion volumes (Svendsen, 2010a, 2012e)) has demonstrated, much can be observed and connected and, beyond that, at least some of it can be theorized. Also discernible from the findings of this book is the central proposition that (at least in the covert intelligence realm) international intelligence liaison is the mechanism pivotal to the increasing 'homogenization', 'international standardization', and eventual 'globalization of intelligence'. This is because it encapsulates attempts towards realizing the essential collective and cooperative security means of responding to the globalized, and hence globally shared and mutual, security threats of the early twenty-first century.

Intelligence liaison, extending to outreach, is additionally the mechanism – in its 'means' (*modi operandi*) form – for enabling further and deeper intelligence liaison on these concerns into the future. This is by figuring in its 'end' or 'solution' (*modus vivendi*) form, as a constant (ongoing) issue monitoring and management mechanism. International intelligence liaison, together with international outreach activities in the overt intelligence realm, therefore offers an incredibly powerful and widely encompassing tool for conducting and managing international relationships, effectively underpinning the globalization of intelligence, as well as providing a suitably dynamic mechanism for handling the product of those interactions, and managing their associated information flows.

Without liaison, undoubtedly the foreign policies of states would flounder. Moreover, interests and/or values – whether they are of a national, regional or even global nature – would be left increasingly unfulfilled. In short, as a tool, intelligence liaison offers much. Equally, exploration(s) of the globalization of intelligence can prove to be highly valuable, if only by demonstrating the phenomenon's multi-purpose and multi-functional utility. Intelligence communities can still effect a greater harnessing of those trends (Svendsen, 2011b, 2012e).

11.0 Final reflections

By recognizing the value of theory, this book attempts to address the under-theorized condition of intelligence liaison. While generally exploring the 'end-condition' of the globalization of intelligence, this book presents a 'theory' of international intelligence liaison that is as comprehensive as is believed to be possibly attainable.

However, as demonstrated, theorization attempts *can only extend so far*. The multiple limitations can be highlighted. If the theory of intelligence liaison is extended further, then it appears to become overstretched to breaking point. In such circumstances, the theory becomes increasingly 'top-heavy' and inadequately grounded in lower foundational, and empirically observable, bases. This increases the likelihood of it becoming over-extended, and it essentially 'falling over', and thereby 'failing'.

The generalizability of the theory similarly drops. This happens because when intelligence liaison, extending to the globalization of intelligence, is applied in the cold light of 'reality', specific details and contexts become increasingly important (see Zuckerman, 2005). Perhaps paradoxically, these factors can then even run counter to general macro, higher-level principles (Scholz and Wang, 2009).[76] They are also most detectable at the micro and lower levels, as the analysis of particular intelligence liaison relationships becomes deeper. Drivers remain variable.

When probed in depth, intelligence liaison, extending more widely to the globalization of intelligence, is never as straightforward, or as obvious, as it may look superficially or at first. It is here that attempts to articulate the *dynamics* of the intelligence liaison phenomenon, extending to the globalization of intelligence, can be most satisfactorily accomplished by employing the lens of a 'theory of optimized intelligence and security outreach'. More arguably in contemporary circumstances, that outreach can be most appropriately characterized as occurring on *exponential* bases. This is closely in harmony with contemporary globalization (writ large) trends.

Finally, the historically enduring phenomenon of intelligence liaison will survive. For the foreseeable future, intelligence liaison is most likely to remain essentially on a trajectory that can be generally characterized as being on 'a continuum with expansion'. What is more apparent is that intelligence liaison – together with its associates, extending to outreach – is so dynamic that it will continue to fascinate, considerably challenging its practitioners and analysts alike well into the future. Forming a useful issue-management and navigation tool, intelligence liaison will continue to flourish, together with elements of its wider processes, notably the 'globalization of intelligence', persisting to simultaneously both challenge and aid us.

Notes

Preface

1. See, e.g., G. Miller, 'With bill at Obama's desk, Congress aims to renew oversight of CIA operations', *WP*, 30 September 2010; A. Goldman and M. Apuzzo, 'At CIA, Grave Mistakes Led To Promotions', *AP*, 9 February 2011; S. Aftergood, 'Senate Review of CIA Interrogation Program "Nearing Completion"', FAS_SN, 24 April 2012; 'Intelligence and Security Committee wants more power', *BBC*, 13 July 2011; D. Welch, 'Wilkie to oversee agencies', *SMH*, 18 November 2010.
2. For similar conceptualizations of 'reach', *Global Reach – Global Power*, Washington, DC: Department of the (US) Air Force, 1992; 'U.S. Forces Show Reach in Crises Response', *Defense.gov*, 5 April 2011; 'Foreign Secretary: "For the first time in decades our diplomatic reach will be extended not reduced"', *FCO.gov.uk*, 11 May 2011. 'Developing the UK's global reach', *FCO.gov.uk*, 29 March 2012.
3. See also 'Richard Lloyd Jones' in V. Stagg, 'Review', 10th Australian Institute of Professional Intelligence Officers (AIPIO), November 2001, Queensland, Australia, 17 March 2002.
4. Defined as a 'contraction of "global" and "local",' which 'refers to the increasing entanglement of these two spheres' – Mooney and Evans (2007).
5. See also '"Hire non-Swedes for sensitive posts": Säpo', *TL*, 7 December 2009; 'Sweden's spy laws need updating: Säpo', *TL*, 24 May 2011.

1 Unpacking Intelligence and Liaison: Understanding basics, drivers and underlying mechanisms

1. 'The Prisoners' Dilemma', *FP*, 25 April 2011.
2. M. Rosen, 'How English evolved into a global language', *BBC*, 20 December 2010.
3. 'INTelligence: Signals Intelligence', *CIA.gov*, August 2010.
4. MASINT is intelligence from 'sensors that measure seismic, acoustic, chemical and biological signatures', that is those emissions related to WMD (Dupont, 2003, p. 18; Richelson, 2001).
5. Davies (2009, pp. 957–969); R. Pengelley, 'Picture perfect', *JIDR*, 14 December 2010.
6. US Joint Chiefs of Staff, 'Geospatial Intelligence Support to Joint Operations', *JP 2-03*, 22 March 2007, p. vii; 'INTelligence: Geospatial Intelligence', *CIA.gov*, September 2010; E. Keymer, 'Mapping the battlespace', *JDW*, 30 June 2011.
7. 'INTelligence: Human Intelligence', *CIA.gov*, October 2010; Johnson (2010a, pp. 308–332; Hitz, 2010, from p. 257); for 'SOCINT', Patton (2010), and other 'culture' refs in Chapter 4 (3.0, bp. 1).
8. On OSINT, R.A. Best, Jr. and A. Cumming, 'Open Source Intelligence (OSINT): Issues for Congress', *CRS*, 5 December 2007; S. Aftergood, 'The

Institutionalization of Open Source Intelligence' and 'Open Up Open Source Intelligence', *FAS_SN*, 24 August 2011.

9. See also Danish Defence Intelligence Service (FE), *Intelligence Risk Assessment 2010*, Copenhagen: September 2010, pp. 5–6.
10. S. Aftergood, 'ODNI Issues New Security Standards for Intel Facilities', *FAS_SN*, 27 October 2010. On 'SCIFs' ('Secure Compartment(aliz)ed Information Facilities'), Svendsen (2010a, p. 42, p. 161).
11. Quoted from The Institute for Telecommunication Services (ITS): 'ITS is the research and engineering branch of the National Telecommunications and Information Administration (NTIA), a part of the U.S. Department of Commerce (DOC)', http://www.its.bldrdoc.gov/, 'Communications Security (COMSEC)', 23 August 1996, http://www.its.bldrdoc.gov/fs-1037/dir-008/_1132.htm, accessed on 22 April 2012.
12. See also 'What's allowed by a "presidential finding"?', *CNN*, 31 March 2011.
13. See also B.A. Gwakh, 'Taliban Employs Modern Weapons in "War of Words"', *RFE/RL/ISN*, 22 March 2011; W. Maclean, 'Propaganda will prove crucial in Libya war', *Reuters*, 23 March 2011.
14. J. Gomez, 'Wary of security, Navy won't talk about bin Laden', *AP*, 15 May 2011.
15. R.A. Best, Jr. and A. Feickert, 'Special Operations Forces (SOF) and CIA Paramilitary Operations: Issues for Congress', *CRS*, 4 January 2005; A. Feickert, 'U.S. Special Operations Forces (SOF): Background and Issues for Congress', *CRS*, 25 January 2008; 'Special Operations Focuses on World's "Unlit Spaces"', *Defense.gov*, 10 February 2011; 'Socom's Impact Outweighs Its Size, Commander Says', *Defense.gov*, 2 March 2011; 'Future funding for special operations forces looks bright, analysts say', *CNN*, 5 May 2011.
16. See also S. Aftergood, 'Special Operations Forces on the Rise', *FAS_SN*, 2 May 2011; 'Petraeus leaves legacy of ramped-up special operations fused with intelligence in Afghanistan', *AP*, 19 July 2011; 'U.S. Seen Boosting Covert Action's Role Against Iran', *GSN*, 12 May 2011; 'SOCOM eyes global capability network', *JIDR*, 10 May 2012.
17. See also '"Narrative verdict" at Linda Norgrove inquest', *BBC*, 15 February 2011; 'Bin Laden death "not an assassination" – Eric Holder', *BBC*, 12 May 2011; J. Warrick and K. Brulliard, 'Obama's national security team was sharply divided over Osama bin Laden raid', *WP*, 8 May 2011.
18. D. Priest, 'Intelligence Officials Defend Secret Overseas Prisons', *WP*, 2 November 2005; 'UAV attacks on Pakistan-based militants reach peak', *JM&R*, 10 January 2011; T. Mckelvey, 'Inside the Killing Machine', *Newsweek*, 13 February 2011; G. Jaffe and K. DeYoung, 'U.S. drone targets two leaders of Somali group allied with al-Qaeda, official says', *WP*, 30 June 2011; A. Goldman and M. Apuzzo, 'Osama Bin Laden's Hunter: CIA Analyst Examined', *AP*, 5 July 2011.
19. 'Liaison' in A.C. Wasemiller, 'The Anatomy of Counterintelligence', in *CSI*, 13, 1, Winter 1969, pp. 15–16, pp. 22–24, via CREST, CIA-RDP78T03194A000300010005-7 (2005/04/28).
20. See also P. Apps, 'Do Western states spy for corporate ends?', *Reuters*, 15 September 2010.
21. See also 'A Look Back ... The Creation of *Studies in Intelligence*', *CIA.gov*, July 2011.

22. C. Irvine, 'Roald Dahl's seductive work as a British spy', *ST*, 31 August 2008; 'N Korea "sex spy" jailed in South', *BBC*, 15 October 2008.
23. NATO Standardisation Agency (NSA), *NATO Glossary of Terms and Definitions*, p. 2-L-3 (emphasis added); US Joint Chiefs of Staff, 'Department of Defense Dictionary of Military and Associated Terms', *JP 1-02*, updated 17 September 2006, p. 312.
24. Department of the (US) Army, Office of the Assistant Chief of Staff, G-2, Intelligence, 'Organization and Functions', *Special Regulations: No.10-120-1*, 10 October 1951, p. 4, via CREST, CIA-RDP57-00384R001000020004-7 (2001/08/23); 'Liaison' in *Records Management Program: Survey Report of the Office of the Director*, April 1953, via CREST, CIA-RDP57-00042A000100320001-2 (2006/11/08).
25. Entry for 'liaison' in the 'Glossary', http://www.mi6.gov.uk/output/glossary.html#L, accessed on 22 April 2012.
26. See also quotation from the '*Butler Report*' in Chapter 2 (4.4).
27. See also 'Pakistan Gives U.S. Generals the Silent Treatment After Osama Raid', *WB*, 10 May 2011.
28. 'Statement on the Binyam Mohammad High Court Judgement', *FCO*, 4 February 2009.
29. M. Townsend and T. Thompson, 'Undercover police cleared "to have sex with activists"', *GU*, 22 January 2011.
30. Definition via *askOxford.com* (the Oxford English Dictionary).
31. Also a non-attributable source.
32. Observation based on paraphrased information from a non-attributable source. On 'reachback', 'Civil support for military operations and emergency responses', *NATO*, January 2008; B. Tigner, 'NATO looks to intensify anti-CBRN efforts', *JDW*, 24 March 2010.
33. E-mail communication with Robert David Steele, former US intelligence officer and CEO of OSS.Net, Inc. and Earth Intelligence Network, conducted Monday, 2 July 2007.
34. 'Friends like these', *JFR*, 21 August 2003.
35. See also G. Kessler, 'A key back channel for U.S., Israeli ties', *WP*, 6 October 2010; M. Mazzetti and E. Schmitt, 'C.I.A. Agents in Libya Aid Airstrikes and Meet Rebels', *NYT*, 30 March 2011.
36. 'US–Arab intelligence co-operation', *JIAA*, 1 July 2007; see also 6.0, in this chapter; B. Harvey, 'CIA's Panetta Held Secret Talks on Syria in Ankara, Sabah Says', *Bloomberg*, 26 April 2011.
37. See also E. Lipton, N. Clark and A.W. Lehren, 'Diplomats Help Push Sales of Jetliners on the Global Market', *NYT*, 2 January 2011; W. Maclean, 'Espionage can help UK economic security – ex-spy chief', *Reuters*, 5 July 2011.
38. S. Aftergood, 'JASON: Can Climate Change Agreements be Verified?', *FAS_SN*, 26 January 2011; H. Schneider and G. Jaffe, 'Unrest tests Egyptian military and its crucial relationship with U.S.', *WP*, 30 January 2011; J.E. Keating, 'Does the CIA Need a Country's Permission to Spy on It?', *FP*, 13 April 2011.
39. R. Watson, 'Syria ends co-operation with US', *BBC*, 24 May 2005; R. Beeston, C. Philp and O. August, 'Britain re-establishes high-level intelligence links with Syria', *Times*, 19 November 2008; 'Turkey's intel severs ties with Mossad', *UPI*, and 'Pakistan urges more intel sharing with Britain', *AFP*, 26 October 2010.
40. S. Fidler and M. Huband, 'A Special Relationship?', *FT*, 6 July 2004.

41. K. Sengupta, 'Rights and wrongs of rendition: MI5 consults "ethical counsellor"', *Independent*, 6 March 2009.
42. 'UK "creates market for torture"', *BBC*, 28 April 2009; 'Rowan Williams in conversation with William Hague', *NewStatesman*, 17 June 2011.
43. See also D. Filkins, M. Mazzetti and J. Risen, 'Brother of Afghan Leader Is Said to Be on C.I.A. Payroll', *NYT*, 28 October 2009; J. Risen, 'Jailed Afghan Drug Lord Was Informer on U.S. Payroll', *NYT*, 11 December 2010.
44. See also F. Gardner, 'Egypt violence exposes secret tools of state repression', *BBC*, 4 February 2011.
45. J. Hughes-Wilson, 'The Realities of Intelligence Sharing in the International Environment', *RUSI*, October 2009.
46. 'UK torture intelligence "dilemma"', *BBC*, 26 March 2009; 'The dark pursuit of the truth', *Economist*, 30 July 2009; G. Corera, 'MI6 "is not complicit" in torture', *BBC*, and R. Norton-Taylor, 'Government officials dismiss fresh calls for torture inquiry', *GU*, 10 August 2009; D. Gardham, 'Britain "will act on torture intelligence"', *DT*, 10 November 2010; J. Daley, 'We can't afford moral certainty about torture', *DT*, 13 November 2010.
47. 'MI5's "torture" evidence revealed', *BBC*, 21 October 2005; R. Verkaik, 'British involvement in rendition of suspects will continue, says Straw', *Independent*, 13 April 2010; D. Riechmann, 'Bush to Veto Bill Banning Waterboarding', *HP*, 8 March 2008; see Chapter 2 sources.
48. 'Tortured Intelligence', *Times*, 11 August 2009; see also '7/7 inquests: MI5 "not responsible for attack"', *BBC*, 21 February 2011; P. Taylor, 'Musharraf "not told of UK's disapproval of torture"', *BBC*, 14 March 2011.
49. Based on information from a non-attributable source; P. R. Pillar, 'Don't Blame the Spies', *FP*, 16 March 2011; M. Mazzetti and S. Shane, 'Old Arab Ties May Harm New Ones', *NYT*, 17 March 2011.
50. UK ISC, *Renditions*, June 2007, p. 13, para.34.
51. See also W. Wark, 'No one to trust', *OttawaCitizen*, 25 November 2009; I. Cobain and F. Karim, 'UK linked to notorious Bangladesh torture centre', *GU*, 17 January 2011.
52. See also B. Raman, former additional secretary in the Cabinet Secretariat, Government of India, 'The dangers of intelligence cooperation', *rediff.com*, 18 July 2002; K. Brulliard and G. Miller, 'Pakistanis disclose name of CIA operative', *WP*, 9 May 2011; E. Pilkington and R. Norton-Taylor, 'Hackers expose defence and intelligence officials in US and UK', *GU*, 8 January 2012.
53. UK ISC, *Renditions*, p. 12, para.29; 'Israeli interrogators in Iraq – An exclusive report', *JFR*, 6 July 2004.
54. Norwegian and Dutch episodes in C. Wiebes' post 'intelligence liaison' on 'intelforum', http://archives.his.com/intelforum/2000-January/msg00144.html, accessed on 22 April 2012.
55. 'Conclusion: Q.' from ISC, Renditions, quoted in HMG, Government Response to the Intelligence and Security Committee's Report on Rendition, July 2007, p. 5.
56. R. Norton-Taylor, 'Linda Norgrove: secrets and lives', and A.A. Shaffer, 'British aid worker Linda Norgove hostage rescue: an expert's analysis', *GU*, and 'Hazards of hostage rescue missions', *BBC*, 11 October 2010.
57. See, e.g., several of the recent sources cited throughout this study.
58. See also B. Raman, 'When spooks of the world unite', *rediff.com*, 21 February 2003.

59. US Joint Chiefs of Staff, 'Joint Operation Planning', *JP 5-0*, 26 December 2006, p. II-7 and p. II-8; R. Karniol, 'Japan to set up liaison office in Washington', *JDW*, 4 October 2006; 'Hamas creates external intelligence arm', *JIAA*, 29 January 2010.
60. See also HMG, *Emergency Preparedness*, London: Cabinet Office, 2005, pp. 24–33; 'Civil Emergency Planning', *NATO*, January 2010; 'European Civil Protection', *EU*, January 2010.
61. 'Hayden Hearing', *CNN*, 18 May 2006.
62. Also a non-attributable source.
63. 'Portugal's top spy resigns in row over cuts to service', *BBC*, 18 November 2010.
64. Quoted in Scott (2004a, p. 322); Sir David Omand's comments in Presenter: Professor Peter Hennessy, 'Analysis: Secrets and Mysteries', *BBC Radio 4*, Broadcast: 19/04/2007; Hennessy (2007).
65. 'Secretary Rice Interview with James Rosen of Fox News Channel', *States News Service*, 10 July 2005.
66. 'Foreign Office will provide additional funding for the BBC World Service', *FCO.gov.uk*, 22 June 2011; C.S. Gray, *Hard Power and Soft Power*, http://www.StrategicStudiesInstitute.army.mil/, accessed on 22 April 2012; 'American "Smart Power": Diplomacy and Development Are the Vanguard', *State.gov*, 28 April 2011.
67. W. Pincus, 'Intelligence spending at record $80.1 billion in first disclosure of overall figure', *WP*, 28 October 2010.
68. J. Sims and B. Gallucci, 'Why intelligence-sharing can't always make us safer', *WP*, 8 January 2010; Chs 3 and 4 of Svendsen (2010a).
69. See also 'Recommendation' in the US National Commission on Terrorist Attacks Upon the United States of America, *9/11 Commission Report*, 22 July 2004, p. 415; K. O'Brien and J. Nusbaum, 'Intelligence gathering on asymmetric threats', *JIR*, 1 October/1 November 2000.
70. US Joint Chiefs of Staff, 'Electronic Warfare', *JP 3-13.1*, 25 January 2007, p. V-2.
71. Dame Stella Rimington, 'Security and Democracy – is there a conflict?', Transcript of the Richard Dimbleby Lecture by the Director General of the Security Service, 12 June 1994.
72. 'Sharing Information with Foreign Partners' in US Government, *National Strategy for Information Sharing*, October 2007, pp. 25–26.
73. For the importance of intelligence standards, see UK ISC, *Annual Report 2006–2007*, January 2008, p. 8.
74. ISO website, http://www.iso.org/ accessed on 22 April 2012; S. Bell, 'Technological standardization: security specific considerations', *RHS&RM*, 18 September 2008.
75. 'Apple "not tracking" iPhone users', *BBC*, 27 April 2011.

2 The Burgeoning Globalization of Intelligence: Intelligence cooperation in practice

1. W.J. Donovan, Director, *Memorandum for the President 2/8/52-ABD*, 7 November 1944, via CREST, CIA-RDP83-01034R000200090008-3 (2006/02/07); *Interpretive Notes of Memorandum for the President*, 18 November 1944, via *ibid.*, esp. p. 8; Troy (1981).

2. C. Dickey, 'A Thousand Points of Hate', *Newsweek*, 2 January 2010; D. Morgan, 'US official says security threat harder to tackle', *Reuters*, 22 September 2010; see also Iran's 'nuclear question' sources.
3. Several other sources have relevance: UK ISC, *Could 7/7 Have Been Prevented?*, May 2009, p. 8; 'Responsibility to protect: An idea whose time has come – and gone?', *Economist*, 23 July 2009; E. Ferris, *The Politics of Protection*, Washington, DC: Brookings, 2011; R. Thakur, 'UN breathes life into "responsibility to protect"', *TorontoStar*, 21 March 2011.
4. See also HMG, *Emergency Preparedness*, London: Cabinet Office, 2005; 'Understanding Civilian Protection: Concepts and Practices' and 'Exploring Civilian Protection', *Brookings/USIP*, 14 September 2010.
5. Sir David Omand, 'Securing the State: A Question of Balance', *CH*, 8 June 2010; D. Priest, 'Are We Safer?', *PBS FRONTLINE*, 18 January 2011.
6. 'UK "must log" phone and web use', *BBC*, 7 June 2009; 'The technology of surveillance', *BBC*, 21 May 2009.
7. See also, e.g., P. Baker, 'Bush Official, in Book, Tells of Pressure on '04 Vote', *NYT*, 21 August 2009; S. Waterman, 'Costs of War: Untimely "Terror"', *ISN_SW*, 29 September 2009.
8. See also F. Gardner, 'Saudi Arabia's shadowy connection', *BBC*, 1 November 2010.
9. See, e.g., D. Cole, 'The Torture Memos: The Case Against the Lawyers', *NYRB*, 56, 15, 8 October 2009; M. Alexander, 'Torture's Loopholes', *NYT*, 21 January 2010; C. Johnson, 'No sanctions for Bush lawyers who approved waterboarding, report will say', *WP*, 31 January 2010; M. Ratner, 'CiF: Bringing the "Bush Six" to justice', *GU*, 7 January 2011; 'The Zelikow Memo: Internal Critique of Bush Torture Memos Declassified', *US NSAr Update*, 4 April 2012.
10. Several other sources available, e.g.: E. Blanche, 'Testimony puts US "renditions" in spotlight', *JIR*, 28 May 2004; 'Statement by the Director of National Intelligence Mr. Dennis C. Blair', *ODNI*, 21 April 2009; J. Markon, 'Justice Dept.'s National Security Division draws mixed reviews 4 years', *WP*, 6 October 2010; 'Licence to Torture', *BBC Panorama*, 10 July 2009; J. Stein, 'CIA lawyer: U.S. law does not forbid rendition', *WP*, 4 November 2010; 'Malign Neglect', *NYT*, 21 May 2011; P. Finn and J. Tate, 'Justice Department to investigate deaths of two detainees in CIA custody', *WP*, 30 June 2011; L. Miller, '"The Interrogator:" A CIA insider's crisis of conscience', *Salon.com*, 3 July 2011; 'Terrorism and the Law', *NYT*, 16 July 2011.
11. Again, several other sources available: 'Mr. Cheney's Blind Spot', *WP*, 7 February 2009; R. Klein, 'Donald Rumsfeld ... Says Harsh Interrogation Helped "In Saving Lives"', *ABC*, 8 February 2011; F. Gardner, 'Anti-terror tactics "weaken law"', *BBC*, 16 February 2009; 'Illegal, and Pointless', *NYT*, 17 July 2009; see multiple media and NGO reports as published around end August to end September 2009; S. Shane and C. Savage, 'Bin Laden Raid Revives Debate on Value of Torture', *NYT*, 3 May 2011.
12. Several further sources: G. Corera, 'MI6 "is not complicit" in torture', *BBC*, 10 August 2009; 'MI5 chief defends torture stance', *BBC*, 16 October 2009; 'UK faces torture collusion claim', *BBC*, 24 November 2009; 'US "hid terror suspect treatment"', *BBC*, 10 March 2010; J. Sunderland, 'Intelligence cooperation: time to ask the hard questions', *HRW*, and S. Swann, 'Government

urged to publish "terror guidelines"' and '"Torture complicity": Key cases', *BBC*, 29 June 2010; I. Cobain, 'Britain joined renditions despite knowing of torture', *GU*, 26 April 2011; D. Casciani, 'Official guidance for questioning suspects held by foreign powers is unlawful', *BBC*, 28 June 2011; 'UK secret interrogation policy revealed', *Jurist*, 5 August 2011.

13. 'Cobra: The UK's emergencies team', *BBC*, 6 April 2006; 'Cobra meeting over Yemen explosives alert', *BBC*, 30 October 2010. On FEMA, http://www.fema.gov/ accessed on 22 April 2012; E. O'Keefe, 'FEMA still in "state of flux," needs to improve coordination efforts, watchdog says', *WP*, 17 March 2011; A.E. Kornblut, 'White House Situation Room lavished with attention following bin Laden raid', *WP*, 12 May 2011.
14. 'Torture claims: David Cameron announces inquiry', *BBC*, and 'UK involvement with detainees in overseas counter-terrorism operations', *UK Cabinet Office*, 6 July 2010; I. Cobain, 'Torture guidance does not breach law, says coalition', *GU*, 27 September 2010; I. Cobain and R. Norton-Taylor, 'Lawyers to boycott UK torture inquiry as rights groups label it a sham', *GU*, and S. Swann, 'Spy chiefs to give public evidence at rendition inquiry', *BBC*, 6 July 2011; 'Campaigners to shun UK inquiry into detainee "torture"', *BBC*, 4 August 2011.
15. See also K. Shebs, 'UK laws post-1997 "compromised" traditional liberties: rights group', *Jurist*, 20 February 2009; 'Anti-terror stop-and-search powers need "safeguards"', *BBC*, 15 June 2011.
16. See also E. Metcalfe, 'No trade-off on torture', *GU*, 5 August 2011.
17. A.O. Selsky, 'Ex-State Dept. lawyer decries torture after 9/11', *AP*, 27 March 2009; 'Shoulder to shoulder', *Economist*, 12 March 2009; B. Brogan and C. Hope, 'Investigation into MI5 torture allegations could jeopardise national security', *DT*, 18 July 2009.
18. See also L. Beehner, 'The United States and the Geneva Conventions', *CFR*, 20 September 2006; J. Belczyk, 'ICRC head calls for greater compliance with Geneva Conventions on 60th anniversary', *Jurist*, 12 August 2009.
19. See also, e.g., the 'Arar case' and its impact on US–Canadian relations: D. Cole, 'He Was Tortured, But He Can't Sue', *NYRB*, 15 June 2010. For other Canadian challenges, see also several media sources covering events over the years 2009–2011 relating to 'terrorism' and 'torture'-related allegations.
20. 'Australia returns passport to ex-Gitmo detainee', *AP*, and N. O'Brien, 'Habib cleared, gets passport back', *SMH*, 27 May 2011.
21. R. Brody, 'Europe must come clean on its involvement in CIA torture', *EuropeanVoice*, 24 September 2009; S. Hui, 'UK lawmakers call for new rendition flight ban', *AP*, 5 November 2009; C. Whitlock, 'CIA detainees again an issue in Lithuania', *WP*, 20 November 2009; A. Kingsbury, 'Milan's Botched CIA Caper and the War on Terrorism', *USN&WR*, 11 November 2010; J. Stein, 'Spanish prosecutors want 13 CIA agents arrested', *WP*, 13 May 2010; S. Bengali, 'Other countries probe Bush-era torture, not U.S.', *McClatchy*, 18 August 2010; D. Cole, 'Obama's Torture Problem', *NYRB*, 6 November 2010; S. Swann, 'What happened in Europe's secret CIA prisons?', *BBC*, 6 October 2010; 'German sues Macedonia over alleged CIA kidnapping', *AP*, 4 January 2011; A. Goldman and M. Apuzzo, 'At CIA, Grave Mistakes Led To Promotions', *AP*, 9 February 2011; 'CIA rendition flights did land in Ireland: Ahern', *BelfastTelegraph*, 17 December 2010; 'Amnesty says EU "failing" over

CIA renditions', *BBC*, 15 November 2010; J. Nylander, 'CIA rendition flights stopped by Swedish military', *SwedishWire*, 5 December 2010; 'CIA rendition deportee: "Sweden is responsible"', *TL*, 15 August 2011; 'Former top US diplomat questions DK govt. claims', *Politiken.dk*, 12 January 2011; S. Raghavan and J. Tate, 'African commission asked to take case challenging CIA rendition program', *WP*, 28 February 2011.

22. See also S. Aftergood, 'GAO Gains a Foothold in Intelligence Oversight', *FAS_SN*, 29 September 2010; 'Spy bosses to face Iraq inquiry', *BBC*, 16 November 2009; 'Who's to blame for torture? Lawyers probe logs', *AP*, 29 October 2010.
23. See also (1) US focus: B. Wittes, R.M. Chesney and R. Benhalim, 'The Emerging Law of Detention', *Brookings*, 25 January 2010; 'AG Holder defends prosecuting terror suspects in civilian courts', *Jurist*, 17 June 2011; J. Abrams, 'Patriot Act Extension Signed By Obama', *AP*, 27 May 2011; 'Overlooking Oversight', *NYT*, 4 June 2011. (2) UK focus: A. Hirsch, 'State and the individual – supreme court takes on weighty first case', *GU*, 5 October 2009; 'Lord Macdonald: UK "over-reacted after 9/11 attacks"', and D. Casciani, 'UK counter-terror review explained', *BBC*, 26 January 2011; UK ISC, *AR 2010–2011*, July 2011, pp. 42–43 and pp. 46–47.
24. P. Sands, 'Accountability is Coming to the USA', *University of Oxford Changing Character of War Newsletter*, 31 July 2009; 'The "James Bond" taking top job at MI6', *BBC*, 1 November 2009.
25. See also M. Bright, 'Laws of war out of date, says Reid', *JDW*, 4 April 2006; W. Maclean, 'UK seeks stronger cyber laws to fight attacks', *Reuters*, 5 July 2011.
26. See also 'US rebuffs Wikileaks Iraq torture claims', *BBC*, 25 October 2010.
27. See also, e.g., R. Winnett, C. Hope, S. Swinford and H. Watt, 'Guantánamo Bay terrorists radicalised in London to attack Western targets', *DT*, 25 April 2011; B. Wheeler, 'UK turns spotlight on far right after Norway killings', *BBC*, 25 July 2011.
28. A. Travis, 'CIA at work in UK, anti-terror chief tells MPs', *GU*, 2 October 2009; S. Mohammed and R. Verkaik, 'CIA given details of British Muslim students', *Independent*, 1 April 2010; D. Casciani and S. Swann, 'The UK's handling of detainees', *BBC*, 15 July 2010; '"Al-Qaeda assassin worked for MI6", secret cables claim', *BBC*, 26 April 2011.
29. See also P. Mercer, 'Australia plans new terror laws', *BBC*, 17 August 2009; 'Australia "faces permanent alert"', *BBC*, 23 February 2010; T. Lester, 'New phone tap powers planned for spy review', *SMH*, 13 May 2010; 'Three guilty of plotting Sydney army base attack', *BBC*, 23 December 2010; D. Welch, 'New laws to widen ASIO spy powers', *SMH*, 19 May 2011.
30. S. Shane, 'Rethinking Our Terrorist Fears', *NYT*, 27 September 2009.
31. H. Carter, 'Torture – new claim of secret UK complicity', *GU*, 26 July 2009; K. DeYoung and M.A. Fletcher, 'U.S. was more focused on al-Qaeda's plans abroad than for homeland, report on airline bomb plot finds', *WP*, 8 January 2010; '7/7 inquests: Coroner rules victims unlawfully killed' and '7/7 inquests: Key points from coroner', *BBC*, 6 May 2011; M.C. Babb, 'U.S. Condemns Attacks in Egypt, Nigeria, Iraq', *America.gov*, 3 January 2011; W. Maclean, 'Moscow shows airport ground attack risk', *Reuters*, 25 January 2011.

32. 'Terrorism Act 2006', *UK Home Office*, 2008; J. Manel, 'Court law "hinders terror police"', *BBC*, 5 July 2009; 'Yemen bomb plot: This is no time to tie up our intelligence agencies', *DT*, 1 November 2010. In the US, S.G. Stolberg, 'Senate Passes Legislation to Renew Patriot Act', *NYT*, 3 March 2006; E. Nakashima and C. Johnson, 'Partial Patriot Act Extension Is Approved by Senate Panel', *WP*, 15 October 2009.
33. D. Gardham, 'MI5 warned that bin Laden was planning attacks on morning of 9/11', *DT*, 5 October 2009; J. Burke, 'Guantánamo Bay files rewrite the story of Osama bin Laden's Tora Bora escape', *GU*, 26 April 2011; G. Corera, 'Bin Laden's Tora Bora escape, just months after 9/11', *BBC*, 21 July 2011; P. Finn, I. Shapira and M. Fisher, 'The Hunt: A different sort of search requires a new set of tactics', *WP*, 6 May 2011; E. Schmitt and T. Shanker, 'In Long Pursuit of Bin Laden, the Raid That Just Missed', *NYT*, 5 May 2011.
34. A. Koch, 'Counter-terrorism co-operation is endangered by US renditions', *JIR*, 16 September 2005; R. Grenier, 'The Spies Who Got Left in the Cold', *NYT*, 10 January 2010; P. Finn, 'ACLU files suit over 2008 detention and treatment of U.S. citizen in U.A.E.', *WP*, 20 August 2010.
35. See also C. Dickey, 'The New TNT', *Newsweek*, 29 September 2009; 'US warns airlines', *AP*, 6 July 2011; 'Allegations of UK Complicity in Torture', *The (UK) Government Reply to ... HL PAPER 152, HC 230*, October 2009; A. Hirsch, 'Liberty in the decade of extraordinary rendition', *GU*, 17 October 2009; S. Rosenberg, 'Risk of attack remains for Germany', *BBC*, 4 March 2010; 'Hague: UK to assess terror defences after Norway', *BBC*, 24 July 2011.
36. See also 'US links al-Qaeda to recent Europe terror plot – report', *BBC*, 1 October 2010; 'Europe put on jihadist alert', *JT&SM*, 8 October 2010; C. Bryan-Low, 'Fears of Extremism Widen to Scandinavia', *WSJ*, and P. Rogers, 'A rage unquenched', *OD*, 16 December 2010; 'Arrests halted "significant" terror plot – Lord Carlile', *BBC*, 21 December 2010; W. Maclean, 'After bin Laden, militants flood net with threats', *Reuters*, 27 June 2011; J. Madslien, 'Norway's far right not a spent force', *BBC*, 23 July 2011; 'Norway holds memorial services...', *AP*, 29 July 2011; 'Sweden advances plan to combat extremism', *TL*, 5 August 2011.
37. See also W. Maclean, 'Europe, U.S. juggle divergent tolerance of risk', *Reuters*, 5 October 2010; 'Western intelligence sees increased chatter on possible small-scale bin Laden revenge attacks', *AP*, and V. Dodd, 'Anti-terrorism: spotting extremists is as difficult now as six years ago', *GU*, 6 May 2011; D. Van Natta, Jr., 'Cities Nationwide Heighten Vigilance on Terror', *NYT*, 13 May 2011.
38. See also the comments of the Head of the Danish Defence Intelligence Service in the DDIS (FE), *Intelligence Risk Assessment 2010*, Copenhagen: September 2010, p. 5; see also the different 'informing, alerting and warning' distinctions drawn in P. Bobbitt, 'Global Warning', *NYT*, 13 October 2010; E. Sullivan, 'Color-coded terror warnings to be gone by April 27', *AP*, 27 January 2011.
39. '45-minute claim "a bit of colour"', *BBC*, 20 January 2010; G. Corera, 'Political questions remain over cargo bombs', *BBC*, 2 November 2010.
40. See also 'Keeping Personal Data Private', *NYT*, 25 November 2009; R. Woodbury, 'Regular citizens have big security role – Napolitano', *Reuters*, 6 November 2010.

41. S. Rotella, 'U.S. learned intelligence on airline attack suspect while he was en route', *LAT*, 7 January 2010; S.S. Hsu, J. Markon and K. Brulliard, 'U.S., Pakistan make arrests in failed Times Square bomb attempt', *WP*, 4 May 2010; 'Pakistan Detains Alleged NYC Bomber Accomplice', *GSN*, 1 October 2010. On military intelligence fusion cells, Capt. Paul Lushekno, U.S. Army, 'Best Defense' blog guest columnist, in T.E. Ricks, 'The answers for Afghanistan are pretty damn simple – and here they are, guys', *FP*, 28 September 2010.
42. M. Townsend, 'MI5 U-turn could hasten scrapping of system', and 'Control orders violate our deepest principles', *TO*, 7 November 2010.
43. R. Norton-Taylor, 'Another blow for MI5 secrecy', *GU*, 30 November 2010; R. Norton-Taylor, 'Supreme court was right to ban use of secret evidence by intelligence services', *GU*, 13 July 2011; 'US AG Holder invokes state secrets privilege in mosque surveillance lawsuit', *Jurist*, 3 August 2011.
44. 'Control orders are essential for security, warns peer', *BBC*, 3 January 2011; A. Travis, 'Control orders: home secretary tables watered-down regime', *GU*, 27 January 2011; 'MPs back control orders extension', *BBC*, 2 March 2011. On 'PREVENT' revisions, 'Updated anti-extremism strategy published' and M. Easton, 'Is fight against terror about violence or extremism?', *BBC*, 7 June 2011.
45. J. Ware, 'The battle for phone tap evidence', *Panorama*, and 'Intercept evidence "not viable"', *BBC*, 10 December 2009; A. Hirsch, 'Work starts to reverse ban on using intercept evidence in criminal trials', *GU*, 16 May 2010.
46. See also 'Law' definition of 'evidence' from *oxforddictionaries.com*, accessed: May 2011; S. Shane and B. Weiser, 'Judging Detainees' Risk, Often With Flawed Evidence', *NYT*, 24 April 2011; 'The Prisoners' Dilemma', *FP*, 25 April 2011; 'Gates: Bin Laden Intel Required Prompt Action', *Defense.gov*, 15 May 2011.
47. M. Mazzetti and H. Cooper, 'Detective Work on Courier Led to Breakthrough on Bin Laden', *NYT*, 5 May 2011; G. Corera, 'Dead or alive? US indecision over killing Bin Laden', *BBC*, 15 July 2011; K. Dozier, 'Osama Bin Laden Documents', *AP*, 8 June 2011.
48. Based on paraphrased information from a non-attributable source; UK ISC, *AR 2009–2010*, Norwich: TSO, March 2010, pp. 17–19; 'The secret services and torture: The price of secrecy', *Economist*, and N. Assinder, 'Gitmo Inmates Settlement: Why Britain Decided to Pay', *TIME*, 18 November 2010.
49. See also UK ISC, *AR 2008–2009*, Norwich: TSO, March 2010, pp. 41–47; E. Ballard, 'Head of UK's MI6 stresses importance of intelligence-sharing', *JDW*, 29 October 2010; ISC, *AR 2010–2011*, p. 6, para.16; B. Curry, 'CSIS ordered to hand over file in terror case', *G&M*, 21 October 2009; C. Freeze, 'Secret U.S. assessment of Omar Khadr disclosed by WikiLeaks', *G&M*, 25 April 2011.
50. M. Scherer, 'Ridge: Second Thoughts, but Not Second-Guessing', *TIME*, 31 August 2009; 'DC metro bomb plot', *BBC*, 11 April 2011; 'Final suspect convicted of JFK airport plot in New York', *BBC*, 27 May 2011.
51. 'Statement by the Office of the Director of National Intelligence Regarding United Kingdom Court Decision', *ODNI*, Washington, DC: 10 February 2010; 'Professor Michael Clarke: Judgment undermines intelligence co-operation', *Independent*, 11 February 2010.
52. UK HMG, *Government Response to the ISC's AR 2009–2010*, Norwich: TSO, March 2010, p. 3, para.G; R. Norton-Taylor, 'David Cameron moves to allay

US fears on intelligence', *GU*, 6 July 2010; R. Norton-Taylor, 'Intelligence agencies go to supreme court over ruling on secret evidence', *GU*, 23 January 2011; C. Woods, 'Government should stop state secrets being aired in court, says spy watchdog', *GU*, 6 January 2012.

53. See also 'US "hid terror suspect treatment"'; 'UK intelligence "unaware" of waterboarding interrogation', *BBC*, 9 November 2010; P. Taylor, 'Musharraf "not told of UK's disapproval of torture"', *BBC*, 14 March 2011. Further tensions, P. Reynolds, 'Wikileaks reveal US diplomats' view of UK as ally', *BBC*, 4 December 2010; S. Shane, 'U.S. Approval of Killing of Cleric Causes Unease', *NYT*, 13 May 2010.
54. UK HMG, Government Response to the ISC's AR 2008–2009, Norwich: TSO, March 2010, p. 7, para.W.
55. See also 'William Hague questioned on Pakistan drone strikes', *BBC*, 17 December 2011; 'Detainee abuse inquiry criticised', *BBC*, 6 January 2012.
56. UK ISC, *Inquiry into Intelligence, Assessments and Advice prior to the Terrorist Bombings on Bali*, December 2002; J. Burns and M. Huband, 'US considers security reforms along UK lines', *FT*, 5 May 2003; HMG, *Threat Levels*, Norwich: TSO, July 2006, pp. 369–386.
57. UK ISC, *AR 2003–2004*, June 2004, p. 27, para.92.
58. *ibid.*, p. 22, para.76; 'UK terror threat level is reduced', *BBC*, 20 July 2009.
59. S. Rogers, 'UK threat level: how has it changed over time?', and R. Norton-Taylor and A.Travis, 'MI5 and police reduce UK terror threat from "severe" to "substantial"', *GU*, 11–12 July 2011.
60. E. Alden, J. Burns, J. Harding and M. Huband, 'More security alerts disrupt main airports', *FT*, 15 February 2003; Burns and Huband, 'US considers security reforms along UK lines'; J. Rogin, 'Zelikow: Former buddies Tenet and Cheney once ran the war on terror', *FP*, 26 March 2010.
61. http://www.fas.org/irp/agency/ttic/, accessed on 22 April 2012; B. Feller, 'Obama chooses new counterterror chief', *AP*, 2 July 2011.
62. 'Transformation through Integration and Innovation', *The National Intelligence Strategy of the United States of America*, October 2005; White House, 'Guidelines and Requirements in Support of the Information Sharing Environment', *Memo. for the Heads of Exec. Depts and Agencies*, 16 December 2005; ODNI, 'Analytic Standards', *ICD No.203*, effective: 21 June 2007; A.E. Kornblut, 'Obama Team Says Zazi Case Illustrates Balanced Approach to Terror Threat', *WP*, 6 October 2009.
63. J. Weaver, 'Sept. 11 attacks helped forge bond between FBI and local police', *Miami Herald*, 11 September 2009; 'CIA Opens Counterproliferation Center', *GSN*, 19 August 2010; 'Integrated, National Network of State and Major Urban Area Fusion Centers', *ISE.gov*, 13 November 2010; K. Dilanian, '"Fusion centers" gather terrorism intelligence – and much more', *LAT*, 15 November 2010.
64. Quoted in R. Beeston and M. Evans, 'Straw is asked why no warning was given on Kenya', *Times*, 30 November 2002; R. Norton-Taylor, 'Kenya terror attack', *GU*, 30 November 2002; P. Conradi and E. Leahy, 'Britain "fails public" on issuing attack warnings', *TST*, 1 December 2002.
65. More on Australia, M. Wesley, 'Between Probity and Proficiency', *CSIS Commentary No. 88*, April 2006 (Unclassified). More on Canada, R. Morden, 'Spies, not Soothsayers', *CSIS Commentary No. 85*, Fall 2003 (Unclassified); S. McLuhan, 'Intelligence Sharing between Canada and the United States',

One Issue, Two Voices, 6, January 2007; 'Canadian and US build intelligence partnership', *JID*, 15 July 2008; L.C. Savage, 'Canada's biggest problem? America', *CFR*, 7 October 2009; G. Weston, 'Canada offered to aid Iraq invasion: WikiLeaks', *CBC.ca*, 15 May 2011.

66. CSIS, *Communicating with Canadians*, c.2006, p. 11; S. Chase, 'Watchdog urges Ottawa to create standalone foreign spy service', *G&M*, 25 October 2010; J. Davis, 'Spy overseer's office abolished', *Canada.com*, 26 April 2012.
67. Beeston and Evans, 'Straw is asked why no warning was given on Kenya'; 'UK stance over Manila threat questioned', *BBC*, 29 November 2002.
68. See also B. Wittes, 'President Obama needs more legal tactics against terrorists', *WP*, 14 May 2010; 'Republican lawmakers urge Obama to define terror suspect detention policy', *Jurist*, 20 July 2011.
69. 'Eight Years Later' and J. Zeleny and H. Cooper, 'Obama Details New Policies in Response to Terror Threat', *NYT*, 8 January 2010; K. Dilanian, 'U.S. counter-terrorism agents still hamstrung by data-sharing failures', *LAT*, 5 October 2010; 'Information Sharing With Fusion Centers Has Improved, but Information System Challenges Remain', *US DHS Report OIG-11-04*, October 2010; S. Aftergood, 'Information Sharing Still a Work in Progress', *FAS_SN*, 12 August 2011; G. Miller, 'Intel panels to take stock of post-9/11 progress', *WP*, 17 August 2011.
70. See also S.M. Patrick, 'Multilateral Achievements since 9/11', *CFR*, 19 August 2011.
71. J.D. Morton, 'Changing Threat to the United States', *National Security Institute Conference*, 2 May 2005; Svenden (2010a, pp. 40–42).
72. Quoted in 'The ideas interview: Faisal Devji', *GU*, 17 October 2005; Lefebvre (2003, p. 527); S. Yousafzai, R. Moreau and C. Dickey, 'The New Bin Laden', *Newsweek*, 23 October 2010; G. Miller and J. Warrick, 'Al-Qaeda threat more diffuse but persistent', *WP*, and J. Burke, 'What now for al-Qaida?', *GU*, 2 May 2011.
73. 'Paper 2: International Terrorism: The Government's Strategy', *UK Government's Strategic Objective*, 22 February 2005, pp. 1–2; 'RBS fined £5.6m for anti-terror failings', *BBC*, 3 August 2010; E. Nakashima, 'Money transfers could face anti-terrorism scrutiny', *WP*, 27 September 2010.
74. See also J. Marcus, 'US prepares for war', *BBC*, 16 September 2001.
75. J. Borger, 'CIA bought foreign cooperation against terrorism, says report', *GU*, 19 November 2005; Priest, 'Foreign Network at Front of CIA's Terror Fight'; S. Ross, '28 Nations Helped U.S. To Detain "Suspects"', *Scoop.co.nz*, 1 April 2010; K.R. Timmerman, 'A shadow warrior falls', *WT*, 17 April 2010.
76. Countries in the G8 are: the UK, the US, Canada, France, Germany, Russia, Japan and Italy – see also 'International co-operation strengthened in the fight against terrorism', *Hermes*, 12 May 2004; 'G8 Gleneagles 2005', *FCO.gov.uk*, 2006.
77. See also 'US Secret Service and Europol partners in fighting organised crime', *EUROPOL*, 7 November 2005; B. Bender, 'Secret Service strained as leaders face more threats', *BostonGlobe*, 18 October 2009.
78. 'Intelligence' refs in 'ASEAN's Stance on Terrorism', http://www.aseansec.org/12636.htm, accessed on 22 April 2012; J.C. Margeson, 'Cooperation Among Foreign Intelligence Services', *Contemporary Perspectives and Review*, 12 January 2007.

79. *UN Press Release*, 28 September 2001; K. O'Brien, 'Co-operation and co-ordination', *JDW*, 11 September 2002; W. Maclean, 'Al Qaeda Yemen wing poses special menace: U.N. official', *Reuters*, 23 November 2009; see also 'peacekeeping intelligence' (PKI) references.
80. 'OSCE promotes public private partnership in combating terrorism', *OSCE*, 1 June 2007; 'Effective anti-terrorism policy requires OSCE comprehensive approach, says Chairperson', *OSCE*, 14 October 2010.
81. See also 'Intelligence sharing in a wider NATO', *JIR*, 1 July 2002; 'New NATO intelligence centre opens in Britain', *UK MoD*, and 'Global Intelligence Assesment [*sic.*] for NATO Countries', *NATO SHAPE*, 16 October 2006; B. Tigner, 'NATO seeks more than a quick fix to its rapid-reaction command structure', *JIDR*, 8 January 2009; 'Improving information management for armed force operations', *NATO*, 23–25 March 2010; 'Situation Centre (SITCEN)', *NATO*, 2 December 2010; 'NATO nations deepen cooperation on intelligence, surveillance and reconnaissance', *NATO*, 17 March 2011.
82. See also 'Interpol says its databases are likely being used after bin Laden raid', *AP*, 11 May 2011.
83. 'International Co-operation: the United Nations, European Union and G8' in 'Paper 2', pp. 4–5.
84. See esp. 'The problems surrounding intelligence liaison in Western intelligence services' in Wiebes (2003); B. Bender, 'US worried by coalition "technology-gap"', *JDW*, 29 July 1998.
85. For problems in NATO, R. Boyes, 'Russian spy in Nato could have passed on missile defence and cyber-war secrets', *TST*, 16 November 2008; B. Tigner, 'NATO chief bullish on prospects for alliance reform', *JDW*, 18 October 2010; 'NATO Tells Turkey Not to Purchase Third-Party Antimissile Tech', *GSN*, 27 July 2011.
86. 'Regional organizations should co-ordinate actions more closely to tackle terrorism, says OSCE anti-terrorism chief', *OSCE*, 8 October 2009; 'New OSCE department for transnational threats established', *OSCE*, January 2012.
87. J. Dempsey, 'Doubts over second phase of war on terrorism', *FT*, 30 November 2001; F.T. Miko, 'Removing Terrorist Sanctuaries', *CRS*, 11 February 2005, p. 24; J. Hooper, 'Europe and US clash over terrorist investigations', *GU*, 22 October 2001; Ward and Hackett (2004).
88. See also D. Farah and D. Eggen, 'Joint Intelligence Center Is Urged', *WP*, 21 December 2003; D. Hamilton, 'Only cooperation can make us safe', *Letter from Washington – Global Europe*, 15 January 2010; 'Europe says Americans slow in sharing intelligence from Osama bin Laden cache in Pakistan', *AP*, 13 May 2011.
89. J. Lichfield, E. Nash, S. Castle and J. Bennetto, 'Europe must share terror intelligence', *Independent*, and R. Norton-Taylor and R. Cowan, 'Madrid bomb suspect linked to UK extremists', *GU*, 17 March 2004; 'European anti-terror body urged', *BBC*, 21 March 2004.
90. J. Burke and I. Traynor, 'Fears of an Islamic revolt in Europe begin to fade', *TO*, 26 July 2009; 'Al-Qaeda dejects recruits', *JT&SM*, 9 October 2009; 'Number of militant recruits on the rise: report', *AFP*, 18 October 2009; 'Al Qaeda Africa wing less a threat to Europe: official', *Reuters*, 17 November 2009.

91. 'Senior European intelligence officer' quoted in Huband, 'Debate gets down to the fundamentals'; M. Seiff, 'MI5 Chief won't share all secrets with EU', *UPI*, 14 September 2005; 'Bureaucracy blocks EU terror fight', *UPI*, 1 August 2005.
92. See also 'Mr Johnny Engell-Hansen (Head of Operations Unit, SitCen)', *Civil Protection and Crisis Management in the European Union – EU Committee, UK House of Lords*, 21 January 2009; P. Muncaster, 'European Commission talks tough on security', *V3.co.uk*, and W. Maclean, 'Europe must do more to counter plots-EU official', *Reuters*, 1 October 2010.
93. 'Conventions against terrorism', *UNODC*, 2006-2009; Amstutz and Teubner (eds) (2009).
94. 'Global action against terrorism', *UNODC*, May 2010.
95. J-P. Laborde, 'Combating Terrorism: The Strategy of the United Nations', *CH*, 13 April 2010; 'UN and international partners to combat trafficking and promote security in West Africa', *UNODC*, 16 December 2010; B. Ki-moon, 'Need for the UN is greater than ever', *SMH*, 31 December 2010.
96. Z. Brzezinski, 'Editorial: A New Age of Solidarity? Don't Count on it', *WP*, 2 November 2001; 'Friends like these', *JFR*, 21 August 2003; Ellis, (2009).
97. See earlier 'control order' sources.
98. Quoted in J. Burns, S. Fidler, M. Huband and H. Williamson, 'A catastrophic failure of intelligence', *FT*, 30 November 2001.
99. See also Guidelines for Identifying and Handling CIA Information During Declassification Review of Records from the Period 1946–54 (undated), p. 6, via CREST, CIA-RDP93B01194R001300060003-9 (2005/08/16).
100. Burns *et al.*, 'A catastrophic failure of intelligence'; Dame Eliza Manningham-Buller, DG MI5, 'The International Terrorist Threat and the Dilemmas in Countering It', *Speech at the Ridderzaal, Binnenhof, The Hague, Netherlands*, 1 September 2005.
101. See also J. Markon, 'FBI, ATF squabbles are hurting bombing inquiries, Justice official says', *WP*, 26 August 2010; A. Osborn, 'Russia's biggest spy agencies at war', *ST*, 26 December 2010; E. MacAskill, 'US agencies fought internal war over handling of detainees', *GU*, 25 April 2011.
102. W. Pincus, 'Settling an intelligence turf war', *WP*, 17 November 2009; K. Dozier, 'CIA chief spices up spy shop's image on reality TV', *AP*, 31 August 2010.
103. See also S.S. Hsu, 'FBI whistleblower trial highlights bureau's post-9/11 transformation', *WP*, 28 September 2010; D. Priest and W.M. Arkin, 'Monitoring America', *WP*, 20 December 2010; 'Elaborating on the security threat', *WP*, 15 January 2011; 'Backward at the F.B.I.', *NYT*, 18 June 2011.
104. Burns *et al.*, 'A catastrophic failure of intelligence'; D. Barrett and P. Hess, 'New papers detail FBI, CIA wrangle over detainees', *AP*, 30 October 2009.
105. Burns *et al.*, 'A catastrophic failure of intelligence'.
106. See also earlier refs and 'The Peacekeeping Situation Centre', *UN website*, February 2010. On PKI, see also J.A. Ravndal, 'Developing Intelligence Capabilities in Support of UN Peace Operations', *NUPI*, 22 December 2009.
107. See also, e.g., 'NATO agrees to split of Regional Command South, Afghanistan', *NATO*, 21 May 2010; L.C. Baldor, 'US, NATO were crucial, unseen hands in Libya fight', *AP*, 23 August 2011.

108. Burns *et al.*, 'A catastrophic failure of intelligence'.
109. A. Oppenheimer, 'Europe – Security one year on', *JTSM*, 13 September 2002.
110. 'Friends like these'.
111. D. Linzer, 'Rule against intelligence sharing is hurting war on terrorism', *AP*, 27 March 2004; Sims (2006, p. 205).
112. G. Corera, 'Changes needed in information sharing', *JIR*, 1 August 2003.
113. e.g., G. Thompson and S. Shane, 'Cables Portray Expanded Reach of Drug Agency', *NYT*, 25 December 2010; M. Schultze-Kraft, 'New Global Drug Policy Depends on Effective Governance', *ISN*, 27 July 2011.
114. M. Abbas, 'Joint drills help Iraq Kurd, Arab police thaw ties', *Reuters*, 26 November 2009; A. Nicoll (ed.), 'The ambitious UK–France defence accord', *IISS_SC*, 16, 41, 16 November 2010; 'British-Australian co-operation helps deliver extra armour to Afghanistan', *UK MoD*, 11 April 2011; 'New Joint Forces Command established', *UK MoD*, 2 April 2012.
115. UK ISC, *AR 2005–2006*, June 2006, p. 16, para.46.
116. See also 'Global action against terrorism', *UNODC*, 2009.
117. Morton, 'Changing Threat to the United States'; http://www.diplomaticsecurity.org/ and http://www.state.gov/m/ds/terrorism/c8583.htm, accessed on 22 April 2012.
118. W.R. Johnson, 'Clandestinity and Current Intelligence', *CSI*, 20, 3, Fall 1976, p. 56, via CREST, CIA-RDP78T03194A000400010019-1 (2005/01/26).
119. *Encyclopedia of Espionage, Intelligence, and Security – Volume I*, Thomson/Gale, 2004, p. 271; D. Benjamin, 'Statement Before the UN Counter-Terrorism Committee', *State.gov*, 20 July 2011.
120. US JCS, 'Multinational Operations', *JP 3-16*, 7 March 2007, p. I-7; 'US Army director places emphasis on collaboration', *JIDR*, 22 September 2010.
121. R.N. McDermott and W.D. O'Malley, 'Countering terrorism in Central Asia', *JIR*, 1 October 2003.
122. 'Stopping the Flow of Money to Terrorists', *Headline Archives*, 25 September 2003; Parker and Taylor (2010); 'Follow the Money', *NYT*, 8 December 2010; V. Pop, 'Commission to propose new EU anti-terrorism tool', *EUObserver.com*, 12 July 2011.
123. 'The prime minister's statement to the House of Commons on the bomb attacks in Bali', *GU*, 15 October 2002; R. Munavia, 'An Approach to Security Sector Reform in Asia' in *Security Sector Reform Moving the Agenda Forward*, March 2003; J. Stevenson in *IISS_AP*, 44, 367, London: IISS, November 2004, p. 67; L.C. Baldor, 'Terrorism threats in Indonesia worry US officials', *AP*, 7 November 2010; R. Epstein, 'Australian police help build secret hit lists', *SMH*, 27 December 2010.
124. 'The prime minister's statement'.
125. See also G. Corera, 'US reforms overlook threat from foreign intelligence', *JIR*, 1 June 2003; 'UK defends counter-terror "cuts"', *BBC*, 21 January 2010; R. Norton-Taylor, 'Al-Qaida faces a "crisis of credibility", claims former MI6 chief', *GU*, 5 July 2011.
126. US National Strategy for Combating Terrorism, February 2003, pp. 29–30.
127. P. Hennessy, 'Analysis: Secrets and Mysteries', *BBC Radio 4*, 19 April 2007.
128. 'Paper 2', pp. 3–4; 'Bali bombing suspect arrested in Pakistan', *JT&SM*, 8 April 2011.

129. Information from a non-attributable source; 'Britons arrested in Ibiza "drugs" raid', *BBC*, 30 August 2010; F. Gardner, 'UK helps Colombian commandos fight cocaine trade', *BBC*, 15 December 2010; 'National Crime Agency details outlined by Theresa May', *BBC*, 8 June 2011; 'Police database will share data on 15 million people', *BBC*, 22 June 2011.
130. P. Muncaster, 'FBI and Soca seek help from security teams', *V3.co.uk*, 21 October 2009; M.D. Kellerhals Jr., 'Nations Must Cooperate More to Combat International Crime', *America.gov*, 6 October 2010; A. Zwaniecki, 'Countries Cooperate to Confront Crime Rings', *America.gov*, 9 November 2010; 'Mexico acknowledges US intel agents, won't discuss reports they help interrogate, tap phones', *AP*, 8 August 2011.
131. Quoted in E. Keymer, 'Police official calls for cyber co-operation', *JDW*, 19 April 2011; S. Shane, 'F.B.I. Admits Hacker Group's Eavesdropping', *NYT*, 3 February 2012.
132. 'Paper 2', pp. 3–4; see also J. Glanz and D. Rohde, 'Report Faults Training of Afghan Police', *NYT*, 4 December 2006; J.M. Sharp and C.M. Blanchard, 'Post-War Iraq: Foreign Contributions to Training, Peacekeeping, and Reconstruction', *CRS*, 18 June 2007; 'UK help on Pakistan security body', *BBC*, 2 October 2009.
133. See also J. Burke, 'Channel tunnel is terror target', *TO*, 24 December 2006.
134. Quoted in R. Blitz, D. Sevastopulo and P. Spiegel, 'The politics of policing', *FT*, 17 August 2005; Shapiro and Suzan (2003); Kepel (2006, pp. 308–313); I. Traynor, K. Willsher and D. Walsh, 'French police arrest 11 Islamic terrorist suspects', *GU*, 5 October 2010; 'Desert storm brewing', *JT&SM*, 2 November 2010.
135. M. Arnold and J. Eaglesham, 'France warms to US foreign policy shift', *FT*, 2 August 2005; Andréani (2004); Svendsen (2010a, p. 43).
136. I. Cobain, 'Police call in foreign terror experts', *GU*, 12 July 2005; E. Sciolino and D. Van Natta, Jr., 'With No Leads, British Consult Allies on Blasts', *NYT*, 11 July 2005; A. Hayman, 'No warning, no links, no leads', *Times*, 20 June 2009; V. Burnett and J. Burns, 'Tip-off prevented terrorist attack ahead of election, claims Pakistan', *FT*, 14 July 2005.
137. See also UK ISC, *Could 7/7 Have Been Prevented?*; 'Greek–British intelligence services deny torture claims', *JTWR*, 12 January 2006.
138. D.A. Denny, 'Counterterrorism requires "all the tools of statecraft"', *TWF*, 15 September 2005.
139. G. Poteat and W. Anderson, 'Declaration of Interdependence', *Weekly Standard*, 5 May 2007.
140. R. Verkaik, 'British involvement in rendition of suspects will continue, says Straw', *Independent*, 13 April 2010; R. Norton-Taylor, 'Ministry of Defence ordered to disclose involvement in US-led rendition', *GU*, 19 April 2011; O. Bowcott, 'Judges accuse Ministry of Defence of stifling challenges over treatment of detainees', *GU*, 12 May 2011.
141. Based on paraphrased information from a non-attributable source; see also K. Dilanian, 'Alleged CIA operative criticizes "extraordinary rendition" of Muslim cleric', *LAT*, 26 May 2011; 'U.S. Prisoner of War, Detainee Operations Need More Advance Planning', *RAND*, 9 June 2011.
142. Maclean, 'Europe, U.S. juggle divergent tolerance of risk'; P. Rogers, 'Al-Qaida: Condition and Prospect', *OD*, 15 October 2010; S. Simon and

J. Stevenson, 'Al-Qaeda Takes It to the Streets', *WP*, 8 October 2010; 'U.S., Pakistan Continue Cooperation on Afghan Border', *Defense.gov*, 10 May 2011.

143. 'Cross Community Issues' in ch. 7 of *Report of the Inquiry into Australian Intelligence Agencies (The 'Flood Report')*, Canberra: Australian Government, 2004; Jones (2010b).
144. See also J. Marcus, 'Afghanistan conflict an "information war"', *BBC*, 11 February 2010; R.A. Falkenrath, 'From Bullets to Megabytes', *NYT*, 26 January 2011.
145. See also 'The new face of airborne SIGINT', *JIDR*, 30 November 2010; R. Sibley, 'Longtime bureaucrat takes helm of top-secret intelligence unit', *vancouversun.com*, 13 January 2012.
146. P. Beaumont, J. Jowit and M. Bright, 'Airline industry on frontline in al-Qaeda's war on the west', *TO*, 4 January 2004; A. Clark, 'Pilots criticise officials as more BA flights cancelled', *GU*, 13 February 2004; 'Foiling jet plot "a close thing"', *BBC*, 8 September 2009; 'Suicide in the sky', *JT&SM*, 9 October 2009; 'Conviction of BA worker reveals Al-Qaeda connection', *JT&SM*, 8 April 2011.
147. B. Woodward, 'Phone call pointed U.S. to compound – and to "the pacer"', *WP*, 7 May 2011.
148. See also R. Baer, 'The Risks of Relying on "Chatter"', *TIME*, 4 March 2009.
149. Much literature is available, see also: 'Spotlight on failed US intelligence', *BBC*, 12 September 2001; R. Norton-Taylor and J. Henley, 'Security agencies attacked over "stunning failure"', *GU*, 13 September 2001; D. Campbell and K. Connolly, 'FBI failed to find suspects named before hijackings', *GU*, 25 September 2001; E. Helmore, 'Agent blasts FBI over 11 September "cover-up"', *TO*, 26 May 2002; J. Burke, 'Warning of 9/11 attack "ignored"', *GU*, 8 September 2002.
150. See also D. Campbell, 'How the plotters slipped US net', *GU*, 27 September 2001.
151. See also A. de Botton, 'Does more information mean we know less?', *BBC*, 14 January 2011; T. Shanker and M. Richtel, 'In New Military, Data Overload Can Be Deadly', *NYT*, 16 January 2011; C. Freeze, 'Spying in the digital age', *G&M*, 28 July 2011; G. Slabodkin, 'Army fights to overcome data onslaught', *DefenseSystems*, 16 August 2011.
152. See also Farah and Eggen, 'Joint Intelligence Center Is Urged'.
153. For NSA 'overreach', C. Savage and J. Risen, 'Federal Judge Finds N.S.A. Wiretaps Were Illegal', *NYT*, 31 March 2010; 'Federal judge awards damages to Islamic charity in NSA wiretapping case', *Jurist*, 22 December 2010; C. Savage, 'F.B.I. Casts Wide Net Under Relaxed Rules for Terror Inquiries, Data Show', *NYT*, 26 March 2011; S. Aftergood, 'Domestic Intelligence Surveillance Grew in 2010', *FAS_SN*, 6 May 2011.
154. See also on NSA, J. Bamford, 'Who's In Big Brother's Database?', *NYRB*, 5 November 2009; E. Nakashima, 'NSA stops collecting some data to resolve issue with court', *WP*, 19 April 2010. For the UK, G. Corera, 'GCHQ denies giant database claims', *BBC*, 30 March 2010; P. Johnston, 'GCHQ: licensed to eavesdrop', *DT*, 27 August 2010; N. Collins, 'GCHQ: the most secretive service', *DT*, 26 August 2010; 'Tim Farron says Lib Dems would "kill" web monitoring plans', BBC, 8 April 2012.

155. 'US CIA chief visits India to discuss security', *AFP*, 2 October 2010; 'India, US pledge to boost intelligence sharing, cooperation in counterterrorism', *AP*, 27 May 2011.
156. 'Signals intelligence', *Sweden.gov.se*, 24 August 2009; see also 'NZ journalist discloses Israeli electron', *SMH*, 6 September 2010; 'Turkey to launch intelligence satellite', *Google News*, 3 October 2010; S. Ito, 'Japan shifts defence focus to China, N.Korea', *AFP*, 17 December 2010.
157. M. Huband, 'US, Britain and Australia to Build Global Intelligence Operation to Counter al-Qaeda', *FT*, 30 June 2004; D. Welch, 'New terrorism centre watching home-grown jihadis', *SMH*, 22 October 2010.
158. 'International Cooperation' in 'ITAC: The Integrated Threat Assessment Centre', *CSIS*, July 2006, p. 3; Government of Canada, 'The Integrated Threat Assessment Centre (ITAC)', *CSIS Backgrounder*, 13, April 2007; 'Liaison and Cooperation' in CSIS, 'Counter-Terrorism', *Backgrounder Series*, 8, August 2002, pp. 10–11; B. Campion-Smith, 'Spy agency CSIS warns of homegrown terror in Canada', *Toronto Star*, 12 May 2010; W. Wark, 'CSIS director blew himself up', *Ottawa Citizen*, 25 June 2010.
159. S. Fidler and M. Huband, 'A special relationship?', *FT*, 6 July 2004.
160. Denmark's 'Centre for Terrorism Analysis' in Tebbit, (2006, pp. iii–iv, paras.11–12); 'US charges two over "terror plot"', *BBC*, 27 October 2009; I. MacDougall, 'Norway al-Qaida case highlights terror strategy', *AP*, 17 July 2010; N. Larson, 'Cartoons made Scandinavia terror threat "much bigger": experts', *AFP/TL*, 3 January 2011; 'Somali cartoonist attacker found guilty', *Politiken.dk*, 21 June 2011; 'Dukaev – 12 years and expulsion', *Politiken.dk*, 31 May 2011; 'TV: Copenhagen video released in Headley case', *Politiken.dk*, 26 May 2011. For the German 'Coordination Center', F.T. Miko and C. Froehlich, 'Germany's Role in Fighting Terrorism: Implications for U.S. Policy', *CRS*, 27 December 2004, pp. 7–9; 'Germany minister now warns of terror attack threat', *Reuters*, 6 November 2010; see also 'Poland's anti-terrorist center gears up to protect Euro 2012', *AP*, 17 May 2011; Sweden's National Centre for Terrorist Threat Assessment (NCT), 'Suicide attack could happen again: prosecutor', *TL*, 3 June 2011; 'Indian cabinet approves new counter-terror centre', *BBC*, 12 January 2012.
161. See also L. Archer, 'War and Terror in the Noughties', *news.com.au*, 2 November 2009; P. Dorling, 'Spies step up co-operation with US, Japan', *SMH*, 22 January 2011; P. Dorling, 'Australia and the US agree on a spy satellite deal', *TAA*, 7 February 2011; B. Chandramohan, 'Revisiting the ANZUS Treaty through Self-Triangulation', *ISN*, 25 November 2010; D. Rothkopf, 'A Special Relationship on the Rise Down Under?', *FP*, 16 November 2011.
162. A. Koch, 'US looks to replace info sharing network', *JDW*, 16 November 2005; 'US to standardize on single intelligence radio', *JIDR*, 1 May 2002; Svendsen (2010a, pp. 27–30).
163. J. Kucera, 'US recognises the value of sharing', *JDW*, 16 February 2005; L. Sariibrahimoglu, 'US, Turkey increase co-operation to counter militants', *JDW*, 5 October 2005; G. Harris, 'Understanding Counterinsurgency Strategy', *ISN*, 8 November 2010; 'Intel, Ops Fusion Aids Warfighters, Roughead Says', *Defense.gov*, 23 March 2011; 'Stavridis Cites Value of Partnerships', *Defense.gov*, 29 March 2011.

164. E.g., P. Beaumont, 'Damning report on intelligence co-operation', *GU*, 7 March 2009; 'IBM involved in failed IT plan for UK spies-report', *Reuters*, 25 September 2009; '"Empire Challenge" Promotes Intelligence Interoperability', *Defense.gov*, 27 May 2011; 'UK develops systems to attack Afghan ISTAR information handling problems', *JIDR*, 25 August 2010; 'US Army seeks to improve timeliness of UAV intelligence', *JDW*, 18 March 2011; 'Europe's MAJIIC project expands ISR remit', *JIDR*, 30 March 2011; 'New US military satellite launched into space, will keep watch over missiles, battlefields', *AP*, 7 May 2011; 'Nimrod R1 aircraft in final flight for RAF', *BBC*, 28 June 2011; M. Hosenball, 'Nine Years After 9/11, Intelligence Sharing Is Still Hobbled', *Newsweek*, 24 September 2010; J. Bliss, 'Terror Intelligence Lacking 10 Years After 9/11, Chairmen Say', *Bloomberg*, 30 March 2011; J. Kouri, 'Intelligence agency cooperation still uncertain, say lawmakers', *Examiner.com*, 16 May 2011; 'Navy: Actually, Most Military Intel Systems Suck', *WB*, 15 June 2011.
165. M.A. Goodman, 'The decline of the independent CIA', *Baltimore Sun*, 18 October 2010; C. Howson, 'Don't Let BI Standardization Lead To Stagnation', *Information Week*, 6 December 2010.
166. 'Gates: "Perfect Fusion" Made bin Laden Raid Succeed', *Defense.gov*, 16 May 2011.
167. 'PM says Norway coopertaing [*sic.*] with foreign intelligence', *Reuters*, 23 July 2011; 'Norway attacks: "Breivik acted alone"', *BBC*, 27 July 2011; D. Barrett, 'British traders helped supply Breivik's arsenal of weapons', *DT*, 30 July 2011; 'Anders Behring Breivik indicted on terror and murder charges', *GU*, 8 March 2012.
168. S. Shane, 'A Year of Terror Plots, Through a Second Prism', *NYT*, 13 January 2010; G. Corera, 'MI5 head warns of serious risk of UK terrorist attack', *BBC*, 17 September 2010.
169. J. Bernstein, 'Nukes for Sale', *NYRB*, 13 May 2010; 'Bomb-making for beginners', *Economist*, 4 November 2010; S. Koelbl, 'Pakistan's Nuclear Bomb: "We May Be Naive, But We Are Not Idiots"', *Spiegel.de*, 28 June 2011 (A.Q. Khan interview); 'Pakistan Rejects Khan's Claims of North Korean Payoffs', *GSN*, 8 July 2011.
170. 'Straw says regime change "never" UK plan', *BBC*, 2 February 2011; for declassified files, 'The U.S. Prepares for Conflict, 2001', *US NSAr*, 22 September 2010; 'Was There Even a Decision?', *US NSAr*, 1 October 2010; J. Prados and C. Ames (eds.), 'Shaping the Debate', *US NSAr*, 4 October 2010.
171. 'Iraq Invasion Not Just About WMD, Chalabi Says', *GSN*, 4 October 2010; 'U.S. Erred in Focusing War Case on Iraqi WMD, Rice Says', *GSN*, 24 January 2011; R. Norton-Taylor, 'Tony Blair's promise to George Bush: count on us on Iraq war', *GU*, 21 January 2011.
172. R.J. Smith and J. Warrick, 'A nuclear power's act of proliferation', *WP*, 13 November 2009.
173. S. Shane, 'In Dispute With Iran, Path to Iraq Is in Spotlight', *NYT*, 30 September 2009.
174. UK Foreign Secretary, 'Countering the Proliferation of Weapons of Mass Destruction', *FCO*, 25 February 2004; 'Nuclear Proliferation: Today's Challenges and US response', *State.gov*, 24 February 2006.
175. E.g., A.F. Woolf, M.B. Nikitin and P.K. Kerr, 'Arms Control and Nonproliferation: A Catalog of Treaties and Agreements', *CRS*, 1 June 2007;

'New US/UK Collaboration to tackle Nuclear and Radiological Threats', *FCO*, 18 February 2008; W. Lippert, 'Geiger counting – Interpol's hunt for radiological and nuclear threats', *JIR*, 7 March 2008; 'UN Security Council Resolution 1887, Non-proliferation', *CFR*, 24 September 2009; J. Baetz, '10 nations urge new push for non-proliferation', *AP*, 30 April 2011.

176. S.S. Hsu, 'In WMD Report, U.S. Gets a C', *WP*, 9 September 2008; J. Cirincione and J. Wolfsthal, 'The Collapse of Bush's Nuclear Strategy', *HP*, 26 September 2008; M. Matishak, 'Obama Touts Administration's Nonproliferation Accomplishments', *GSN*, 26 January 2011.
177. Several sources available: 'Stopping illicit WMD traffic', *JID*, 29 September 2006; 'Six Moldovan "uranium smugglers" arrested', *BBC*, 29 June 2011.
178. A. Koch, 'Non-proliferation in global "crisis"', *JDW*, 12 March 2003; S. Jones, 'Non-proliferation leadership: Brussels or Washington?', *JIR*, 1 March 2002; M.B. Sheridan, 'At nuclear conference, U.S. expects little, gains little', *WP*, 31 May 2010.
179. B. Jones, 'The need for a new response to WMD proliferation', *Independent*, 16 August 2004; J. Tirone, 'Pakistani Bomb Got Help From UN as Lax Oversight Weakened Nuclear Watchdog', *Bloomberg*, 15 December 2010.
180. On the PSI, 'State Dept. Fact Sheet Outlines Proliferation Security Initiative', *State.gov*, March 2006; 'The Proliferation Security Initiative (PSI) At a Glance', *ACA*, June 2004; 'Proliferation Security Initiative', via http://www.globalsecurity.org/, accessed on 22 April 2012; N. Hordern, 'Stopping the flow of WMD', *JIR*, 1 August 2003; T. Ország-Land, 'Russia joins maritime security drive', *JT&SM*, 14 July 2006.
181. http://www.dfait-maeci.gc.ca/foreign_policy/global_partnership/menu-en.asp, Ministry of Foreign Affairs, Canada, April 2006; 'Global partners fail to agree on WMD strategy', *JID*, 2 September 2008.
182. UNSCR 1540 is: 'a non-proliferation resolution by which… all States shall refrain from supporting by any means non-State actors that attempt to acquire, use or transfer nuclear, chemical or biological weapons and their delivery systems', http://www.un.org/News/Press/docs/2004/sc8076.doc.htm, April 2006; W. Boese, 'Implications of UN Security Council Resolution 1540', *ACA*, 15 March 2005.
183. 'EU Non-proliferation and Export Controls', http://www.sipri.org/contents/expcon/eu_page.html, accessed: 7/04/2006; 'Joint statement by the European Union and United States on the Joint Program of work on the non-proliferation of weapons of mass destruction', 20 June 2005, http://www.usembassy.org.uk/terror576.html, in the UK website, accessed: 16 March 2006; 'EU Ministers Call for WMD Readiness', *GSN*, 8 November 2010.
184. 'Treaty on the Non-Proliferation of Nuclear Weapons (NPT)', http://www.iaea.org/Publications/Documents/Treaties/npt.html, accessed on 22 April 2012; 'Joint Statement on First P-5 Follow-Up Meeting to the NPT Review Conference', *State.gov*, 1 July 2011.
185. 'Convention on the Prohibition of the Development, Production and Stockpiling of Bacteriological (Biological) and Toxin Weapons and on Their Destruction', signed April 1972, in force March 1975, http://www.opbw.org/, accessed on 22 April 2012.
186. 'The Organisation for the Prohibition of Chemical Weapons (OPCW)', 1997, http://www.opcw.org/, accessed on 22 April 2012; E. Katz, 'Chemical

reaction – Challenges of the Chemical Weapons Convention', *JIR*, 1 June 2007.

187. This initiative helps cover WMD *delivery systems*. P. Kerr 'Code of Conduct Aims to Stop Ballistic Missile Proliferation', *Arms Control Today*, January/February 2003; 'ICBM [Intercontinential ballistic missiles] threat is growing, warns CIA', *JM&R*, 1 October 2001; A. Koch, 'USA fears "secondary WMD proliferation"', *JDW*, 5 September 2001; J.E. McLaughlin, 'Watch for More and More Medium- and Long-Range Missiles', *IHT*, 29 August 2001; CSIS, 'Proliferation Issues', *Backgrounder Series*, 7, April 2003; J. Pollack, 'Missile control', *BAS*, 1 August 2011.
188. On the 'Missile Technology Control Regime', http://www.mtcr.info/english/index.html, accessed on 22 April 2012; B. Gopalaswamy and J. Scheffran, 'Time for a missile test ban', *BAS*, 24 June 2009.
189. 'The Case for the Comprehensive Nuclear Test Ban Treaty', *State.gov*, 10 May 2011; 'Statement of the United States to the CTBTO Preparatory Commission', *State.gov*, 14 June 2011; J. Park, D.A. Grejner-Brzezinska, and R. von Frese, 'A new way to detect secret nuclear tests: GPS', *BAS*, 18 August 2011.
190. J. Medalia, 'Comprehensive Nuclear-Test-Ban Treaty', *CRS*, 18 September 2008; P. Baker, 'Arms Talks Now Turn to Short-Range Weapons', *NYT*, 24 December 2010.
191. 'US and Russia launch international nuclear security initiative', *JID*, 23 November 2006; M.B. Sheridan, 'New nuclear arms policy shows limits U.S. faces', *WP*, 7 April 2010.
192. 'UN probes US Syria reactor claim', *BBC*, 25 April 2008; 'Exercise on CBRN Defence at NATO HQ', *NATO*, 15 April 2008; R. Lee, 'Sharing Intel for a Nuclear Cooperation Regime', *ISN*, 5 August 2009; F. Pouladi, 'Iran accuses UN atomic watchdog of sending "spies"', *AFP*, 4 December 2010; R.F. Worth and D.E. Sanger, 'U.N. Nuclear Inspectors' Visit to Iran Is a Failure, West Says', *NYT*, 3 February 2012.
193. S. Wilson and M.B. Sheridan, 'Obama leads summit effort to secure nuclear materials' and D.E. Hoffman, 'As U.S. attempted to remove nuclear material from Chile, earthquake struck', *WP*, 11 April 2010.
194. A. Koch, 'Investigators suspect nuclear smuggling network is still active', *JIR*, 1 July 2006; 'US sanctions on AQ Khan "allies"', *BBC*, 12 January 2009; E. Lake, 'Nuke-smuggling network in demand', *WT*, 28 July 2010; E. Lake, 'Musharraf defends handling of Khan', *WT*, 14 November 2010.
195. S. Aftergood, 'A.Q. Khan Discusses Pakistan's Nuclear Program', *FAS_SN*, 8 September 2009.
196. M. Kakutani, 'Ground War: The Iraq Surge Grunts Knew', *NYT*, 6 October 2009.
197. See also 'U.S. and British Combined to Delay Pakistani Nuclear Weapons Program in 1978–1981', *US NSAr*, 27 July 2011.
198. See also 'CIA Delayed Breakup of Khan Network for Decades, Journalists Assert', *GSN*, 5 January 2011; 'U.K. Official Fired For Discussing Nuclear Probe', *GSN*, 24 August 2010.
199. J. Warrick (chair), D.Albright, R. Mowatt-Larssen and R. Wirtz, 'After the Khan Network', *Carnegie International Nonproliferation Conference Panel Transcript*, 7 April 2009; 'Three Swiss Engineers Charged With Aiding Khan Nuke Proliferation Ring', *GSN*, 13 December 2011; 'North Korea Using

Front Companies For Nuke Program, U.N. Panel Finds', *GSN*, 20 April 2011; J. Solomon, 'North Korean Pair Viewed as Key to Secret Arms Trade', *WSJ*, 31 August 2010.

200. R.J. Smith and J. Warrick, 'Pakistani scientist depicts more advanced nuclear program in North Korea', *WP*, 28 December 2009.
201. Fidler and Huband, 'A special relationship?'; 'How the US has investigated the Iraq war', *BBC*, 24 November 2009; Svendsen (2010a, pp. 116–158); 'Pre-war Iraq "not threat to UK", former MI5 boss says', *BBC*, 29 August 2011.
202. M. Huband, 'MI6 and CIA seek to draw a line under very bad year', *FT*, 23 December 2004; P. Heap, 'The truth behind the MI6 façade', *GU*, 2 October 2003; T.L. Friedman, 'Long Live Lady Luck', *NYT*, 6 November 2010; D. Welch, 'Terrorism border alert list is fallible, ASIO chief admits', *SMH*, 28 May 2011; 'Revenge of the Zombie Terrorist', *WB*, 9 June 2011.
203. 'The big lie', *SMH*, 19 June 2004.
204. 'Blair "unaware" of WMD threat', *BBC*, 4 February 2004; 'Blair accused over WMD evidence', *BBC*, 11 July 2004; Butler Committee (2004, pp. 137–8); P. Waugh, 'Ministers were repeatedly told that there were "huge" gaps...', *London Evening Standard*, 25 November 2009; A. Cowell, 'Blair's Book Reveal "Tears" but No Regrets on Iraq', *NYT*, 1 September 2010; S. Aftergood, 'Revisiting the Decision to Go to War in Iraq', *FAS_SN*, 18 October 2010; C. Woodhouse, 'No. 10 "warned not to meddle in intelligence during Kosovo war"', *London Evening Standard*, 25 January 2011; C. Ames, 'Intelligence experts tried to stop Iraq dossier exaggeration', *GU*, 20 May 2011.
205. 'Weapons dossier "sent back six times"', *BBC*, 6 June 2003.
206. See also 'UK "accepted" Iraq action in 2002' and 'Bush "hardened Blair Iraq stance"', *BBC*, 26 November 2009; 'Hoon denies Iraq war inevitable', *BBC*, 19 January 2010.
207. 'Q&A: The weapons evidence', *BBC*, 20 July 2004.
208. 'If British armed forces chiefs weren't seeing intelligence, who was?', *DT*, 5 September 2010.
209. However, see also 'Inquiry calls over Iraq dossier', *BBC*, 12 March 2009.
210. 'Campbell defends Iraq war dossier', *BBC*, 12 January 2010; 'Iraq inquiry: Campbell dossier evidence questioned', *BBC*, and R. Norton-Taylor, 'Iraq dossier drawn up to make case for war – intelligence officer', *GU*, 12 May 2011; C. Ames, 'Memo reveals intelligence chief's bid to fuel fears of Iraqi WMDs', *TO*, 26 June 2011; 'Iraq inquiry: Campbell "like an unguided missile"', *BBC*, 14 July 2011; 'Non-military options over Iraq neglected says diplomat', *BBC*, 12 July 2010.
211. 'No 10 defends spy chief Scarlett', *BBC*, 2 August 2004.
212. G. Corera, 'Death of the 45-minute claim', *BBC*, 12 October 2004; 'British Spy Agency Cleared Iraqi WMD Intel Under Pressure: Officials', *GSN*, 15 July 2011.
213. J. Blitz, 'Whitehall heard "drumbeats" of Iraq war', *FT*, 24 November 2009; 'Al-Qaeda link to Iraq "rejected"' and 'Iraq war eve WMD doubt revealed', *BBC*, 25 November 2009.
214. 'Iraq intelligence "not very substantial" says Prescott', *BBC*, 30 July 2010.
215. See also '"Curveball" Confesses to Lying on Iraqi WMD', *GSN*, M. Chulov and H. Pidd, 'Curveball admissions vindicate suspicions of CIA's former Europe chief' and C. Ross, 'CiF: Curveball and the manufacture of a lie',

GU, 15 February 2011; 'Powell Calls For Explanation on Faulty Iraq WMD Intelligence', *GSN*, and H. Pidd, 'Curveball doubts were shared with CIA, says ex-German foreign minister', *GU*, 17 February 2011; 'Secret U.S. mission hauls uranium from Iraq', *AP*, 7 May 2008.

216. 'International efforts to combat Al Qaeda terrorism', UK House of Commons Foreign Affairs Committee, *Foreign Policy Aspects of the War Against Terrorism*, Norwich: TSO, 2006, p. ev3, para.12.
217. See also 'Iraq war legality', *BBC*, 28 April 2005; 'Goldsmith admits Iraq legal shift' and 'Secrecy "frustrating" Iraq panel', *BBC*, 27 January 2010; R. Norton-Taylor, 'Blair shut me out, says former legal chief Lord Goldsmith', *GU*, 17 January 2011; 'Iraq inquiry "disappointed" by Bush-Blair note secrecy', *BBC*, 18 January 2011; P. Reynolds, 'Straw's Iraq clash with lawyers', *BBC*, 26 January 2010; 'Iraq my "hardest choice" – Straw', *BBC*, 21 January 2010; 'Iraq inquiry told about top diplomat's reservations' and 'Iraq inquiry publishes legal advice to Blair on war', *BBC*, 30 June 2010; 'Ex-MI5 boss says war raised terror threat', *BBC*, 20 July 2010.
218. 'Blix hopes for truth over Iraq', *BBC*, 5 June 2003; 'WikiLeaks Show WMD Hunt Continued in Iraq – With Surprising Results', *WB*, 23 October 2010.
219. 'Clegg clarifies stance after saying Iraq war "illegal"', *BBC*, 21 July 2010.
220. 'Iraq war "legitimacy" questioned', *BBC*, 27 November 2009; 'Blix says US arguments for Iraq invasion "absurd"', *BBC*, 27 July 2010.
221. See also S. Fidler, 'The way we war', *FT*, 7 June 2008; 'The Case of the Cash Hungry Contractor', *FBI*, 13 July 2009; D.E. Hoffman, 'Half a Ton of Uranium – and a Long Flight', *WP*, 21 September 2009; 'The New "Informal" Multilateral Era', *CFR*, 24 September 2009.
222. J. Acton, 'The myth of proliferation-resistant technology', *BAS*, 65, 6, November/December 2009; S. Mydans, 'Thailand Extradites Russian Arms Suspect to U.S.', *NYT*, 16 November 2010; D.E. Sanger and E. Schmitt, 'Pakistani Nuclear Arms Pose Challenge to U.S. Policy', *NYT*, 31 January 2011; E. Perez, 'Pakistani Man Charged Over Shipments to Pakistan's Nuclear Program', *WSJ*, 9 March 2011; 'U.S. Prepared to "Snatch" Pakistani Nukes, Report Claims', *GSN*, 4 August 2011; R. Weitz, 'Pakistan's nuclear security troubles', *JIAA*, 26 July 2011.
223. F. Frattini, G. Shultz and S. Nunn, 'The nuclear tipping point', *GU*, 23 September 2009; 'The Subject Was Nuclear Weapons', *NYT*, 25 September 2009; 'New Pentagon Intel Office to Target Nuclear, Extremist Threats', *GSN*, 24 April 2012.
224. '"Lack of thought" into Iraq war', *BBC*, 16 March 2008; H. Blix, 'CiF: Blair's blind faith in intelligence', *GU*, 28 January 2010; C. Hoyt, 'Semantic Minefields', *NYT*, 16 May 2010.
225. 'Tony Blair is recalled to give evidence', *BBC*, 8 December 2010; N. Morris, 'Labour put limits on Iraq Inquiry to keep the US happy', *Independent*, 1 December 2010; P. Reynolds, 'Brown: The unasked questions', *BBC*, 5 March 2010; 'Egyptian Leader Asserted Iraq had Bioweapons, Bush Memoir Says', *GSN*, 12 November 2010; 'ElBaradei Blasts Bush Administration Over Iraq War', *GSN*, 25 April 2011; 'Condoleezza Rice Discusses Iraq With Lawrence O'Donnell', *HP*, 6 May 2011; N. Watt, 'Chilcot to "heavily criticise" Tony Blair over Iraq war', *GU*, 31 July 2011.
226. 'Straw to face Iraq inquiry again', *BBC*, 8 February 2010; 'Gen. Hugh Shelton: Bush Officials Pushed For Iraq War "Almost To The Point Of Insubordination"

(VIDEO)', *HP*, 24 October 2010; M. Kakutani, 'In Bush Memoir, Policy Intersects With Personality', *NYT*, 3 November 2010; 'Rumsfeld Acknowledges "Misstatement" on Iraqi WMD' and 'Prewar U.S. Report Admits Lack of "Hard" Proof on Iraqi WMD', *GSN*, 8/9 February 2011.

227. W.J. Broad and D.E. Sanger, 'Restraints Fray and Risks Grow as Nuclear Club Gains Members', *NYT*, 15 October 2006; C.D. Ferguson, 'Next customer, please', *BAS*, 66, 6, 2010, pp. 36–42; 'Libya to give weapons to 1 mln people: state media', *AlertNet*, 20 March 2011; B. Klapper, 'White House wants NATO to hunt for [Libyan] WMD', *AP*, 26 August 2011; J. Marcus, 'Syria's long path to the Security Council', *BBC*, 9 June 2011.
228. 'US faces problems in future deterrence, says STRATCOM commander', *JM&R*, 4 October 2010; D. Byman, 'Deterring Enemies in a Shaken World', *NYT*, 4 September 2011.
229. 'North Korea's uranium programme heightens concern', *IISS_SC*, 17, 2, January 2011; W.P. Strobel, 'Struggle over Iran's nuclear capabilities playing out in courts, intelligence centers', *McClatchy*, 18 April 2010; J. Warrick, 'U.S. accuses Iran of aiding al-Qaeda', *WP*, 29 July 2011; 'Ahmadinejad: Iran No Intention Of Building Atomic Bomb', *Reuters*, 3 August 2011.
230. 'Growing Shadows in an Unsettled Iraq', *CFR*, 30 June 2011; M.S. Schmidt, 'Threat Resurges in Deadliest Day of Year for Iraq', *NYT*, 15 August 2011.
231. See also J. Palmer, 'Call for debate on killer robots', *BBC*, 3 August 2009; J. Markoff, 'War Machines: Recruiting Robots for Combat', *NYT*, 27 November 2010; 'Artificial intelligence: No command, and control', *Economist*, 25 November 2010.
232. M. Bronner, 'Former Iraqi Weapons Monitor Describes U.S. Abuse For First Time', *HP*, 23 July 2009; E. Cody, 'Europe's antiterrorism agencies favor human intelligence over technology', *WP*, 12 May 2010; 'Stan McChrystal's Very Human Wired War', *WB*, 26 January 2011.
233. B. Berkowitz, 'The Big Difference Between Intelligence and Evidence', *WP*, 2 February 2003.
234. 'Blair: Iraq war was test case', *BBC*, 5 January 2004; R. Norton-Taylor, 'Blair: man of faith, in his own ideas', *GU*, 23 April 2009.
235. Quoted in S. Jeffries, '"I Do Give A Damn"', *GU*, 6 October 2005.
236. 'The Proliferation Security Initiative', *State.gov*, March 2006; D.E. Sanger, 'U.S. Said to Turn Back North Korea Missile Shipment', *NYT*, 12 June 2011.
237. 'Experts meet in Omaha to consider ways to disrupt WMD transfers', *States News Service*, 21 March 2005.
238. J. Warrick, 'Intelligence Head Says Next President Faces Volatile Era', *WP*, 31 October 2008; S. Talbott, 'America's Next President Must Master the Tyranny of the Urgent', *FT*, 4 November 2008.
239. See also: 'Sanctions Still Useful in Iran Nuclear Standoff, Israeli Defense Chief Says', *GSN*, 13 December 2010; 'Intel Agencies Update Report on Iranian Nuclear Work', *GSN*, 16 February 2011.
240. 'International Cooperation Needed To Lower Proliferation Risks As Nuclear Energy Grows', *Science Daily*, 2 October 2008.
241. K.N. Luongo, 'Confronting twenty-first-century nuclear security realities', *BAS*, 10 November 2009; W. Burr, 'The United States and Pakistan's Quest for the Bomb', *US NSAr*, 22 December 2010.

242. P. Krugman, 'The Politics of Spite', *NYT*, 5 October 2009; further *vis-à-vis* the media: J. Weisberg, 'The O'Garbage Factor', *Newsweek*, 17 October 2009; N. Fenton, 'The Future of the News', *OD*, 18 November 2009.
243. S. Shane, 'Divisions Arose on Rough Tactics for Qaeda Figure', *NYT*, 18 April 2009; S. Shane and M. Mazzetti, 'In Adopting Harsh Tactics, No Inquiry Into Their Past Use', *NYT*, 22 April 2009.
244. See also Lt. Col. N. Freier, 'The Strategy Deficit', http://www.StrategicStudiesInstitute.army.mil/, accessed on 22 April 2012; L.H. Kahn, 'When science is lacking, good leadership is critical', *BAS*, 27 October 2009; Svendsen (2010b, pp. 367–399); R. Cooper, 'The Utility of Force by General Sir Rupert Smith', *TST*, 18 September 2005.
245. Many further sources exist: D. Priest, 'Bush's "War" On Terror Comes to a Sudden End', *WP*, 23 January 2009; 'Excerpts of Joe Biden speech', *BBC*, 7 February 2009; T. Starks, 'Intelligence Policy: New Perspective or Familiar Approach?', *CQ*, 16 February 2009; 'US drops "enemy combatant" term', *BBC*, 13 March 2009; Bono, 'Rebranding America', *NYT*, 18 October 2009; D. Cole, 'What to Do About Guantánamo?', *NYRB*, 14 October 2010; 'The new detainee dilemma', *WP*, 26 December 2010; P. Finn and A.E. Kornblut, 'Obama creates indefinite detention system for prisoners at Guantanamo Bay', *WP*, 8 March 2011; P. Finn and A.E. Kornblut, 'Guantanamo Bay: Why Obama hasn't fulfilled his promise to close the facility', *WP*, 23 April 2011; C. Savage, W. Glaberson and A.W. Lehren, 'Classified Files Offer New Insights Into Detainees', *NYT*, 24 April 2011; D. Leigh and J. Ball, 'Obama grapples with fate of last 172 prisoners', *GU*, and B. Wittes, 'Assessing the Risk of Guantánamo Detainees', *Brookings*, 25 April 2011; D. Cole, 'Guantánamo After Bin Laden', *NYRB*, 12 May 2011; P. Finn and D.Q. Wilber, 'Guantanamo detainees see legal progress reversed', *WP*, 1 July 2011.
246. S.S. Hsu and J. Warrick, 'Obama's Battle Against Terrorism To Go Beyond Bombs and Bullets', *WP*, 6 August 2009; 'Striking a Balance on Counterterrorism Policies', *CFR*, 10 August 2009; 'Editorial: Obama administration's anti-terror architecture: Too much like Bush', *LAT*, 10 April 2011; R. Tiron and T. Capaccio, 'Obama Chooses "Safe" U.S. National Security Team with Panetta, Petraeus', *Bloomberg*, 28 April 2011; K.J. Greenberg, 'The war on terror: Obama-style', *CBS*, 24 June 2011; K. DeYoung, 'Brennan: Counterterrorism strategy focused on al-Qaeda's threat to homeland', *WP*, 30 June 2011; 'Correcting for Bush's mistakes', *Boston Globe*, 16 July 2011; M. Zenko, 'U.S. National Security Strategy: Rhetoric and Reality', *CFR*, 15 August 2011; 'Obama's New Defense Plan: Drones, Spec Ops and Cyber War', *WB*, and W. Pincus, 'Brave new world of weaponry', *WP*, 5 January 2012.
247. M.D. Shear, 'At West Point, Obama offers new security strategy', *WP*, 23 May 2010; *US National Security Strategy*, Washington, DC: May 2010; 'Obama's NSS: Promise and Pitfalls', *CFR*, 28 May 2010; 'Next Generation NATO', *Carnegie Europe*, 17 May 2010.
248. Quoted in M. Dobbs, 'Myths of the missile crisis', *BBC*, 7 July 2008.
249. S.S. Hsu and J. Agiesta, 'Intelligence chief says FBI was too hasty in handling of attempted bombing', *WP*, 21 January 2010; N. O'Brien, 'Afghanistan intelligence flawed, says ex-CIA man', *SMH*, 31 August 2010; P. Apps,

'Security alone not enough to foil parcel bombers', *Reuters*, 3 November 2010.

250. P. Reynolds, 'The subtle shift in British foreign policy', *BBC*, 13 July 2007; R. Fox, 'A dangerous ally', *GU*, 8 September 2008.
251. See also 'National security and intelligence structure study', *UK Cabinet Office*, 28 January 2011.
252. See also 'National Security Council Established', *FCO*, and 'Establishment of a National Security Council', *Number10.gov.uk*, 12 May 2010; 'National Security Council hold "intensive" discussions on Afghanistan', *FCO*, 2 June 2010; M. Cavanagh, 'How to fix the National Security Council', *Spectator*, 15 May 2011; ISC, *AR 2010–2011*, pp. 4–5, paras.9–10; 'The first 18 months of The National Security Council', *IISS Voices*, 30 November 2011.

3 Overview: From intelligence to *globalized* intelligence during an era of terror, crises, and organized crime

1. See also V. Gienger and T. Capaccio, 'Iraq Troop Exit From Cities Shifts War Burden', *Bloomberg*, 30 June 2009.
2. 'Pre-emption' is defined as: applying *a priori*, rather than *post facto*, intelligence, law enforcement and/or security service crime defeating, disrupting and/or frustrating actions. See also 'UK "to boost diplomatic presence" around the world', *BBC*, 11 May 2011.
3. For the 'problems' confronted, 'Active Engagement, Modern Defence', *NATO Strategic Concept*, November 2010; *US National Security Strategy*, Washington, DC: May 2010; see also UK strategies in Chapters 2 and 5. Further insights, J. Gettleman, 'The Pirates Are Winning!', *NYRB*, 14 October 2010; 'EU Ministers Call for WMD Readiness', *GSN*, 8 November 2010; J. Ukman, 'New U.S. effort targets "transnational organized crime" as threat to national security', *WP*, 25 July 2011.
4. UK Association of Chief Police Officers (ACPO), 'Introduction to Intelligence-Led Policing', *ACPO Practice Advice*, 2007; 'Intelligence, Tips Drive Operations in Afghanistan', *US DoD*, 17 September 2010; 'Brigade Leaders Cite Value of Intelligence', *Defense.gov*, 2 May 2011; 'The Plan To Kill The Al Qaeda Leader', *Reuters*, 13 May 2011; C. McGreal, 'Al-Qaida document cache reveals toll of US drone strikes on Bin Laden's plans', *GU*, 3 May 2012.
5. See also 'Who is guarding the guardians of the law?', *TAA*, and I. Wing, 'Intelligence is not a dirty word', *Canberra Times*, 20 October 2008.
6. K. DeYoung and G. Jaffe, 'U.S. "secret war" expands globally as Special Operations forces take larger role', *WP*, 4 June 2010; R. Norton-Taylor, 'War is a bummer, chief of defence staff tells MPs', *GU*, 11 May 2011.
7. Acknowledgement is due to J.R. Wijnmaalen, NL, for highlighting the concept of 'action-research'; see also S. Aftergood, 'Document Exploitation as a New Intelligence Discipline' and 'Defense Intelligence and Counterinsurgency', *FAS_SN*, 24 May 2011.
8. See also Chapters 2 and 5; G. Ebbutt, 'UK must make better use of open source intelligence', *JIDR*, 3 February 2010; S. Condon, 'Homeland Security lacking "open source" intelligence', *CNET*, 12 September 2008; 'Taliban resistance "under-estimated" by Britain', *BBC*, 11 May 2011.

9. 'Globalising homeland security', *JID*, 6 October 2006; Hopper (2006, from p. 77); Roberts (2006, pp. 135–138); 'Pakistani Terror Organization Looks to Extend Reach', *GSN*, 6 April 2011.
10. 'Reforming the intelligence services: The spy game', *Economist*, 19 March 2005, p. 12.
11. See also UK ISC, *Renditions*, June 2007, pp. 11–13; J. Meserve, 'TSA to expand number of employees who will have secret clearances', *CNN*, 23 September 2010.
12. 'US-Arab intelligence co-operation', *JIAA*, 1 July 2007; 'Saudi says it warned of al-Qaida threat from Yemen', *AP*, 19 October 2010; D. De Luce, 'Jordan warned CIA about informer who bombed Afghan base', *AFP*, 20 October 2010; 'Al-Qaida targeting Morocco', *UPI*, 6 January 2011; W. Maclean, 'Tunisia puts focus on West-Arab security ties', *Reuters*, 16 January 2011; C. Dickey, 'Intelligence Test', *Newsweek*, 12 June 2011.
13. Sir Richard Dearlove KCMG OBE, 'Our Changing Perceptions of National Security', *Peter Nailor Memorial Lecture on Defence*, Gresham College, London, 25 November 2009; 'Post 9/11 shows dramatic improvement in policing, intelligence sharing in West', *Sify*, 6 October 2010.
14. I. Villelabeitia, 'Turkey appoints top spy as security threats shift', *Reuters*, 28 May 2010.
15. Cf. UK ISC quoted in Svendsen (2010, p. xix); L.C. Baldor, 'CIA rolls out plan to beef up spy techniques', *AP*, 26 April 2010; D. Oakes, 'Secret plan gives extra powers to spies', *SMH*, 28 April 2010; 'Japan "boosting intelligence on Chinese military"', *AFP*, 17 April 2010; M. Steen, 'Dutch spies boost operations abroad', *FT*, 20 April 2010; 'Fiji to set up new intelligence unit', *Radio NZ*, 9 May 2010; J. Keaten, 'France's spy service bulks up amid terror threats', *AP*, 28 December 2010; 'As troops withdraw, US spying scaled back in Iraq: official', *AFP*, 31 August 2010; 'Mexico, US open joint office to combat drug gangs', *AFP*, 1 September 2010.
16. UK ISC, *AR 2010–2011*, July 2011, p. 33, para.113 (emphasis added).
17. 'Experts discuss the [US] government's growing intelligence network', *WP*, 25 July 2010; R. Baer, 'Time to Tame Washington's Intelligence Beast', *TIME*, 19 July 2010; 'Medvedev gives more power to security services', *AP*, 29 July 2010; 'Breaking a Promise on Surveillance', *NYT*, 29 July 2010.
18. R.S. Mueller, Director, FBI, 'From 9/11 to 7/7', *CH*, 7 April 2008, pp. 4–6; 'FBI in Pakistan Investigating Possible Shahzad Ties', *CBS*, 8 May 2010; D. Gardham, 'British intelligence cracks trans-Atlantic terrorist network', *DT*, 9 November 2009; Svendsen (2012c).
19. ODNI, The 2006 Annual Report of the United States Intelligence Community, February 2007, p. 18.
20. D. Priest, 'Foreign Network at Front of CIA's Terror Fight', *WP*, 18 November 2005; S. Ross, '28 Nations Helped U.S. To Detain "Suspects"', *Scoop.co.nz*, 1 April 2010; K.R. Timmerman, 'A shadow warrior falls', *WT*, 17 April 2010.
21. UK ISC, *Renditions*, p. 56.
22. T. Weber, 'Davos 2011: We're all hyper-connected, now what?', *BBC*, 29 January 2011; 'Digital Nation', *PBS FRONTLINE*, 8 February 2011; Sir D. Omand, G. Herbert and N. Inkster, 'Controlling Information', *CH*, 13 April 2011; 'Bin Laden raid was revealed on Twitter', *BBC*, 2 May 2011; 'Darpa Apes Nick Fury to Map Social Networks', *WB*, 3 May 2011; M. Shiels, 'Cisco

predicts internet device boom', *BBC*, 1 June 2011; 'Facebook connections map the world', *BBC*, 14 December 2010; E. Messmer, 'Two new security books ponder: Just how vulnerable are we?', *pcadvisor.co.uk*, 4 January 2012.

23. See also B. Gourley, 'New IARPA Program Aims To Discover Tech Trends', *smartdatacollective.com*, 11 October 2011.
24. 'Mining social networks', *Economist*, 2 September 2010; 'Intelligence agencies urged to track social media sites', *BBC*, 28 January 2011; P. Apps, 'Should spies spend more time on Twitter?', *Reuters*, 8 February 2011; 'Intelligence chiefs: Social media helped in monitoring recent revolts', *CNN*, 16 February 2011; 'Armed Forces Minister – national security in the digital age', *UK MoD*, 5 July 2011; I. Mackenzie, 'Is technology to blame for the London riots?', *BBC*, 8 August 2011; J. Best, 'Police say Twitter and BBM gave riot "intelligence"', *ZDNetUK*, 17 August 2011.
25. 'Stan McChrystal's Very Human Wired War', *WB*, 26 January 2011; 'Network Would Link Defense Functions, People', *Defense.gov*, 25 April 2011; 'US looks to distribute humanitarian equipment network', *JIDR*, 21 April 2011.
26. Several examples exist: 'Sudan: the CIA's unlikely ally', *JID*, 18 May 2005; 'Strange partners: Sino-US intel co-operation', *JID*, 29 September 2008; 'Training courses for security personnel', Sri Lankan Ministry of Defence, 2006; B. Neild and agencies, 'UN Sri Lanka report alleges war crimes', *GU*, 26 April 2011; T. Harding, 'SAS trains Libyan troops', *DT*, 11 September 2009; A. Mostrous, 'Gaddafi regime fed names of jihadists to the CIA and to Britain', *Times*, 22 March 2011; W.A. Terrill, *The Conflicts in Yemen and U.S. National Security*, http://www.StrategicStudiesInstitute.army.mil/, January 2011; 'Bahrain touted intelligence ties with Israel: WikiLeaks', *AFP*, 8 April 2011; D. Leigh, 'China among regimes invited to interrogate captives', *GU*, 25 April 2011; 'Malaysia and Saudi Arabia sign security pact: report', *AFP*, 20 April 2011; I. Cobain and R. Norton-Taylor, 'MI5 "gave Libyan spies details of dissidents in Britain"', *GU*, 23 April 2012.
27. Quoted in Reveron (2006, p. 455); J.S. Porth, 'Like-Minded States Must Work Together To Thwart Terrorist Agenda', *TWF*, 24 April 2006.
28. 'Secretary Powell's Roundtable with European Editors', *FDCH*, 29 April 2004; D. Birch, 'Official: NATO and Pakistan sharing tactical plans', *AP*, 26 February 2010; 'China, U.S. Swapping Intel on North Korea, Cables Say', *GSN*, 11 April 2011.
29. S. Kaufman, 'U.S. Allies, Good Security Helped Prevent Cargo Bomb Attacks', *America.gov*, 1 November 2010.
30. This describes situations whereby individual interconnections may work more substantially on multiple more 'restricted' bilateral or trilateral bases, following a 'hub-and-spokes' model, and fashioned depending on the specific case or issue being focused upon.
31. Several further sources exist: 'ASEAN defense chiefs agree on intelligence sharing', *Jakarta Post*, 31 March 2011; T. Moss, 'Regional overview – Southeast Asia', *JDW*, 6 May 2011; 'ASEAN agrees data-sharing to fight Islamic militants', *Reuters*, 28 September 2011; 'ASEAN intelligence chiefs meet in Cambodia to further cooperation', *Philippine Star*, 27 March 2012. Also: A. Levine, 'Gulf countries agree to boost defence co-operation', *JDW*, 6 November 2008; 'CIS security, intelligence chiefs agree to deter religious extremism together', *Interfax*, 16 September 2010; 'Defense, intelligence officials from 13 countries

discuss security in Black Sea region', *AP*, 4 April 2011; 'Mediterranean perspective in focus at OSCE meeting on future of European security', *OSCE*, 14 October 2010; 'Enhanced diplomacy, regional organizations key to countering terrorism, OSCE expert tells security conference', *OSCE*, 18 February 2009; 'Intelligence-sharing centre opened in Kazakhstan', *UNODC*, 10 December 2009; 'Saharan states open military HQ', *BBC*, 21 April 2010; 'Maghreb states establish joint intelligence centre', *JIW*, 1 October 2010; L. Gelfand, 'Yemen and Djibouti tighten military ties in face of security threats', *JDW*, 27 October 2010; D.C. Giacopelli, 'Regional military force established to crack down on Lord's Resistance Army', *OD*, 18 October 2010; 'Agreement on Nordic declaration of solidarity', *Norway MFA*, 5 April 2011; 'Guatemala calls for Nato-style regional force', *FT*, 20 July 2011.

32. Much literature is available: For EU-ASEAN cooperation, see as discussed, e.g., in Svendsen (2008a, pp. 132–133). For Europe-Asia regional cooperation, 'OSCE, Asian Partners discuss comprehensive approach to security', *OSCE*, 18 May 2010; R. Muzalevsky, 'Kazakhstan – From Regional Discourse to Global Security', *ISN*, 21 March 2011. For EU-Africa developments, Vines (2010); R. Allani, D. Monan, N. Mueller, I. Puscas and L. Watanabe, 'EU and Maghreb Countries: Counterterrorism Cooperation', *ISN*, 6 April 2011. For African security cooperation, see Williams (2010).
33. 'ASEAN Efforts to Counter Terrorism', *ASEAN*, 2005 (emphasis added); Tan (2007); D. Mahadzir, 'Malaysia and US host intelligence conference', *JDW*, 26 September 2007.
34. E. Marat, 'Fissures in the force – Multilateral co-operation can only go so far', *JIR*, 1 June 2007.
35. 'US Secret Service and Europol partners in fighting organised crime', *EUROPOL*, 7 November 2005; K. Archick, 'U.S.-EU Cooperation Against Terrorism', *CRS*, 16 October 2006; 'US-EU Counterterrorism Cooperation', US-EU Mission, 2006; 'North Atlantic Council meeting with Political and Security Committee of the European Union', *NATO*, 21 May 2010; B. Vaughn, 'U.S. Strategic and Defense Relationships in the Asia-Pacific Region', *CRS*, 22 January 2007, p. 9; 'OSCE workshop promotes international co-operation, public-private partnerships to protect critical energy infrastructure from terrorist attacks', *OSCE*, 11 February 2010.
36. Acknowledgement is due to Robert Dover for valuably highlighting this phrase. For some 'unevenness', with different rates of development: 'Planned SCO exercises hit by Uzbek absence', *JIW*, 19 November 2009; 'Saudi ex-spy chief calls for anti-Qaeda centre in Gulf', *AFP*, 3 December 2010.
37. See also: E. Kaplan, 'Hometown Security', *CFR*, 2 January 2007; E. Kaplan, 'New York Spurs Counterterrorism Efforts', *CFR*, 28 December 2006; B. Hope, 'Police Counterterror Official Touts Importance of Local Role', *New York Sun*, 18 August 2006; M. Downing, 'Counterterrorism and Crime Fighting in Los Angeles', *WINEP*, 22 October 2009.
38. See also D. Linzer, 'In New York, a Turf War in the Battle Against Terrorism', *WP*, 22 March 2008; 'Christopher Dickey: Intelligence The NYPD Way', *NPR*, 15 February 2009; 'NYPD testing wireless dirty bomb detection system...', *AP*, 28 July 2011; M. Harwood, 'Vegas Tourism Board Pays for Fusion Center Intelligence Analyst', *SecurityManagement*, 12 August 2009; 'Organised Crime in New Zealand – Global threat, local impact', *NZPolice*, 23 September 2010.

39. e.g., 'Osama Bin Laden's death: Political reaction in quotes' and M.I. Khan, 'Bin Laden neighbours describe Abbottabad compound', *BBC*, 2 May 2011; 'Norway attacks: World reaction to bombing and shooting', *BBC*, 22 July 2011.
40. 'US-Arab intelligence co-operation'.
41. ODNI, The 2006 Annual Report of the United States Intelligence Community, p. 18.
42. ODNI, *The 2006 Annual Report of the United States Intelligence Community*, p. 18; 'Personnel Reimbursement for Intelligence Cooperation and Enhancement of Homeland Security Act', *Congressional Record (House)*, Washington, DC: 29 July 2008, pp. H7191–H7192.
43. See also ODNI 'Information Sharing Environment' (ISE) efforts, details via www.ise.gov/, accessed: August 2010.
44. Chief of SIS, quoted in UK ISC, *Annual Report 2006–2007*, January 2008, p. 12; W. Hughes and M. Pyman, 'Organised Crime: Joint Responsibility', *TWT*, April 2011, pp. 16–18.
45. 'ODNI Marks Five-Year Anniversary With Ceremony', *ODNI*, 21 April 2010; 'Neary on where the Office of the Director of National Intelligence went wrong', *WP*, 6 April 2010.
46. UK ISC, *AR 2006–2007*, p. 11, para.31.
47. See also 'Standing guard', *JIDR*, 13 January 2011; B. Wittes, 'Databuse', *Brookings*, 1 April 2011; 'US Army looks to deploy "Sense Through The Wall" devices', *JDW*, 1 April 2011.
48. A. Travis, series of articles in *GU*, 25 February 2009; S. Lee, 'Secret Ops, Domestic Spying OK – As Long As Someone's Watching the Watchmen', *Wired*, 21 September 2009; 'Body scanners raise privacy fears', *BBC*, 17 January 2010; 'Searching Your Laptop', *NYT*, 15 November 2010; E. MacAskill and R. Booth, 'CIA sought material on UN chief', *GU*, 4 December 2010; C. Savage, 'F.B.I. Agents Get Leeway to Push Privacy Bounds', *NYT*, 12 June 2011; M. Ward, 'Bruce Schneier warns "profits killing personal privacy"', *BBC*, 12 October 2010; L. Phillips, 'EU to force social network sites to enhance privacy', *GU*, 16 March 2011; K. Dilanian, 'Senator vows to block surveillance bill over privacy concerns', *LAT*, and 'Greens flag concerns with cybercrime reforms', *ABC (Australia)*, 2 August 2011.
49. See also W. Pincus, 'Agency Seeks Greater Surveillance Power Overseas', *WP*, 28 July 2007; J. Preston, 'Officers on Border Team Up to Quell Violence', *NYT*, 25 March 2010; 'Al Qaeda members land in Somalia from Yemen – government', *Reuters*, 7 April 2010; R.A. Best Jr., 'Securing America's Borders', *CRS*, 7 December 2010; 'France and Italy push for reform of Schengen treaty', *BBC*, 26 April 2011.
50. Priest, 'Foreign Network at Front of CIA's Terror Fight'; P. Dodds, 'Spy agencies infiltrate al-Qaida', *AP*, 5 November 2010.
51. Priest, 'Foreign Network at Front of CIA's Terror Fight'.
52. Priest, 'Foreign Network at Front of CIA's Terror Fight'.
53. See also 'Indonesian in court in Danish embassy case', *Politiken.dk*, 6 January 2011; 'Obama Meets With Rasmussen on Afghanistan', *Defense.gov*, 14 March 2011; 'Tasks of the Danish Defence Intelligence Service', *Danish MoD (www.fmn.dk)*, 4 April 2011.
54. S. Fidler, 'The human factor', *FT*, 7 July 2004; R. Solholm, 'Norway and Spain to share new satellite', *Norway Post*, 9 September 2010.

55. See also 'Panetta: Intelligence Community Needs to Predict Uprisings', *Defense.gov*, 11 February 2011; D.M. Luna, 'Combating Transnational Criminal Threats and Illicit Pathways', *State.gov*, 15 November 2011.
56. See also L. Siberry, 'Protective Security', *RHS&RM*, 13 August 2009; US DHS, *National Infrastructure Protection Plan*, 2009; S.S. Hsu, 'Airlines Set to Ask More of Passengers', *WP*, 13 August 2009; E. Nakashima, 'Terrorist watch list: One tip now enough to put name in database, officials say', *WP*, 29 December 2010; 'UK terrorism security threat level raised at airports', *BBC*, 7 January 2011; 'US warns airlines', *AP*, 6 July 2011; 'Homeland Security warns about potential threats against utilities', *CNN*, 20 July 2011; C. Williams, 'Airline passengers' sensitive data to be handed to US', *DT*, 19 April 2012; D. Cassata, 'A divided Congress confronts a rising cyberthreat', *AP*, 23 April 2012.
57. 'Swift rebuke', *WP*, 1 March 2010; T. Brokaw, 'The Wars That America Forgot About', *NYT*, 17 October 2010.
58. See also 'Comments and Suggestions on Draft ICS 77-2146/a', pp. 1–2, attached to H.H. Saunders, INR, US State Department, 'Subject: Comments on PRM-11 Task 2 Draft Paper', *Memorandum to:* ***, 5 May 1977, via CREST, CIA-RDP79M00095A000300020009-1 (2002/09/03).
59. See also T. Shorrock, 'The corporate takeover of U.S. intelligence', *Salon*, 1 June 2007; D. Priest and W.M. Arkin, 'Secret America' series, *WP*, 19–21 July 2010; 'Top Secret America: A note on this project', *WP*, 18 July 2010; C. Strohm, 'Gates moves to overhaul, boost military intelligence', *GovernmentExecutive.com*, 7 January 2011; J. Goldberg, 'In Defense of James Clapper', *The Atlantic*, 23 December 2010.
60. See also M. Alexander, 'I'm Still Tortured by What I Saw in Iraq', *WP*, 30 November 2008; J. Egeland and M. Aguirre, 'Torture: America's policy, Europe's shame', *OD*, 17 June 2009; 'UN rights experts call for end to secret prisons', *Jurist*, 4 June 2010; D. Leigh, J. Ball, I. Cobain and J. Burke, 'Guantánamo leaks lift lid on world's most controversial prison', *GU*, 25 April 2011.
61. See also S. Aftergood, 'Information Sharing as a Form of Secrecy', *FAS_SN*, 17 August 2009; E. Nakashima, 'Administration Seeks to Keep Terror Watch-List Data Secret', *WP*, 6 September 2009; 'Intelligence, Secrecy Drove bin Laden Operation', *Defense.gov*, 2 May 2011.
62. See also Speech by Sir John Sawers, serving Chief ('C') of the UK Secret Intelligence Service (SIS/MI6) (2009–date), 'Britain's Secret Frontline', *FCO*, 28 October 2010; N. Grimley, 'D for discretion', *BBC*, 22 August 2011.
63. See also W. Burr, 'More dubious secrets', *US NSAr*, 17 July 2009; S. Aftergood, 'Navy: Excessive Security Can Degrade Effectiveness', *FAS_SN*, 12 August 2011. On the 2010 'Wikileaks affair' and its impact, E. Nakashima, 'With better sharing of data comes danger', *WP*, 29 November 2010; E. Schmitt, 'White House Orders New Computer Security Rules', *NYT*, 6 October 2011.
64. See also S. Aftergood, 'U.S. is "Incapable of Keeping a Secret," Rumsfeld Concluded in 2005', *FAS_SN*, 15 July 2011.
65. See also R.A. Best Jr., 'Intelligence Estimates', *CRS*, 24 November 2010.
66. See also 'A Reminder for the F.B.I.', *NYT*, 26 September 2010; 'Pentagon says intel contractors went too far', *AP*, 29 October 2010.
67. 'Co-operation crucial for security, French Minister of State for European Affairs tells OSCE', *OSCE*, 20 May 2010.
68. See several references to WikiLeaks throughout this study – N.B. generalizations about the overall impact of WikiLeaks' disclosures are difficult to make

so can only be made on a case-by-case basis; see also 'FBI probes Anonymous intercept of US-UK hacking call', *BBC*, 3 February 2012. 'Expect more online attacks, Anonymous hackers say', *BBC*, 8 April 2012.

69. S. Aftergood, 'Meeting Set on Sharing of Classified Info', *FAS_SN*, 10 January 2011; S. Aftergood, 'Two Cultures of Secrecy and Disclosure', *FAS_SN*, 14 June 2011.
70. See also J. Ware, 'US forces kill Osama Bin Laden in Pakistan', *BBC Panorama*, 2 May 2011.
71. M. Landler and S. Shane, 'U.S. Sends Out Warning to People Named in Cable Leaks', *NYT*, 6 January 2011; J.S. Nye, Jr., 'The Right Way to Trim', *NYT*, 4 August 2011.
72. D. Murphy, 'Deadly Filipino "slugfest" between soldiers and Islamists', *CSM*, 13 August 2009.
73. See also 'US counter-terrorism assistance programmes', *JID*, 14 September 2007; 'US senator presses for more help on Mexico border', *Reuters*, 26 September 2010; N. Watt, 'Protests as UK security put at heart of government's aid policy', *GU*, 29 August 2010.
74. See also 'OSCE workshop in Vienna promotes international legal framework against terrorism', *OSCE*, 29 April 2010.
75. For more on related NATO SSR efforts, 'NATO adopts standards for intelligence, surveillance and reconnaissance', *NATO*, 12 October 2005; 'The Partnership for Peace', *NATO*, 8 March 2007; 'Progress on intelligence sector reform', *NATO*, 30–31 January 2008; T. Skinner, 'Joined-up thinking: NATO C4ISR', *JDW*, 9 July 2009; 'NATO celebrates World Standards Day', *NATO*, 20 October 2009; 'France and NATO to validate interoperability of Afghan surveillance capabilities', *NATO C3 Agency*, 15 April 2010; 'Sweden joins NATO combined battle labs', *JIDR*, 21 April 2010; K. Hoffmann, 'IBM Creates Cloud-Computing System for NATO Command', *Bloomberg*, 22 December 2010; 'Developing NATO's cyber defence policy' and A.F. Rasmussen, SG, '"Partners increase our security"', *NATO*, 25/26 January 2011.
76. See also 'The International Special Training Centre (ISTC) Exhibiting at Defendory International', *MarketWatch*, 7 October 2008.
77. R. Galpin, 'GCHQ staff teach "future spies" in schools', *BBC*, 9 March 2011; R. Marsh, 'Feds need more computer defense experts, Napolitano says', *CNN*, 22 April 2012.
78. See also S. Gallagher, 'Data standard gains traction for intelligence sharing', *defensesystems.com*, 26 February 2010.
79. '"Thousands" pose UK terror threat', *BBC*, 5 November 2007; 'Al-Qaeda "seek to infiltrate MI5"', *BBC*, 1 August 2009; 'Canada's spy chief warns of Cold War-level espionage', *AFP*, 15 June 2011; R. Solholm, 'Counter intelligence in Norway', *Norway Post*, 19 March 2010; 'We are vigilant about spying risk, says William Hague', *BBC*, 6 December 2010; 'Hague: UK is under cyber-attack', *BBC*, 4 February 2011; 'Poland intelligence officials says 300 foreign diplomats in country are agents', *CP*, 10 March 2011.
80. W. Pincus, 'Afghan intelligence contracts apply some limits', *WP*, 27 July 2010.
81. A.-M. Slaughter, 'Interests vs. Values? Misunderstanding Obama's Libya Strategy', *NYRB*, 30 March 2011.
82. See also 'Looking at security in a whole new way, with Partners', *NATO*, 15 February 2011; 'Needed Reform: The Case of NATO', *ISN*, 11 January 2012.

83. See also 'Nigeria and UK announce counter-terrorism co-operation agreement', *JIW*, 20 July 2011; 'Britain, Algeria boost counter-terrorism strategy: minister', *AFP*, 12 November 2010; 'UK-Bolivia agreement on drugs', *UK Home Office*, 20 January 2011; 'Russia's Lavrov urges anti-terror cooperation with British intelligence', *RIA Novosti*, 2 March 2011.
84. Also on New Zealand Intelligence, 'Director's Address to Wellington Intelligence Seminar', *NZ Security Intelligence Service (SIS)*, 23 May 2007; 'Landslide vote to bolster SIS surveillance powers', *Stuff.co.nz*, 5 July 2011; A. Young, 'US–NZ relationship has come of age, says Key', *NZ Herald*, 25 July 2011; 'US–NZ agreements to increase intelligence-sharing', *NZ Herald*, 2 May 2012.
85. See also 'Russia's global dreams', *JFR*, 15 October 2008; W. Pincus, 'Leaked memo offers insight to Russian security agencies', *WP*, 6 December 2010.
86. See also 'Strait spying', *JIR*, 28 March 2011; D. Grammaticas, 'China cyberwarfare capability a "formidable concern"', *BBC*, 11 March 2011; 'Prosecutors charge German man with spying on Uighur exiles for Chinese intelligence agency', *AP*, 8 April 2011; M. Moore, 'China opens string of spy schools', *DT*, 26 June 2011.
87. See also 'The Stockholm-Mogadishu connection', *JIW*, 12 August 2009; 'Muslim Council head "clueless" over terror plot', *TL*, 10 January 2011.
88. See also R. Douthat, 'Trust but E-Verify', *NYT*, 29 May 2011; 'Ministry of Defence foiled 1,000 cyber attacks says Fox', *BBC*, 7 June 2011.
89. See also T. Shanker, 'Pentagon Will Help Homeland Security Department Fight Domestic Cyberattacks', *NYT*, 20 October 2010.
90. 'Liaison and Cooperation' in CSIS, 'Counter-Terrorism', *Backgrounder Series*, 8, August 2002, p. 11.
91. 'Ivan Lewis on Today Programme', *FCO*, 4 August 2009.
92. See also 'Allegations of UK Complicity in Torture', *The (UK) Government Reply to ... HL PAPER 152, HC 230*, October 2009; 'MI5 chief defends torture stance', *BBC*, 16 October 2009; 'UK faces torture collusion claim', *BBC*, 24 November 2009; R. Verkaik, 'British involvement in rendition of suspects will continue, says Straw', *Independent*, 13 April 2010.
93. R. Norton-Taylor, 'MI5 faces crisis of credibility as torture denials are discredited', *GU*, 10 February 2010; 'MI5 denies Binyam case "cover-up"' and 'MI5 Binyam claim "ludicrous lies"', *BBC*, 12 February 2010.
94. P. A. Buxbaum, 'Achieving Intelligence Dominance', *ISN_SW*, 14 July 2010; 'Adapting America's Security Paradigm and Security Agenda', *National Strategy Information Center Report*, Washington, DC: July 2010.
95. See illustration in US Government, *National Strategy for Information Sharing*, October 2007, p. 5; 'Jordanian-US intelligence co-operation', *JID*, 9 November 2007.
96. Priest, 'Foreign Network at Front of CIA's Terror Fight'.
97. See also S. Shane and R.F. Worth, 'Earlier Flight May Have Been Dry Run for Plotters', *NYT*, 1 November 2010.
98. C. Freeze and J. Wingrove, 'Canada's top spy to retire in June', *G&M*, 14 April 2009; L. Khalil, 'Is New York a Counterterrorism Model?', *CFR*, 10 September 2009; J. Stein, 'NYPD Intelligence making FBI blue', *WP*, April 2010; A. Feuer, 'The Terror Translators', *NYT*, 17 September 2010; 'CIA denies helping police spy on New York Muslims', *CNN*, 26 August 2011; see other NYPD refs; 'Maldivian police monitor jihadist network activity', *JT&SM*, 10 January 2011.

99. See also 'Declassified UKUSA Signals Intelligence Agreement Documents Available', *NSA*, and 'UKUSA Agreement Release 1940–1956', *NSA/CSS website*, 24 June 2010; 'Newly released GCHQ files: UKUSA Agreement', *The (UK) National Archives*, June 2010; G. Corera, 'Details of secret US-UK "spying pact" released', *BBC*, and R. Norton-Taylor, 'Not so secret: deal at the heart of UK-US intelligence', *GU*, and R.G. Satter, 'Details of Cold War intelligence pact published', *AP*, 25 June 2010.
100. See also 'Q&A: Challenges, solutions faced by Western intelligence', *Reuters*, 28 October 2010.
101. See, e.g., 'Canadian [*sic.*] and US build intelligence partnership', *JID*, 15 July 2008; 'Canadian PM Harper and Obama to meet in Oval Office', *BBC*, 4 February 2011; 'Canada builds a future with equipment and experience gained in Afghanistan', *JIDR*, 12 August 2011; see also Chapter 2, including refs to Australia.
102. See also I. Morris, 'Location, location and how the West was won', *BBC*, 10 November 2010.

4 Anatomy and Introducing Theory: Why 'reach' matters

1. See also the list in E. Rosenbach and A.J. Peritz, 'Intelligence and International Cooperation' in their *Confrontation or Collaboration? Congress and the Intelligence Community*, Cambridge, MA: Belfer Center/Harvard Kennedy School, July 2009.
2. See also 'C. People and Culture' in 'The Changing Face of Intelligence: NATO Advanced Research Workshop – Report', *The Pluscarden Programme*, St Antony's College, Oxford, 9–10 December 2005, p. 3.
3. Frank Birch quoted in a memo to Denniston, Head of Government Communications and Cipher School (GC&CS) in C. Grey and A. Sturdy, *The Organisation of Bletchley Park 1939–1945*, OIG: 2006, p. 15.
4. 'Britain defends no-ransom policy', *BBC*, 1 February 2010; Sir David Omand, 'Securing the State: A Question of Balance', *CH*, 8 June 2010.
5. ODNI, 'Transformation through Integration and Innovation', *The National Intelligence Strategy of the United States of America*, October 2005. For Japan, K. Kotani, 'Recent Discussions on Japanese Intelligence Reform', *RUSI*, 10 July 2009.
6. See also 'Security Classification Guidance on Liaison Relationships with Foreign Intelligence Organizations and Foreign Security Services', *DCID 1/10*, effective 14 December 1982 (released: May 2002); US Joint Chiefs of Staff, 'Joint Operations', *JP 3-0*, 17 September 2006, pp. II-7-8.
7. See also R. Crilly, 'Pakistan seeks formal agreement with CIA', *Scotsman*, 10 July 2011.
8. See also US National Disclosure Policy (NDP), such as NDP-1 National Policy and Procedures for the Disclosure of Classified Military Information to Foreign Governments and International Organizations, overseen by the US National Disclosure Policy Committee (NDPC), 16 June 1992.
9. For intelligence liaison 'rules' and 'guidelines', Dame Stella Rimington, 'Security and Democracy – is there a conflict?', *Transcript of the Richard Dimbleby Lecture by the Director General of the Security Service*, 12 June 1994; *DCID 1/10*.

10. See also 'Allies and espionage', *JID*, 15 March 2002; 'British M.P.'s Link 10 Attaches to C.I.A.', *NYT*, 20 March 1975, and UPI, 'There Are No Friends In World of Spying', *Baltimore News American*, 16 March 1975 – both articles reproduced in CIA, *News, Views and Issues*, c.April/May 1975, via CREST, CIA-RDP77-00432R000100360006-2 (2001/08/08).
11. See also N. Paton Walsh, R. Norton-Taylor and E. MacAskill, 'The Cold War is over, but rock in a park suggests the spying game still thrives', *GU*, 24 January 2006; A. David, 'US spy in rendition trial: "I followed orders"', *AP*, 30 June 2009; B. Bouzane, 'Diplomatic expulsions often fly under radar, says intelligence expert', *Vancouver Sun*, 18 May 2011; E. Schmitt, T. Shanker and D.E. Sanger, 'U.S. Braced for Fights With Pakistanis in Bin Laden Raid', *NYT*, 9 May 2011.
12. Also information from a non-attributable source.
13. '"Iran arms smuggler" captured by Nato in Afghanistan', *BBC*, 24 December 2010.
14. See also US National Intelligence Council (NIC) and EU Institute for Security Studies (ISS), *Global Governance 2025: At a Critical Juncture*, September 2010, p. iii.
15. For an outreach process flow chart, 'Planning and Evaluating Outreach', p. 1, PDF via http://nnlm.gov/evaluation/guide/introduction.pdf, accessed on 22 April 2012.
16. See also 'The DDIS Intelligence Risk Assessment 2010', *Danish Defence Intelligence Service (FE)*, 13 September 2010 (2011 ed., 7 November 2011 [in English]).
17. HMG, *Government Response to the ISC's Report on Rendition*, July 2007, p. 6.
18. See also on diplomacy, Sir J. Greenstock, 'The rules of the game', *TLS*, 28 October 2009; Sir I. Roberts, 'The Development of Modern Diplomacy', *CH*, 23 October 2009.
19. G. Corera, 'MI5 expanding outside London', *BBC*, 11 December 2007; G. Corera, 'Real spooks with new role after 9/11', *BBC*, 4 December 2007.
20. Omand, 'Securing the State: A Question of Balance'.
21. See also E. Nakashima and C. Whitlock, 'With Air Force's new drone, "we can see everything"', *WP*, 2 January 2011; C. Savage, 'U.S. Pushes to Ease Technical Obstacles to Wiretapping', *NYT*, 18 October 2010; S.S. Hsu, 'Wiretap approvals decline, but Justice's workload is rising', *WP*, 25 December 2010. For other countries, I. Thomson, 'UK government to store all internet traffic data', *V3.co.uk*, 21 October 2010; 'Swedes' emails to be stored for six months', *TL*, 11 November 2010.
22. See also T. Pfaff, *Resolving Ethical Challenges in an Era of Persistent Conflict*, http://www.StrategicStudiesInstitute.army.mil/, accessed on 22 April 2012; L. Carmichael, 'US moral authority undercut by war on terror', *AFP*, 17 August 2011.
23. See also Omand, 'Securing the State'; H. Ullman, 'The (new) morality of the (new) American way of war', *UPI*, 6 July 2011.
24. See also 'Times: US advisers training Pakistani troops', *AP*, 23 February 2009; J. Forero, 'Colombia stepping up anti-drug training of Mexico's army, police', *WP*, 22 January 2011.
25. 'US-Arab intelligence co-operation', *JIAA*, 1 July 2007.

26. Also on 'altruism' and 'egoism', J. Lichtenberg, 'Is Pure Altruism Possible?', *NYT*, 19 October 2010.
27. For alleged 'under-reach', e.g., P. Stewart, 'U.S. lacks intel on North Korea, including succession', *Reuters*, 16 September 2010; P. Cruickshank, 'New info on post-9/11 hunt for bin Laden emerges', *CNN*, 14 September 2010; L. O'Donnell, 'Bin Laden living comfortably in Pakistan: CNN', *AFP*, 18 October 2010; '7 July bombers bought special mobile phones', *BBC*, 14 October 2010; 'Intelligence agencies struggling with problems', *Jakarta Post*, 14 March 2011.
28. See also J. Stewart, 'Global data storage calculated at 295 exabytes', *BBC*, 11 February 2011; J. Tessler, 'AT&T: iPhone Is A Strain On The Network...', *AP*, 21 April 2011.
29. See also, e.g., 'Interview: Tyler Drumheller', *PBS Frontline*, 15 February 2006.
30. See also, e.g., N. Rolander, 'Norway Police Warned of Rising Far-Right Extremism', *WSJ*, 23 July 2011; 'Mass rallies for Norway victims', J. Madslien, 'Unanswered questions in Norway tragedy', *BBC*, and S. Pogatchnik, 'Norway Police's Response To Massacre Criticized', *AP*, 26 July 2011; 'Norway attacks: "Breivik acted alone"', *BBC*, 27 July 2011; 'Meticulous planning of killer forces Norway officials to re-examine surveillance, controls', *AP*, 4 August 2011.
31. See also DDIS 2011, pp. 48–49.
32. For cases, e.g., 'Norwegians not under surveillance', *NP*, 7 November 2010; J. Isherwood, 'PET aware of monitoring since 2004', *Politiken.dk*, 16 November 2010; D. Landes, 'Prosecutor drops probe into US embassy "spying"', *TL*, 4 April 2011.
33. S.S. Hsu, 'U.S. Should Simplify Terror Warning System, Panel Says', *WP*, 16 September 2009.
34. See also B. Hoffman, 'We Can't Win If We Don't Know the Enemy', *WP*, 25 March 2007.
35. See also S. Kleinman and M. Alexander, 'Try a Little Tenderness', *NYT*, 11 March 2009. Cases: C. Johnson, 'Christmas Day bomb suspect Abdulmutallab providing intelligence, sources say', *WP*, 3 February 2010; W. Pincus and C. Johnson, 'Interagency teams can now question terror suspects', *WP*, 6 February 2010; A. Entous, 'Obama starts deploying interrogation teams', *Reuters*, 19 May 2010 S. Aftergood, 'DNI Advisors Favor Non-Coercive "Intelligence Interviewing"', *FAS_SN*, 27 August 2010; 'Intelligence Interviewing', *US Intelligence Science Board (ISB) Study on Educing Information*, April 2009; W. Pincus, 'Guide for interrogators tells how FBI agent turned suspect into informant', *WP*, 30 August 2010.
36. For 'reach-dynamics' in liaison interactions, P. Benson, 'In wake of CIA suicide bomber, what went wrong depends on who you ask', *CNN*, 25 October 2010; J. Hughes-Wilson, 'New Intelligence Blunders?', *RJ*, 155, 1, February 2010; 'Family of shot man criticises MI5', *BBC*, 26 February 2010; J. Burke and D. Walsh, 'Osama bin Laden wives interviewed by US intelligence', *GU*, 13 May 2011.
37. See also 'Norway commission to investigate Breivik attacks', *BBC*, 27 July 2011.
38. D. Gardham, 'Security and Intelligence services get funding to counter new threats', *DT*, 19 October 2010; D. Welch, 'Intelligence review stays on hold, fuelling upset', *SMH*, 6 January 2012.

39. See also 'Danish NH_4NO_3 laws to be checked', *Politiken.dk*, 25 July 2011.
40. See also C. Yates, 'Would you trust the human eye to spot a bomb?', *BBC*, 5 January 2010; 'U.S. Spies Want Algorithms to Spot Hot Trends', *WB*, 1 October 2010; '"Political correctness" fostered extremists', *BBC Today*, 27 April 2011.
41. For alleged 'overreach', e.g.: 'Councils "still abusing spy laws"', *BBC*, 21 July 2009; S. Lyall, 'Ever-Present Surveillance Rankles the British Public', *NYT*, and R. Evans, P. Lewis and M. Taylor, 'How police rebranded lawful protest as "domestic extremism"', *GU*, 25 October 2009; D. Bigo, 'The globalisation of counter-terror', *Le Monde Diplomatique*, 14 January 2009; 'We have a history of excessive use of intelligence, military resources', *Jakarta Post*, and 'Activists Warn of Anti-Terror Agency's Powerful Reach', *Jakarta Globe*, 12 September 2010; S. Aftergood, 'The New Nobility: Russia's Security State', *FAS_SN*, 13 September 2010; 'Police face legal threat over Birmingham "spy" cameras', *BBC*, 18 October 2010; J. Lichfield, 'Sarkozy accused of using security service to spy on journalists', *Independent*, and 'Spying and corruption in Colombia', *Economist*, 4 November 2010; 'France accuses Iran of violence at Tehran embassy', *BBC*, 16 November 2010; 'The intelligence services have grown too powerful', *Independent*, 17 November 2010; G. Tremlett, 'Wikileaks: US pressured Spain over CIA rendition and Guantánamo torture', *GU*, 1 December 2010; M. Slackman, 'Officials Pressed Germans on Kidnapping by C.I.A.', *NYT*, 8 December 2010; P. Yost, 'Gov't: Surveillance errors in few cases', *AP*, 3 December 2010; J. Massola, 'Report criticises spies' handling of secrets, as complaints against agencies rise steeply', *TA*, 15 October 2010.

5 Where Next? Suggestions for the future

1. Commentator Rocco Rosano, 'intelforum' post, 12 November 2000, http://archives.his.com/intelforum/2000-November/msg00130.html
2. See also R.A. Best, Jr., 'Director of National Intelligence Statutory Authorities', *CRS*, 16 December 2011.
3. See also M. Frankel, 'A Response to Ken Lieberthal's Report on the Intelligence Community', *Brookings*, 19 October 2009; 'Spooks Get New Workout Routine...', *WB*, 7 June 2011.
4. See also G. Miller, 'Obama praises CIA workers' role in bin Laden killing', *WP*, 18 May 2011; 'Gates: Bin Laden Mission Reflects Perseverance, Determination', *Defense.gov*, 27 May 2011; 'Panetta Discusses Security Challenges in Stratcom Visit', *Defense.gov*, 5 August 2011.
5. R. Woodbury, 'Regular citizens have big security role-Napolitano', *Reuters*, 6 November 2010.
6. See also K. Dozier, 'Building a network to hit militants', *AP*, 5 January 2011; 'ASIO to share collected intelligence with other government bodies', *SMH*, 2 March 2011; J.P. Bjelopera, 'Terrorism Information Sharing and the Nationwide Suspicious Activity Report Initiative', *CRS*, 28 December 2011.
7. J. Warrick and W. Pincus, 'CIA Finds Holes in Pre-9/11 Work', *WP*, 22 August 2007.
8. See also 'Bulgaria's Intelligence Services under Common Cap', *Standart News* (Bulgaria), 16 May 2010; 'DOD, Homeland Security Collaborate in Cyber Realm', *Defense.gov*, 3 June 2011.

9. US ODNI ISE, www.ise.gov; P. Benson, 'Director of national intelligence names deputy to boost collaboration', *CNN*, 20 August 2010; M. Hosenball, 'Nine Years After 9/11, Intelligence Sharing Is Still Hobbled', *Newsweek*, 24 September 2010; '[Program Manager] Opens Public Dialogue on the ISE at CSIS Forum', *ISE Blog*, 5 October 2010; T. Costlow, 'Bin Laden operation underscores importance of info sharing', *Defense Systems*, 2 May 2011; S. Aftergood, 'ODNI Describes Emerging Tools for Data Fusion, Analysis', *FAS_SN*, 10 May 2011; ODNI, *2010 Data Mining Report*, Washington, DC: 2011.
10. See also US ODNI, *The National Intelligence Strategy of the United States of America*, October 2005; J. Rollins, 'Fusion Centers', *CRS*, 18 January 2008; 'Unifying Intelligence to Protect Americans', *FBI.gov*, 12 March 2009.
11. 'War by Other Means', *RAND Counterinsurgency – Final Report*, Santa Monica, CA: RAND, 2008, p. 41; J. Stein, 'Obama Faces Gaping Holes in U.S. Intelligence', *Spy Talk*, and G. Bruno, 'Getting Smart on Intelligence Reform', *CFR*, 14 January 2009.
12. US Government, *National Strategy for Information Sharing*, October 2007; US ODNI, 'Subject: (U) Intelligence Information Sharing', *Intelligence Community Policy Memo. No. 2007-500-3*, 22 December 2007; ODNI, *Information Sharing Strategy*, 22 February 2008; R.A. Best Jr., 'Intelligence Issues for Congress', *CRS*, 6 July 2009; E. Sullivan, 'Officials See Rise In Militia Groups Across US', *AP*, 12 August 2009; T. McCulloch, 'Mind the gap', *JIR*, 11 February 2010; 'Lynn Opens Countertrafficking Command Center', *Defense.gov*, 19 April 2011.
13. 'Continued Progress in Reforming Intelligence', *ODNI*, 15 January 2009; 'Intellipedia Gurus Win 2009 Homeland Security Medal', *CIA.gov*, 8 October 2009; 'NATO pins hopes on image-sharing project to detect IEDs', *JDW*, 4 December 2009; F. Gardner, 'Tracking key terror suspects', *BBC*, 13 May 2011.
14. US ODNI, *The National Intelligence Strategy*, August 2009, pp. 12–13 and pp. 14–15; I.A.R. Lakshmanan, 'Al-Qaeda Hobbled by Improved Anti-Terror, Intelligence Efforts', *Bloomberg*, 30 September 2009.
15. ODNI, *2009 Data Mining Report*, Feb.–Dec. 2009, p. 6; K.N. Paul, ODNI Program Manager, 'Annual Report to The Congress', *ISE*, Washington, DC: July 2010.
16. K. Peterson, 'Intelligence Agents Borrow Wall Street Trading Technology', *WSJ*, 28 May 2010; 'Pentagon picks 11 firms for intelligence IT work', *Reuters*, 14 May 2010; S. Fritsch, 'Technology and Global Affairs', *ISP*, 12, 1, February 2011, pp. 27–45.
17. UK ISC, *Could 7/7 Have Been Prevented?*, May 2009, p. 8; Field (2009); P. Taylor, '7/7: No more locked doors', *GU*, 6 May 2011. In Australia, D. Welch, 'ASIO gets new wiretap powers in caring-sharing plan', *SMH*, 12 October 2010; D. Welch, 'New terrorism centre watching home-grown jihadis', *SMH*, 22 October 2010.
18. UK ISC, *AR 2008–2009*, March 2010, p. 8, para.20; UK ISC, *AR 2010–2011*, July 2011, p. 76, paras.257–258.
19. E. Keymer, 'Police official calls for cyber co-operation', *JDW*, 19 April 2011.
20. UK HMG, *Government Response to the ISC's Annual Report 2008–2009*, Norwich: TSO, March 2010, p. 7, para.V; Daun and Jäger (2006).
21. 'UK intelligence chief calls for greater collaboration', *JIDR*, 13 June 2011.

22. See also J. Morrison, 'Watching over our spies requires more intelligence', *TST*, 16 July 2006; A. Dowd, 'Canada promises better handling of terror cases', *Reuters*, 7 December 2010.
23. S. Rotella, 'U.S. learned intelligence on airline attack suspect while he was en route', *LAT*, 7 January 2010; S. Aftergood, 'Agencies Boost Surveillance of Classified Networks', *FAS_SN*, 14 March 2011; E. Montalbano, 'Government Eyeing Security Technology To Prevent Another Wikileaks', *Information Week*, 21 March 2011; S. Aftergood, 'DNI Orders "Integrated Defense" of Intelligence Information', *FAS_SN*, 23 March 2011; M. Ward, 'Tracking the internal threats', *BBC*, 6 April 2011; S. Aftergood, 'House Intel Bill Mandates Insider Threat Detection', 'Defense Employees Told to Report Suspicious Activities', and 'Total Number of Security Clearances Still Unknown', *FAS_SN*, 5/24/27 May 2011; 'Report clears spy agency, despite skirted rules', *CTV.ca*, 29 July 2011.
24. See also J.D. McCausland, *Developing Strategic Leaders for the 21st Century*, http://www.StrategicStudiesInstitute.army.mil/, accessed on 22 April 2012.
25. S. Vedantam, 'What the Bard and Lear Can Tell a Leader About Yes Men', *WP*, 19 March 2007.
26. See also '7 July bombers spotted on CCTV after exhaustive hunt', *BBC*, 13 October 2010.
27. See also S. Shane, 'Obama Faces a New Push to Look Back', *NYT*, 13 July 2009; D. Froomkin, 'Is Torture In America's Future As Well As In Our Country's Past?', *HP*, 4 July 2011; 'US review for 11 September attacks anniversary', *JIW*, 18 August 2011.
28. J. Steele, 'Only a full inquiry can avert another disaster like Iraq', *GU*, 24 January 2008; P. Reynolds, 'Iraq inquiry: tolerant or critical?', *BBC*, and P. Dodds, 'Iraq War Inquiry Set To Begin In Britain', *AP*, 24 November 2009; http://www.iraqinquiry.org.uk/, accessed on 22 April 2012; P. Biles, 'Iraq inquiry: The ten key moments from public hearings', *BBC*, 3 February 2011.
29. See also A. Sparrow, 'Opposition anger over 2011 date for Iraq war report', *GU*, 30 July 2009.
30. See also G. Hassan and A. Barnett, 'Britain's neo-liberal state', *OD*, 29 November 2008; 'Blair leak fears curbed Cabinet Iraq talks – O'Donnell', *BBC*, 28 January 2011.
31. R. Norton-Taylor, 'Advisers "regret" not warning Tony Blair enough about dangers of invading Iraq', *GU*, 19 January 2011; 'Iraq strategy made people "very unhappy" – ex-spy chief', *BBC*, 20 January 2011; 'Jaw-jaw, war-war and law-law', *GU*, 22 January 2011; 'Tony Blair was warned of "Iraq danger" by civil servant', *BBC*, 25 January 2011.
32. See, e.g., J.F. Burns, 'British Leader Rebuts Commanders' Concerns About a Long Libya Campaign', *NYT*, 21 June 2011.
33. See also J. Owen, 'Warning of "lone terrorist" threat', *Independent*, 26 June 2011; 'Cost of wars in Iraq and Afghanistan tops £20bn', *BBC*, 20 June 2010; D. Froomkin, 'Reassessing The Cost Of The Post-9/11 Era, Post Bin Laden', *HP*, 11 May 2011; 'Counting the cost', *JIR*, 9 June 2011; 'Can the Europeans Defend Themselves?', *NYT*, 14 June 2011.
34. See also on the UK Strategic Defence and Security Review 2010: S. Rayment, 'National security strategy's real test will come when the next shock arrives', *ST*, 17 October 2010.

35. '"Lack of thought" into Iraq war', *BBC*, 16 March 2008.
36. 'Blair: Iraq war was test case', *BBC*, 5 January 2004.
37. ODNI, *National Intelligence: A Consumers Guide*, 28 May 2009; R.D. Steele, 'Human Intelligence: All Humans, All Minds, All the Time', http://www.StrategicStudiesInstitute.army.mil/, accessed on 22 April 2012.
38. W. Pincus, 'As missions are added, Stratcom commander keeps focus on deterrence', *WP*, 30 March 2010; T. Shanker and E. Schmitt, 'U.S. Military Intelligence Puts Focus on Afghan Graft', *NYT*, 12 June 2010; 'The overgrowth of intelligence programs since Sept. 11', *WP*, 21 July 2010; 'Challenges, solutions faced by Western intelligence', *Reuters*, 28 October 2010; W. Maclean, 'After bin Laden, militants flood net with threats', *Reuters*, 27 June 2011; V. Dodd, R. Norton-Taylor and J. Halliday, 'MI5 joins social messaging trawl for riot organisers', *GU*, 15 August 2011; 'Why America's Spies Struggle To Keep Up', *NPR*, 11 January 2012.
39. Also, e.g., J. Doward, G. Hinsliff and M. Townsend, 'Confidential memo reveals US plan to provoke an invasion of Iraq', *TO*, 21 June 2009.
40. 'Misdirection of National Intelligence', *NYT*, 21 July 2010.
41. M. Zenko, 'Don't Rush the Afghan Debate', *CSM*, and H. Cincotta, 'Senate Vote Marks Next Step in Complex Effort to Close Guantánamo', *America.gov*, 30 October 2009.
42. 'Intelligence Community: Overview', *UK Cabinet Office*, October 2009; 'Improving the Central Intelligence Machinery', *UK Cabinet Office Briefing Paper*, July 2009.
43. UK HMG, *National Intelligence Machinery*, November 2010; UK ISC, *AR 2010–2011*, pp. 36–41; 'Supporting the National Security Council', *Recommendations Report of UK Cabinet Office Study*, 10 October 2011.
44. Epigraph to his novel *Howards End*, London: Edward Arnold, 1910.
45. See also S. Waterman, 'Connecting the Clichés', *ISN_SW*, 12 January 2010; E. Lipton, E. Schmitt and M. Mazzetti, 'Review of Jet Bomb Plot Shows More Missed Clues', *NYT*, 18 January 2010; 'Al-Qaida critic struggles to get name off FBI wanted terrorist profile', *AP*, 29 June 2011.
46. Capt. (Ret.) Patrick Hennessey, 'The Widening Gap between the Civilian and Military Worlds', *RUSI*, 14 December 2009.
47. See also 'What They're Looking For Inside Osama's Thumb Drives', *WB*, 6 May 2011.
48. e.g., R.S. Boyd, 'Feds thinking outside the box to plug intelligence gaps', *McClatchy*, 30 March 2010; US National Intelligence Council (NIC) and EU Institute for Security Studies (ISS), *Global Governance 2025: At a Critical Juncture*, September 2010.
49. See also 'Risk Communication in Security Policy', *CSS Analyses*, 62, October 2009; J. Giroux, 'We all have a role to play', *FrontLine Security*, Summer 2009, pp. 24–27; S. Kaufman, 'America Must Lead Through Engagement, Obama Says', *America.gov*, 27 January 2010; M.D. Kellerhals, Jr., 'Obama Reaches Out to Muslim World', *America.gov*, 9 November 2010; P. S. Goodman, 'In Case of Emergency: What Not to Do', *NYT*, 21 August 2010; K. Nguyen, 'In disasters, it's good to talk but harder to listen', *Alert Net*, 19 January 2011.
50. See also M.L. Wald, 'Disaster Plan Problems Found at U.S. Nuclear Plants', *NYT*, 12 May 2011; 'Virtual Worlds Form Defense Training Frontier', *Defense.gov*, 9 May 2011.

51. S. Shane, 'State Dept. Daily Is Window on a Jittery Planet', *NYT*, 6 December 2010; R. Hardy, 'Will Osama Bin Laden continue to haunt the US?', *BBC*, and J. Borger, 'After Osama Bin Laden, is the world a safer place?', *GU*, 2 May 2011; 'Operational Uncertainties Require Flexibility, Gates Says', *Defense.gov*, 6 May 2011; L. Sly, 'Reversals challenge hope of Arab Spring', *WP*, 13 May 2011.
52. See also '"Reaching Out" – Promoting Community Engagement', and 'A New Approach to Counter-Radicalization', *CFR*, 1 April 2011; A. McDuffee, 'Google Ideas think tank gathering former extremists to battle radicalization', *WP*, 24 June 2011.
53. 'Spy Agency Wants Videogame to Help Think Straight', *WB*, 26 January 2011; 'DARPA reveals new angle on holographic displays', *JIDR*, 6 April 2011; M. Mazzetti, 'Obama Said to Fault Spy Agencies' Mideast Forecasting', *NYT*, 4 February 2011.
54. P. Rogers, 'A new military paradigm', *OD*, 6 January 2011.
55. See also J. Solana and M. Kaldor, 'Time for the Human Approach', *OD*, 17 November 2010; R.D. Kaplan, 'The Humanist in the Foxhole', *NYT*, 14 June 2011.
56. See also A. Giridharadas, 'Are Metrics Blinding Our Perception?', *NYT*, 21 November 2009; C. Thompson, 'Can Game Theory Predict When Iran Will Get the Bomb?', *NYT*, 16 August 2009; J.M. Broder, M.L. Wald and T. Zeller Jr., 'At U.S. Nuclear Sites, Preparing for the Unlikely', *NYT*, 28 March 2011.
57. J. Waldron, 'Reality Check', *LRB*, 10 April 2008; A. Holland, 'Checking Blair's "Calculus of Risk"', *OD*, 2 February 2010; W. Pincus and E. O'Keefe, 'Anti-terrorism chief rebukes politicians who use cases as talking points', *WP*, 8 February 2010; Hood *et al.* (2004, pp. 59–144).
58. See also T. Hegghammer, 'Jihadi studies', *TLS*, 2 April 2008; P. Finn, 'Most Guantanamo detainees low-level fighters, task force report says', *WP*, 29 May 2010.
59. See also W.J. Broad, 'U.S. Rethinks Strategy for the Unthinkable', *NYT*, 15 December 2010.
60. See also B. Carey, 'Teasing Out Policy Insight From a Character Profile', *NYT*, 28 March 2011; '[UN] Operational Guidelines on the Protection of Persons in Situations of Natural Disasters', *Brookings*, 10 January 2011.
61. '"Kinetic" is defined as involving a spectrum of associated activities, ranging from moving quickly and firmly against targets and suspects – not least during their disruption and interdiction – to including, but not exclusively meaning, "killing". Proportionality and breadth and extent of response questions also figure in the overall equation' – Svendsen (2010a, p. 207, n. 502).
62. See also 'FBI to play larger role in US counter-terror ops: report', *AFP*, 28 May 2009.
63. See also 'MoD "must adapt" to new threats', *BBC*, 15 May 2009; M. Mazzetti, R.F. Worth and E. Lipton, 'Bomb Plot Shows Key Role Played by Intelligence', *NYT*, 31 October 2010; A. Lyon, 'Military reflex alone can't quell Yemen militants', *Reuters*, 1 November 2010.
64. See also P. Hurtado, 'FBI Uses Triage to Shift From Terror to Madoff, Subprime Probes', *Bloomberg*, 22 December 2008; Z.A. Goldfarb, 'Feds highlight successes against investment fraud', *WP*, 7 December 2010; A.C. Bakshi, 'Former CIA Director on intelligence priorities', *CNN Blog*, 14 April 2011.
65. Several further sources apply: 'Climate Change as a Security Issue', *NYT*, 14 August 2009; F. Harvey and D. Carrington, 'Governments failing to

avert catastrophic climate change, IEA warns', *GU*, 25 April 2012; R. Stein, 'Reports Criticize Pandemic Planning', *WP*, 21 September 2009; M. Helft, 'Google Uses Searches to Track Flu's Spread', and V. Klinkenborg, 'Map Upon Map', *NYT*, 12 November 2008; 'Google uses new tool to track dengue fever hubs', *BBC*, 31 May 2011; T.L. Friedman, 'Connecting Nature's Dots', *NYT*, 23 August 2009; E. Ferris, 'Natural Disasters: Thinking Beyond Immediate Response', *Brookings*, 2 October 2009; M. Klapper and J.J. Riley, 'Haiti Lessons: A Search and Rescue Corps...', *NYT*, 13 February 2010; B. Herbert, 'What's Wrong With Us?', *NYT*, 16 February 2010; A.C. Revkin, 'Disaster Awaits Cities in Earthquake Zones', *NYT*, 25 February 2010; 'Curbing disaster risk is "everybody's business," Ban says on International Day', *UN*, 13 October 2010; 'Enhancing Preparation for and Management of Global Threats', *CH Project*, 2010; R. Solholm, 'Arctic challenges ahead', *Norway Post*, 26 January 2011.

6 Clarifying the Globalization Nexus: Explaining the 'globalization of intelligence' in the broader context and theory conclusions

1. See also 'Commanders Cite Unpredictable Future Threats', *Defense.gov*, 4 March 2011; S. Erlanger, 'The Legacy of 1989 Is Still Up for Debate', *NYT*, and F. Halliday, 'The Other 1989s', *OD*, 9 November 2009.
2. See also 'US intelligence missions for review', *JDW*, 8 October 1994; J. Mackinlay and J. Olsen, 'Squaring the Circle', *JIDR*, 1 October 1995; B. Tarnoff, 'Diamond's "The CIA and the Culture of Failure"', *San Francisco Chronicle*, 5 September 2008; J. Lyons, 'Spy agency ASIS "run down"', *TA*, 9 September 2008; J. Kirkup, 'Intelligence agencies face first budget cut in a decade', *DT*, 22 October 2010; 'Intelligence group warns gov't against cutting spy budget in ways that could weaken efforts', *AP*, 24 May 2011.
3. See also M.D. Shear and D. Balz, 'Obama Appeals for Global Cooperation', *WP*, 24 September 2009; 'The Icelandic Plume', *NYT*, 19 April 2010.
4. 'The CIA's World-View', *JFR*, 16 February 1989; Richelson (1990); 'The Foreign Policy Lessons of 11/9', *CFR*, 12 June 2008; T.L. Friedman, 'The Power in 11/9', *NYT*, 18 October 2009; T. Garton Ash, '1989!', *NYRB*, 56, 17, 5 November 2009; Treverton (2009, pp. 15–48); P. Dorling, 'Australian spies snoop on China's expanding Star Wars arsenal', *SMH*, 21 December 2010.
5. B. Starr, 'CIA to refocus as new top team is announced', *JDW*, 1 August 1997; T. Karon, 'The CIA's Stormy Crystal Ball', *TIME*, 20 December 2000.
6. On the negative fallout from overall globalization, see also S. Logan, 'DEA Uncovers Drug-Terror Nexus', *ISN_SW*, 21 January 2010; D. Lee, 'Exposing the world of Japan's yakuza mafia', *BBC*, 5 October 2010.
7. See also D. Ignatius, 'What the CIA needs in David Petraeus', *WP*, 6 July 2011.
8. See also R.(D.) Cheney, 'Remarks by the Vice President to The World Economic Forum', *FDCH*, 24 January 2004.
9. See also 'UK "needs to find new world role"', *BBC*, 22 April 2010; A. Burnett, 'Britain's Hung Foreign Policy', *FP*, 7 May 2010; R. Norton-Taylor, 'Al-Qaida and Taliban threat is exaggerated, says security thinktank', *GU*, 7 September 2010; A. Faiola, 'Obama's London visit comes amid British reckoning', *WP*, 24 May 2011.

10. See also J.R. Cerami and J.A. Engel (eds), *Rethinking Leadership and "Whole of Government" National Security Reform* and P. R. Cuccia, *Implications of a Changing NATO*, http://www.StrategicStudiesInstitute.army.mil/, accessed on 22 April 2012; M. Fisher and L. Sly, 'Pressure for change builds across Arab world', *WP*, 28 February 2011.
11. See also S. Aftergood, 'CIA Whistleblower Complaint Declassified', *FAS_SN*, 4 August 2009.
12. See also K. Dozier, 'Spec-Ops troops learn to be gumshoes', *AP*, 3 January 2012.
13. See also B. Ki-moon, UN Secretary General, 'Our power lies in unity', *GU*, 23 September 2008; H. Gusterson, 'The bursting global security bubble', *BAS*, 24 September 2008; S.S. Hsu, '9/11 Commission Leaders Push for More Action on Security', *WP*, 25 July 2009; P. Rogers, 'Britain's Security Future', *OD*, 20 September 2010; 'Defence cuts could jeopardise Britain's security relationship with America', *Economist*, 26 May 2011; G. Corera, 'Spies facing budget squeeze and more oversight', *BBC*, 13 July 2011; D. Welch, 'Spy bases shut down to "save money"', *SMH*, 20 November 2010; J. Moore, 'Intelligence Officials Expect "Belt Tightening"', *Executivegov.com*, 11 February 2011; N. Hopkins, 'Hackers have breached top secret MoD systems, cyber-security chief admits', *GU*, 3 May 2012.
14. See also J. Chen, 'Five Real Missions for 007', *FP*, November 2008; 'A Plan for Action', *Managing Global Insecurity Report*, November 2008; P. Rogers, 'A world in the balance', *OD*, 13 November 2008.
15. See also A. Rogers, 'Security threats are "global"', *JIR*, 1 November 2004.
16. T. Judt, 'What Have We Learned, If Anything?', *NYRB*, 55, 7, 1 May 2008; A.J. Echevarria, II, *Preparing for One War and Getting Another?*, http://www.StrategicStudiesInstitute.army.mil/, accessed on 22 April 2012; Professor Sir Adam Roberts, President, The British Academy, 'Reinventing the Wheel', *The Gresham Special Lecture*, 7 June 2011.
17. See also 'Recent conflicts, new threats underline need for adapted military doctrine', *OSCE*, 24 May 2011.
18. C. Drew, 'Drone Flights Leave Military Awash in Data', *NYT*, 11 January 2010; D.S. Cloud, 'Anatomy of an Afghan war tragedy', *LAT*, 10 April 2011.
19. See also G. Adams, 'Strategic planning comes to the State Department', *BAS*, 30 July 2009; C.S. Gray, *Schools for Strategy*, http://www.StrategicStudiesInstitute.army.mil/, accessed on 22 April 2012.
20. See also B. Kendall, 'Does "the West" still exist?', *BBC*, 17 March 2007.
21. See also J.R. Bennett, 'Private intel, the new gold rush', *ISN_SW*, 1 July 2008; P. Hess, 'CIA fires nongovernment interrogators, contract security guards at shuttered secret prisons', *AP*, 10 April 2009; E. Lichtblau and J. Risen, 'N.S.A.'s Intercepts Exceed Limits Set by Congress', *NYT*, 16 April 2009; J. Tate, 'CIA's brain drain', *WP*, 12 April 2011.
22. See also G. Corera, 'Is al-Qaeda still relevant?', *BBC*, 7 April 2011; 'Interview with Head of German Intelligence', *spiegel.de*, 9 May 2011; D. Ignatius, '10 years after 9/11, al-Qaeda is down but not out', *WP*, 24 August 2011; J. Burke and F. Fukuyama, 'Twin Towers and terrorism', *TO*, 11 September 2011; D. Hayes, '9/11, Ten years on', *OD*, 7 September 2011.
23. CIA, *Strategic Intent 2007–2011: One Agency, One Community*, 2007, p. 6; D. Snow and J. Pearlman, 'Future military threat remote: intelligence

head', *SMH*, 26 September 2008; 'Risky business', *JIR*, 11 December 2008; Colombani and Naím, (2010); Thomas (2010); Patrick (2010); C. Mead and A. Snider, 'Why the CIA is spying on a changing climate', *McClatchy*, 10 January 2011. For the 'polymorphous' nature of 'modern warfare', Lonsdale (2008, p. 36); Thornton (2007); Heuser (2010). For UK threats, R. Norton-Taylor, 'Top-tier threats to Britain's security', *GU*, 18 October 2010; 'British police in training for Mumbai-style attack', *DT*, 15 March 2011; W. Maclean, 'Decade on from 9/11, West's threat list grows', *Reuters*, 26 January 2011.

24. See also M. Musgrove, '"Citizen cartographers" map the microcosms of the world', *WP*, 31 January 2010.
25. See also E. Ford, 'Time to rethink government for the 21st century', *Times*, 2 January 2009; C. Dickey, 'Revolution 2.0', *Newsweek*, 5 January 2009; G. Rachman, 'Economic risk and geopolitical risk share agenda at World Economic Forum', *FT*, 29 January 2011; P. Rogers, 'The global crisis: between Cairo and Davos', *OD*, 3 February 2011.
26. P. Williams, *From the New Middle Ages to a New Dark Age*, http://www.StrategicStudiesInstitute.army.mil/, accessed on 22 April 2012.
27. See also US *Quadrennial Defense Review*, 2006; *The National Security Strategy of the United States of America*, March 2006; J. Westhead, 'Planning the US "Long War" on terror', *BBC*, 10 April 2006.
28. See also M. Slackman, 'Arab Unrest Propels Iran as Saudi Influence Declines', *NYT*, 23 February 2011; D.S. Cloud, 'Gates warns against future land wars like Iraq, Afghanistan', *LAT*, 25 February 2011; 'North Korean Nukes Might Fit on Missiles, Aircraft: U.S.', *GSN*, 11 March 2011.
29. Several further sources exist: K. Haider, 'Pressure mounts on Pakistan's military over bin Laden', *Reuters*, and 'Latest Pakistani Assurances on Nuclear Security Draw Mixed Reaction', *GSN*, 11 May 2011; 'Pakistan Spy Agency Denies Aiding Mumbai Attacks', *GSN*, 25 May 2011; J. Marcus, 'After Karachi', *BBC*, 23 May 2011; 'Pentagon Says Pakistani Ties Crucial, Nuke Security at Stake', *GSN*, 17 June 2011; A. Rashid, 'Ten years of meltdown in Pakistan', *BBC*, 2 October 2011; E. Schmitt, 'Lull in Strikes by U.S. Drones Aids Militants in Pakistan', *NYT*, 7 January 2012.
30. See also R. Norton-Taylor, 'Terrorism: the threat shifts to Yemen – and Africa', *GU*, 3 November 2010. For Somalia, 'UN focuses on Somalia with multi-agency piracy plan', *JIDR*, 8 February 2011; W. Maclean, 'West cheers Qaeda loss, but Somali chaos endures', *Reuters*, 13 June 2011; M. Mazzetti and E. Schmitt, 'U.S. Expands Its Drone War Into Somalia', *NYT*, 1 July 2011; B. Bennett, 'Al Qaeda's Yemen branch has aided Somalia militants, U.S. says', *LAT*, 18 July 2011.
31. T. Blair, 'Prime Minister's speech: Doctrine of the International community at the Economic Club, Chicago', *No.10 Downing Street*, 24 April 1999; K. Ghattas, 'Brown's speech looks beyond Bush', *BBC*, 19 April 2008; J. Garvie, 'Globalization and its cures', *TLS*, 18 February 2009; J. Napolitano, Secretary, U.S. Homeland Security, 'Common Threat, Collective Response', *CFR*, 29 July 2009; 'Global Cooperation Need Seen For Climate Warming, Piracy Fight', *World Sentinel*, 8 November 2009.
32. UK Foreign Secretary Margaret Beckett, 'The Challenge of Multilateralism', *FCO.gov.uk*, 3 July 2006; 'A New Era of Security Cooperation: NATO Secretary General's Speech…', *NATO*, 24 April 2008; Zartman and Touval (2010).

33. See also 'Information superiority key to success of operations', *NATO*, 6 May 2008; A. Rathmell, 'Multilateral Approaches to Security' and J. Ker-Lindsay and A. Cameron (eds.), 'Turkey's Added Value', *RUSI*, October 2009.
34. See also H. Young, 'Once lost, these freedoms will be impossible to restore', *GU*, 11 December 2001; 'McChrystal: We've Shot "An Amazing Number" Of Innocent Afghans', *HP*, 2 April 2010.
35. See also M. Kaldor, '"New thinking" needs new direction', *OD*, 25 September 2008; P. Rogers, 'The war on terror: seven years on (part one)', *OD*, 25 September 2008; J. Risen and E. Lichtblau, 'Early Test for Obama on Domestic Spying Views', *NYT*, 18 November 2008; S. Gorman, 'White House to Abandon Spy-Satellite Program', *WSJ*, 23 June 2009; L. Nathan, 'Intelligence in South Africa', *TWT*, August/September 2009; Murphy, 'Is Homeland Security spending paying off?', *LAT*, 28 August 2011.
36. See also 'Google and Government Monitoring', *NYT*, 2 May 2010; 'Wikileaks: Many at Guantanamo "not dangerous"', *BBC*, 25 April 2011; P. Yost, 'US cannot say how many had communications watched', *AP*, 29 July 2011.
37. Recent coverage on fluctuating US-PK relations includes: 'Clinton, Panetta Note Concerns on U.S. Partnership with Pakistan', *GSN*, 17 August 2011; see also G. Kessler, 'Despite diplomatic tensions, U.S.-Israeli security ties strengthen', *WP*, 16 July 2010.
38. See also G. Miller, 'CIA expanding presence in Afghanistan', *LAT*, 20 September 2009.
39. See also F. Dahl, 'Under pressure, Syria offers nuclear cooperation', *Reuters*, 30 May 2011.
40. See also, e.g., F. Zakaria, 'Wanted: A New Grand Strategy', *Newsweek*, 8 December 2008; 'Excerpts of Joe Biden speech', *BBC*, 7 February 2009; T. Starks, 'Intelligence Policy: New Perspective or Familiar Approach?', *CQ*, 16 February 2009; 'The long goodbye – Closing time at Guantánamo Bay', *JIR*, 12 March 2009; 'US drops "enemy combatant" term', *BBC*, 13 March 2009; P. Rogers, 'America's politics of defence', *OD*, 12 March 2009; B. Mendelsohn, 'International Cooperation in the War on Terrorism', *ISN_SW*, 28 June 2010.
41. See also R. Donadio, 'Battling an Image and Reality', *NYT*, 29 January 2010; 'ASIS sets sights on people smugglers', *SMH*, 10 May 2011.
42. See also C.J. Chivers, 'As Marines Move In, Taliban Fight a Shadowy War', *NYT*, 2 February 2010.
43. See also D. Casciani, 'UK Border Agency criticised over intelligence use', *BBC*, 13 May 2011.
44. See also A. Kingsbury, 'Making Intelligence More Diverse, One Spy at a Time', *USN&WR*, 15 February 2009; 'CIA trying to hire more diverse group of agents', *CNN*, 18 May 2011.
45. K. Allen, 'Boom time for PR', *GU*, 14 September 2006.
46. See also 'New Policy Makes Information Sharing a Factor in Employees' Performance Reviews', *ODNI*, 6 October 2008; W. Pincus, 'Change Expands Eligibility for Intelligence Hires', *WP*, 29 October 2008.
47. Based in part on information from a non-attributable source.
48. C. Whitlock, 'Afghans oppose U.S. hit list of drug traffickers', *WP*, 24 October 2009.
49. See also, e.g., B. Gourley, 'New IARPA Program Aims to Discover Tech Trends', *smartdatacollective.com*, 11 October 2011; J. Markoff, 'Government Aims to Build a "Data Eye in the Sky"', *NYT*, 10 October 2011.

50. See also J. Amos, 'Skynet satellite system extended', *BBC*, 9 March 2010; J. Amos, '"Muscular" UK Space Agency set up', *BBC*, 23 March 2010; 'Norwegian satellite to be launched', *Norway Post*, 30 June 2010; 'US Strategic Command accepts control of WGS-3 satellite', *JDW*, 1 July 2010; 'US aid agency to enlist satellites to boost development', *AFP*, 5 August 2011; for 'IS[TA]R' aspects, J. Beale, 'Jet that's a "spy in the sky"', *BBC*, 16 July 2010.
51. See also K. Mahbubani, 'The Case Against the West', *FA*, May/June 2008; F. Zakaria, 'The Future of American Power', *FA*, May/June 2008; J. Pomfret, 'The Chinese are "changing us"', *WP*, 14 November 2009; D.E. Sanger, 'Huge Deficits May Alter U.S. Politics and Global Power', *NYT*, 2 February 2010.
52. See also J. Markoff, 'Internet Traffic Begins to Bypass the U.S.', *NYT*, 30 August 2008; J. Warrick and W. Pincus, 'Reduced Dominance Is Predicted for U.S.', *WP*, 10 September 2008; C. Kang, 'Comments on net neutrality irk AT&T', *WP*, 25 November 2009.
53. See also 'Barriers to conflict' *JIR*, 1 July 2006; M. Mazzetti and G. Thompson, 'U.S. Widens Role in Mexican Fight', *NYT*, 25 August 2011; 'Plans for tougher border controls', *BBC*, 26 January 2007; 'Virtual Failure on the Border', *NYT*, 30 October 2010; I. Traynor, 'EU warns Denmark over border controls', *GU*, 17 May 2011; E. Bronner, 'Israeli Troops Fire as Marchers Breach Borders', *NYT*, 15 May 2011; A. Kimery, 'US, Canada Announce Comprehensive Border Security Plan', *hstoday.us*, 8 December 2011. On 'cyber' dimensions, J. Giles, 'UK is ideal home for electronic Big Brother', *New Scientist*, 7 April 2009; P. Jackson, 'Why the US is fielding a cyber army', *BBC*, 15 March 2010; G. Rachman, 'An undeclared war in cyberspace', *FT*, 4 October 2010; T. Espiner, 'UK helps Australia's cyber-spy unit get to work', *ZDNet*, 11 March 2011; D. Welch, 'Australia the victim of "massive" cyber espionage', *SMH*, 1 August 2011; P. Apps, 'In cyber warfare, policy lags technology', *Reuters*, 24 November 2010; 'Cyber Attack', *CBC*, 2 June 2011; 'UK beefs up cyber warfare plans', *BBC*, 31 May 2011; B. Schiller, 'Cybersecurity: politics, interests, choices', *OD*, 13 July 2011; R. Windrem, 'US intelligence agencies getting better at classifying cyber-attacks', *MSNBC*, 15 July 2011; N. Shachtman, 'A crime wave in cyberspace', *WP*, 23 July 2011.
54. H.A. Crumpton, US Coordinator for Counterterrorism, 'Remarks', *RUSI*, 16 January 2006; see also M. Kakutani, 'Surveying a Global Power Shift', *NYT*, 29 January 2012.
55. Quoted in M. Allen, 'Bush and Blair warn Taliban of Retaliation', *WP*, 3 October 2001.
56. See also 'Global focus – Admiral Mike Mullen', *JIR*, 1 October 2009.
57. See, e.g., 'Obama, Cameron Discuss Security Aspects of U.S., UK Ties', and 'Shared Values Define U.S.-U.K. Ties, Obama Tells Parliament', *Defense.gov*, 25 May 2011; 'US, UK continue cyber collaboration', *JDW*, 23 March 2012.
58. R. Norton-Taylor, 'UK "deluded" in relying on US for defence, warns think-tank', *GU*, 30 June 2009.
59. US ODNI, *National Intelligence Strategy*, Washington, DC: August 2009, p. 18.
60. See also M. Rodenbeck, 'View from Cairo', *ISN*, 7 October 2008; J. Lichtenberg, 'Is Pure Altruism Possible?', *NYT*, 19 October 2010.
61. See also D. Brooks, 'Nice Guys Finish First', *NYT*, 16 May 2011.
62. For critique, e.g., T. Engelhardt, 'Dumb question of 21st century: Is it legal?', *CBS*, 31 May 2011; see also D. Ignatius, 'How do you prevent a terror attack?', *WP*, 27 July 2011.

63. C. Johnson, 'Guidelines Expand FBI's Surveillance Powers', *WP,* 4 October 2008; D. Leppard, 'There's no hiding place as spy HQ plans to see all', *TST,* 5 October 2008; 'Local Law Enforcement's Counterterrorism Initiatives Have Evolved into All-Hazards Strategies', *RAND,* 28 October 2010; W. Maclean, 'Militant mix of experts, novices blurs risk picture', *Reuters,* 31 October 2010; N. Hager, 'Israel's omniscient ears', *Le Monde Diplomatique,* 4 September 2010; 'Army Wants Spy Blimps to Psych Out Insurgents', *WB,* 4 March 2011.
64. 'US intelligence agencies seize policy initiative', *JFR,* 21 February 2008.
65. 'Risk Governance Deficits', *International Risk Governance Council Report,* Autumn 2009; D. LeBlanc, 'Whether terrorism, flu or earthquake, Canada lacks a plan, Fraser finds', *G&M,* 4 November 2009.
66. *Vis-à-vis* the media: R. Fisk, 'The truth about the Middle East is buried beneath the headlines', *Independent,* 31 October 2009; N. Fenton, 'The Future of the News', *OD,* 18 November 2009; T. Koppel, 'Olbermann, O'Reilly and the death of real news', *WP,* 14 November 2010; T.L. Friedman, 'Too Good to Check', *NYT,* 16 November 2010.
67. See also D. Casciani, 'Terror watchdog says UK is "safe haven" for suspects', *BBC,* 3 February 2011; 'UK "should cut links to European Court of Human Rights"', *BBC,* 7 February 2011.
68. See also J. Borger, 'Al-Qaida may have lost some gloss, but it has not been beaten', *GU,* 14 December 2010; D. Gardham, 'Al-Qaeda bomb techniques are constantly evolving', *DT,* 17 December 2010.
69. 'The Warning', *PBS Frontline,* 20 October 2009.
70. See also A. Mumford, 'Puncturing the Counterinsurgency Myth', September 2011, and G. Hughes, 'The Military's Role in Counterterrorism', May 2011, both papers via: http://www.StrategicStudiesInstitute.army.mil/, accessed on 22 April 2012.
71. I. Eland, 'Reining in the empire', *WT,* 31 August 2008.
72. See also W. Pincus, 'Under plan, intelligence agencies would be consulted before reading of rights', *WP,* 13 February 2010.
73. See also G. Weston, 'Canada offered to aid Iraq invasion: WikiLeaks', *CBC.ca,* 15 May 2011.
74. 'Personnel Management Issues' in UK ISC, *AR 1997–98,* 1998, para.36.
75. A.E. Kornblut, 'Obama Team Says Zazi Case Illustrates Balanced Approach to Terror Threat', *WP,* 6 October 2009.
76. See also J. Bartlett, 'Common sense Nobel', *OD,* 29 October 2009.

Select Bibliography

Abbott, C., P. Rogers and J. Sloboda (2007) *Beyond Terror* (London: Rider).

Adams, J. (1994) *The New Spies* (London: Hutchinson).

Adamson, F.B. (2006) 'Crossing Borders', *International Security*, 31, 1 (Summer).

Agrell, W. (2006) 'Sweden and the Dilemmas of Neutral Intelligence Liaison', *Journal of Strategic Studies*, 29, 4 (August).

Agrell, W. (2009) 'Intelligence Analysis after the Cold War – New Paradigm or Old Anomalies?', ch. 5 in G.F. Treverton and W. Agrell (eds.), *National Intelligence Systems* (Cambridge: Cambridge University Press).

Agrell, W., and G.F. Treverton (2009) 'The Science of Intelligence', ch. 11 in G.F. Treverton and W. Agrell (eds.), *National Intelligence Systems.*

Aid, M.M. (2003) 'All Glory is Fleeting', *Intelligence and National Security*, 18, 4 (Winter).

Aid, M.M. (2009) *The Secret Sentry* (New York: Bloomsbury).

Aid, M.M. (2012) *Intel Wars* (New York: Bloomsbury).

Albright, D., and C. Hinderstein (2005) 'Unraveling the A.Q. Khan and Future Proliferation Networks', *The Washington Quarterly*, 28, 2 (Spring).

Albright, D. (2010) *Peddling Peril* (New York: Free Press).

Aldrich, R.J. (2001) *The Hidden Hand* (London: John Murray).

Aldrich, R.J. (2002) 'Dangerous Liaisons: Post-September 11 Intelligence Alliances', *Harvard International Review*, 24, 3 (Fall).

Aldrich, R.J. (2005) 'The Secret State', ch. 19 in P. Addison and H. Jones (eds.), *A Companion to Contemporary Britain 1939–2000* (London: Blackwell).

Aldrich, R.J. (2009a) 'Global Intelligence Co-operation versus Accountability: New Facets to an Old Problem', *Intelligence and National Security*, 24, 1 (February).

Aldrich, R.J. (2009b) 'US–European Intelligence Co-operation on Counter-Terrorism: Low Politics and Compulsion', *British Journal of Politics and International Relations*, 11, 1 (February).

Aldrich, R.J. (2009c) 'Beyond the Vigilant State: Globalisation and Intelligence', *Review of International Studies*, 35, 4 (October).

Aldrich, R.J., and P.H.J. Davies (2009) 'The Future of UK Intelligence and Special Operations', *Review of International Studies*, 35, 4 (October).

Aldrich, R.J. (2010) *GCHQ* (London: HarperPress).

Aldrich, R.J. (2011a) 'International Intelligence Co-operation in Practice', ch. 2 of H. Born, I. Leigh and A. Wills (eds.), *International Intelligence Co-operation and Accountability* (London: Routledge).

Aldrich, R.J. (2011b) '"A Profoundly Disruptive Force": The CIA, Historiography and the Perils of Globalization', *Intelligence and National Security*, 26, 2 and 3.

Ale, B. (2009) *Risk* (London: Routledge).

Alexander, D. (2002) *Principles of Emergency Planning and Management* (Harpenden, Herts: Terra).

Alexander, M.S. (1998) 'Introduction: Knowing your Friends, Assessing your Allies – Perspectives on Intra-Alliance Intelligence', *Intelligence and National Security*, 13, 1 (Spring).

Allen, E.P. (2008) 'Of Note: To Deny and Deceive: The Limits of Counterdeception – an Addendum', *SAIS Review*, XXVIII, 1 (Winter–Spring).
Alpert, G.P., and M. Dames (2011) 'Intra-agency and Inter-agency Co-operation in International Police Work', *Police Practice and Research*, 12, 2.
Altinay, H. (ed.) (2011) *Global Civics* (Washington, DC: Brookings).
Ambler, E. (1939) *The Mask of Dimitrios* (London: Penguin [2009]).
Amoore, L., and M. de Goede (eds.) (2008) *Risk and the War on Terror* (London: Routledge).
Amstutz, M., and G. Teubner (eds.) (2009) *Networks: Legal Issues of Multilateral Co-operation* (Oxford: Hart).
Andregg, M. (2010) 'Ethics and Professional Intelligence', ch. 44 in L.K. Johnson (ed.), *The Oxford Handbook of National Security Intelligence* (Oxford: Oxford University Press).
Andrew, C.M., and D. Dilks (eds.) (1984) *The Missing Dimension* (Basingstoke: Macmillan).
Andrew, C. (2004) 'Intelligence analysis needs to look backwards before looking forward', *History & Policy* (June).
Andrew, C., R.J. Aldrich and W.K. Wark (eds.) (2009) *Secret Intelligence: A Reader* (London: Routledge).
Andréani, G. (2004) 'The "War on Terror": Good Cause, Wrong Concept', *Survival*, 46, 4 (December).
Aradau, C., and R. Van Munster (2011) *Politics of Catastrophe* (London: Routledge).
Argomaniz, J. (2011) *The EU and Counter-Terrorism* (London: Routledge).
Armstrong, D., T. Farrell and H. Lambert (2012) *International Law and International Relations* (Cambridge: Cambridge University Press, 2nd ed.).
Arnold, M.J. (2008) 'Intervention', ch. 11 in Snyder (ed.), *Contemporary Security and Strategy.*
Arquilla, J., and D. Ronfeldt (eds.) (2001) *Networks and Netwars* (Santa Monica, CA: RAND).
ASIP Editorial (2010) 'Promoting Intergroup Cooperation', *Analyses of Social Issues and Public Policy* (8 November).
Atkinson, S.R. (2010) 'Returning Science To The Social', *The Shrivenham Papers*, 10 (UK Defence Academy, July).
Aughey, S. (2011) 'Obama and Human Rights: Continuity and Change', *The World Today* (January).
Avant, D.D., M. Finnemore and S.K. Sell (eds.) (2010) *Who Governs the Globe?* (Cambridge: Cambridge University Press).
Aydinli, E., and J.N. Rosenau (eds.) (2005) *Globalization, Security, and the Nation State* (Albany, NY: SUNY Press).
Aydinli, E. (ed.) (2010) *Emerging Transnational (In)Security Governance* (London: Routledge).
Baer, R. (2002) *See No Evil* (New York: Crown).
Baker, A., and G. Phillipson (2011) 'Policing, profiling and discrimination law', *Journal of Global Ethics*, 7, 1.
Ball, D. (2002) 'Desperately Seeking Bin Laden: The Intelligence Dimension of the War Against Terrorism', ch. 5 in K. Booth and T. Dunne (eds.), *Worlds In Collision* (Basingstoke: Palgrave).
Ball, K., and F. Webster (eds.) (2003) *The Intensification of Surveillance* (London: Pluto).

Ball, R. (2011) 'The Strategic Utility of New Zealand Special Forces', *Small Wars & Insurgencies*, 22, 1 (March).
Bamford, J. (2002) *Body of Secrets* (London: Arrow).
Bar-Joseph, U., and R. McDermott (2008) 'Change the Analyst and Not the System', *Foreign Policy Analysis*, 4.
Barkawi, T. (2006) 'Terrorism and North-South Relations', *RUSI Journal* (February).
Bayley, D.H. (2006) *Changing the Guard* (Oxford: Oxford University Press).
Baylis, J., J.J. Wirtz and C.S. Gray (eds.) (2010) *Strategy in the Contemporary World*, 3rd ed. (Oxford: Oxford University Press).
Bell, S. (2007) 'The UK's Risk Management Approach to National Security', *RUSI Journal*, 152, 3 (June).
Bennett Jones, O. (2009) *Pakistan: Eye of the Storm*, 3rd ed. (New Haven, CT: Yale University Press).
Bensahel, N. (2003) *The Counterterror Coalitions* (Santa Monica, CA: RAND).
Bentley, M. (2011) 'WMD Terrorism: Defining "Mass Destruction" in US Law', *Politics*, 31, 2 (June).
Berardo, R. (2009) 'Processing Complexity in Networks', *Policy Studies Journal*, 37, 3 (July).
Bergen, P., B. Hoffman and K. Tiedemann (2011) 'Assessing the Jihadist Terrorist Threat to America and American Interests', *Studies in Conflict and Terrorism*, 34, 2 (February).
Bergenäs, J. (2010a) 'The Role of Regional Organizations in Combating WMD Terrorism', *G8/G20 Magazine* (Summit 2010).
Bergenäs, J. (2010b) 'The Nuclear Domino Myth', *Foreign Affairs* (31 August).
Bergenäs, J. (2010c) 'Fighting Security Challenges With Regional Cooperation', *World Politics Review* (8 December).
Berkowitz, B. (2003) *The New Face of War* (New York: Free Press).
Berkowitz, D., and A.E. Goodman (1991) *Strategic Intelligence in American National Security* (Princeton, NJ: Princeton University Press).
Bernkopf Tucker, N. (2008) 'The Cultural Revolution in Intelligence: Interim Report', *The Washington Quarterly*, 31, 2 (Spring).
Berridge, G.R. (2010) *Diplomacy*, 4th ed. (Basingstoke: Palgrave).
Betts, R.K. (1982) *Surprise Attack* (Washington, DC: Brookings).
Betts, R.K. (2009) 'Analysis, War, and Decision: Why Intelligence Failures are Inevitable', ch. 6 in P. Gill, S. Marrin and M. Phythian (eds.), *Intelligence Theory* (London: Routledge).
Betts, R.K. (2010) 'Conflict or Cooperation?', *Foreign Affairs* (November/December).
Betts, R.K., and T. Mahnken (eds.) (2003) *Paradoxes of Strategic Intelligence* (London: Routledge).
Biddle, S. (2007) 'Speed kills?', *Journal of Strategic Studies*, 30, 1 (February).
Bieler, A., and A.D. Morton (2001) 'The Gordian Knot of Agency-Structure in International Relations: A Neo-Gramscian Perspective', *European Journal of International Relations*, 7, 1.
Bisley, N. (2008) 'Great Powers and the International System', ch. 12 in Snyder (ed.), *Contemporary Security and Strategy*.
Black, J. (2006) *The Dotted Red Line* (London: Social Affairs Unit).
Blackburn, S. (2003) *Ethics* (Oxford: Oxford University Press).
Blair, T. (2007) 'A Battle for Global Values', *Foreign Affairs* (January/February).
Blakeley, R. (2011a) 'Why Not Torture Terrorists?', *International Journal of Human Rights*, 15, 4.

Blakeley, R. (2011b) 'Dirty Hands, Clean Conscience?', *Journal of Human Rights*, 10, 4.
Blank, L.R., and G.P. Noone (2008) *Law of War Training* (Washington, DC: USIP, March).
Bolt, N. (2009) 'Unsettling Networks', *RUSI Journal*, 154, 5 (October).
Booth, K. (2007) *Theory of World Security* (Cambridge: Cambridge University Press).
Born, H., and I. Leigh (2005) *Making Intelligence Accountable* (Oslo, Norway: Parliament of Norway).
Born, H., and I. Leigh (2007) 'Democratic Accountability of Intelligence Services', *Democratic Control of Armed Forces (DCAF) Policy Paper*, 19.
Born, H., L.K. Johnson and I. Leigh (2005) *Who's Watching the Spies?* (Washington, DC: Potomac).
Born, H., I. Leigh and A. Wills (eds.) (2011) *International Intelligence Cooperation and Accountability* (London: Routledge).
Bosch, O. (2004) 'Weapons Proliferation and Resolution 1540', *The World Today*, 62, 4 (May).
Bosch, O., and P. van Ham (eds.) (2007) *Global Non-Proliferation and Counter-Terrorism* (Washington, DC: Brookings, CH, and Clingendael Institute).
Boulden, G.P. (2002) *Thinking Creatively* (London: DK).
Bourne, M. (2011) 'Controlling the Shadow Trade', *Contemporary Security Policy*, 32, 1.
Bousquet, A. (2008) 'Chaoplexic warfare or the future of military organization', *International Affairs*, 84, 5.
Bousquet, A.J. (2009) *The Scientific Way of Warfare* (London: Hurst).
Bousquet, A., and R. Geyer (2011) 'Complexity and the International Arena', and subsequent essays, *Cambridge Review of International Affairs*, 24, 1 (March).
Bowen, W.Q. (2006) 'Libya and Nuclear Proliferation: Stepping Back from the Brink', *IISS Adelphi Paper*, 380 (London: Routledge/IISS).
Bowen, W.Q., and J. Brewer (2011) 'Iran's Nuclear Challenge: Nine Years and Counting', *International Affairs*, 87, 4 (July).
Bowman, M.E. (2006–07) 'Dysfunctional Information Restrictions', *Intelligencer* (Fall/Winter).
Bracken, P., I. Bremmer and D. Gordon (eds.) (2008) *Managing Strategic Surprise* (Cambridge: Cambridge University Press).
Brattberg, E. (2012) 'Coordinating for Contingencies: Taking Stock of Post-9/11 Homeland Security Reforms', *Journal of Contingencies & Crisis Management*, early view: http://onlinelibrary.wiley.com/doi/10.1111/j.1468-5973.2012.00662.x/abstract
Brennan, J. (2010) 'Securing the Homeland by Renewing American Strength, Resilience, and Values', *Remarks* (26 May).
Briggs, R. (2010) 'Community Engagement for Counterterrorism', *International Affairs*, 86, 4 (June).
Broderick, J. (2007) 'Intelligence and Civil Protection in the UK', *Democracy and Security*, 3, 3 (September).
Brown, C., and K. Ainley (2005) 'US Hegemony and World Order', ch. 12 in *Understanding International Relations*, 3rd ed. (Basingstoke: Palgrave).
Brzezinski, Z. (2009) 'An Agenda for NATO', *Foreign Affairs* (September/October).
Burgess, J.P. (2008) 'Non-Military Security Challenges', ch. 4 in C.A. Snyder (ed.), *Contemporary Security and Strategy*, 2nd ed. (Basingstoke: Palgrave).

Butler Committee (2004) *Report into the Review of Intelligence on Weapons of Mass Destruction* (14 July).

Buzan, B., J. De Wilde and O. Wæver (1998) *Security: A New Framework for Analysis* (Boulder, CO: Lynne Riemmer).

Buzan, B., and L. Hansen (2009) *The Evolution of International Security Studies* (Cambridge: Cambridge University Press).

Byman, D., and M. Waxman (2002) *The Dynamics of Coercion* (Cambridge: Cambridge University Press).

Byman, D. (2008) 'An Autopsy of the Iraq Debacle', *Security Studies*, 17, 4.

Calleo, D.P. (2008) 'The Tyranny of False Vision: America's Unipolar Fantasy', *Survival*, 50, 5.

Canton, B. (2008) 'The Active Management of Uncertainty', *International Journal of Intelligence and CounterIntelligence*, 21, 3.

Cardillo, R. (2010) 'Intelligence Community Reform: A Cultural Evolution', *CIA Studies in Intelligence*, 54, 3 (September).

Carl, L.D. (1996) *CIA Insider's Dictionary* (Washington, DC: NIBC).

Carment, D., and M. Rudner (eds.) (2006) *Peacekeeping Intelligence* (London: Routledge).

Chandler, D. (2002) *From Kosovo to Kabul* (Sterling, VA: Pluto).

Chesterman, S. (2006) 'Does the UN have Intelligence?', *Survival*, 48, 3 (Autumn).

Chesterman, S. (2008) 'I Spy', *Survival*, 50, 3.

Chesterman, S. (2009) 'Intelligence Cooperation in International Operations', *New York University School of Law, Public Law and Legal Theory Research Paper No. 09–34* (May).

Chesterman, S. (2010) 'Privacy and Surveillance in the Age of Terror', *Survival*, 52, 5 (October).

Chivers, C.J. (2011) 'Small Arms, Big Problems', *Foreign Affairs* (January/February).

Cialdini, R.B. (2010) 'Roots, Shoots, and Fruits of Persuasion in Military Affairs', *Analyses of Social Issues and Public Policy*, 17 (December).

Cilluffo, F.J., J.B. Cozzens and M. Ranstorp (2010) *Foreign Fighters: Trends, Trajectories & Conflict Zones* (Washington, DC: GWU HSPI, October).

Clark, R.M. (2009) *Intelligence Analysis: A target-centric approach*, 3rd ed. (Washington, DC: CQ).

Clark, V. (2010) *Yemen* (New Haven, CT: Yale University Press).

Clauser, J., and J. Goldman (rev./ed.) (2008) *An Introduction to Intelligence Research and Analysis* (Lanham, MD: Scarecrow).

Clemente, D. (2011) 'WikiLeaks: Unsteady Drip', *The World Today* (March).

Clemente, J.D., and S. Marrin (2005) 'Improving Intelligence Analysis by Looking to the Medical Profession', *International Journal of Intelligence and CounterIntelligence*, 18, 4.

Clemente, J.D., and S. Marrin (2006–07) 'Modeling an Intelligence Analysis Profession on Medicine', *International Journal of Intelligence and CounterIntelligence*, 19, 4 (Winter).

Clifford-Jones, I. (2009) 'Affirming Climate Change's Place in the National Security Framework', *RUSI Homeland Security and Resilience Monitor* (13 August).

Clift, A.D. (2003) 'Intelligence in the Internet Era', *CIA Studies in Intelligence*, 47, 3.

Clift, A.D. (2010) 'The Evolution of International Collaboration in the Global Intelligence Era', ch. 13 in Johnson (ed.), *The Oxford Handbook of National Security Intelligence*.

Clinton, H.R. (2010) 'Leading Through Civilian Power', *Foreign Affairs* (November/December).

Clough, C. (2004) '*Quid Pro Quo:* The Challenges of International Strategic Intelligence Cooperation', *International Journal of Intelligence and CounterIntelligence*, 17, 4.

Clutterbuck, L. (2006) 'Developing A Counter-Terrorism Network: Back to the Future?', ch. 2 in P. Katona, J. Sullivan and M.D. Intriligator (eds.), *Countering Terrorism and WMD* (London: Routledge).

Cohen, H.J. (2008) 'In Sub-Saharan Africa, Security Is Overtaking Development as Washington's Top Policy Priority', *American Foreign Policy Interests*, 30, 2.

Coker, C. (2002) 'Globalisation and Insecurity in the Twenty-first Century', *IISS Adelphi Paper*, 345 (London: IISS/Oxford University Press, June).

Coker, C. (2009) *War in an Age of Risk* (Cambridge: Polity).

Cole, D., and J.X. Dempsey (2006) *Terrorism and the Constitution*, 3rd ed. (New York: New Press).

Cole, J. (2010) 'Securing Our Future', *RUSI Journal*, 155, 2 (April/May).

Coletta, D. (2008) *Trusted Guardian* (Aldershot: Ashgate).

Collins, P. (2002) *Virtual and Networked Organizations* (Oxford: Capstone).

Colombani, J.-M., and M. Naím (2010) 'Scarcity and Foreign Policy', *Carnegie Europe* (25 October).

Cook, A. (2009) *Emergency Response to Domestic Terrorism* (London: Continuum).

Cooper, N. (2011) 'Humanitarian Arms Control and Processes of Securitization', *Contemporary Security Policy*, 32, 1.

Cooper, N., and D. Mutimer (2011) 'Arms Control for the 21st Century: Controlling the Means of Violence', *Contemporary Security Policy*, 32, 1.

Cooper, S., D. Hawkins, W. Jacoby and D. Nielson (2008) 'Yielding Sovereignty to International Institutions', *International Studies Review*, 10.

Corera, G. (2006) *Shopping for Bombs* (London: Hurst).

Corera, G. (2011) *The Art of Betrayal* (London: W&N).

Cornish, P. (2007a) 'The UK Contribution to the G8 Global Partnership Against the Spread of Weapons and Materials of Mass Destruction, 2002–06', *International Security Programme Report* (Chatham House, London: January).

Cornish, P. (ed.) (2007b) *Domestic Security, Civil Contingencies and Resilience in the United Kingdom* (London: Chatham House, International Security Programme, June).

Crawford, M. (2011) 'Exploring the Maze', *Survival*, 53, 2.

Crawford, T.W. (2010) 'Intelligence Cooperation' in R.A. Denemark (ed.), *The International Studies Encyclopedia* (Oxford: Wiley/Blackwell).

Crelinsten, R.D. (2006) *Intelligence and Counter-Terrorism in a Multi-Centric World* (Stockholm: SNDC/FHS).

Cronin, A.K. (2002/03) 'Behind the Curve: Globalization and International Terrorism', *International Security*, 27, 3 (Winter).

Cronin, A.K. (2010) 'The Evolution of Counterterrorism: Will Tactics Trump Strategy?', *International Affairs*, 86, 4 (June).

Curtis, M. (2003) *Web of Deceit* (London: Vintage).

Cusimano, M.K. (ed.) (2000) *Beyond Sovereignty* (Boston, MA: Bedford/St. Martin's).

Daalder, I.H. (ed.) (2007) *Beyond Preemption* (Washington, DC: Brookings).

Dahl, E.J. (2005) 'Warning of Terror: Explaining the Failure of Intelligence Against Terrorism', *Journal of Strategic Studies*, 28, 1 (February).

Dahl, E.J. (2010) 'Missing the Wake-up Call', *Intelligence and National Security*, 25, 6 (December).
Dahl, E.J. (2011) 'The Plots that Failed', *Studies in Conflict & Terrorism*, 34, 8.
Dalby, S. (2011) 'Critical Geopolitics and the Control of Arms in the 21st Century', *Contemporary Security Policy*, 32, 1.
Daniel, D.C.F. (2005) 'Denial and Deception', ch. 8 in J. Sims and B. Gerber (eds.), *Transforming U.S. Intelligence* (Washington, DC: Georgetown University Press).
Daun, A., and T. Jäger (2006) 'Geheimdienstkooperation in Europa', *Welt Trends*, 51, 14 (Sommer).
Davies, N. (2009) *Flat Earth News* (London: Vintage).
Davies, P.H.J. (2002) 'Ideas of Intelligence: Divergent National Concepts and Institutions', *Harvard International Review*, 24, 3 (Fall/September).
Davies, P.H.J. (2004a) 'Intelligence Culture and Intelligence Failure in Britain and the United States', *Cambridge Review of International Affairs*, 17, 3 (October).
Davies, P.H.J. (2004b) *MI6 and the Machinery of Spying* (London: Frank Cass).
Davies, P.H.J. (2009) 'Imagery in the UK: Britain's Troubled Imagery Intelligence Architecture', *Review of International Studies*, 35, 4 (October).
Davies, P.H.J. (2011) 'Twilight of Britain's Joint Intelligence Committee?', *International Journal of Intelligence and CounterIntelligence*, 24, 3.
Davis, I., and A. Persbo (2004) 'After the Butler Report: Time to take on the Group Think in Washington and London', *BASIC Papers*, 46 (July).
Davis, J. (2002) 'Improving CIA Analytic Performance: Strategic Warning', *Occasional Papers*, 1, 1, Sherman Kent Center for Intelligence Analysis (September).
Davis, J. (2007) 'Strategic warning', ch. 13 in L.K. Johnson (ed.), *Handbook of Intelligence Studies* (London: Routledge).
Davis, P.K. (2008) 'Defense planning and risk management in the presence of deep uncertainty', ch. 6 in Bracken, Bremmer and Gordon (eds.), *Managing Strategic Surprise*.
de Blij, H. (2009) *The Power of Place* (Oxford: Oxford University Press).
de Jong, B., W. Platje and R.D. Steele (eds.) (2003) *Peacekeeping Intelligence* (Oakton, VA: OSS).
Dearlove, Sir Richard, former Chief ('C') SIS/MI6 (1999–2004) (2010) *Testimony to Chilcot Iraq Inquiry* (16 June).
Deary, I.J. (2001) *Intelligence* (Oxford: Oxford University Press).
Deflem, M. (2010) *The Policing of Terrorism* (London: Routledge).
DeKeseredy, W.S. (2009) 'Canadian Crime Control in the New Millennium', *Police Practice and Research*, 10, 4 (August).
Denemark, D. (2012) 'Trust, Efficacy and Opposition to Anti-terrorism Police Power: Australia in Comparative Perspective', *Australian Journal of Political Science*, 47, 1.
Dershowitz, A.M. (2006) *Preemption* (London: Norton).
Dias, K. (2011) 'The Responsibility to Prevent: Are New Norms Emerging in Humanitarian Intervention?', *CIGI* (20 April).
Doig, A. (2005) 'Joining up a response to terrorism? ... And agency shall speak to agency', *Crime, Law and Social Change*, 44.
Dolnik, A. (2010) 'Fighting to the Death: Mumbai and the future Fidayeen Threat', *RUSI Journal*, 155, 2 (April/May).
Dorey, P. (2005) *Policy Making in Britain* (London: Sage).

Dorn, A.W. (2010) 'United Nations Peacekeeping Intelligence', ch. 17 in Johnson (ed.), *The Oxford Handbook of National Security Intelligence.*
Dover, R., and M.S. Goodman (eds.) (2009) *Spinning Intelligence* (London: Hurst).
Dover, R., and M.S. Goodman (eds.) (2011) *Learning from the Secret Past* (Washington, DC: Georgetown University Press).
Dover, R., and M. Phythian (2011) 'Lost over Libya: The 2010 Strategic Defence and Security Review – An Obituary', *Defence Studies*, 11, 3 (September).
Downes, C. (2010), 'Unintentional Militarism: Over-reliance on Military Methods and Mindsets in US National Security and its Consequences', *Defense & Security Analysis*, 26, 4.
Dumbrell, J. (2010) 'American Power: Crisis or Renewal?', *Politics*, 30, S1 (December).
Dunne, T., and K. Mulaj (2010) 'America after Iraq', *International Affairs*, 86, 6 (November).
Dupont, A. (2003) 'Intelligence for the Twenty-First Century', *Intelligence and National Security*, 18, 4 (Winter).
Dupont, A., and W.J. Reckmeyer (2012) 'Australia's National Security Priorities: Addressing Strategic Risk in a Globalised World', *Australian Journal of International Affairs*, 66, 1.
Dutch Review Committee for the Intelligence and Security Services (2009) 'On the Cooperation of GISS [Dutch General Intelligence and Security Service (AIVD)] with Foreign Intelligence and/or Security Services', *Review Report CTIVD no. 22A.*
Duyvesteyn, I. (2011) 'Hearts and Minds, Cultural Awareness and Good Intelligence: The Blueprint for Successful Counter-insurgency?', *Intelligence and National Security*, 26, 4.
Egnell, R. (2010) 'Winning "Hearts and Minds"?', *Civil Wars*, 12, 3 (September).
Ehrman, J. (2009) 'Toward a Theory of CI: What are We Talking About When We Talk about Counterintelligence?', *CIA Studies in Intelligence*, 53, 2 (June).
Elie, J. (2004) 'Intelligence and the Cold War', *SAIS Review*, XXIV, 1 (Winter/Spring).
Ellis, D.C. (2009) 'On the Possibility of "International Community"', *International Studies Review*, 11.
Ellis, J.D., and G.D. Kiefer (2004) *Combating Proliferation* (Baltimore, MD: John Hopkin's University Press).
Eriksen, J.W. (2010) 'Should Soldiers Think before They Shoot?', *Journal of Military Ethics*, 9, 3 (September).
Etienne, J. (2011) 'Compliance Theory: A Goal Framing Approach', *Law & Policy* (April).
Etzioni, A. (2007) *Security First* (New Haven, CT: Yale University Press).
Evans, G. (2009) 'Rethinking Military Intelligence Failure – Putting the Wheels Back on the Intelligence Cycle', *Defence Studies*, 9, 1 (March).
Evans, G., and J. Newnham (1998) *Dictionary of International Relations* (London: Penguin).
Eznack, L. (2011) 'Crises as Signals of Strength', *Security Studies*, 20, 2.
Fallows, J. (2006) *Blind into Baghdad* (New York: Vintage).
Farrell, T. (2010) 'Humanitarian Intervention and Peace Operations', ch. 15 in Baylis *et al.* (eds.), *Strategy in the Contemporary World.*

Fägersten, B. (2010) 'Bureaucratic Resistance to International Intelligence Cooperation – The Case of Europol', *Intelligence and National Security*, 25, 4 (August).
Fairclough, N. (2006) *Language and Globalization* (London: Routledge).
Feakin, T. (2009) 'National Security in an Age of "Shock and Aftershock"', *RUSI Homeland Security and Resilience Monitor* (13 August).
Feiling, T. (2009) *The Candy Machine* (London: Penguin).
Felbab-Brown, V. (2009) *Shooting Up* (Washington, DC: Brookings).
Ferris, E. (2011) *The Politics of Protection* (Washington, DC: Brookings).
Field, A. (2009) 'Tracking Terrorist Networks', *Review of International Studies*, 35, 4 (October).
Fingar, T. (2008) 'Speech at the Council on Foreign Relations', *Media Highlights* (Wednesday, 19 March – UNCLASSIFIED).
Fingar, T. (2011) *Reducing Uncertainty* (Stanford, CA: Stanford University Press).
Finlan, A. (2009) *Special Forces, Strategy and the War on Terror* (London: Routledge).
Fischhoff, B., and J. Kadvany (2011) *Risk: A Very Short Introduction* (Oxford: Oxford University Press).
Fisk, R. (2005) *The Great War for Civilisation* (London: Fourth Estate).
Flynn, S.E. (2007) *The Edge of Disaster* (New York: Random House).
Flynn, S.E. (2008) 'America the Resilient', *Foreign Affairs* (March/April).
Foley, F. (2009a) 'Reforming Counterterrorism', *Security Studies*, 18, 3 (July).
Foley, F. (2009b) 'The Expansion of Intelligence Agency Mandates', *Review of International Studies*, 35, 4 (October).
Foot, R. (2006) 'Human Rights in Conflict', *Survival*, 48, 3 (Autumn).
Frankel, M. (2011) 'The ABCs of HVT', *Studies in Conflict & Terrorism*, 34, 1 (January).
Frantzen, D. (2010) 'Interrogation Strategies, Evidence, and the Need for *Miranda*: A Study of Police Ideologies', *Police Practice and Research*, 11, 3 (June).
Freedman, L. (1995) 'Alliance and the British Way in Warfare', *Review of International Studies*, 21.
Freedman, L. (2006) 'The Transformation of Strategic Affairs', *IISS Adelphi Paper*, 379 (London: Routledge).
Freedman, L. (2008) *A Choice of Enemies* (London: W&N).
Freeman, Jr., C.W. (2011) 'The Arab Reawakening: Strategic Implications', *Middle East Policy*, 18, 2 (Summer).
Friedman, T.L. (2005) *The World Is Flat* (London: Penguin).
Frost, R.M. (2005) 'Nuclear Terrorism After 9/11', *IISS Adelphi Paper*, 378.
Fuchs-Drapier, M. (2011) 'The European Union's Solidarity Clause in the Event of a Terrorist Attack', *Journal of Contingencies and Crisis Management*, 19, 4 (December).
Fukuyama, F. (2007) 'Challenges of Uncertainty', ch. 1 in *Blindside* (Washington, DC: Brookings).
Furedi, F. (2006) *Culture of Fear Revisited*, 4th ed. (London: Continuum).
Gaddis, J.L. (2005) *The Cold War* (London: Penguin).
Gade, E.K. (2010) 'Defining the Non-Combatant', *Journal of Military Ethics*, 9, 3 (September).
Gal-Or, N. (1985) *International Cooperation to Suppress Terrorism* (London: Taylor & Francis).

Galeotti M. (ed.) (2005) *Global Crime Today* (London: Routledge).
Gallaher, C., C.T. Dahlman, M. Gilmartin, A. Mountz and P. Shirlow (2009) *Key Concepts in Political Geography* (London: Sage).
Gannon, J.C., Chairman, US NIC (2001) 'The Role of Intelligence Services In a Globalized World', *Conference Sponsored by Friedrich Ebert Stiftung* (Berlin, Germany, 21 May).
Gardner, Sqn Ldr S. (2006) 'Operation IRAQI FREEDOM – Coalition Operations', *Royal Air Force Historical Society Journal*, 36.
Gaskarth, J. (2011) 'Entangling Alliances? The UK's Complicity in Torture in the Global War on Terrorism', *International Affairs*, 87, 4 (July).
Gavrilis, G. (2010) *The Dynamics of Interstate Boundaries* (Cambridge: Cambridge University Press).
Gearty, C. (2005) '11 September 2001, Counter-terrorism, and the Human Rights Act', *Journal of Law and Society*, 32, 1 (March).
George, R. (2010) 'Intelligence and Strategy', ch. 8 in Baylis *et al.* (eds.), *Strategy in the Contemporary World.*
Gerber, B.J. (2007) 'Disaster Management in the United States', *Policy Studies Journal*, 35, 2.
Gerspacher, N. (2008) 'The History of International Police Cooperation', *Global Crime*, 9, 1–2 (February–May).
Ghemawat, P. (2007) 'Why the World Isn't Flat', *Foreign Policy* (March/April).
Gibson, S.D. (2005) 'In the Eye of the Perfect Storm', *Risk Management*, 7, 4.
Giegerich, B. (ed.) (2010) *Europe and Global Security* (London: IISS/Routledge).
Gill, B. (2011) 'The Global Security Governance System…', *SIPRI* (May).
Gill, P. (2007) 'Knowing the Self, Knowing the Other', ch. 6 in Johnson (ed.), *Handbook of Intelligence Studies.*
Gills, B.K. (2010) 'The Return of Crisis in the Era of Globalization: One Crisis, or Many?', *Globalizations*, 7, 1–2.
Glenny, M. (2008) *McMafia* (London: Vintage).
Glenny, M. (2011) *Darkmarket* (London: Bodley Head).
Goodman, M.S. (2006) 'Intelligence Education: Studying and Teaching About Intelligence: The Approach in the United Kingdom', *CIA Studies in Intelligence*, 50, 2.
Graff, G.M. (2012) *The Threat Matrix: The FBI at War* (London: Back Bay).
Graham, Senator B., and J. Nussbaum (2008) *Intelligence Matters* (University Press of Kansas).
Graham, B., J. Talent, G. Allison, R. Cleveland and S.G. Rademaker (2008) *World at Risk* (New York: Vintage).
Graham Jr., T., and K.A. Hansen (2007) *Spy Satellites* (Seattle, WA: University of Washington Press).
Gray, C.S. (2007a) 'Out of the Wilderness', *Comparative Strategy*, 26, 1 (January).
Gray, C.S. (2007b) *War, Peace and International Relations* (London: Routledge).
Gray, C.S. (2008) 'Coping With Uncertainty', *Comparative Strategy*, 27, 4 (July).
Gray, C.S. (2010a) 'Strategic Thoughts for Defence Planners', *Survival*, 52, 3 (June).
Gray, C.S. (2010b) 'Moral Advantage, Strategic Advantage?', *Journal of Strategic Studies*, 33, 3 (June).
Gray, J. (2002) *False Dawn* (London: Granta).
Gray-King, E. (2009) *Risk Management* (London: DSC).
Grayling, A.C. (2009) *Liberty in the Age of Terror* (London: Bloomsbury).

Gregor, W.J. (2010) 'Military Planning Systems and Stability Operations', *PRISM*, 1, 3 (May).
Grey, C. (2012) *Decoding Organization: Bletchley Park, Codebreaking and Organization Studies* (Cambridge: Cambridge University Press).
Gross, M.L. (2008) 'The Second Lebanon War', *Journal of Military Ethics*, 7, 1.
Gruber, L. (2000) *Ruling the World* (Princeton, NJ: Princeton University Press).
Guelke, J. (2009) 'Privacy and the Defence of Democracy', *RUSI Homeland Security and Resilience Monitor* (13 August).
Gupta, A.K., and M. Becerra (2003) 'Impact of Strategic Context and Inter-Unit Trust on Knowledge Flows within the Multinational Corporation' ch. 2 in B. McKern (ed.), *Managing the Global Network Corporation* (London: Routledge).
Gustafson, K. (2010) 'Strategic Horizons', *Intelligence and National Security*, 25, 5 (October).
Guyatt, N. (2003) *Another American Century?* (London: Zed).
Haacke, J. (2009) 'The ASEAN Regional Forum: from dialogue to practical security cooperation?', *Cambridge Review of International Affairs*, 22, 3.
Haass, R.N. (2008) 'The Age of Nonpolarity', *Foreign Affairs* (May/June).
Haass, R.N. (2009) *War of Necessity, War of Choice* (New York: S&S).
Haass, R.N. (2011) 'Weakened U.S. in Stormy Mideast', *US Council on Foreign Relations* (29 April).
Habegger, B. (2009) 'Horizon Scanning in Government' and 'Strategic Foresight in Public Policy', *Center for Security Studies – ETH Zürich* (February and August).
Haddick, R. (2009) 'Send in the Spies', *Foreign Policy* (2 October).
Haddick, R. (2011) 'Rise of the Irregulars', *Foreign Policy* (10 June).
Hafez, M.M. (2006) *Manufacturing Human Bombs* (Washington, DC: USIP Press).
Hafez, M.M. (2007) *Suicide Bombers in Iraq* (Washington, DC: USIP Press).
Hagelin, B. (2009) 'Science, Security and Spies', *European Security*, 18, 4 (December).
Hager, N. (1996) *Secret Power* (Nelson, NZ: CPP).
Hall, W.M., and G. Citrenbaum (2012) *Intelligence Collection* (Westport, CT: Praeger Security International).
Hamel-Green, M. (2009) 'Nuclear-weapon-free Zone Initiatives', *Global Change, Peace & Security*, 21, 3 (October).
Hannah, G., K. O'Brien and A. Rathmell (2005) *Intelligence and Security Legislation for Security Sector Reform* (Cambridge: RAND Europe, June).
Hannay, D. (2009) 'Three Iraq Intelligence Failures Reconsidered', *Survival*, 51, 6 (December).
Harcourt, B.E. (2007) *Against Prediction* (Chicago, IL: UCP).
Hardin, G. (1968) 'The Tragedy of the Commons', *Science* (13 December).
Harding, J. (2009) *Alpha Dogs* (London: Atlantic Books).
Harding, R. (2010) 'Globalization in the Age of Terror', *Diplomatic Courier* (24 March).
Harrison, F. (2006) 'Sharing Information is not Enough', *Defense Intelligence Journal*, 15, 1.
Hastedt, G.P., and B.D. Skelley (2009) 'Intelligence in a Turbulent World', ch. 7 in Gill *et al.* (eds.), *Intelligence Theory*.
Hastings Dunn, D. (2008) 'The Double Interregnum', *International Affairs*, 84, 6.
Hatlebrekke, K.A., and M.L.R. Smith (2010) 'Towards a New Theory of Intelligence Failure? The Impact of Cognitive Closure and Discourse Failure', *Intelligence and National Security*, 25, 2 (April).

Hayman, A., and M. Gilmore (2009) *The Terrorist Hunters* (London: Bantam).
Haywood, R., and R. Spivak (2012) *Maritime Piracy* (London: Routledge).
Head, M. (2002) 'Critique And Comment: "Counter-Terrorism" Laws: A Threat To Political Freedom, Civil Liberties And Constitutional Rights', *Melbourne University Law Review*, 34.
Heath, J. (2006) 'The Benefits of Cooperation', *Philosophy & Public Affairs*, 34, 4.
Hedström, P. (2005) *Dissecting the Social: On the Principles of Analytical Sociology* (Cambridge: Cambridge University Press).
Hedström, P., and P. Bearman (eds) (2009) *The Oxford Handbook of Analytical Sociology* (Oxford: Oxford University Press).
Hegghammer, T. (2010) *Jihad in Saudi Arabia* (Cambridge: Cambridge University Press).
Heisbourg, F. (2011) 'Leaks and Lessons', *Survival*, 53, 1 (February/March).
Held, D., and A. McGrew (2007) *Globalization/Anti-Globalization*, 2nd ed. (Cambridge: Polity).
Hemming, S. (2010) 'The Practical Application of Counter-terrorism Legislation in England and Wales: A Prosecutor's Perspective', *International Affairs*, 86, 4.
Henderson, R.D'A. (2003) *Brassey's International Intelligence Yearbook* (Washington, DC: Brassey's).
Hennessy, P. (2003) *The Secret State* (London: Penguin).
Hennessy, P. (2005) 'Informality and Circumscription: The Blair Style of Government in War and Peace', *The Political Quarterly*, 76, 1 (January).
Hennessy, P. (ed.) (2007) *The New Protective State* (London: Continuum).
Hennessy, P. (2010) *The Secret State: Preparing For The Worst 1945–2010* (London: Penguin).
Hennessy, P. (2011) 'The Horizon Scanner's Craft', *Chatham House Transcript* (23 June).
Herman, M. (1996) *Intelligence Power in Peace and War* (Cambridge: Cambridge University Press/Chatham House – Royal Institute of International Affairs, London).
Herman, M. (1999) 'Modern Intelligence Services: Have they a place in ethical foreign policies?', *Conflict Studies Research Centre Paper M18* (September).
Herman, M. (2001) *Intelligence Services in the Information Age* (London: Frank Cass).
Herman, M. (2002) '11 September: Legitimising Intelligence?', *International Relations*, 16, 2.
Herman, M. (2003a) 'Counter-Terrorism, Information Technology and Intelligence Change', *Intelligence and National Security*, 18, 4 (Winter).
Herman, M. (2003b) 'Intelligence after 9/11: A British View of the Effects', *Canadian Security Intelligence Service (CSIS) Commentary No. 83* (17 July).
Herman, M. (2004) 'Ethics and Intelligence after September 2001', ch. 12 in L. Scott and P. D. Jackson (eds.), *Understanding Intelligence in the Twenty-First Century: Journeys in Shadows* (London: Routledge).
Hersh, S.M. (2004) *Chain of Command* (London: Penguin).
Heuser, B. (2010) *The Evolution of Strategy* (Cambridge: Cambridge University Press).
Heywood, A. (2004) *Political Theory*, 3rd ed. (Basingstoke: Palgrave).
Hibbs, M. (2011) 'New Global Rules for Sensitive Nuclear Trade', *Carnegie* (28 July).
Hill, C. (2003) *The Changing Politics of Foreign Policy* (Basingstoke: Palgrave).

Hill, C. (2010) 'Tough Choices', *The World Today* (April).
Hirsh, M. (2002) 'Bush and the World', *Foreign Affairs*, 81, 5 (September/October).
Hislope, R., and A. Mughan (2012), *Introduction to Comparative Politics: The State and its Challenges* (Cambridge: Cambridge University Press).
Hitz, F.P. (2005) *The Great Game: The Myth and Reality of Espionage* (New York: Knopf).
Hitz, F.P. (2008) *Why Spy? Espionage in an Age of Uncertainty* (New York: St. Martin's Press).
Hitz, F.P. (2010) 'Human Source Intelligence', ch. 16 in Johnson (ed.), *The Oxford Handbook of National Security Intelligence.*
Hobbs, P. (2009) *Project Management* (London: DK).
Hood, C., H. Rothstein and R. Baldwin (2004) *The Government of Risk* (Oxford: Oxford University Press).
Hopper, P. (2006) *Living with Globalization* (Oxford: Berg).
Hough, P. (2008) *Understanding Global Security*, 2nd ed. (London: Routledge).
Howard, M. (2006–07) 'A Long War?', *Survival*, 48, 4 (Winter).
HQUSAA (2012) 'Information Collection', *US Army Field Manual (FM) 3–55* (April).
Hughes-Wilson, J. (2010) 'Book Review: James Igoe Walsh…', *RUSI Journal*, 155, 2 (April/May).
Hulnick, A.S. (1991–92) 'Intelligence Cooperation in the Post-Cold War Era: A New Game Plan?', *International Journal of Intelligence and CounterIntelligence*, 5, 4 (Winter).
Hulnick, A.S. (2006) 'What's Wrong with the Intelligence Cycle', *Intelligence and National Security*, 21, 6 (December).
Hunt, C.T., and A.J. Bellamy (2011) 'Mainstreaming the Responsibility to Protect in Peace Operations', *Civil Wars*, 13, 1 (March).
Hutton, W. (2003) *The World We're In* (London: Abacus).
Ifft, E. (2007) 'Deterrence, Blackmail, Friendly Persuasion', *Defense and Security Analysis*, 23, 3 (September).
Ignatieff, M. (2005) *The Lesser Evil* (Princeton, NJ: Princeton University Press).
IISS (2007) *Strategic Survey 2007* (London: IISS/Routledge).
IISS (2009) *Strategic Survey 2009* (London: IISS/Routledge).
Immerman, R.H. (2011) 'Transforming Analysis', *Intelligence and National Security*, 26, 2 and 3.
Indyk, M.S. (2009) 'Developments in Iran and North Korea', *Brookings* (19 September).
Inkster, N., and A. Nicoll (2010) 'Keep Calm and Carry On', *Survival*, 52, 2 (April).
Inkster, N. (2010a) 'The Protecting State', *Survival*, 52, 5 (October).
Inkster, N. (2010b) 'Intelligence Assumes a Front-line Position in SDSR', *IISS* (19 October).
Inkster, N. (2011a) 'The Death of Osama bin Laden', *Survival*, 53, 3.
Inkster, N. (2011b) '9/11/11: A Decade of Intelligence', *Survival*, 53, 6.
Jackson, B.A. (2008) *Marrying Prevention and Resiliency* (Washington, DC: RAND).
Jackson, P. (2010) 'On Uncertainty and the Limits of Intelligence', ch. 28 in Johnson (ed.), *The Oxford Handbook of National Security Intelligence.*

Jakobsen, P.V. (2011) 'Pushing the Limits of Military Coercion Theory', *International Studies Perspectives*, 12, 2 (May).
Jakobsen, P.V. (2012) 'Reinterpreting Libya's WMD Turnaround – Bridging the Carrot-Coercion Divide', *Journal of Strategic Studies* (May).
Jarvis, L., and M. Lister (2010) 'Stakeholder Security', *Contemporary Politics*, 16, 2 (June).
Jenkins, B.M., and J.P. Godges (eds.) (2011) *The Long Shadow of 9/11* (Santa Monica, CA: RAND).
Jervis, R. (2010a) *Why Intelligence Fails* (Ithaca, NY: Cornell University Press).
Jervis, R., reply by T. Powers (2010b) 'The CIA and Iraq – How the White House Got Its Way: An Exchange', *New York Review of Books* (15 July).
Johnson, L.K. (2003) 'Bricks and Mortar for a Theory of Intelligence', *Comparative Strategy*, 22, 1.
Johnson, L. (2006) 'The Liaison Arrangements of the Central Intelligence Agency', ch. 2 in A.G. Theoharis and R.H. Immerman (eds.), *The Central Intelligence Agency: Security Under Scrutiny* (US: Greenwood).
Johnson, L.K. (ed.) (2007) *Handbook of Intelligence Studies* (London: Routledge).
Johnson, L.K. (2009) 'Sketches for a Theory of Strategic Intelligence', ch. 3 in Gill *et al.* (eds.), *Intelligence Theory*.
Johnson, L.K. (2010a) 'Evaluating "Humint": The Role of Foreign Agents in U.S. Security', *Comparative Strategy*, 29, 4 (September).
Johnson, L.K. (ed.) (2010b) *The Oxford Handbook of National Security Intelligence* (Oxford: Oxford University Press).
Johnson, L. (2012), *National Security Intelligence* (Cambridge: Polity).
Johnstone, S., and J. Mazo (2011) 'Global Warming and the Arab Spring', *Survival*, 53, 2.
Jones, B. (2010) *Failing Intelligence* (London: Dialogue).
Jones, B.D., S. Forman and R. Gowan (eds.) (2010) *Cooperating for Peace and Security* (Cambridge: Cambridge University Press).
Jones, C. (2007) 'Intelligence Reform: The Logic of Information Sharing', *Intelligence and National Security*, 22, 3 (June).
Jones, D.M., and M.L.R. Smith (2010) 'Whose Hearts and Whose Minds?', *Journal of Strategic Studies*, 33, 1 (February).
Jones, T.M., and P. Sheets (2009) 'Torture in the Eye of the Beholder', *Political Communication*, 26, 3 (July).
Kahn, D. (2006) 'The Rise of Intelligence', *Foreign Affairs* (September/October).
Kam, E. (1988) *Surprise Attack* (Cambridge, MA: Harvard University Press).
Katz, J.I. (2008) 'Lessons Learned from Nonproliferation Successes and Failures', *Comparative Strategy*, 27, 5 (October).
Keefe, P.R. (2010) 'Privatized Spying: The Emerging Intelligence Industry', ch. 18 in Johnson (ed.), *The Oxford Handbook of National Security Intelligence*.
Kennedy, H. (2004) *Just Law* (London: Vintage).
Kennedy, P. (1993) *Preparing for the Twenty-First Century* (New York: Random House).
Kent, R. (2010) 'Disaster Planning: It's Good to Talk', *Prospect*, 175 (22 September).
Keohane, R.O., and J.S. Nye, Jr. (1998) 'Power and Interdependence in the Information Age', *Foreign Affairs*, 77, 5 (September/October).
Kepel, G. (1997) *Allah in the West* (Cambridge: Polity).

Kepel, G. (2006) *Jihad*, 4th ed. (London: I.B. Tauris).
Kerbel, J. (2008) 'Lost for Words', *Parameters* (Summer).
Kerton-Johnson, N. (2008) 'Justifying the use of force in a post-9/11 world: striving for hierarchy in international society', *International Affairs*, 84, 5.
Khanna, P. (2009) *The Second World* (London: Penguin).
Kibbe, J.D. (2004) 'The Rise of the Shadow Warriors', *Foreign Affairs* (March/April).
Kibbe, J.D. (2007) 'Covert Action and the Pentagon', *Intelligence and National Security*, 22, 1 (February).
Kilcullen, D.J. (2007a) 'Subversion and Countersubversion in the Campaign against Terrorism in Europe', *Studies in Conflict & Terrorism*, 30.
Kilcullen, D.J. (2007b) 'Countering global insurgency', *Journal of Strategic Studies*, 28, 4.
Kilcullen, D. (2009a) *The Accidental Guerrilla* (London: Hurst).
Kilcullen, D.J. (2009b) 'Terrain, Tribes, and Terrorists: Pakistan, 2006–2008', *Brookings* (September).
Kitchen, V.M. (2010) *The Globalisation of NATO* (London: Routledge).
Klein, E. (1967) *A Comprehensive Etymological Dictionary of the English Language* (Volume II, L–Z, London: Elsevier).
Knopf, J.W. (2008) 'Wrestling with Deterrence: Bush Administration Strategy After 9/11', *Contemporary Security Policy*, 29, 2.
Koblentz, G.D. (2011) 'Predicting Peril or the Peril of Prediction? Assessing the Risk of CBRN Terrorism', *Terrorism and Political Violence*, 23, 4 (August).
Krause, K. (2011) 'Leashing the Dogs of War', *Contemporary Security Policy*, 32, 1.
Kriendler, J. (2006) *NATO Intelligence and Early Warning* (Shrivenham: UK Defence Academy, March).
Kroenig, M. (2010) *Exporting the Bomb* (Ithaca, NY: Cornell University Press).
Kull, S. (2011) *Feeling Betrayed* (Washington, DC: Brookings).
Kupatadze, A. (2010) 'Organized Crime and the Trafficking of Radiological Materials: The Case of Georgia', *The NonProliferation Review*, 17, 2 (July).
Kutz, M.R. (2008) 'Contextual Intelligence: An Emerging Competency for Global Leaders', *Regent Global Business Review* (August).
Kydd, A. (2005) *Trust and Mistrust in International Relations* (Princeton, NJ: Princeton University Press).
LaFeber, W. (2002) 'The Bush Doctrine', *Diplomatic History*, 26, 4 (Fall).
Laidler, K. (2008) *Surveillance Unlimited* (Cambridge: Icon).
Lander, S. (2004) 'International Intelligence Cooperation: An Inside Perspective', *Cambridge Review of International Affairs*, 17, 3 (October).
Langewiesche, W. (2007) *The Atomic Bazaar* (New York: Farrar, Straus & Giroux).
Lansford, T. (2007) 'Multinational Intelligence Cooperation', ch. 21 in J.J.F. Forest (ed.), *Countering Terrorism and Insurgency in the 21st Century* (Westport, CT: Praeger).
Lawson, G., C. Armbruster and M. Cox (eds.) (2010) *The Global 1989* (Cambridge: Cambridge University Press).
Leblond, P. (2005) 'Globalization and World Insecurity', *International Studies Review*, 7.
Lebovich, A. (2011) 'The LWOT', *Foreign Policy* (8 April).
Lefebvre, S. (2003) 'The difficulties and dilemmas of international intelligence cooperation', *International Journal of Intelligence and CounterIntelligence*, 16, 4.

Lefebvre, S. (2010) 'Canada's Legal Framework for Intelligence', *International Journal of Intelligence and CounterIntelligence*, 23, 2 (June).
Lefebvre, S. (2012) 'Challenges to the Theory and Practice of Intelligence', *International Journal of Intelligence and CounterIntelligence*, 25, 1 (Winter).
Legro, J.W. (2005) *Rethinking the World* (Ithaca, NY: Cornell University Press).
Lehmkuhl, D. (2008) 'Control Modes in the Age of Transnational Governance', *Law & Policy*, 30, 3 (July).
Levite, A. (1987) *Intelligence and Strategic Surprise* (New York: Columbia University Press).
Libicki, M.C. (2007) *Conquest in Cyberspace* (Cambridge: Cambridge University Press).
Lindblom, C.E. (1959) 'The Science of "Muddling Through"', *Public Administration Review*, 19 (Spring).
Lindblom, C.E. (1979) 'Still Muddling, Not Yet Through', *Public Administration Review*, 39.
Lindgren, M., and H. Bandhold (2009) *Scenario Planning* (Basingstoke: Palgrave).
Liu, X., S. Hong, and Y. Liu (2012) 'A Bibliometric Analysis of 20 Years of Globalization Research: 1990–2009', *Globalizations*, 9, 2 (April).
Long, A. (2008) *Deterrence* (Santa Monica, CA: RAND).
Lonsdale, D. (2008) 'Strategy', ch. 1 in D. Lonsdale, D. Jordan, J.D. Kiras, I. Speller, C. Tuck and C.D. Walton, *Understanding Modern Warfare* (Cambridge: Cambridge University Press).
Lotrionte, C. (2008) 'The Fault, dear Brutus, is not in individuals, but in our system', *SAIS Review*, XXVIII, 1 (Winter–Spring).
Lowenthal, M.M. (2006) *Intelligence*, 3rd ed. (Washington, DC: CQ) (5th ed. 2011).
Lowenthal, M.M. (2008) 'Towards a Reasonable Standard for Analysis: How Right, How Often on Which Issues?', *Intelligence and National Security*, 23, 3.
Lowenthal, M.M. (2010) 'The Policymaker-Intelligence Relationship', ch. 27 in Johnson (ed.), *The Oxford Handbook of National Security Intelligence*.
Lubell, M. (2007) 'Familiarity Breeds Trust: Collective Action in a Policy Domain', *Journal of Politics*, 69, 1 (February).
Luongo, K.N., and I. Williams (2007) 'The Nexus of Globalization and Next-Generation Nonproliferation: Tapping the Power of Market-Based Solutions', *The NonProliferation Review*, 14, 3 (November).
Lupton, D. (1999) *Risk* (London: Routledge/Key Ideas).
Lynch, M.P. (2011) 'After Truth Gives Way', *The Philosophical Quarterly* (2 February).
Lyon, D. (2007) *Surveillance Studies* (Cambridge: Polity).
McCauley, C., and S. Moskalenko (2010) 'Recent U.S. Thinking About Terrorism and Counterterrorism', *Terrorism and Political Violence*, 22, 4 (October).
McChrystal, S.A. (2011) 'It Takes a Network', *Foreign Policy* (March/April).
McCourt, D.M. (2010) 'Rethinking Britain's Role in the World for a New Decade', *British Journal of Politics and International Relations* (14 December).
McCrisken, T. (2011) 'Ten Years on: Obama's War on Terrorism in Rhetoric and Practice', *International Affairs*, 87, 4 (July).
McDowell, D. (2009) *Strategic Intelligence* (Lanham, MD: Scarecrow).
McFate, M. (2010) 'Culture', ch. 14 in T. Rid and T. Keaney (eds.), *Understanding Counterinsurgency* (London: Routledge).

McInnes, C., and S. Rushton (2010) 'HIV, AIDS and Security: Where Are we Now?', *International Affairs*, 86, 1 (January).
McKeeby, D.I. (2006) 'International Intelligence Exchange Top Priority, Says Hayden', *The Washington File* (18 May).
Mckenzie, A. (2012) '"New Wars" Fought "Amongst the People": "Transformed" by Old Realities?', *Defence Studies*, 11, 4.
McKern, B. (2003) 'Organizational Innovation in Multinational Corporations', ch. 1 in *Managing the Global Network Corporation* (London: Routledge).
McLachlan, D. (1968) *Room 39: Naval Intelligence in Action 1939–45* (London: W&N).
McMaster, H.R. (2010) 'Remaining True to Our Values', *Journal of Military Ethics*, 9, 3 (September).
Mabee, B. (2009) *The Globalization of Security* (Basingstoke: Palgrave).
Mackey, C., and G. Miller (2004) *The Interrogator's War* (London: John Murray).
Mackinlay, J. (2002) 'Globalisation and Insurgency', *IISS Adelphi Paper*, 352.
Mackinlay, J. (2009) *The Insurgent Archipelago* (London: Hurst).
Maddrell, P. (2009) 'Failing Intelligence', *International Journal of Intelligence and CounterIntelligence*, 22, 2.
Madsen, F.G. (2009) *Transnational Organized Crime* (London: Routledge).
Manningham-Buller, Dame E. (2007) 'Partnership and Continuous Improvement in Countering Twenty-First Century Terrorism', *Policing*, 1, 1.
Mansfield, M. (2010) 'Reflections on Service', *CIA Studies in Intelligence*, 54, 2 (June).
Maoz, Z. (2011) *Networks of Nations* (Cambridge: Cambridge University Press).
Marrin, S. (2009) 'Training and Educating U.S. Intelligence Analysts', *International Journal of Intelligence and CounterIntelligence*, 22, 1 (March).
Marrin, S. (2011a) 'The 9/11 Terrorist Attacks: A Failure of Policy Not Strategic Intelligence Analysis', *Intelligence and National Security*, 26, 2 and 3.
Marrin, S. (2011b) *Improving Intelligence Analysis: Bridging the Gap between Scholarship and Practice* (London: Routledge/Studies in Intelligence Series).
Martin, A. (2007) 'The lessons of Eastern Europe for modern intelligence reform', *Conflict, Security & Development*, 7, 4.
Martin, A., and P. Wilson (2008) 'The Value of Non-Governmental Intelligence', *Intelligence and National Security*, 23, 6 (December).
Matei, F.C. (2009) 'The Challenges of Intelligence Sharing in Romania', *Intelligence and National Security*, 24, 4 (August).
Mathewson, I. (2010) 'Evaluating the 2010 Strategy Review: The Role of Intelligence', *Chatham House* (October).
May, E.R. (2005) 'The Twenty-first Century Challenge for U.S. Intelligence', ch. 1 in Sims and Gerber (eds.), *Transforming U.S. Intelligence*.
Mazarr, M.J. (2008) 'The Folly of "Asymmetric War"', *The Washington Quarterly*, 31, 3 (Summer).
Mendelsohn, B. (2011) 'Al-Qaeda's Franchising Strategy', *Survival*, 53, 3.
Michaelsen, C. (2010), 'Australia and the Threat of Terrorism in the Decade after 9/11', *Asian Journal of Political Science*, 18, 3.
Miller, P. (2010) 'In Defense of Secrecy', *Foreign Policy* (14 December).
Miller, W.L. (2011) 'Religion, Risk and Legal Culture: Balancing Human Rights against a "War on Terror"', *British Journal of Politics and International Relations* (April).

Miskel, J.F. (2008) *Disaster Response and Homeland Security* (Stanford, CA: Stanford University Press).

Mitchell, W. (2011) 'PROJECT KITAE: Battlespace Agility in Helmand: Network vs. Hierarchy C2', *Royal Danish Defence College (FAK) Research Papers* (August).

Mithas, S., and J. Whitaker (2007) 'Is the World Flat or Spiky?', *Information Systems Research*, 18, 3.

Mittelman, J.H. (2010) *Hyperconflict* (Stanford, CA: Stanford University Press).

Montgomery Hyde, H. (with Foreword by [James Bond author] Ian Fleming) (1962) *Room 3603* (Guildford, CT: Lyons).

Mooney, A., and B. Evans (eds.) (2007) *Globalization: The Key Concepts* (London: Routledge).

Moore, J.N., and R.F. Turner (eds.) (2010) *Legal Issues in the Struggle Against Terror* (Durham, NC: Carolina Academic Press).

Moran, J. (2005) 'State Power in the War on Terror', *Crime Law and Social Change*, 44.

Moran, J., and M. Phythian (2005) 'In the Shadow of 9/11', *Crime Law and Social Change*, 44.

Morffew, C. (2006) 'NATO Defense Reform and Reconstruction', ch. 9 in J. Dufourcq and D.S. Yost (eds.), *NATO-EU Cooperation in Post-Conflict Reconstruction* (Rome, Italy: NATO Defense College, May).

Morris, J. (2010) 'Law, Politics, and the Use of Force', ch. 5 in Baylis *et al.* (eds.), *Strategy in the Contemporary World.*

Mulholland, W.R. (1973) 'Trials, Tribulations and some Lingering Doubts: Liaison Training', *CIA Studies in Intelligence*, 17, 2 (Summer).

Müller-Wille, B. (2006) 'Intelligence and Democratic Accountability', *European Security*, 15, 4 (December).

Mumford, A. (2012) 'Minimum Force meets Brutality: Detention, Interrogation and Torture in British CounterInsurgency Campaigns', *Journal of Military Ethics*, 11, 1.

Munton, D. (2009) 'Intelligence Cooperation Meets International Studies Theory: Explaining Canadian Operations in Castro's Cuba', *Intelligence and National Security*, 24, 1 (February).

Murakami, H. (2002) *Underground* (London: Vintage).

Murphy, C.N., and J. Yates (2009) *The International Organization for Standardization: Global governance through voluntary consensus* (London: Routledge).

Mutimer, D. (2011) 'From Arms Control to Denuclearization', *Contemporary Security Policy*, 32, 1.

Nagl, J.A., and B.M. Burton (2010) 'Thinking Globally and Acting Locally', *Journal of Strategic Studies*, 33, 1 (February).

Naím, M. (2005) *Illicit* (New York: Doubleday).

Naím, M. (2009) 'Globalization', *Foreign Policy* (March/April).

Nathan, L. (2010) 'Intelligence bound', *International Affairs*, 86, 1 (January).

Netten, N., and M. van Someren (2011) 'Improving Communication in Crisis Management by Evaluating the Relevance of Messages', *Journal of Contingencies and Crisis Management* (April).

Newbery, S., B. Brecher, P. Sands and B. Stewart (2009) 'Interrogation, Intelligence and the Issue of Human Rights', *Intelligence and National Security*, 24, 5.

Nicander, L.D. (2011) 'Understanding Intelligence Community Innovation in the Post-9/11 World', *International Journal of Intelligence and CounterIntelligence*, 24, 3.

Nicoll, A. (ed.) (2010a) *IISS Strategic Survey 2010* (London: Routledge/IISS).

Nicoll, A. (ed.) (2010b) 'Terrorist Threats in Europe: Hype or Reality?', *IISS Strategic Comment*, 16, 35 (October).
Nicoll, A. (ed.) (2010c) 'US Intensifies Drone Strikes in Pakistan', *IISS Strategic Comment*, 16, 36 (October).
Nicoll, A. (ed.) (2012) 'The MTCR: staying relevant 25 years on', *IISS Strategic Comment* (24 February).
Nolte, W.M. (2010) 'Intelligence Analysis in an Uncertain Environment', ch. 25 in Johnson (ed.), *The Oxford Handbook of National Security Intelligence*.
Norrlof, C. (2010) *America's Global Advantage* (Cambridge: Cambridge University Press).
Notholt, S. (2009) 'Pandemic Flu: the UK Response', *RUSI Homeland Security and Resilience Monitor* (13 August).
Nussbaum, B. (2007) 'Protecting Global Cities', *Global Crime*, 8, 3 (August).
Nye, Jr., J.S. (2002) 'The American National Interest and Global Public Goods', *International Affairs*, 78, 2.
Nye, Jr., J.S. (2004) *Soft Power* (New York: PublicAffairs).
Nye, Jr., J.S. (2011a) 'Are America's best days really behind us?', *Foreign Policy* (8 March).
Nye, Jr., J.S. (2011b) 'The War on Soft Power', *Foreign Policy* (12 April).
O'Brien, K.A. (2009) 'Managing National Security and Law Enforcement Intelligence in a Globalised World', *Review of International Studies*, 35, 4 (October).
O'Brien, K.A. (2010) *The South African Intelligence Services* (London: Routledge).
O'Brien, R., and M. Williams (2007) *Global Political Economy*, 2nd ed. (Basingstoke: Palgrave).
O'Hanlon, M., and K.M. Campbell (2006) *Hard Power* (New York: Basic Books).
Odgaard, L. (2012) *China and Coexistence: Beijing's National Security Strategy for the Twenty-First Century* (Washington, DC/Baltimore: Woodrow Wilson Center Press/Johns Hopkins University Press).
Ogilvie-White, T. (2010) 'The Defiant States', *The NonProliferation Review*, 17, 1.
Ogilvie-White, T., and D. Santoro (2011) 'Disarmament and Non-proliferation', *Survival*, 53, 3.
Oleson, P. C. (2009) 'Book Review: *Strategic Intelligence...*', *CIA Studies in Intelligence*, 53, 3 (September).
Omand, D. (2005) 'Reflections on Secret Intelligence', *Gresham College Transcript* (20 October).
Omand, D. (2006) 'Ethical Guidelines in Using Secret Intelligence for Public Security', *Cambridge Review of International Affairs*, 19, 4 (December).
Omand, D. (2009) 'The Limits of Avowal', ch. 10 in Treverton and Agrell (eds.), *National Intelligence Systems*.
Omand, D. (2010) *Securing the State* (London: Hurst).
Onions, C.T., G.W.S. Friedrichsen and R.W. Burchfield (eds.) (1966) *The Oxford Dictionary of English Etymology* (Oxford: Oxford University Press).
Pany, M.B. (2012), *Intelligence-Kooperation in der EU* (Germany: GRIN Verlag).
Parker, M., and M. Taylor (2010) 'Financial Intelligence: A Price Worth Paying?', *Studies in Conflict and Terrorism*, 33, 11 (November).
Paskal, C. (2011) 'Rebuilding Sandcastles', *The World Today* (July).
Patomäki, H. (2008) *The Political Economy of Global Security* (London: Routledge).
Patrick, S. (2010) 'Irresponsible Stakeholders?: The Difficulty of Integrating Rising Powers', *Foreign Affairs* (November/December).
Patton, K. (2010) *Sociocultural Intelligence* (London: Continuum).

Paul, T.V., and N.M. Ripsman (2004) 'Under Pressure? Globalisation and the National Security State', *Millennium*, 33.
Peake, H. (2011) 'Review: *Intelligence Cooperation and the War on Terror*', *CIA Studies in Intelligence*, 55, 1 (March).
Penttilä, R.E.J. (2003) 'The Role of the G8 in International Peace and Security', *IISS Adelphi Paper*, 43, 355 (10 May).
Perkovich, G. (2006) 'The End of the Nonproliferation Regime?', *Current History* (November).
Perry, D.L. (2009) *Partly Cloudy: Ethics in War, Espionage, Covert Action, and Interrogation* (Lanham, MD: Scarecrow).
Perry, W.L., and J. Moffat (2004) *Information Sharing Among Military Headquarters* (Santa Monica, CA: RAND).
Peters, B.G. (2001) *The Politics of Bureaucracy*, 5th ed. (London: Routledge).
Petersen, K.L. (2012) *Corporate Risk and National Security Redefined* (London: Routledge).
Phillips, S. (2011) *Yemen and the Politics of Permanent Crisis* (London: Routledge/IISS).
Phythian, M. (2005) 'Intelligence, policy-making and the 7 July 2005 London bombings', *Crime Law and Social Change*, 44.
Pillar, P.R. (2006) 'Intelligence, Policy, and the War in Iraq', *Foreign Affairs*, 85, 2 (March/April).
Pillar, P.R. (2010) 'The Perils of Politicization', ch. 29 in Johnson (ed.), *The Oxford Handbook of National Security Intelligence.*
Pillar, P.R. (2011a) *Intelligence and U.S. Foreign Policy*: Iraq, 9/11, and Misguided Reform (Columbia University Press).
Pillar, P.R. (2011b) 'Bringing Closure to a Disruptive Decade', *ISN* (31 May).
Pillar, P.R. (2012) 'Think Again: Intelligence', *Foreign Policy* (January/February).
Pinto, O. (1955/1961) *Spycatcher* (London: Panther).
Plümper, T., and E. Neumayer (2009) 'The Friend of my Enemy is my Enemy', *European Journal of Political Research*, 49, 1 (October).
Pollard, N.A. (2009) 'On Counterterrorism and Intelligence', ch. 6 in Treverton and Agrell (eds.), *National Intelligence Systems.*
Pollack, J.D. (2011) *No Exit* (London: IISS/Routledge).
Popplewell, R.J. (1995a) 'Lacking Intelligence', *Intelligence and National Security*, 10, 4 (October).
Popplewell, R.J. (1995b) *Intelligence and Imperial Defence* (London: Frank Cass).
Porter, P. (2010) 'Geography, Strategy and the National Interest: The Maps are too Small', *The World Today* (May).
Posner, R.A. (2004) *Catastrophe: Risk and Response* (Oxford: Oxford University Press).
Pouliot, V. (2011) 'Multilateralism as an End in Itself', *International Studies Perspectives*, 12, 1 (February).
Priest, G. (2000) *Logic* (Oxford: Oxford University Press).
Prunckun, H. (2010) *Handbook of Scientific Methods of Inquiry for Intelligence Analysis* (Lanham, MD: Scarecrow).
Raab, C.D. (2011) 'Networks for Regulation', *Journal of Comparative Policy Analysis*, 13, 2.
Ralph, J. (2011) 'After Chilcot', *British Journal of Politics and International Relations*, 13, 3 (August).

Ralston, B., and I. Wilson (2006) *The Scenario Planning Handbook* (Mason, Ohio: Thomson SW).
Ramsay, M. (2011) 'Dirty hands or dirty decisions?', *International Journal of Human Rights*, 15, 4.
Ransley, J., and L. Mazerolle (2009) 'Policing in an era of uncertainty', *Police Practice and Research*, 10, 4 (August).
Rasmussen, M.V. (2006) *The Risk Society at War* (Cambridge: Cambridge University Press).
Ratcliffe, J. (2008) *Intelligence-Led Policing* (Uffculme: Willan).
Redmond, P. J. (2010) 'The Challenges of Counterintelligence', ch. 33 in Johnson (ed.), *The Oxford Handbook of National Security Intelligence.*
Rees, W., and R.J. Aldrich (2005) 'Contending Cultures of Counterterrorism: Transatlantic Divergence or Convergence?', *International Affairs*, 81, 5 (October).
Rees, W. (2006) *Transatlantic Counter-terrorism Cooperation* (London: Routledge).
Rees, W. (2011) *The US-EU Security Relationship* (Basingstoke: Palgrave Macmillan).
Reinares, F. (2010) 'The Madrid Bombings and Global Jihadism', *Survival*, 52, 2 (April).
Reveron, D.S. (2006) 'Old Allies, New Friends: Intelligence-Sharing in the War on Terror', *Orbis*, 50, 3 (Summer).
Reveron, D.S. (2008) 'Counterterrorism and Intelligence Cooperation', *Journal of Global Change and Governance*, 1, 3 (Summer).
Richelson, J.T. (1990) 'The Calculus of Intelligence Cooperation', *International Journal of Intelligence and CounterIntelligence*, 4, 3 (Fall).
Richelson, J.T. (2001) 'MASINT: the New Kid In Town', *International Journal of Intelligence and CounterIntelligence*, 14, 2.
Richelson, J.T. (2008) *The US Intelligence Community*, 5th ed. (Boulder, CO: Westview 6th ed. (2011)).
Richelson, J.T. (2010) 'Technical Collection in the Post-September 11 World', ch. 7 in Treverton and Agrell (eds.), *National Intelligence Systems.*
Rid, T., and T. Keaney (eds.) (2010) *Understanding Counterinsurgency* (London: Routledge).
Riedel, B. (2008/10) *The Search for al Qaeda* (Washington, DC: Brookings).
Riedel, B. (2011a) 'On the Line', *Brookings* (27 June).
Riedel, B. (2011b) 'Oslo's Clash of Civilizations', *Brookings* (25 July).
Rimington, S. (2001) *Open Secret* (London: Hutchinson).
Ringland, G. (2006) *Scenario Planning*, 2nd ed. (London: Wiley).
Ringmose, J., K. Pedersen, L. Mouritsen and P. Dahl Thruelsen (2008) *The Anatomy of Counterinsurgency Warfare* (Copenhagen: RDDC/FAK, October).
Ripsman, N.M., and T.V. Paul (2005) 'Globalization and the National Security State: A Framework for Analysis', *International Studies Review*, 7.
Ripsman, N.M., and T.V. Paul (2010) *Globalization and the National Security State* (Oxford: Oxford University Press).
Riste, O. (2009) 'The Intelligence-Policy Maker Relationship and the Politicization of Intelligence', ch. 8 in Treverton and Agrell (eds.), *National Intelligence Systems.*
Ritzer, G. (2009) *Globalization: A Basic Text* (Oxford: Wiley-Blackwell).
Roberts, A. (2002) 'Counter-terrorism, Armed Force and the Laws of War', *Survival*, 44, 1 (Spring).

Roberts, A.S. (2003) 'Entangling Alliances', *Cornell International Law Journal*, 36, 2 (November).

Roberts, A. (2006) *Blacked Out* (Cambridge: Cambridge University Press).

Roberts, A. (2009) 'Geneva Conventions Sixty Years On', *The World Today* (August/September).

Roberts, A. (2010) 'The Rise and Fall of the Guardians', *Foreign Affairs* (January/February).

Robertson, K.G. (1987) 'Intelligence, Terrorism and Civil Liberties', *Conflict Quarterly*, 7, 2 (Spring).

Rogers, P. (2009) 'International Threats, National Security', *RUSI Homeland Security and Resilience Monitor* (13 August).

Rosenau, W. (2006) 'Liaisons Dangereuses?', ch. 4 in D. Hansén and M. Ranstorp (eds.), *Cooperating Against Terrorism* (Stockholm: SNDC/FHS).

Rosenberg, H., and C.S. Feldman (2008) *No Time to Think* (London: Continuum).

Rosenberg, J. (2008) 'The Interpretation of Probability in Intelligence Estimation and Strategic Assessment', *Intelligence and National Security*, 23, 2.

Ross, C. (2007) *Independent Diplomat* (London: Hurst).

Rovner, J. (2011a) 'Faulty Intelligence', *Foreign Policy* (22 June).

Rovner, J. (2011b) *Fixing the Facts: National Security and the Politics of Intelligence* (London: Cornell University Press).

Rudner, M. (2002) 'The Globalisation of Terrorism', *Canadian Issues* (September).

Rudner, M. (2004a) 'Challenge and Response', *Canadian Foreign Policy*, 11, 2 (Winter).

Rudner, M. (2004b) 'Hunters and Gatherers: The Intelligence Coalition Against Islamic Terrorism', *International Journal of Intelligence and CounterIntelligence*, 17, 2.

Rudner, M. (2007) 'Canada's Communications Security Establishment, Signals Intelligence and Counter-terrorism', *Intelligence and National Security*, 22, 4 (August).

Russell, R.L. (2007a) *Sharpening Strategic Intelligence* (Cambridge: Cambridge University Press).

Russell, R.L. (2007b) 'Achieving all-source fusion in the Intelligence Community', ch. 14 in Johnson (ed.), *Handbook of Intelligence Studies*.

Russell, R.L. (2010) 'Competitive Analysis', ch. 23 in Johnson (ed.), *The Oxford Handbook of National Security Intelligence*.

Sanders, R. (2011) '(Im)plausible legality', *International Journal of Human Rights*, 15, 4.

Sands, P. (2006) *Lawless World* (London: Penguin).

Saul, J.R. (2009) *The Collapse of Globalism* (London: Atlantic).

Schell, J. (2003) *The Unconquerable World* (London: Penguin).

Schmidle, N. (2011) 'Getting Bin Laden', *The New Yorker* (8 August).

Scholte, J.A. (2005) *Globalization*, 2nd ed. (London: Palgrave).

Scholz, J.T., and C-L. Wang (2009) 'Learning to Cooperate', *Australian Journal of Political Science*, 53, 3 (June).

Schraagen, J.M., M. Huis in 't Veld and L. De Koning (2010) 'Information Sharing During Crisis Management in Hierarchical vs. Network Teams', *Journal of Contingencies and Crisis Management*, 18, 2 (June).

Schroeder, P.W. (1976) 'Alliances, 1815–1945' in K.L. Knorr (ed.), *Historical Dimensions of National Security Problems* (Kansas University Press).

Schwab, K. (2006) 'Globalisation and the Knowledge Revolution', *The World Today*, 62, 12 (December).

Schweizer, P. (1993) *Friendly Spies* (New York: Atlantic Monthly).

Scott, L. (2004a) 'Secret Intelligence, Covert Action and Clandestine Diplomacy', *Intelligence and National Security*, 19, 2, (Summer).

Scott, S.V. (2004b) *International Law in World Politics* (London: Lynne Rienner).

Selverstone, M.J. (2010) 'Organizing and Reorganizing for National Security', *Diplomatic History*, 34, 5 (November).

Sepp, K.I. (2010) 'Special Forces', ch. 10 in Rid and Keaney (eds.), *Understanding Counterinsurgency.*

Shapiro, J., and B. Suzan (2003) 'The French Experience of Counter-Terrorism', *Survival*, 45, 1 (Spring).

Shapiro, J.N., and D.A. Siegel (2010) 'Is this Paper Dangerous?', *Security Studies*, 19, 1 (January).

Shapiro, J.N., and R. Darken (2010) 'Homeland Security: A New Strategic Paradigm?', ch. 14 in Baylis *et al.* (eds.), *Strategy in the Contemporary World.*

Shapiro, S. (2004) 'Intelligence Services and Political Transformation in the Middle East', *International Journal of Intelligence and CounterIntelligence*, 17.

Shell Global Business Environment (2003) 'Scenarios: An Explorer's Guide', *Exploring the Future* (London: Shell International).

Shelley, L. (2010) *Human Trafficking* (Cambridge: Cambridge University Press).

Shulsky, A.N., and G.J. Schmitt (2002) *Silent Warfare*, 3rd ed. (Washington, DC: Potomac).

Shukman, H. (ed.) (2000) *Agents for Change* (London: St Ermin's).

Siberry, L. (2009) 'Protective Security', *RUSI Homeland Security and Resilience Monitor* (13 August).

Sims, J., and B. Gerber (eds.) (2005) *Transforming U.S. Intelligence* (Washington, DC: Georgetown University Press).

Sims, J., and B. Gerber (eds) (2009) *Vaults, Mirrors, and Masks: Rediscovering U.S. Counterintelligence* (Washington, DC: Georgetown University Press).

Sims, J. (2005a) 'Understanding Friends and Enemies', ch. 2 in *ibid.*

Sims, J. (2005b) 'Understanding Ourselves', ch. 3 in *ibid.*

Sims, J.E. (2006) 'Foreign Intelligence Liaison: Devils, Deals, and Details', *International Journal of Intelligence and CounterIntelligence*, 19 (Summer).

Sims, J. (2007) 'Intelligence to Counter Terror: The Importance of All-Source Fusion', *Intelligence and National Security*, 22, 1 (February).

Sirkin, H.L., J.W. Hemerling and A.K. Bhattacharya (2008) *Globality* (London: Headline).

Siry, S., and D. Reveron (2001) 'Intelligence and Post-conflict Reconstruction in Bosnia-Herzegovina', *Low Intensity Conflict and Law Enforcement*, 10, 2 (Summer).

Sloan, G. (2012) 'Military doctrine, command philosophy and the generation of fighting power: genesis and theory', *International Affairs*, 88.

Smith, D., and D. Elliot (eds.) (2006) *Key Readings in Crisis Management* (London: Routledge).

Smith, M. (2004) *The Spying Game* (London: Politico's).

Smith, M. (2005) 'Intelligence-sharing failures hamper war on terrorism', *Jane's Intelligence Review* (1 July).

Smith, M.D. (2009) 'Truth in Intelligence: A Cautionary Tale', *International Journal of Intelligence and CounterIntelligence*, 22, 2 (June).

Smith, R. (2006) *The Utility of Force* (London: Penguin).
Snyder, G.H. (1990) 'Alliance Theory: A Neorealist First Cut', *Journal of International Affairs*, 44, 1 (Spring).
Spear, J. (2011) 'More Business as Usual?', *Contemporary Security Policy*, 32, 1.
Steele, R.D. (2004) 'Information Peacekeeping and the Future of Intelligence', *International Journal of Intelligence and CounterIntelligence*, 17, 2.
Steele, R.D. (2007) 'Foreign Liaison and Intelligence Reform: Still in Denial', *International Journal of Intelligence and CounterIntelligence*, 20, 1.
Steger, M.B. (2009) *Globalization*, 2nd ed. (Oxford: Oxford University Press).
Steinberg, J.B. (2007) 'Weapons of Mass Destruction and the Use of Force', ch. 2 in Daalder (ed.), *Beyond Preemption.*
Stephenson, Sir William (1976) 'Point of Departure: A Foreword by Intrepid', in W. Stevenson, *A Man Called Intrepid* (Basingstoke: Macmillan).
Stinnett, D.M., B.R. Early, C. Horne and J. Karreth (2011) 'Complying by Denying', *International Studies Perspectives*, 12, 3 (August).
Stohl, C. (1995) *Organizational Communication* (London: Sage).
Stone, D. (2008) 'Global Public Policy, Transnational Policy Communities, and Their Networks', *Policy Studies Journal*, 36, 1.
Strachan, H. (2005) 'The Lost Meaning of Strategy', *Survival*, 47, 3 (October).
Strachan, H. (2008a) 'Strategy as a Balancing Act', *RUSI Journal*, 153, 3 (June).
Strachan, H. (2008b) 'Strategy and the Limitation of War', *Survival*, 50, 1.
Strachan, H. (2010) 'Strategy or Alibi?', *Survival*, 52, 5 (October).
Strachan, H. (2011) 'Strategy and contingency', *International Affairs*, 87, 6.
Strong, Maj.-Gen. Sir K. (1968) *Intelligence at the Top* (London: Cassell).
Sullivan, B., M. Snyder and J. Sullivan (eds.) (2007) *Cooperation* (Oxford: Wiley-Blackwell).
Suskind, R. (2006) *The One Percent Doctrine* (London: S&S).
Sutherland, B. (ed.) (2011) *Modern Warfare, Intelligence and Deterrence: The Technologies That Are Transforming Them* (Oxford: Wiley/*The Economist*).
Svendsen, A. (2008a) 'The Globalization of Intelligence Since 9/11: Frameworks and Operational Parameters', *Cambridge Review of International Affairs*, 21, 1 (March).
Svendsen, A.D.M. (2008b) 'The Globalization of Intelligence Since 9/11: The Optimization of Intelligence Liaison Arrangements', *International Journal of Intelligence and CounterIntelligence*, 21, 4.
Svendsen, A.D.M. (2009a) 'Painting Rather than Photography: Exploring Spy Fiction as a Legitimate Source Concerning UK–US Intelligence Co-operation', *Journal of Transatlantic Studies*, 7, 1 (March).
Svendsen, A.D.M. (2009b) 'Connecting Intelligence and Theory: Intelligence Liaison and International Relations', *Intelligence and National Security*, 24, 5 (October).
Svendsen, A.D.M. (2010a) *Intelligence Cooperation and the War on Terror: Anglo-American Security Relations after 9/11* (London: Routledge/Studies in Intelligence Series).
Svendsen, A.D.M. (2010b) 'Strategy and Disproportionality in Contemporary Conflicts', *Journal of Strategic Studies*, 33, 3 (June).
Svendsen, A.D.M. (2010c) 'Re-fashioning Risk: Comparing UK, US and Canadian Security and Intelligence Efforts Against Terrorism', *Defence Studies*, 10, 3 (September).
Svendsen, A.D.M. (2010d) 'Introducing "RESINT": A "missing" and "undervalued" "INT" in all-source intelligence efforts?', *2nd International Conference of*

the International Society of Military Sciences (ISMS) Paper, Stockholm: SNDC/FHS (10–11 November).

Svendsen, A.D.M. (2011a) 'The CIA and the "Globalisation of Intelligence"', paper presented at *Landscapes of Secrecy Conference*, University of Nottingham, UK (April).

Svendsen, A.D.M. (2011b) 'Intelligence Liaison: An Essential Navigation Tool', ch. in J. Schroefl, B.M. Rajaee and D. Muhr (eds.), *Hybrid and Cyber War as Consequences of the Asymmetry* (Frankfurt a.M.: Peter Lang).

Svendsen, A.D.M. (2011c) 'On "a continuum with expansion"? Intelligence co-operation in Europe in the early twenty-first century', *Journal of Contemporary European Research (JCER)*, 7, 4 (December).

Svendsen, A.D.M. (2011d) '"Exemplary 'friends and allies'"? Unpacking UK–US Relations in the Early Twenty-First Century', *Journal of Transatlantic Studies*, 9, 4 (December).

Svendsen, A.D.M. (2011e) 'Special Issue on "The CIA and US Foreign Relations Since 1947..."', *H-Diplo/ISSF Roundtable Reviews*, III, 6 (December).

Svendsen, A.D.M. (2011f) 'NATO, Libya Operations and Intelligence Co-operation – a Step Forward?', *Baltic Security and Defence Review*, 13, 2 (December).

Svendsen, A.D.M. (2012a) 'On "a continuum with expansion"? Intelligence Co-operation in Europe in the Early 21st Century', in C. Kaunert and S. Leonard (eds.), *European Security, Terrorism and Intelligence: Towards Europeanization of Security* (Basingstoke: Palgrave).

Svendsen, A.D.M. (2012b) '"Strained" Relations? Evaluating Contemporary Anglo-American Intelligence and Security Co-operation', ch. in S. Marsh and A. Dobson (eds.), *Contemporary Anglo-American Relations* (London: Routledge).

Svendsen, A.D.M. (2012c) 'The Federal Bureau of Investigation and change: Addressing US Counter-terrorism Intelligence', *Intelligence and National Security*, 27, 3 (June).

Svendsen, A.D.M. (2012d) 'Collective Intelligence' in G. Moore (ed.), *Encyclopaedia of U.S. Intelligence (EUSI)* (New York: Routledge).

Svendsen, A.D.M. (2012e) *The Professionalization of Intelligence Cooperation: Fashioning Method out of Mayhem* (Basingstoke: Palgrave).

Swannell, J. (ed.) (1992) *Oxford Modern English Dictionary* (Oxford: Oxford University Press).

Swyngedouw, E. (2004) 'Globalisation or "glocalisation"? Networks, territories and rescaling', *Cambridge Review of International Affairs*, 17, 1.

Tan, A.T.H. (2007) 'Singapore's Cooperation with the Trilateral Security Dialogue Partners in the War Against Global Terrorism', *Defence Studies*, 7, 2.

Taylor, B. (2010) 'Sanctions as Grand Strategy', *IISS Adelphi Paper*, 411 (London: Routledge/IISS).

Taylor, P.J. (2004) *World City Network: A Global Urban Analysis* (London: Routledge).

Taylor, S.A. (2007) 'The Role of Intelligence in National Security', ch. 14 in A. Collins (ed.), *Contemporary Security Studies* (Oxford: Oxford University Press).

Tebbit, K. (2006) *Benchmarking of the Danish Defence Intelligence Service* (Copenhagen/København, Denmark: April).

Tenet, G., and B. Harlow (2007) *At the Center of the Storm* (New York: HarperCollins).

Thomas, S.M. (2010) 'A Globalized God', *Foreign Affairs* (November/December).
Thomas, S.T. (1988) 'Assessing Current Intelligence Studies', *International Journal of Intelligence and CounterIntelligence*, 2, 2.
Thornton, R. (2007) *Asymmetric Warfare* (Cambridge: Polity).
Till, G. (2008) 'The Evolution of Strategy and the New World Order', ch. 6 in C.A. Snyder (ed.), *Contemporary Security and Strategy*, 2nd ed. (Basingstoke: Palgrave).
TNPR Editorial (2006) 'Keeping the NPT together', *The NonProliferation Review*, 13, 1 (March).
Todd, P., and J. Bloch (2003) *Global Intelligence* (London: Zed).
Tovey, M. (ed.) (2008) *Collective Intelligence: Creating a Prosperous World at Peace* (Oakton, Va: Earth Intelligence Network).
Treverton, G.F. (2003a) 'Reshaping Intelligence to Share with "Ourselves"', *Canadian Security Intelligence Service (CSIS) Commentary No. 82* (July – Unclassified).
Treverton, G.F. (2003b) *Reshaping National Intelligence For an Age of Information* (Cambridge: Cambridge University Press).
Treverton, G.F. (2005) *The Next Steps in Reshaping Intelligence* (Santa Monica, CA: RAND).
Treverton, G.F., S.G. Jones, S. Boraz and P. Lipscy (2006) *Toward a Theory of Intelligence* (Santa Monica, CA: RAND).
Treverton, G.F. (2009a) *Intelligence for an Age of Terror* (Cambridge: Cambridge University Press).
Treverton, G.F. (2009b) *Approaches to 'Outreach' for intelligence*, (Stockholm: SNDC/FHS).
Treverton, G.F., and W. Agrell (eds.) (2009) *National Intelligence Systems* (Cambridge: Cambridge University Press).
Treverton, G.F. (2010) 'Addressing "Complexities" in Homeland Security', ch. 21 in Johnson (ed.), *The Oxford Handbook of National Security Intelligence*.
Treverton, G.F. (2011) 'What Should We Expect of Our Spies?', *Prospect* (25 May).
Treverton, G.F., E. Nemeth, and S. Srinivasan (2012) *Threats Without Threateners?* (Santa Monica, CA: RAND).
Treverton, G.F., and J.J. Ghez (2012) *Making Strategic Analysis Matter* (Santa Monica, CA: RAND).
Troy, T.F. (1981) *Donovan and the CIA* (Washington, DC: CIA Center for the Study of Intelligence) via CREST, CIA-RDP90-00708R000600120001-0 (2000/04/18).
Turner, I (2011) 'Freedom From Torture in the "War on Terror": Is it Absolute?', *Terrorism and Political Violence*, 23, 3.
UK Her Majesty's Government (HMG) (2010) *A Strong Britain in an Age of Uncertainty* (Norwich: TSO, 18 October).
US House Permanent Select Committee on Intelligence (PSCI) and the Senate Select Committee on Intelligence (SSCI) (2002) *Report of the Joint Inquiry into the Terrorist Attacks of September 11, 2001* (December).
van Creveld, M. (2006) 'The Fate of the State Revisited', *Global Crime*, 7, 3–4 (August-November).
Vagts, A. (1967) *The Military Attaché* (Princeton, NJ: Princeton University Press).
Valencia, M. (2006) 'Is the PSI really the cornerstone of a new international norm?', *Naval War College Review*, 59, 4 (Autumn).
Valtonen, V. (2010) 'Collaboration of Security Actors – an Operational-Tactical Perspective', *2nd International Conference of the International Society of Military*

Sciences Paper, Stockholm: Swedish National Defence College (SNDC/FHS) (10–11 November).

Vandepeer, C. (2009) 'Intelligence Analysis as Decision-making: A Case Study of the 2002 Bali Bombings', *www.goa-intelligence.org* (22 January) [accessed 20/4/2012].

Various (2010) 'The Politics of Getting the Defence and Security Review We Need', *The Political Quarterly*, 81, 3 (July–September).

Vidino, L. (2011) *Radicalization, Linkage, and Diversity* (Santa Monica, CA: RAND).

Vines, A. (2010) 'Rhetoric from Brussels and Reality on the Ground: the EU and Security in Africa', *International Affairs*, 86, 5 (September).

Vucetic, S. (2010) 'Anglobal Governance?', *Cambridge Review of International Affairs*, 23, 3 (September).

Wacks, R. (2008) *Law* (Oxford: Oxford University Press).

Wallace, R.J. (2010) 'Hypocrisy, Moral Address, and the Equal Standing of Persons', *Philosophy and Public Affairs*, 38, 4 (Fall).

Walsh, J.I. (2007) 'Defection and Hierarchy in International Intelligence Sharing', *Journal of Public Policy*, 27, 2.

Walsh, J.I. (2008) 'Intelligence Sharing for Counter-Insurgency', *Defense and Security Analysis*, 24, 3.

Walsh, J.I. (2009) *The International Politics of Intelligence Sharing* (New York: Columbia University Press).

Walsh, P. (2011) *Intelligence and Intelligence Analysis* (London: Routledge).

Wanandi, J. (2002) 'A Global Coalition against International Terrorism', *International Security*, 26, 4 (Spring).

Ward, A., and J. Hackett (eds.) (2004) 'Al-Qaeda Targets Europe', *IISS Strategic Comments*, 10, 2 (March).

Ward, A., and J. Hackett (eds.) (2006) 'Cooperative Intelligence', *IISS Strategic Comments*, 12, 4 (May).

Wark, W.K. (2003) 'Learning to Live with Intelligence', *Intelligence and National Security*, 18, 4 (Winter).

Wark, W. (2004–05) 'Learning Lessons (and How) in the War on Terror', *International Journal*, 60, 1 (Winter).

Warner, M. (2002) 'Wanted: A Definition of "Intelligence"', *CIA Studies in Intelligence*, 46, 3.

Warner, M. (2009a) 'Building a Theory of Intelligence Systems', ch. 2 in Treverton and Agrell (eds.), *National Intelligence Systems*.

Warner, M. (2009b) 'Intelligence as Risk Shifting', ch. 2 in Gill *et al.* (eds.), *Intelligence Theory*.

Warner, M. (2012) 'Intelligence and Reflexivity: An Invitation to a Dialogue' (and the other articles in), *Intelligence and National Security*, 27, 2 & 3 (April & June).

Warrick, J. (2011) *The Triple Agent* (New York: Doubleday).

Wasemiller, A.C. (1969) 'The Anatomy of Counterintelligence', in *CIA Studies in Intelligence*, 13, 1 (Winter).

Waterman, S. (2010) 'Connecting the Clichés', *ISN Security Watch* (12 January).

Waters, M. (1995) *Globalization* (London: Routledge).

Watters, B.S.C. (2011) 'The Utility of Social Science and Management Theory on Military Operations: of Portacabins and Polo Fields', *Defence Studies*, 11, 1.

Watts, L.L. (2004) 'Conflicting Paradigms, Dissimilar Contexts', *CIA Studies in Intelligence*, 48, 1.

Watts, L.L. (2011) 'A Mind War: Intelligence, Secret Services and Strategic Knowledge in the 21st Century', *CIA Studies in Intelligence*, 55, 4 (Extracts, December)

Weaver, W.G., and R.M. Pallitto (2010) 'Extraordinary Rendition', ch. 20 in Johnson (ed.), *The Oxford Handbook of National Security Intelligence.*

Webb, J.B. (2010) 'Review: *The International Politics of Intelligence Sharing*', *CIA Studies in Intelligence*, 54, 4 (December).

Weber, S., N. Barma, M. Kroenig and E. Ratner (2007) 'How Globalization Went Bad', *Foreign Policy* (January/February).

Weitsman, P.A. (2004) *Dangerous Alliances* (Stanford, CA: Stanford University Press).

West, D.M. (2011) *The Next Wave* (Washington, DC: Brookings).

Westerfield, H.B. (ed.) (1995) *Inside CIA's Private World* (New Haven, CT: Yale University Press).

Westerfield, H.B. (1996) 'America and the World of Intelligence Liaison', *Intelligence and National Security*, 11, 3 (July).

Weston, K. (2009) 'The Changing Nature of Counter-Terrorism Policing', *RUSI Homeland Security and Resilience Monitor* (13 August).

Whang, T. (2011) 'Playing to the Home Crowd? Symbolic Use of Economic Sanctions in the United States', *International Studies Quarterly* (June).

Whetham, D. (ed.) (2011) *Ethics, Law and Military Operations* (Basingstoke: Palgrave).

Wiebes, C. (2003) *Intelligence and the War in Bosnia 1992–95* (London: Lit Verlag).

Wilder, D.C. (2011) 'An Educated Consumer Is Our Best Customer', *CIA Studies in Intelligence*, 55, 2 (June).

Wilkie, A. (2004) *Axis of Deceit* (Melbourne: Black Inc. Agenda).

Williams, E. (2008) 'Out of Area and Very Much in Business?', *Comparative Strategy*, 27, 1.

Williams, P.D. (2010) 'Explaining and understanding security cooperation in Africa', *African Security Review*, 19, 2.

Wilson, P. (2005) 'The Contribution of Intelligence Services to Security Sector Reform', *Conflict, Security and Development*, 5, 1 (April).

Wilson, P. (2007) 'Preparing to Meet New Challenges', ch. 9 in S. Tsang (ed.), *Intelligence and Human Rights in the Era of Global Terrorism* (London: PSI).

Wippl, J.W. (2012) 'Intelligence Exchange Through InterIntel', *International Journal of Intelligence and CounterIntelligence*, 25, 1 (Winter).

Wirtz, J.J. (1993) 'Constraints on Intelligence Collaboration: The Domestic Dimension', *International Journal of Intelligence and CounterIntelligence*, 6, 1.

Wirtz, J.J. (2008) 'Hiding in Plain Sight: Denial, Deception, and the Non-State Actor', *SAIS Review*, XXVIII, 1 (Winter–Spring).

Wirtz, J.J. (2009) 'Theory of surprise', ch. 5 in Gill *et al.* (eds.), *Intelligence Theory*.

Wirtz, J.J., and J.J. Rosenwasser (2010) 'From Combined Arms to Combined Intelligence', *Intelligence and National Security*, 25, 6 (December).

Wittes, B. (ed.) (2009) *Legislating the War on Terror* (Washington, DC: Brookings).

Wittes, B. (2010) *Detention and Denial* (Washington, DC: Brookings).

Wolf, Jr., C., B.G. Chow and G.S. Jones (2008) *Enhancement by Enlargement* (Santa Monica, CA: RAND).
Woodward, B. (2011) *Obama's Wars* (London: S&S).
Yang, Q., D. Yao, J. Garnett and K. Muller (2010) 'Using a Trust Inference Model for Flexible and Controlled Information Sharing During Crises', *Journal of Contingencies and Crisis Management*, 18, 4 (December).
Yost, D. (ed.) (2007) (Essays in) *International Affairs*, 83, 3 (May).
Young, A.R. (2010) 'Perspectives on the Changing Global Distribution of Power', *Politics*, 30, S1 (December).
Zakaria, F. (2009) *The Post-American World* (London: Penguin).
Zartman, I.W., and S. Touval (eds.) (2010) *International Cooperation* (Cambridge: Cambridge University Press).
Zegart, A.B. (2011) *Eyes on Spies* (Stanford, CA: Hoover).
Zinn, J.O., and P. Taylor-Gooby (eds.) (2006) *Risk in Social Science* (Oxford: Oxford University Press).
Zinn, J.O. (2008) 'The Contribution of Sociology to the Discourse in Risk and Uncertainty', ch. 1 in *Social Theories of Risk and Uncertainty* (Oxford: Blackwell).
Zuckerman, A.S. (ed.) (2005) *The Social Logic of Politics* (Philadelphia, PA: Temple University Press).

Index

Page numbers in **bold** indicate illustrations